This is the first comprehensive study of the life and works of Muhammad Baqer as-Sadr – an Iraqi scholar who made an important contribution to the renewal of Islamic law and politics in the contemporary Middle East. Executed in 1980 by the regime of Saddam Hussein, Sadr was the most articulate thinker as well as a major political actor in the revival of Shi'i learning, which placed Najaf in southern Iraq at its centre.

Dr Chibli Mallat examines in depth the intellectual development of Sadr and his companions, who included Ayatollah Ruhullah al-Khumaini. He assesses how Sadr reformed the system of religious education and developed innovative approaches to the key areas of study of law, economics and banking. The author convincingly demonstrates how Sadr's ideas and activities were influential in the rise of political Islam across the Middle East, particularly in countries with strong Shi'i constituencies such as Iran, Iraq and Lebanon, and played an important part in the Iranian revolution of 1979.

Given the renewed interest in Islam as a religious, political and social phenomenon, this is a most timely book and will be widely read by students and specialists of law, economics and the politics of the Middle East as well as of the history of ideas.

Cambridge Middle East Library: 29

THE RENEWAL OF ISLAMIC LAW

Cambridge Middle East Library

The *Cambridge Middle East Library* aims to bring together outstanding scholarly work on the history, politics, sociology and economics of the Middle East and North Africa in the nineteenth and twentieth centuries. While primarily focusing on monographs based on original research, the series will also incorporate broader surveys and in-depth treatments.

A list of books in this series will be found at the end of this volume

THE RENEWAL OF ISLAMIC LAW

Muhammad Baqer as-Sadr, Najaf and the Shiʿi International

CHIBLI MALLAT

School of Oriental and African Studies, University of London

CAMBRIDGE
UNIVERSITY PRESS

PUBLISHED BY THE PRESS SYNDICATE OF THE UNIVERSITY OF CAMBRIDGE
The Pitt Building, Trumpington Street, Cambridge, United Kingdom

CAMBRIDGE UNIVERSITY PRESS
The Edinburgh Building, Cambridge CB2 2RU, UK
40 West 20th Street, New York NY 10011–4211, USA
477 Williamstown Road, Port Melbourne, VIC 3207, Australia
Ruiz de Alarcón 13, 28014 Madrid, Spain
Dock House, The Waterfront, Cape Town 8001, South Africa

http://www.cambridge.org

First published 1993
First paperback edition 2003

A catalogue record for this book is available from the British Library

Library of Congress cataloguing in publication data

Mallat, Chibli.
The renewal of Islamic law: Muhammad Baqer as-Sadr, Najaf, and the Shi'i International / Chibli Mallat.
p. cm. – (Cambridge Middle East library; 29)
Includes bibliographical references and index.
ISBN 0 521 43319 3 hardback
1. Islamic law. 2. Sadr, Muhammad Bāqir. 3. Shī'ah. I. Title. II. Series.
LAW (ISLAM 7 Mall 1993)
340.5′9 – dc20 92–23821 CIP

ISBN 0 521 43319 3 hardback
ISBN 0 521 53122 5 paperback

Contents

Acknowledgments *page* viii
Note on transliteration and dates ix

General introduction: The law in the Islamic Renaissance and the role of Muhammad Baqer as-Sadr 1

Part I Islamic law and the constitution

Introduction to Part I 23
1 Archetypes of Shi'i law 28
2 On the origins of the Iranian constitution: Muhammad Baqer as-Sadr's 1979 treatises 59
3 The first decade of the Iranian constitution: problems of the least dangerous branch 79

Part II Islamic law, 'Islamic economics', and the interest-free bank

Introduction to Part II 111
4 Law and the discovery of 'Islamic economics' 113
5 Muhammad Baqer as-Sadr and Islamic banking 158
Conclusion: The costs of renewal 188

Notes 190
Bibliography 228
Index 243

Acknowledgments

This work is owed, primarily, to my parents, whose generosity and encouragement allowed me to complete it. I should like to dedicate it to them.

Several persons have also helped me in many ways. I should like to thank in particular Professors John Wansbrough and Tony Allan, for their constant and sympathetic support. Special gratitude goes to Albert Hourani and Dr Roger Owen, whose dedicated advice saw the work to the press. Several persons have read the manuscript and offered their welcome suggestions to improve it: Professor Roy Mottahedeh, Dr Robin Ostle, Dr Norman Calder, Professor William Twining, Mr Chris Rundle and my colleague in the department, Ian Edge, as well as anonymous readers at Cambridge University Press. At the Press, the professionalism of Dr Gill Thomas helped sustain my efforts. The Hariri foundation offered financial help to help complete the work, and I should like to acknowledge the friendliness and support of Mona Kni'o at the London branch of the Foundation. Jane Connors, Liz Hodgkin, and Jad Swidan read part of the manuscript and contributed valuable suggestions, and my colleagues Ja'far Delshad and Jawdat al-Qazwini offered their insiders' view and their friendship from the very beginning of the research. My wife helped me put the work in shape and provided relentless support. To all, I would like to express my deep gratitude. I am of course responsible for the mistakes and imperfections which remain.

Note on transliteration and dates

Italic and capitals

I have adopted for Arabic and Persian words the standard transliteration of the *International Journal of Middle Eastern Studies*, but I have omitted the diacritics, except in the bibliography and index. /ʿ/ is used for *ʿayn* and /ʾ/ for *hamza*.

Arabic and Persian words have been italicised throughout, except for usual non-italicised items which are current in English (such as the Qur'an), and institutions like the Iranian Majles (Parliament). In this case, they also begin with a capital. Following Henry Corbin (*En Islam Iranien*, 4 vols., Paris, 1971–2), the word *Imam* is capitalised only in reference to the Twelve *Imams* of the Shiʿi tradition.

Also, as in Batatu's standard work on Iraq (*The Old Social Classes and the Revolutionary Movements in Iraq*, Princeton, 1978), we have found it more accurate to write as-Sadr rather than al-Sadr, at-Tabataba'i rather than al-Tabataba'i etc.

Abbreviations

Q	Qur'an
BSOAS	*Bulletin of the School of Oriental and African Studies*
IJMES	*International Journal of Middle Eastern Studies*
SI	*Studia Islamica.*

Dates

If a single date is used, reference is to the Gregorian Christian calendar. When a *hijri* (Hegire) date is used, it is followed by the corresponding Gregorian date. No specification is made to Hijri *qamari* (lunar calendar) or to Hijri *shamsi* (solar calendar generally used in modern Iran) since the context is generally sufficient to distinguish the use of each, which is in any case followed by the AD date.

General introduction: The law in the Islamic Renaissance and the role of Muhammad Baqer as-Sadr

Law as *Lingua Franca*

In recent years, a renewed interest in Islam as a worldwide active social phenomenon has appeared. This has resulted in a flurry of works of sundry types on the theme of resurgence, revivalism, re-emergence of political Islam, also dubbed revolutionary Islam, radical Islam, militant Islam, Islamic fundamentalism, or more simply Islamism.[1]

The issue of Islam as a socially turbulent phenomenon was approached by countries and disciplines: history, sociology, anthropology, politics.[2] Questions were being posed in the worried and intrigued West, but they were also being asked in the East, where answers had an immediate political relevance. Naturally, the concerns were different according to the groups' varied interests. The common underlying concern, however, was for stability, or its converse, foiled or successful revolution. Depending on the position of a group in a particular state, fear, concern, or hope alternated.

This research tries to look into the thought of the resurgent Islams behind the first layer of enthusiasm or despair, to determine how the new vindicated outlook was shaped, and to examine whether there were any new ideas in the alternative system at all. In this longer perspective of the history of ideas, ideas could be 'new' only in comparison with earlier outlooks. A comparative, as well as a prospective work was therefore needed. This meant not only asking questions of a chronological type, whether current ideas were new compared to those reformists advocated fifty or a hundred years ago, but also whether the claim of a different strand of thought which was specifically Islamic could be defended before a more universal jury.

One striking feature of the Islamic renewal is the legal form emphasised in its own language. Whether voiced by laymen or religious scholars, the appeal to Islam has directly addressed Islamic law: the *shari'a*. The concern of the Islamist advocates has primarily taken a legalistic form. The *'ulama*'s (plural of *'alim*, or *fuqaha'*, plural of *faqih*, jurists) emphasis on the law might not be surprising, since they would in effect be defending their speciality. This is particularly true when the body of the *'ulama* as such is under attack by the rapid changes brought about by the twentieth century. But upholders of revolutionary Islam were not solely scholars of the law, and the reasons for the appeal to the *shari'a* by people who were not essentially trained in classical law are rooted in the special place of the *shari'a* in the tradition.[3]

Certainly Islam has offered as a civilisation areas of extreme sophistication in all walks of life, including scientific and literary disciplines. Yet, strong as the scientific tradition may have been, it has objectively lagged behind the advances of the scientific disciplines in the West. This is not true of the literary disciplines, some of which prove essentially incompatible with a categorisation in terms of progress. Typical of the 'humanities' field is literature: the poetry of al-Mutanabbi, Abu Tammam, Hafiz, and Firdawsi remains unsurpassed. In these fields, there can be no 'advance'.

Other disciplines partake of the two traditions. They are both comparatively static and prone to 'advances' which render preceding research in their field, as in pure science, relatively obsolete. The pertinence of progress in their case is more uncertain. Such is the case of the '*continent histoire*',[4] in which Ibn Khaldun (d. 808/1406) appears as a scientific analyst of the rise and fall of nations. One is reluctant none the less to describe *the Muqaddima* as a 'scientific' text. It belongs to a type of historiography which starts with Ibn Khaldun and flourishes in the nineteenth and twentieth-century histories with major works emphasising economic structures, modes of production and exchange, and long waves.[5] But the language of *the Muqaddima* offers a string of brilliant insights rather than the systematic model of interconnected concepts which distinguish scientific laws.

These remarks may be too general for a precise classification of major disciplines in the Islamic tradition, but they serve the limited purpose in this essay of 'discarding' the work of historians like Tabari (d.923), Ibn al-Athir (d.1234), and Ibn Khaldun, in so far as they have resisted the impact of breaks ('*coupures*') and breakthroughs which characterise science.[6]

More specifically in the study of the thought of revolutionary Islam, the relative[7] irrelevance of the historiographic tradition appears mostly in the general lack of reference to that tradition within Islamic movements.

To this caveat it must be added that the question which is important for the currents of Islamic resurgence is not of a diachronic nature. The validity of historical research and the criteria of its scientificity are secondary to the purely 'synchronic' dimension at stake. Synchrony here means the relationship to contemporaneity. In the case of Ibn Khaldun, the whole of *the Muqaddima* appears irrelevant because it fails to answer the basic need of a contemporary movement in search of Islamic legitimacy: how can the modern Islamic polity be shaped? *The Muqaddima*, Maqrizi's (d.1442) or Tabari's histories, or the great works of the geographers cannot give ready answers. Muslim historians and geographers can only be precursors. The material they offer is too raw. It needs to be fundamentally reworked to appear relevant for questions of the late twentieth century.

One field, in contrast, where the riches of the Muslim tradition appear inextinguishable, and, at the same time, of immediate relevance for the contemporary Islamic polity is the law.

Ibn Manzur (d. 711H/1311 AD), the most famous Arab lexicographer, mentions in his dictionary *Lisan al-'Arab* under the root '*sh r '*' that '*shari'a* is the place from which one descends to water ... and *shari'a* in the acception of Arabs is the law of water (*shur'at al-ma'*) which is the source for drinking which is regulated by people who drink, and allow others to drink, from'.[8] A later classical dictionary is even more specific: '*Ash-shari'a*', writes Zubaydi,

> is the descent (*munhadar*) of water for which has also been called what God has decreed (*sharra'a*: legislate, decree) for the people in terms of fasting, prayer, pilgrimage, marriage etc ... Some say it has been called *shari'a* by comparison with the *shari'a* of water in that the one who legislates, in truth and in all probability, quenches [his thirst] and purifies himself, and I mean by quenching what some wise men have said: I used to drink and remained thirsty, but when I knew God I quenched my thirst without drinking.[9]

The connection between *shari'a* as a generic term for Islamic law, and *shari'a* as the path as well as the law of water, is not a coincidence, and the centrality of water in Islam is obvious in the economic as well as ritualistic sense. What is more important however, is that the jurists – the exponents and expounders of the *shari'a* – did not fail to develop, in answer to this centrality, a highly sophisticated system of rules, covering the whole field of what the contemporary world perceives as 'law'.

From a purely religious law, the *shari'a* therefore developed into the common law of the Muslim world, extending its realm to encompass what modern law would identify as statutes, customs, legal deeds, court decisions, arbitration awards, responsa literature known as *fatwa*s, etc. With the secular distinctions introduced by the European Enlightenment, the *shari'a* lost ground in the Middle East as a common law with no clearly identifiable separation between the religious and the non-religious, but a strict separation of the two realms remains to date impossible. Yet the religious persons at the centre of the Islamic renewal are more jurisconsults than theologians, a fact of importance for developments in the late twentieth-century Muslim world.

In the process of renewing the *shari'a* by the jurisconsults, developments were rife both in terms of form and substance. In substance, as in Salvador Dali's advice to young painters eager to do something 'new', novelty was secured naturally. A twentieth-century author cannot fail to be 'new'. In form, the tentacles of the modern state invested the area previously reserved for individual jurists. The process of codification, which started haltingly in the *qanunnameh*s of the early Ottoman empire, was established, and the debate over the place and role of the *shari'a* extended to all the artisans of legal literature in the contemporary period: legislators, judges and scholars. The sway of 'classical' Islamic law did however vary widely.

In some areas, the consistency and relevance of classical Islamic law are remarkable. Such is the case of the law of succession, where, but for minor modifications, the law applied at present has kept to the same blueprint elaborated by the early jurists of the first and second centuries.[10]

Other areas of the law have been completely discarded. The most significant example attaches to the law of trade in relation to slaves. Jurists of the classical age have written long sections on the rights of slaves as opposed to the rights of free persons, and the special position of slaves in the law permeates several fields, including torts, crime, booty in international law, and property.[11]

Less dramatic than slave law, but similar in many ways, has been the whole area relating to the *'ibadat*, the legal dispositions in the classical texts which regulate acts of worship. In a sense, these rules remain untouched by historical change, and the conduct of a *'ibada* like prayer cannot be affected fundamentally by the new age. Under what is now considered as law, these areas are irrelevant. The *'ibadat* have stopped being a legal precinct. Similarly, there is little or no debate as to the regulation of *hajj* (pilgrimage), and even though its importance remains great, as the polemic between Saudi Wahhabis and Iranian Shi'is in recent years indicates,[12] the problem is purely of a political nature. Classical law does not bear on the controversial areas of the *hajj*.

Other areas of the legal spectrum, still, appear of only marginal relevance. Such is the case, in the present world of nation-states, of the whole field of international law, where the dichotomy between *dar al-harb* (war territory) and *dar al-islam* (peace territory) at the heart of the classical theory has become completely marginal.[13] Similarly, classical criminal law appears, but for some exceptions, not to be followed in the majority of the world's Muslim countries.[14]

The Islamic Renaissance feeds on different legal fields. Although a clear-cut distinction can hardly be made in a vast body of literature which claims to be universal, the importance of only a few legal areas has come to the fore in the years of the renewal. Other areas have been left out. Following the taxonomy just described, international law, criminal law, *'ibadat*, torts and civil law generally, have all remained outside the sphere of interest of the Islamic Renaissance. Similarly, currently relevant parts of the classical *shari'a*, such as the family and succession, have on the whole changed very little since the late 1950s, when important reforms took place in most Muslim countries.[15] Two general areas, in contrast, have been opened to careful scrutiny. They are the constitutional part of public law, and the large field opened up by modern economics: labour law, land law in its specific economic dimension, industrial production and relations, and banking.

The Islamic revival has taken place essentially in these domains. Of course, as in all systematic exercises, there have been many forays into other fields outside the law, including Islamic arts and sciences. In the strict legal domain, writings on civil law, on torts[16] and contracts,[17] were published, and criminal and international law were discussed. These areas did not constitute, however, the crux of the Islamic Renaissance, because the upheaval that the world has witnessed in the Middle Eastern intellectual scene has been much more connected with economic and constitutional issues than with more neutral areas of the civil, criminal, or international law disciplines. Recent turmoil has affected primarily constitutional and economic law, and this is where the intellectual legal production has been at its best and most creative. The Renaissance in Islamic law has been prompted in these two fields, as against other areas which have remained untouched by the revival efforts.

Although it is difficult to explain this selective phenomenon, an essential factor that comes to mind is related to the conditions of the revival. At the heart of it, and at the heart of the renewed interest in Islamic thought worldwide, is without doubt the success and durability of the Islamic Revolution in Iran. Without Iran, Islam would have not come centre stage in the same way, and the vast literature accompanying it would not have come so forcefully into being. The Renaissance, with its emphasis on break and change, has come because of the emergence of a State, the Islamic Republic of Iran, where the received tradition had not developed sufficient conceptual tools.[18]

The establishment of the Iranian State has been directly affected by those legal elements which are central to the concerns of the Iranian revolutionaries now in power. Their interest, because of the peculiar nature of the Revolution, bears precisely on the 'Islamic' formation of State agents, in other words on the Constitution. Because they claim their State to be special and exclusive, the first task confronting the Iranian revolutionaries was the peculiarity of the 'Islamic' State. The other fundamental task was the implementation of a discourse of change in the country's economy. The language of the Iranian Revolution has been premised on an idea of justice which needed implementation, and the tool of the implementation was the law.

These are therefore two priorities of the Islamic Revolution: the 'Islamic' way the institutions of the country are formed, and the 'Islamic' way the production and distribution of wealth is carried out.[19] From the outset of the new regime, an overwhelming interest lay in economics and constitutional law. But the field did not come about as a *deus ex machina*. The Iranian Revolution, like all the revolutions in the world in search of authenticity, had to look back to the tradition for precedents.

Good research on the intellectual roots of the Iranian Revolution has already been achieved, and has uncovered two main strands of revolutionary forerunners. These strands can be described under two headings: the *sufi*, and the *faqih*, traditions. On the one hand, the *sufi* tradition is apolitical and emphasises the philosophical-mystical dimensions of Islam. On the other hand, the *faqih* tradition is deeply concerned with the relationship between government and governed, and is rooted in the legal riches of Islamic culture.

The *sufi* tradition, which fed on such works as Muhammad Husayn Tabataba'i (d. 1983) and Henry Corbin (d. 1978), appears best in the existentialism-influenced background of 'Ali Shari'ati (d. 1977). The Shari'ati legacy is probably most alluring in terms of its humanistic appeal, and it has been the focus of much scholarship in the West in the first years after the revolution.[20] As its relevance to the new Iranian State proved increasingly minimal, and however important a rallying point it represented to the disgruntled opponents of the Shah before the revolution, the *faqih* tradition supplanted it. Law was a much better tool to understand the institutionalisation of the new system.

The *faqih* tradition at the root of the Islamic Renaissance is therefore more appealing from the point of view of the tangible reality of things. As a field where tradition is centuries old, legal scholarship offers an important domain of investigation for the contemporary world.

Yet all the branches of modern law were not equally developed. There is no better example of unequal development than the richness of the field of constitutional law and the virgin territory constituted by economic and financial law.

Theory of government in Islam has ranked high in the concerns of scholars and *'ulama*, and solid work has been produced in this area of modern Islamic thought.[21]

Constitutional theory from an Islamic perspective is important for modern times, particularly in the case of Iran, where the turmoil between 1905 and 1911 was very much enmeshed with the fate of the *mashruta*. The *mashruta*, being the 'Dean of Middle Eastern Constitutions',[22] has been the subject of much scholarship.[23] The constitutional debate has not of course been limited to Iran, but the Iranian events enhanced the received version of government and resource management in a way which shifted the debate to the Shi'i world in an unprecedented manner.[24]

Much work has been produced on government and economics from the legal point of view in Cairo, as well as in the Maghreb. However these works never became truly important, because they never had the chance of finding some practical application from inside the power of a state. It is only retrospectively that Khumaini's *wilayat al-faqih* became significant.[25] Its relevance in effect, and the interest of scholarship in it, were actualised only when its author suddenly seized power. Until 1979, the Iranian leader's reflections on Islamic government represented one pamphlet amongst many others.

But things are not so simple. The dialectic of a text and of an upheaval that claims it as intellectual foreboding and basis does not permit a single answer. The French rhyme of the 1789 Revolution about 'stumbling because it was Voltaire and Rousseau's fault' expresses well the one side of this difficult dialectic.[26] The song claims it was because of the revolutionary thought of the *philosophes* that the revolution took place. But, on the other side of the dialectic, would the Social Contract be anything more than an utopia without Robespierre's actualisation of Jean-Jacques Rousseau?

All other matters remaining equal, the Iranian Revolution offers a similar dialectic. Khumaini's lectures would have passed relatively unnoticed, had Khumaini not come to power in Tehran. But neither would the revolution in Iran have taken the same constitutional form, without the blueprint of the Ayatollah's lectures. It may even be suggested that the revolution in Iran would not have taken place without Khumaini's lectures, the audience which paid attention to them, and the various circles which discussed and elaborated on his theory and tactics.

To carry the comparison with the *philosophes* further, it is suspected that a Rousseau never comes on his own. Who came with Khumaini? This is where the relevance of Shi'i thought as a whole becomes logically compelling. The action was not restricted to a single individual. Beyond the immediate persona of Khumaini, many protagonists prepared the intellectual terrain, and the case of Shari'ati comes naturally to mind as a prime example. But Shari'ati was no jurist, and the function of Shari'ati's texts was mainly cultural.[27] Khumaini's acolytes stemmed from a different background, which was legal both in its formation and its expression. Hence the relevance of Shi'ism. Khumaini is a Shi'i *'alim*, a *mujtahid*. It is in the legal circles in which he and his colleagues were educated that the investigation will yield up the clues to the Iranian constitutional and economic order.

In the Islamic Renaissance as a whole, it is important to bring some perspective to Khumaini by putting him in the wider perspective of the milieu of which he was part. This milieu is rooted in the law colleges of the Shi'i world, most prominent of which was Najaf in the South of Iraq. It is in Najaf that the Islamic legal renewal took place in the 1960s and 1970s. In Najaf, Khumaini himself was one scholar among many.

For a long time, and until he emerged in the light of the Paris exile in the fall of 1978, Khumaini had remained more or less at the periphery. Despite his access to the position of *Ayat Allah* (literally the sign of God, the highest position in the Shi'i legal hierarchy), he was not an innovative jurist by the standards of Shi'i scholarship. Khumaini has little or nothing to say about banking or economics and, even in constitutional law, his main contribution in the Najaf lectures of 1970 was too polemical to offer any significant watershed for the field. Khumaini must be understood as a part, albeit important, of a larger and deeper wave, which is in essence constituted by the 'Shi'i international' formed by the teachers and graduates of the Iranian and Iraqi law colleges.[28]

There was in the Shi'i world a man of much higher intellectual calibre than Khumaini, a man whom Khumaini acclaimed, upon his execution by the Iraqi Ba'th party in April 1980, as 'the prize of Islamic universities':[29] Muhammad Baqer as-Sadr.

Muhammad Baqer as-Sadr: a bio-bibliographical presentation

A decade ago, it would have probably still been necessary to defend the choice of a *'alim* who was completely unknown in the Western world, and who, for a few scholars in the Middle East, merely meant a book, *Iqtisaduna* (*Our Economic System*), and a tragic existence which ended in execution in obscure circumstances in Iraq.

The picture in the late 1980s has radically changed, as the reputation of Sadr, by now well established among his followers currently in exile (mostly in Iran), has crossed the Mediterranean towards Europe and the United States. In 1981, Hanna Batatu had already drawn attention in an article in *The Middle East Journal* in Washington to the importance of Sadr for the underground Shi'i movements in Iraq.[30] In 1984 *Iqtisaduna* was translated, in part, into German, with a long introduction on the Shi'i *'alim* by a young

German orientalist.[31] It soon became impossible to ignore his importance in the revival of Islamic political movements, in Iraq, in the Shi'i world, and in the Muslim world at large. A comparative book on the Islamic movements put Sadr centre stage in relation to Iraq.[32] Then acknowledgment came in Israel,[33] and in France, where a well-informed new journal on the Middle Eastern scene consecrated a long dossier to Muhammad Baqer as-Sadr in 1987.[34]

Muhammad Baqer as-Sadr was born, according to his Arab biographers,[35] in 25 Dhu al-Qi'da 1353/1 March 1935 in Kazimiyya, Iraq, to a family famous in the Shi'i world for its learning. His great-grandfather Sadr ad-Din al-'Amili (d. 1264/1847) was brought up in the Southern Lebanese village of Ma'raka, then emigrated to study in Isfahan and Najaf, where he was buried. His grandfather Isma'il was born in Isfahan in 1258/1842, moved in 1280/1863 to Najaf then Samarra', where he is said to have replaced al-Mujaddid ash-Shirazi in the local *hauza* (Circle of Shi'i scholars). He died in Kazimiyya in 1338/1919. His son Haydar, the father of Muhammad Baqer as-Sadr, was born in Samarra' in 1309/1891, and studied under his father and under *Ayat Allah* al-Ha'iri al-Yazdi in Karbala. He died in Kazimiyya in 1356/1937, leaving a wife, two sons and a daughter. Though a relatively well-known *marja'*, he seems to have died penniless. 'The family, until more than a month after [his] death, were still unable to secure their daily bread, *kanu ha'irin fi luqmat al-'aysh*.'[36]

The 'international' scholarly background, and the relative poverty into which Sadr was born, are the two important elements which determined the context of Sadr's upbringing. The economic hardship that the family faced upon the early death of Haydar as-Sadr came to Muhammad Baqer when he was still an infant.[37] Other members of his family looked after his education, and he grew up under the supervision of his uncle on his mother's side,[38] Murtada Al Yasin, and of his older brother, Isma'il (1340/1921–1388/1968).[39]

In Kazimiyya, Muhammad Baqer went to a primary school called Muntada an-Nashr, where, according to reports of schoolmates, he established himself early on as a subject of interest and curiosity to his teachers, 'so much so that some students took to imitating him in his walk, speech and manner of sitting in class'.[40]

Post mortem descriptions are often eulogistic, and must be taken with circumspection. Against the testimonies of these panegyrics, there is unfortunately no material for contrast, since the government in Iraq does not even acknowledge the existence of Sadr, let alone his intellectual or political achievements. One is therefore limited to the texts themselves, and to the hagiographies of students and followers close to the deceased *'alim*. However unlikely this may be, several reports mention, for example, that Sadr wrote a first treatise at age eleven. 'Abd al-Ghani al-Ardabili, quoted in Ha'iri's biography, refers to this book as a treatise on logic.[41] The earliest published work that can be traced dates however from 1955.[42] This study, an analysis on the episode of Fadak and its significance in Shi'i history, shows great maturity in the young scholar's thoughts in terms of method and substance. The content however betrays a sectarian Shi'i tone which soon disappeared from Sadr's language, until it came back to the fore at the time of the confrontation with the Ba'th in the late 1970s.[43]

In 1365/1945, the family moved to Najaf, where Sadr would remain for the rest of his life. The importance of Najaf had already been established in the twenties as the city and its *'ulama* emerged as the central focus of resistance against the British invasion.[44] A lull followed after a relative defeat against the King in 1924, when major jurists took the route of exile, but most returned a few years later to resume their study and teaching away from political turmoil.

The picture changed radically in the 1950s, as the quietism of the *mujtahid*s, instructed by their inability to stand up to the confrontation with Baghdad, received a serious challenge in the years leading to the 1958 Revolution from an unsuspected quarter, the Communists.[45]

The Communist challenge to the *'ulama* received the attention of one of the most prominent leaders in Najaf, Muhammad Husayn Kashif al-Ghita'. Kashif al-Ghita' greeted in 1953 the American and British ambassadors in the city with complaints about the Western shortsighted attitude to the Middle East. Western policy, he explained to them, was responsible for the fertile ground left open to the development of Communism. This was due to Western support for the Zionist presence in Palestine, and to the government in Baghdad which allowed the perpetuation of the dire poverty of the people and *'ulama*.[46]

Sadr found himself in the midst of a bitter intellectual confrontation between traditional Najaf and the Communists, and his world view was formed with this twofold intellectual background: a Socialist–Communist call prevailing in the whole of the Middle East, which permeated the concern in his writings with the 'social question';[47] and the traditional education of the *'ulama*, including the relatively strict structure of their hierarchy.

More will be said below of the classical education in Najaf in the 1950s and 1960s, because of the importance of the colleges in the constitutional system of the Shi'i world, and the analysis of *Iqtisaduna* will show how Sadr tried to counter the communist appeal to redress the 'social balance'. The constitutional section will also try to use significant aspects of Sadr's early and late life as a contrasting example of the Shi'i *mujtahid*s' hierarchy. In the remainder of this section, the system offered by Sadr's works will be introduced by a rapid overview of his prolific production, against the developments on the Iraqi scene as perceived from Najaf.

The strict, more traditional dimension of Sadr's works appears in several publications which span his life. Most conspicuous are his books on the jurisprudential discipline of *usul al-fiqh*, of which two samples can be considered. One sample belongs to the early years of Najaf, where Sadr wrote an introduction to the history and main characteristics of the discipline, *al-Ma'alim al-Jadida fil-Usul*.[48] This book, which became widely used for introductory teaching at Najaf, was published in 1385/1964. It remains one of the more interesting and accessible works in the field.[49] Sadr himself authored more complicated *usul* works. In 1397/1977, the first tome of a series of four volumes on *'ilm* (the science of) *al-usul*, which were destined to prepare the students for the higher degree of *bahth al-kharej* (graduate research), appeared in Beirut and Cairo.[50] Sadr suggests that he prepared these works to facilitate the task of students, who were otherwise subject to the 'pressure in the language'[51] of the four basic works in use for over a half century in Najaf.[52] *Al-Ma'alim al-Jadida* and the *Durus* series represent the didactic side of Sadr's interest in *usul al-fiqh*. They were intended for the apprentice *'alim* who would find the direct approach to the requirements necessary before *bahth al-kharej* too difficult, and to the lay person generally interested in the overview of the discipline. But Sadr also wrote more advanced works in *usul*, some of which were published posthumously. Most of these advanced works were in the form of notes taken by his students. This is the case of Kazim al-Husayni al-Ha'iri, who compiled a first volume of *Mabaheth al-Usul* in 1407/1987,[53] and of one of Sadr's favourite disciples, Mahmud al-Hashimi, who assembled the section of Sadr's lectures on *Ta'arud al-Adilla ash-Shar'iyya* in a book published in 1977.[54]

The works on *usul* being traditionally student compilations of the lecturers' notes, there is little doubt that many of Sadr's classes must have been recorded, and there will probably appear more *usul* works by Sadr in the future. Biographical sources also mention a first volume in a series entitled *Ghayat al-Fikr fi 'Ilm al-Usul* (*The highest thought in the science of usul*),[55] and it is doubtful that the entire works of Sadr in this field, which he started teaching in Najaf on the higher *kharej* level in 1378/1958[56] will ever be completely recovered.

Akin to these difficult works are Sadr's more general investigations in jurisprudence (*fiqh*), and in logic and philosophy.

The interest in these two areas stems from various concerns. The interest in logic was part of the exercise in *usul*, with a more universal dimension which was meant to offer a response to the same discipline in the West. The main work in this domain is Sadr's *al-Usus al-Mantiqiyya lil-Istiqra'*.[57] Sadr tries to take on the field of logic on its own terms, and *al-Usus al-Mantiqiyya* is filled with references to Russell and to mathematical symbols and equations, leading up to the revelation of the 'true objective' of the work: 'to prove... that the logical bases on which are built all the scientific conclusions derived from observation and experience are the very logical bases on which is built the conclusion on the evidence of a creator and organiser of this world... This conclusion, as any other scientific conclusion, is inductive in its nature.'[58] This work is actually part of the larger system which Sadr was trying to construct on the basis of Islam, and the dabbling in logic with *al-Usus al-Mantiqiyya*, as well as with other smaller contributions,[59] was perhaps the least successful achievement of the system, for Sadr was not well equipped to take on such arcane discipline. It must be noted none the less that the display of technical terms in Arabic is rather remarkable in a field where even terms-of-art are still in the making.

Sadr is better known for his work on philosophy, *Falsafatuna*, which has recently been translated into English.[60] How much the substance of *Falsafatuna* has enriched the philosophical debate in the Muslim world, and whether the work is up to par with the great philosophers in history, is doubtful. The book bears the imprint of the pressing conditions which produced it. Sadr is said to have completed the research and writing in less than a year.[61] In some passages where the authentic Islamic tradition in philosophy surfaces, however, the book reveals the diversity and originality of Sadr's mind. An example drawn from a parallel adapted by Sadr from Mulla Sadra Shirazi (the famous Iranian philosopher, author of *al-Asfar al-Arba'a*, d. 1640) will give an idea of both the constraints of Sadr's philosophical system and its relative originality.

It is now well established that *Falsafatuna* was written in 1959 in reaction to the growing Communist tide in Iraq, particularly among the more disenfranchised Shi'is.[62] Sadr's first purpose was to stem the tide by offering a better understanding and a closer look at Marxism's own system and terminology. *Falsafatuna* appears as a detailed critique, from an Islamic point of view, of the most sophisticated expression of materialist philosophy available then in the Arab world. An appendix to the first edition of the book reveals Sadr's Marxist sources.[63] For a Shi'i *mujtahid*, the effort is remarkable, but the longer term prospects of a book based on a Stalinist-cum-Politzerian dialectical materialism were doomed. Reading *Falsafatuna* now gives a distinct flavour of a *dépassé* language.

What appears to be more interesting than the struggle over the Engels and Stalin philosophical classics of the 1950s (in their Arabic version) is the use in contrast, from time to time, of the philosophical categories of a thinker of Mulla Sadra's stature.

The use of Mulla Sadra's *haraka jawhariyya* is most patent in the chapter of *Falsafatuna* dealing with 'the movement of development'.[64] This chapter typically opens with two quotes from Stalin and Engels on the superiority of Marxist philosophy (dialectical materialism) in its approach to nature as a developing process of contradictions. The quotation sets dialectical materialism in contrast to the idealist school of philosophy, which considers nature in its fixed, unevolving and unevolved form.

First, Sadr points out the fallacy, in the Marxist approach, of impoverishing the philosophical tradition: '...As if the poor metaphysicist had been shorn of all types of understanding... and came not to feel like anybody else... the ways of change and transformation in the world of nature'.[65]

Greek history, says Sadr, has always been mindful of the concept of development in nature. It was never a question for the philosophical debate among the Greeks whether nature develops or not. The debate, with Zeno on the one hand, and the Aristotelian school on the other, was between the first school's emphasis on stages of transformation which carry the object through several discrete phases, and Aristotle's emphasis on movement as a gradualist realisation of the potentiality of the object. This Aristotelian emphasis on the development in nature by the realisation of potentialities was refined by Mulla Sadra's concept of *haraka jawhariyya*.

For Sadr, the concept of motion in the universe received a deeper treatment by Mulla Sadra through an analysis of causality which rests on the concept of development. Mulla Sadra introduced 'a general theory of movement and proved philosophically that movement ... does not only affect the manifestations of nature and its surface epiphenomena'. It goes deeper to the

evolution at the heart of nature and its essentialist motion (*haraka jawhariyya*). This is because the surface movement in its outward manifestations, in that its meaning is renewal and waste, must also have a direct cause which is itself a renewed and unfixed matter, since the causality of fixed matters is itself fixed, and the causality of the changing and renewed is changing and renewed. There can be no fixed direct cause to movement. Otherwise the elements of movement would never come to waste, but stay stagnant and motionless.[66]

Sadr tries to show that the idea of contradiction in the dialectics of Communism is redundant:

Motion in its dialectical understanding rests on the basis of contradiction, and the opposition of contradictions. These conflicts and contradictions are the inner force which pushes movement and creates development. In contrast to this, our philosophical understanding rests on a notion of movement which is considered a course [of passing] from degree to a corresponding degree, without these corresponding degrees ever meeting in one specific stage of the course of the movement.[67]

This example taken from *Falsafatuna* gives an idea of Sadr's arguments and the marshalling of 'Islamic philosophy' in the work. Without assessing the validity of the proposed Islamic system, it is sufficient to say that its subject matter and first *raison d'être* is negative, and this underlying concern weakens the work, although it proved no doubt very valuable to the opposition to Communist ideology in the Iraq of the early 1960s. *Falsafatuna* is so obsessed with Marxist categories that its Islamic language becomes affected by it. In hindsight, of course, criticism is easy: Stalin, Politzer and even Engels' arguments have long become out of fashion in philosophical circles, and their decay has negatively affected Sadr's philosophical treatise itself, which accorded them an importance they do not deserve.

Falsafatuna remains a good example of Sadr's comprehensive efforts to build a full Islamic system of thought. As in the works of logic, the test of time has weakened the arguments, but both efforts remain a unique example of Sadr's diversity of thought. Little in them results from the *mujtahid* tradition, and this is perhaps why they do not appear to be as original and authentic as the other treatises, in which the professionalism of Sadr could emerge more forcefully.

In *fiqh* works by contrast, Sadr was producing what he was expected to produce, namely works of a general legal nature which represent his position as a *mujtahid*. It might be surprising to some extent to find Sadr to be different from other established *mujtahid*s in this respect, who, unlike him, have all tried to offer a comprehensive work of *fiqh* embracing their vast legal knowledge of Shi'i law.[68] The absence of such a *risala 'amaliyya* in his case is attributed to his young age. Sadr was not fifty when he was executed. But there are signs of a work of that nature in his commentary on Muhsin al-Hakim's two volumes *Minhaj as-Salihin* in 1976 and 1980,[69] which were probably completed in the early 1970s, as well as in his three volumes of comments on the nineteenth-century classic by Muhammad Kazem at-Tabataba'i (d. 1327/1919), *al-'Urwa al-Wuthqa*.[70] More importantly, Sadr did release the first volume of a comprehensive work of *fiqh* of his own, *al-Fatawa al-Wadiha*, which he meant as a *risala 'amaliya*.[71] This book was the first in a series which was interrupted, and deals merely with the *'ibadat* section of *fiqh*.

The *fiqh* works can be said to depart little from the tradition, and one cannot see easily how much innovation could be developed in commentaries on works of such respected figures as Hakim and Tabataba'i. But the *Fatawa Wadiha* includes an interesting introductory chapter,[72] which reveals Sadr's readiness to depart from the tradition, even in such established schemes as the century-old dichotomy between *'ibadat* and *mu'amalat*. This departure from the traditional classification is presented as follows:

The rules of the *shari'a*, despite their interconnection, can be divided into four categories:

(1) *'Ibadat*, i.e. purity, prayer, fasting, religious retreats (*i'tikaf*), *hajj*, *'umra* (*hajj* outside the holy month), and repentances (*kaffarat*).

(2) Property law (*amwal*), which is two kinds:

- (a) Public property, by which we mean any property dedicated to a public interest. It includes *zakat* and *khums*, which, despite the fact of their being acts of worship (*'ibadatayn*), have a salient financial aspect. Public property also includes *kharaj* and *anfal* etc. The analysis in this part revolves around the types of public property and the rules related to each and to their expenditure.
- (b) Private property, by which we mean the property of individuals. The analysis of its rules is twofold:

  one: The legal causes for possession or acquisition of a private right whether the property is tangible, (*'ayni*) i.e. outside (*kharij*) property, or an obligation (*fidh-dhimma*), which is property which involves the obligation of another person such as a guarantee or a fine, *gharama*. Into this domain enter the rules of revival (*ihya'*), possession, hunting, servitudes (*taba'iyya*), inheritance, guarantee, fines, including secured contracts, assignments (*hawala*), loans, insurance, and others.

  two: The rules on the disposing of money, including sale, arbitration (*sulh*), companies, trust (*waqf*), and similar transactions.

(3) Private behaviour (*suluk khass*), by which we mean any personal (*shakhsi*) behaviour of an individual, a behaviour which is not directly related to property, and which does not form part of man's worship of his Creator. The rules of private behaviour are twofold:

- (a) Those related to the regulation of the relationship between man and woman. They include marriage, repudiation (*talaq*), *khul'*, *mubara'a*, *zihar*, *ila'* [variations in the law of divorce], etc.

(b) Those related to the regulation of private behaviour in other spheres, including the rules concerning food, drink, clothing, accommodation, social behaviour (*adab al-mu'ashara*), the rules on *nidhr* (religious vow), *yamin* (oath), promise, hunting, animal slaughter, enjoining the good and forbidding the evil, and other similar rules, interdictions, and injunctions.

(4) Public (*'amm*) behaviour, by which we mean the behaviour of the ruler (*wali al-amr*) in the sphere of government, justice, war, and various international relations. Included are the rules of public governance (*al-wilaya al-'amma*), justice, testimonies, penal provisions (*hudud*), *jihad* ('holy' war), etc.[73]

This text is remarkable for the comprehensive structuring of the legal system along lines which differ significantly from the traditional way. All the substantive rules are mentioned, but the *'ibadat-mu'amalat* dichotomy gives way to a more sophisticated and more logical system, which excludes even traditional *'ibadat* rules, such as the 'pillar' of Islam, *zakat*, from their accepted ambit. By re-ordering traditional categories into a consistent taxonomy that excludes *zakat* and *khums* from the *'ibadat* category, and by devising a 'private' sphere section to account for rules of marriage described only a year earlier within the *mu'amalat* genre,[74] the new scheme insulates *'ibadat*, and opens the way to re-ordering the century-old legal classification.

Sadr never completed *al-Fatawa al-Wadiha*, and Islamic law will probably remain bereft of an authority of his stature to affect and re-adapt the traditional scheme. But his legal expertise was not confined to re-ordering the *usul* and *fiqh* disciplines. Where he was most innovative appears in the two areas which form the bulk of the present book, the field of economics, including an important work on Islamic banking,[75] and the constitution.[76]

Before turning to the details of his contributions in this field, the other works of Sadr's encyclopaedic production will be mentioned.

Muhammad Baqer as-Sadr worked on Qur'anic exegesis and on history, and some of his publications in this field are remarkably rich. This is the case of the lectures given in 1979–80 on the 'objective exegesis of the Qur'an', where a combination of historical, political, and methodological remarks on the text and significance of the Qur'an are at work.[77] Similarly, the more historical analyses of Sadr – from *Fadak fit-Tarikh* to his lectures on the Twelve Imams, the 1977 pamphlets on Shi'ism, the various articles on Islamic education, on the Qur'an, and on the political tasks at various stages of the development of the opposition at Najaf – all offer rich insights into the general system on which Sadr was working from his earlier days and into the Iraqi world of hopes and constraints.[78]

But Sadr, like Khumaini, was not on his own. There will appear in the course of this essay several other names from Najaf, of other scholars from the Shi'i world, and also of other (non-Shi'i) luminaries who are important to the Renaissance of Islamic law. Before turning to their contributions, the political context of Muhammad Baqer as-Sadr and his companions will show the extent of the stakes at play.

The political context

The present work is primarily an investigation into the components of the intellectual Renaissance of Najaf, with Muhammad Baqer as-Sadr as one of its most prominent thinkers. The other striking feature of the renewal was its political dimension, and the close interplay between what happened in the obscure alleys and dusty colleges of Najaf, and the Middle East world at large. When Sadr was executed, with his sister Bint al-Huda, probably on 8 April, 1980, the event was a culminating point for the Islamic challenge in Iraq. With Sadr's death, Iraq lost its most important Islamic activist.[79]

The Islamic movement based in Iraq can be followed through the three stages of its intellectual and political development. Back in the late 1950s, the religious circles of Najaf were essentially reactive. As previously mentioned, when *Falsafatuna* was published in 1959, it coincided with the anxious calls by the Najaf *'ulama*, including Muhsin al-Hakim and Sadr's uncle Murtada Al Yasin, to reject the communist appeal.[80] The silence of the *'ulama* until that date was itself a legacy of twentieth-century Iraqi history. The last time the *'ulama* had exercised an active political opposition was in 1923–4, a few years after the great Iraqi revolt of 1920. Then the most famous leaders of Najaf and Karbala went into exile after their confrontation with King Faisal and the British representatives who ruled Iraq. Except for Shaikh Mahdi al-Khalisi, who died in Persian exile in 1925, most returned to Iraq a few years later, and paid with silence the price of their reinsertion. Political mutism remained for three decades, while Shi'i integration in the new Nation-State was proceeding slowly but surely. But in 1959, with the *'ulama*'s audience at an all-time low, the leaders of Najaf and Karbala faced the danger of complete marginalisation as they were threatened into oblivion by the inroads of communism into the fabric of their followers. At the same time, their general perception of 'Abd al-Karim Qasem, who sometimes relied on the Communist wave to strengthen his own power, was inimical. For the *'ulama*, the combination of suspicion towards central rule and the spectre of communism turned direct involvement in politics into a condition for survival. In the reaction to communism and Qasem, Pandora's box was opened.

That first reactive phase of the late 1950s was followed by a period of hesitation and consolidation. Through the following decade of turbulent coups and rapid changes of regimes, an active wing of the *'ulama* pursued its political course, both intellectually and organisationally. The competition between Najaf and Baghdad took many forms. Several documents and testimonies show the efforts in Najaf, Karbala, and Baghdad to heighten awareness of the *'ulama*'s assertive bid in the population at large.

In addition to their hostility to Qasem for being too soft on Communists, the attempt of central rule to diminish further the *mujtahid*s' sway on sensitive issues like matrimonial and family law by implementing an integrated Code of Personal Status was received in Najaf with dismay, even by the well-established and relatively apolitical *'ulama*. The role of the old Muhsin al-Hakim in the opposition to Qasem's Code is paramount, and it took the form of a full-length critique of the 1959 Code by one of his close collaborators, who was himself the scion of an important family of scholars from Najaf.[81]

In the case of Muhammad Baqer as-Sadr, the publication of *Falsafatuna* and *Iqtisaduna* propelled him as the foremost theoretician of the Islamic Renaissance. The philosophical and economic alternative system was to be completed by a social and institutional leg. In *Falsafatuna* and *Iqtisaduna*, a third important volume was promised, which was to be called, on the same pattern, *Mujtama'una* (*Our* [*Islamic*] *Society*).[82] The book was never published, and it is doubtful it was ever written. Instead, we have a number of articles by Sadr on societal themes, which were published in *al-Adwa'*, a journal published at Najaf, and collected after his death as *Risalatuna* (*Our Message*).[83]

The full series of the journal itself is not available, but Sadr's editorials in *Risalatuna* do not betray great originality, and his later articles of the time of the Iranian revolution proved to be of much greater significance. But the mere existence of an openly political journal like *al-Adwa'* in the hitherto sedate Najaf was significant. The reconstitution of the picture of collaborators to the journal is also enlightening for the network of leaders which was then being formed in Southern Iraq.

Two other authors in *al-Adwa'* were Bint al-Huda and Muhammad Husayn Fadlallah. On the collaboration of Bint al-Huda, we have the testimony of her *Collected Works*, also a posthumous publication, which reproduces some of the articles she originally published in 1960 and in 1961.[84] 'It is with great pleasure', she wrote, 'that I meet my female audience at the beginning of each month.'[85] Bint al-Huda was then in charge of the 'feminist rubric', in which she developed, along with her many novels, a vision of the Muslim woman in the ideal Islamic society. A book on Bint al-Huda published in 1985 gives more precise indications on the date of *al-Adwa'*. Here the first issue, which features Bint al-Huda's contribution, is dated 9 June 1960.[86]

Muhammad Husayn Fadlallah, a prominent scholar and leader of the Shi'i community in Lebanon, is another fellow of the small Najaf circle, and he used to write 'the second editorial' of *al-Adwa'* every month.[87] Some of his contributions were also collected in books which were published much later.[88] Fadlallah recalls the enthusiasm of the *Adwa'* period, but also the pressure exercised by the Shi'i establishment which, in combination with the concern of the central government, forced the discontinuation of the journal.[89]

Al-Adwa' was discontinued towards 1963–4, but the testimony of a collection entitled *Min Hadi an-Najaf* (from the guidance of Najaf), which was published in the second half of the 1960s, shows how the network of militant *'ulama* proceeded on the margins of the Najaf establishment.

The books of the collection extant include discussions on themes like the political significance of pilgrimage, the misreadings of the Qur'an by the Orientalists, Islamic literature, the socio-political legacy of the Revolt of Imam Husayn, and the importance of fasting as a symbolic stance against injustice and wrong doing. These works were authored by scholars from Najaf who were destined to political prominence in the 1980s, such as Muhammad Mahdi Shamseddin (the head of the Lebanese Higher Shi'i Council), Mahmud al-Hashimi and Muhammad Baqer al-Hakim (the leaders of the Tehran-based Supreme Council for the Islamic Revolution in Iraq).[90]

Yet the political involvement of the new generation of *'ulama* was constrained by the wariness of older and better established figures, who had much sympathy for the new enthusiasm, were grateful for its success in countering Communist influence, but were also aware of the dangers of unbridled militancy. Testimonies from militant circles shed light on the hesitations of the older *'ulama* (most prominent amongst whom was *Ayat Allah* Abul-Qasem al-Khu'i) who, as in Muhammad Husayn Fadlallah's recollections, succeeded in the mid-1960s to put a curb on political activities. But as the central government was getting increasingly authoritarian and sectarian, the hesitation slowly gave way to the ascendancy of activism.

Then came the third phase, which started when the Ba'th arrived to power in the Summer of 1968. In the now open confrontation, which ended up in the death of Sadr and the destruction of all forms of worldly activity in Najaf, a series of strikes, demonstrations, arrests and repression increased the tension until break point. In the recollection of the protagonists, the first trigger came in the form of a confrontation between Najaf and Baghdad over the establishment of a University at Kufa. The project of the University had been part of the great expansion in Iraq of the educational system, and the active work towards the eradication of illiteracy and the development of higher education. The leaders of Najaf, who saw the establishment of a University in the neighbouring historic city of Kufa as a worthwhile opportunity, pressed the issue forward and were successful in raising the necessary funds for the university from wealthy Shi'i businessmen.[91]

The Ba'th government saw otherwise. Administrative stalling on the Kufa project was accompanied by the increased curb on political activity throughout the country. In retrospect, it is clear that the central government of Ahmad Hasan al-Bakr and Saddam Hussein could not tolerate a project which rendered close control by the repressive apparatus difficult, but its rejection of the project could not be plainly directed against an educational endeavour. The way for a repressive government, for whom the peripheral threat clearly consisted in a Southern Shi'i and a Northern Kurdish one, was to attack the circles of Najaf on the charge of an 'American-Zionist conspiracy'. Mahdi al-Hakim, the son of the Great *Ayat Allah* Muhsin, was the first target of the attack. With Muhammad Bahr al-'Ulum, another close collaborator of his father, a life of underground and exile was beginning. This took place in late 1968 and 1969.

Muhsin al-Hakim was understandably angry, and efforts to patch up the quarrel between him and the Ba'th proved useless. He was reportedly 'on strike' when the government chose to send to Lebanon in 1969 a '*alim* of the Kashif al-Ghita' family as 'Najaf representative', to the great dismay of some Lebanese Shi'i circles.[92] The stage for the next two decades was set. Governmental packing of Najaf was one way, which continued well into the Iran–Iraq war with the same 'Ali Kashif al-Ghita' presiding over numerous 'Islamic popular meetings' held in Baghdad. Dividing between South and North was another successful plank. There was great resentment in Najaf over the rapprochement between Saddam Hussein and the Kurdish leader Mulla Mustafa Barzani, which culminated in the March 1970 agreement: Muhsin al-Hakim and other personalities had expressed dismay towards the heavy-handed treatment of the Kurds by the central government in the preceding years, and the 1970 Agreement was perceived as an ungrateful let down at a time when the Ba'th and the '*ulama* were at daggers drawn. When in June 1970 crowds assembled in Najaf to mourn the death of Muhsin and to voice their disbelief in the accusation that Mahdi was an agent of the CIA,[93] Muhammad Bahr al-'Ulum and Mahdi al-Hakim were in exile and unable to return to Iraq for the mourning ceremonies.

From 1970 onwards troubles recurred yearly against the Iraqi government in Najaf. Muhammad Baqer as-Sadr was arrested several times, and subjected to interrogation and brutal treatment. In the last such instance, in June 1979, as he was preparing to go at the head of a delegation to greet *Ayat Allah* Khumaini in Tehran, he was detained and confined to house arrest. He remained under house arrest until his transfer to Baghdad on 5 April 1980. That date coincided with the second attack on high governmental officials in one week. On 1 April 1980, Tariq 'Aziz, who was then a prominent Ba'thist (but not yet foreign minister), was the target of a grenade attack on the occasion of a speech at Mustansariyya University in Baghdad. 'Aziz was wounded but survived. Students in the rally were not so lucky and, on the occasion of their mourning at the Baghdad Waziriyya University on 5 April, a grenade was again hurled into the crowd. This was for the government the signal for the final confrontation with what they considered the root of his problems. Najaf was invested in the evening, and Muhammad Baqer as-Sadr transferred to Baghdad. Najaf lore recalls that Sadr escaped abduction and imprisonment back in June thanks to Bint al-Huda's rallying the mourners gathered at the *sahn* ('Ali's mosque in Najaf) with the cry 'your imam is being kidnapped'. This time, the government secured the silence of Sadr's sister by taking her along to Baghdad, and by executing her with her brother. Muhammad Baqer's body was reported to have been buried at dawn on 9 April in the presence of relatives from Najaf; thus the presumption of his death a day earlier. But many questions remain unanswered.

Thus ended the build-up of the confrontation inside Iraq between Najaf and Baghdad. The assassination was the focal point for a renewed struggle, which had now extended to the whole Middle Eastern stage. In Lebanon, Kuwait, Iran, Pakistan, India, the Sudan, there fell in the following decade several victims of the war between Muhammad Baqer as-Sadr's friends and Saddam Hussein's supporters.

At a more global level, the confrontation turned into Armageddon, as the Ba'th government first fuite en avant came in the Iran–Iraq war, which was started with the invasion of Iran five months later, on 22 September 1980. Then came the invasion of Kuwait, and, in the wake of the Iraqi rout, the Iraqi *intifada* (revolt) of March 1991, where pictures of Sadr were paraded in the cities of the South during the brief period when they were freed from brutal rule.

Had history gone back full circle? Only time will tell. But the emergence of the Islamic movement in Iran, Iraq and Lebanon cannot be understood without the network which originated and developed in the city of Najaf. A glance at the most prominent figures of the movement in the late 1970s and in the 1980s will show that, without exception, they had studied, resided, or visited their colleagues in Najaf.

With such a complex web of personal and institutional relations as was woven in the Iraqi city, many developments in the Middle East since the access to power in Iran of the most famous Najaf resident, Ruhullah al-Khumaini, bore in a direct or indirect way the imprint of Najaf. The internal Iraqi, Lebanese, and Iranian developments, as well as the international developments which came in the wake of the establishment of the Islamic Republic, were influenced by the legacy of the network.

This, in a nutshell, is the political background of the Renaissance in Najaf. Since the episode of the University of Kufa, the scene of the confrontation has changed into unprecedented globalism. The universal character of the Islamic political challenge started in Najaf would however not have been, without the peculiar intellectual and cultural dimension which it carries. In the midst of dramatic events which were increasingly assuming a global reach, it is important to bear in mind that the Najaf Renaissance was an intellectual phenomenon, involving primarily jurists and legal production. This is the less known dimension of the turbulent Middle East, which is the subject of this book.

At the centre of the cultural renewal and the shaping of the system was 'the Shi'i International', itself the product of the networks of Najaf. In Najaf, Muhammad Baqer as-Sadr, the prize of the Universities as Ruhullah Khumaini called him posthumously, emerges as the founder of a new constitutional and economic system.

PART I

Islamic law and the constitution

Introduction to Part I

No intellectual theme has been more prominent in the Middle East of the twentieth century than the idea of the state. In one way or another, most ideas debated have been closely connected to the ideal form of the state, and nearly all the directions that such a debate could have taken have been probed. The gamut of political theories concerning the state was so wide that it allowed for any ideology, no matter how remote from the society where it was proposed and how thinly connected to its cultural milieu, to find an association with or to curry favour as the ideology of some Middle Eastern group.

It is true that most other countries of the world have witnessed to some extent a similarly wide range of state theories. But a characteristic of the Middle East lay in the difficulty of accepting the classical nation-state which, by the late 1950s, was established in most countries of the world. To date, the reluctance of the debate to deal with nation-states in their present form has been a major indication of the resilience of radically different projections and their claim to order societies in the Middle East according to alternative schemes.

Parallels can of course be found with other areas. South East Asia and Africa have had similar problems of state identity, and the Vietnam and Korean crises, as well as the South-African situation, have seen divisions and controversies which foreshadow and echo the Middle Eastern situation. But the ultimate goal of these crises remained the nation-state. The problem which faced (or faces) these areas was not so deep-rooted as to negate an acceptable and geographically defined state within which the crisis would develop. In those countries, the state as such was not put into question, and crises and problems were articulated on a different ground: socialism or communism versus capitalism, colonial domination v. liberation, racial and tribal control v. integration, pluralistic democracy v. dictatorship... Disagreement ran along these themes, and presupposed an accepted entity over which discord prevailed, and control was sought.

In the case of the twentieth-century Middle East, these themes were important, but there was one further and more critical dimension: the very existence of the state. Alongside those ideological grounds of the debate, many groups rejected the essential form of nation-state accepted elsewhere. This rejection signified that beyond the political problems that were puzzling enough per se, lay a more fundamental area of contention over the state configuration itself. For these ideologies, the nation-state as such was put into question.

It can be argued that the overall picture indicates that the slow but firm establishment of the nation-state on the classical model of decolonisation has taken root even in the Middle East. But this model was regularly challenged by ideologies and demands generally linked to larger entities connecting several nation-states through an integrative utopia.[1] The rejectionist utopia itself has followed the oscillation of a pendulum between two broad forms, (Pan)Arabism and (Pan)Islamism, and can be illustrated by the three consecutive points reached by the pendulum over the century: from the late 1800s to the third decade of the twentieth century, Islamism, or rather Panislamism, was the dominant form of nation-state rejection. From the mid-1920s to the death of Jamal 'Abd an-Naser in 1970, the rise of Panarabism relegated Panislamism to the background. And since the 1970s, the pendulum has returned to favour the rejection of the nation-state in its Islamic form.

With the end of the Iran–Iraq War, the tide of Islamism might have given way again to a dominance of the Panarab rejectionist call, but as with all long trends, perspective remains necessary for assessment. It is also probable that whatever the oscillations of the pendulum of rejection, the other side of the balance will win the day: no trend has been more patent in recent years than the consolidation of the nation-state, and its slow but irrevocable affirmation. But this also still needs some time and distance, and any crisis could wreak havoc on its slow build-up. To date however, even though there have been significant instances where the utopia came closer to reality, as in the Arab confrontation state alignments in wars against Israel in 1967 and in 1973, the nation-state has remained the bedrock, and the rejectionist alternative in all its forms has remained the utopia. The state, in any case, is at the heart of intellectual concern, and both in the Islamic rejectionist utopia and in the converse acceptance of a given nation-state, the *shari'a* has had an important word to say about the forms that the state can and should take. From the balance between nation-state and united utopia, two corresponding poles for the reassertion of the *shari'a* have emerged.

The first pole is externally oriented. It is directly related to strands of the *shari'a* opposing the received notion of nation-state. This is the quest for Islamic utopia. In short, this opposition can be stated as the demand for a suprastatal Islamic order which is reminiscent of the *dar al-harb/ dar al-islam* (abode of war/abode of peace) prototype of the classical jurists' writings. According to this model, a union of all Muslim countries in a single entity is sought, which would resemble the great Islamic empires of the historical tradition: the existing nation-states should vanish before a central Islamic supra-authority which would be responsible for taking over the fate of the Muslim community, the *umma*.

The second pole is internally oriented, and puts the actual mechanisms of an existing state to the test of the *shari'a*. In this approach, the state is a received and accepted notion. The *shari'a* does not then worry about whether a given nation-state is legitimate within its present boundaries. It accepts these boundaries, avoids putting them into question, and concerns itself with the form and the details of the law as it emanates or should emanate from state authority. In short, it deals with the Islamic state without questioning the relevance of its boundaries.

In our study of the *shari'a*'s constitutional impact, the utopian rejectionist aspect of the debate over the state is deliberately ignored.

Although it is of great interest to review the present discussions among Islamic groups concerning the necessity for Muslims to unite into an integrated supra-statal entity, and to examine how these groups base their utopia in the law, such an exercise appears more in the nature of 'international relations' than in a properly legal endeavour. Many valuable studies have been devoted to the early and late forms of Panislamism throughout the century,[2] but it might well be that the *shari'a* is incapable of articulating a discrete theory of international law which is properly Islamic.

Shaybani's *as-Siyar al-Kabir*[3] is generally mentioned as one of the earliest forms of Islamic 'international public law' and used as a measuring rod for the analysis of modern Islamic utopias, but the suggestion of exercising *qiyas* (analogy) over this type of legal literature remains of limited value for the modern world of nation-states. A comparison with the early jurists' international law literature works as a cultural, rather than as a legal, referent. Furthermore, such comparisons are not essentially different from the Panarab suprastatal discourse in its repeated references to the episodes of the glorious past of the unity against the Crusaders. Both comparative uses betray a historical–cultural terminology, rather than any legally articulated discourse. Because of the cultural emphasis in this approach, even for the states which use the utopia of Panislam as a guiding directive (one thinks mostly of Iran in recent times, but there are other 'solidarity' exercises based on Islam, which are at work in Pakistan, Saudi Arabia, Libya, and Iraq), the *shari'a* functions as ideology and not as law.

It is therefore mostly with the second pole, the internal one, that the analysis is concerned in the following constitutional chapter. The starting point takes as an accepted axiom the existence of a given nation-state, including the normal attributes of sovereignty, given boundaries, and international recognition. With no quarrel over the normal twentieth-century attributes of this state, and no emphasis on its subsumption under an international Islamic order, the only question left for the law is an internal one, which is essentially related to the state as supreme rule-maker and coercer. The *shari'a* then purports to construct a cogent definition of this dimension of the Islamic state.

This is the point where the legal halo in Islam appears decisive. All Islamic groups depart from a single shared definition of the Islamic state: 'The Islamic state is a state ruled by Islamic law.'

The definition of the 'rule by Islamic law' in that Islamic state is therefore the matrix of state theory in Islam. This matrix can be broadly described as being constituted by two key elements, which respond to the question of

(1) what Islamic law is and (2) who decides the nature and content of Islamic law.

Thus presented, the matrix allows the analysis to reduce the issues to examining the theory and practice of who the decision-makers are in a given Islamic state, thereby answering the second point concerning who says what Islamic law is. It is much more difficult to articulate the substance of Islamic law, and consequently to answer question one on the nature of Islamic law, since the *shari'a* is by essence all-encompassing. The following chapters try to shed light on the thorny issues connected with the question of 'who decides what Islamic law is'. Part II will develop some of the Renaissance's answers to the substance of Islamic law in economic and financial matters.

In our presentation of recent constitutional developments, the analysis does not proceed in historical or chronological order. Rather, a reverse decoding is attempted, which selects manifestations which appear at variance with the normal use of Islamic legal terminology, then elaborates on their significance in comparative and historical perspective. Three selections are made for their constitutional significance in the *shari'a*.

The first selection consists of a number of texts written over the past three decades by a contemporary Shi'i *'alim*, Muhammad Bahr al-'Ulum. The peculiarity of these texts appears in the variations of Bahr al-'Ulum's approach to the same legal controversy. This controversy has developed as the most significant split between Shi'i schools, and culminated in the eighteenth century. The two schools are the Usuli school, which came victorious in the debate, and the Akhbari school, which is said to have dominated the sixteenth to eighteenth century until its foundering under the critique of the Shi'i jurist al-Wahid al-Behbehani (d.1205/1791).

It is hard to find original texts which are self-labelled Usuli or Akhbari. What is generally acknowledged is that a serious rift has taken place in Shi'i law, and that, but for minor pockets of Akhbarism, Usulism is the sole school extant.

In recent years, however, and there is no better example of this than the writings of Muhammad Bahr al-'Ulum, emphasis has shifted from a simple acknowledgment of the rift between Akhbaris and Usulis, to a noted rapprochement which obliterates the traditionally recognised differences.

The value of such an analysis goes beyond the mere description of the two schools' tenets, and sheds light on the larger picture of contemporary Shi'i law, especially from the point of view of whom is entitled to say what the law is. The arguments of the controversy clarify the Shi'i legal structure in its present dominant Usuli form.

Next to the insistence on the closeness of Akhbarism and Usulism despite the deep historical disputes, the second manifestation of an odd use of the language encountered in modern Shi'i texts derives from the way some episodes of the life of Muhammad Baqer as-Sadr have been reported. An intriguing remark of one of Sadr's biographers is the occasion for the study of the hierarchy of knowledge in the Shi'i jurisprudential apparatus and the training and curriculum of the Shi'i *'ulama*.

A third odd use in the discourse of contemporary Shi'i jurists, which is drawn from an exchange of letters in 1979–80 between Muhammad Baqer as-Sadr and Ruhullah al-Khumaini and from variations on honorific titles which are conspicuous in this correspondence, sets the stage for the final element in the structure of decision-making in legal interpretation. This correspondence is the occasion of an investigation into the ways an acknowledged jurist can reach the highest point of the hierarchy, which is the position of 'Leadership' so central to the Islamic state defined as a state of (Islamic) law. The study can then proceed to a further stage, which involves the making of the modern Iranian constitution.

It is generally acknowledged that one very important text that foreshadowed the Iranian system of government is *Ayat Allah* Ruhullah al-Khumaini's *Velayat-e Faqih*, which was originally delivered as a series of lectures in Najaf in 1970. There is little doubt that the Iranian system has adopted some of Khumaini's conclusions in this text. But a more significant contribution immediately preceded the Iranian revolution and, unlike Khumaini's opus, corresponded to some of the most detailed propositions one finds in the Iranian Constitution.[4] This work of Muhammad Baqer as-Sadr has recently received more recognition in the West as a significant contribution to Islamic constitutionalism.[5]

Before this stage, however, the process by which Sadr himself reached this final blueprint must be examined, against the background of other prominent Islamic scholars of the century, with regard to two major concerns expressed in the field: how he based his constitutional scheme in the Qur'an (stage 1), and how his view of the more abstract State theory developed from his earliest texts through to 1979 (stage 2).

Whatever the similarities with Sadr's texts, or with Khumaini's lectures on Islamic Government, the accession to power of Khumaini's (and Sadr's) disciples in Tehran infused new life into the law. The Constitution in Iran, like any legal text, started an existence of its own, and responded to a logic that was different in its essence from the pure realm of theoretical jurisprudence.

In 1988, many contradictions which were already apparent in some of the earlier texts, as well as in the structure of the Shi'i legal hierarchy, were given expression in Iran in a series of important developments prompted by the highest circles of the system, including the Leader himself, Khumaini. The same year saw, in the aftermath of these exchanges, a radical departure from the Iranian text of 1979, with the emergence of a new constitutional body, and the relative demise of the powerful Council of Guardians. In the summer of 1989, the death of Khumaini and the adoption of a major revision of the Constitution in Iran marked a new phase in Iran.

1 Archetypes of Shi'i law

The relevance of the Usuli/Akhbari controversy

A received notion of contemporary Shi'i law is the major division in the history of Ja'farism[1] between two schools of law, the Usuli and the Akhbari *madhhab*s (schools), and the dominance of each alternatively since the emergence of Shi'i *fiqh*. Since the end of the eighteenth century however, it is generally acknowledged that Shi'i law came under complete control of the Usuli school.

Recently, there has been a renewed interest in the two schools, and some good research carried out on the earlier periods of Akhbari dominance, at the beginning of the Safavid period,[2] as well as the critical period in the eighteenth century[3] that saw the triumph of the eponym of the present Usuli school, Al-Wahid al-Behbehani, about whom very little is known.[4]

The present analysis is less concerned by the establishment, rise and wane of Akhbarism and Usulism than with the present perception of the debate by modern Shi'i jurists. The emphasis on the contemporary perception is partly related to the difficulty in accessing early documents. But it is also premised on the necessity to emphasise methodologically the relevance of the controversy on the present structure of Shi'i law. Whatever the earlier dissensions and their historical dimension, the differences have to some extent become mooted, since the Akhbari school has been discarded for over two centuries. Usulism rules unchallenged. The extremely limited geographical sway of Akhbarism confines its role, by contrast, to that of a revelator of Usuli characteristics: the distinguishing features of contemporary Usuli Shi'i law can be more clearly perceived in the light of their contrast with Akhbarism.

It is not possible to find in the present legal texts of the Shi'i world a defence of Akhbarism in relation to any particular legal view. But in recent years, some Shi'i '*ulama* have 'revisited' the Akhbari-Usuli controversy.[5] The most thorough testimony, and the one which tells most about the present perspectives in Shi'i circles on the controversy, has consisted of a series of studies over three decades by a jurist closely associated with the Najaf Renaissance, Muhammad Bahr al-'Ulum.

Born in 1927 to a family famous for its scholarship,[6] Muhammad Bahr al-'Ulum appears already in the early 1960s as a close collaborator of *Ayat Allah* Muhsin al-Hakim (d. 1970), for whom he wrote a detailed critique of the personal status law just passed in Iraq.[7] With the son of Muhsin, Mahdi (who was assassinated in the Sudan in 1988), he was one of the first *'ulama* of the Najaf Renaissance who took the route of exile after the access to power in Baghdad of the Ba'th party. After a period spent in Iran and in Egypt, where he submitted a doctoral thesis on *The Vices of Consent in Islamic Law*,[8] he settled among the Iraqi exile community in England and acts as one of its leading spiritual guides.

Bahr al-'Ulum addressed the Usuli–Akhbari controversy on three occasions, in 1964, in 1978, and in 1987–8.[9] In these essays, the historical core of the emergence of Akhbarism and its development has remained generally similar, but the areas of difference as he perceived them in the three instances were significantly different.

The renewal of Akhbarism manifested itself in the eleventh century AH in the writings of Mirza Muhammad Amin al-Astarabadi, who, after studying in Najaf, went on to Medina and then to Mecca to found his own school.[10]

Astarabadi was a 'dedicated Akhbari',[11] and he tried to find roots for his school in the early days of Shi'ism after the *ghayba* (the occultation of the twelfth Imam in the ninth century). He argued that the Akhbari school was dominant until Kulayni (d. 329/941) and as-Saduq (d. 381/991), and that it only receded in the fourth century AH, after some Shi'i scholars started introducing the concept of *'aql* (which can be translated briefly as reason, rationality) in the logical system of the law, the *usul*.

The struggle against the science of *usul* as then received[12] was based on the rejection of 'common elements and Usuli methods that might distance them from the legal texts',[13] and on Astarabadi's perception of an unacceptable veering towards Sunnism by the propounders of *usul* among the Shi'i *'ulama*. Bahr al-'Ulum argues that the underlying reason for this struggle was related to the precedence of the Sunnis in developing *usul*, which the Shi'is did not need before the *ghayba*, since the Imams were still capable of decreeing the proper law to follow without any help from methodological construction. This view is illustrated in the use by the Shi'is of Sunni Usuli concepts, a matter disfavoured by purists like Astarabadi. For Astarabadi and the Akhbaris, Sunni precedence in the discipline meant Sunni pre-eminence, and rendered the whole field of usul suspect. 'An example is the word *ijtihad*, which our Imami *'ulama* took from Sunni *fiqh* and developed. The Akhbaris, who did not realise the essential transformation in the meaning of the word, concluded that the science of *usul* among our pairs had adopted the same general direction followed by Sunni scientific thought. They therefore rejected *ijtihad*'.[14]

In Bahr al-'Ulum's 1964 account, the essence of Akhbarism appears in the school's rejection of *ijtihad* in the interpretive process, and in its literal standing by the reports (*akhbar*) ascribed to the Prophet and to the Imams in the four Shi'i *hadith* compilations.[15] For Akhbarism, as read by Bahr al-'Ulum, these texts are beyond questioning, and there is consequently no need to devise a science of interpretation that might endanger their authenticity by unnecessary glosses.

The room for interpretation generally accorded to the jurists by the Shi'is, through the combination of *ijtihad* as a general process and *'aql*[16] as its primary tool, appears at the core of the eighteenth-century controversy between Astarabadi and Behbehani.

But the differences cover a much wider field, and extend to minute details in legal methodology, which tend to indicate that the depth of the rift between the two schools was important historically. But for modern Shi'i jurists, typified by Muhammad Bahr al-'Ulum, the rift appeared less and less considerable. The differences between Akhbaris and Usulis were slowly toned down by logical and legal arguments.

Akhbaris and Usulis: the differences

Some authors have reported up to several dozen major points of difference between Akhbarism and Usulism. Following Yusuf al-Bahrani, Muhammad Bahr al-'Ulum reduces them to twenty-nine points, which are added to the six historical and psychological differences that characterise the shape of the rift between the two schools. Akbarism, it is suggested, forbids *ijtihad*, reduces the sources of law to the Qur'an and the *Sunna*, and, for some Akhbaris, only to the *Sunna*. Only the twelve Imams' interpretation matters, and their manifest *hadith* will prevail over the uncertain or general text of the Qur'an. Indeed the whole discipline of *usul* is superfluous and both *usul* and *ijtihad* are rejected as Sunni devices which are alien to the Twelvers. The relationship of Shi'i society to the Hidden Imam during the Great Occultation is done through a literal and exclusive understanding of the texts of the Twelve Imams. No intermediary is needed, and no *mujtahid*s.

For the Usulis in clear contrast, the Qur'an and the *Sunna* must be supplemented by *ijma'* (consensus) and *'aql* (reason). The role of the *mujtahid* and his practice of *usul* as an elaborate science of interpretation are paramount. The Qur'anic text will prevail over the more specific *hadith*, and it will be up to the *mujtahid* to reconcile the possible contradictions. On the social level, it is necessary to follow a living *mujtahid* like the Imam, and this rule is so important that it will be generally prohibited to be the follower (*muqallid*) of a dead scholar, however prominent he may have been: 'Imitation of the dead is forbidden'.[17]

The most significant differences can be regrouped, from the perspective of the form of present Shi'i law, in the two following interconnected themes, which bear on the (1) legal-technical and (2) social structure of Shi'ism.

(1) *Legal*: The differences in legal interpretation derive from the acceptance by the Usulis of *ijtihad*. *Ijtihad* can be described as the elaboration of law with the help of logic, by a constantly creative process. The process of elaboration is necessary for the Usulis, and forbidden by the Akhbaris. The sources of the law which are therefore acknowledged by the Akhbaris are reduced to the two which do not require (in theory) any interpretive effort, the *Kitab* (the Book, the Qur'an) and the *Sunna*. Some Akhbaris, according

to Muhammad Bahr al-'Ulum, actually recognise only the *Sunna* as a source of law, because the *Sunna* is the only scientifically sound and non-contradictable element, coming as it does without need for elaboration from the *Ma'sum* (the Imam). In contrast, the Usulis admit four basic sources of law, the *Kitab*, the *Sunna*, *ijma'*, and *qiyas*. *Hadith* is also matter for contention. The Akhbaris divide *hadith* into strong and weak, whereas the Usulis distinguish between four *hadith* layers.[18]

(2) *Social*: From these technical and legal differences, derive important consequences on the social structure of the Shi'i legal community. In the same way *ijtihad* appears as the central point of controversy between Usulis and Akhbaris, the existence and authority of the *mujtahid*s are the dividing element in the social configuration resulting from the schools' differences. Since science is the prerogative of the sole Imam, the non-Imam will inevitably be a fallible judge. This is readily acknowledged by both schools, but the Akhbaris force the premise into its full logical conclusion, and science, as the knowledge of things certain, becomes therefore impossible for Akhbarism in the absence of the Imam. The whole society is bound to imitate the *Ma'sum*, and the fact of his absence during the *ghayba* does not alter the picture. Since only the *Ma'sum* is abreast of religious affairs, the role of any other person, including the most learned jurist, becomes superfluous. In Akhbari society, there is no place for the *mujtahid*.

The full singularity of Usulism appears in contrast to this aspect of the Akhbari argument. For the Usulis, *ijtihad* is necessary, and the specialist of *ijtihad* becomes ipso facto superior in knowledge and status to the non-specialist, who is relegated to the second rank of imitator. Society is therefore divided between *muqallid*s and *mujtahid*s, and the *muqallid*s must follow the *mujtahid*s in the same way they follow the Imam. Another significant corollary of this supremacy of the *mujtahid* is the duty for the *muqallid*, not only to follow a *mujtahid*, but also to follow a living *mujtahid*. In Akhbari Usul, only the twelve Imams can be imitated. A fortiori, there is no requirement for the *taqlid* of any *mujtahid*, past or present. For the Usulis, in contrast, the imitation of the dead *mujtahid* is forbidden. The reproduction of *ijtihad* as a creative process is thereby guaranteed.

Thus appears, in Bahr al-'Ulum's account of 1964, the perception of the two schools of law and the significance of their differences. By the late 1970s, however, the picture had significantly changed. In a major work on *ijtihad*, published in 1977,[19] the subject was again discussed, but Bahr al-'Ulum's assessment of the controversy was now clearly based on belittling the differences between Akhbarism and Usulism.

The argument proceeds in the chapter on 'The Akhbariyya and the prohibition of *ijtihad*'[20] by a division of the long history of the Akhbari trend into three major periods. The first period is blurred in the sources. Perusal of the earliest texts mentioning Akhbarism shows a brief and inconclusive quotation of Hilli (d. 726/1325) and, in a much later text by the important Akhbari jurist mentioned earlier, al-Astarabadi (d. 1036/1626), Astarabadi's projection of his own Akhbari tenets back to the early scholars and compilers of recognised Shi'i *hadith* works, al-Kulayni and al-Qummi.[21]

The second period is more significant. It starts with Astarabadi, who heavily criticised the Usulis in *al-Fawa'ed al-Madaniyya*:

> The correct position was that of our Akhbari forebears ... the Qur'an has mostly come by way of obfuscation (*ta'miya*) of the people's minds (*adhhan ar-ra'iyya*), and so did most of the prophetic rules (*sunan nabawiyya*), and we have no way to know about legal rules, whether principal or secondary,[22] except to hear the two Sadeqs [the two Imams Muhammad al-Baqer and Ja'far as-Sadeq]. It is forbidden to deduce theoretical conclusions from the manifest [texts] in the Qur'an, or from the manifest texts of the Prophet's *Sunna* as long as their contexts (*ahwal*) are not known according to the *ahl adh-dhikr* [the Imams].[23]

This passage clearly shows, comments Bahr al-'Ulum, that the only accepted sources for Akhbarism are the *Kitab* and the *Sunna* as told by the Imams. 'This means the prohibition for the *faqih* to interpret and deduce (*ijtihad wa istinbat*) except in the limits drawn from the *akhbar* related to the Imams'.[24]

The third period introduced the compromising position of Yusuf al-Bahrani.[25] This 'stage of moderation' serves Bahr al-'Ulum as a model for the assessment of the controversy. The major differences between the two schools are analysed to show that they are in reality much less significant than the drawn out history of the tug-of-war between the schools seems to suggest.[26]

The new analysis is nowhere more developed than in Muhammad Bahr al-'Ulum's recent reconsideration of the Akhbariyya.[27]

Absolute rapprochement

Bahr al-'Ulum's most recent study of the subject shows the significance of his departure from his earlier views on Akhbarism: 'The allegation of the prohibition of *ijtihad* of the Akhbaris is unfounded, and their practice contradicts this allegation.'[28] Usulis are deemed not to be different from Akhbaris, as the rapprochement has become even more absolute than in Muhammad Bahr al-'Ulum's 1977 opus on *Ijtihad*. Bahr al-'Ulum does not only try to relativise the differences, as he did then through an emphasis on the moderate attitude of Yusuf al-Bahrani. This time, the analysis is set towards complete obliteration of the two schools' differences.

The process by which this diametrically opposite conclusion to the 1964 description is reached consists of a mixture of legal and functional arguments. In 1964, the differences between the two schools appeared considerable both from a legal and a social point of view. To deflect them, Bahr al-'Ulum reduced the differences between the Akhbaris and the Usulis to two main headings, which correspond to our description of the differences between Akhbarism and Usulism as technical-legal and social.

(1) *Legal*: The legal differences are now approached by Muhammad Bahr al-'Ulum in a way that blurs them so much that they disappear. 'The

essential debate – as it appears to me – is limited to the two parties' views on the [accepted] methods of the law (the tools of legislation, *adillat at-tashri'*). For the Akhbaris, they are only the *Kitab* and the *Sunna*, whereas they are four for the *mujtahid*s [the Usulis], that is, in addition, *ijma'* and *'aql*, and other corollary methods like *istishab*, *istihsan* etc.'[29]

But *ijma'*, Muhammad Bahr al-'Ulum argues quoting Muhammad Rida al-Muzaffar,[30] 'in that it is *ijma'*, contains no scientific value, as long as it does not unveil (*yakshuf*) the word of the *Ma'sum*. If it unveils with certainty (*qat'*) the *Ma'sum*'s word, the evidence (*hujja*) is in truth the [matter] unveiled (*munkashaf*) and not the [method of] unveiling (*kashef*). *Ijma'* therefore enters the realm of the *Sunna* and does not constitute an independent argument (*dalil*) beside it.'[31] In other words, *ijma'* as consensus is subsumed under the *Sunna*, and does not represent a new methodological tool which would be so autonomous as to constitute a separate source or method of the law.

For the Usuli–Akhbari controversy, such an incorporation of *ijma'* carries important consequences, and reveals an unsuspected characteristic of modern Shi'ism. Bahr al-'Ulum actually suggests that Akhbarism was right in its rejection of the originality of *ijma'*, and that there is no ground for the assertion of its autonomy as a source of law. Seen in this light, *ijma'* cannot be considered logically or historically as 'a source of Islamic law'.[32]

As for *'aql*, Bahr al-'Ulum uses a logical argument which also deflects the differences between Usulism and Akhbarism. This time, however, the argument undermines the Akhbari, not the Usuli, assertion. Like Muhammad Taqi al-Hakim,[33] Muhammad Bahr al-'Ulum considers that ''*aql* is the source of arguments (*hujaj*). Arguments lead unto it, as the sole reference (*marja'*) in the principles of religion and in some of the branches (*furu'*), which the Legislator cannot issue a rule in, such as orders of submission (*ita'a*), and the subsequent subdivisions of duties as to knowledge and ignorance... '[34] In other words, *'aql* is the inevitable organiser of religious principles, and the way by which secondary rules can be reached. It is the inevitability of resorting to reason even for relatively basic rules that makes the Akhbari jurist, willy nilly, a *mujtahid*.

(2) *Social*: The second important difference, which we have described as social, focuses in the recent manuscript, as well as, less emphatically, in the earlier work of Muhammad Bahr al-'Ulum on *ijtihad*,[35] on the jurist's function and role in society. Bahr al-'Ulum had argued in 1964 that the *mujtahid* was not necessary for Akhbarism, as he, unlike the Imam, is fallible. There was consequently no need for an interpreter who would introduce law to the non-initiate. In contrast, Bahr al-'Ulum argues now for a reconciliation on the ground that 'the Akhbari *faqih* is a *mujtahid* without admitting it, because when he goes back to the two essential sources [of the law, the *Kitab* and the *Sunna*], he needs to exercise a faculty (*malaka*) to understand the legal rule, and transmit it to his *muqallid* (imitator)'.[36] As in the argument over *'aql*, Bahr al-'Ulum uses a logical device to show that whatever the theory of *ijtihad*, and whether it is accepted or rejected by the schools, it

remains inevitable that at least some construing and interpretive exercise should be undertaken in any reading of the law. The jurist, any jurist, is a *mujtahid malgré lui*.[37]

Conclusion: The significance of the controversy

The development of the contemporary perception of the Usuli/Akhbari controversy in Muhammad Bahr al-'Ulum's works has instructive value going beyond marshalling legal arguments for the one or other school, or the advocacy of their ultimate concordance. As argued in the introduction to this section, the importance of the Akhbari/Usuli controversy for the present research lies less in the reconstruction of the historical 'truth' of the debate, than in the emphasis on its contemporary impact.

The reading of the controversy casts new light on the institutional and legal structure of present day Shi'ism. When Bahr al-'Ulum concluded that a jurist can but be an interpreter, a *mujtahid*, in that even a minimal reading exercise involves extrapolation, he subsumed the difference between Akhbarism and Usulism under a more general argument which has important implications for the modern theory of Islamic law.

According to his argument, whenever the jurist, in society, reads the law, he must interpret it. When the Akhbaris tried to limit the jurist's power, they were defeated because they were trying to solve an essential – and unsolvable – contradiction. A jurist, whose task and duties in society are so diminished as in the Akhbari theory, must ultimately abdicate his title. If a jurist must remain of use, there is no alternative but to assume his legal interpretive social role. It is not possible to limit *ijtihad* by imposing constraints on logic, as the Akhbaris do by denying *'aql*. Nor is it possible suddenly to declare interpretation illegal by decree, as in the received absurd notion of the so-called 'closing of the gate of *ijtihad*'.[38]

Two caveats might add perspective to the Shi'i controversy and to Islamic law in general. The first is functional. If a jurist is in any case a *mujtahid malgré lui*, as suggested by Bahr al-'Ulum, then the whole relevance of the celebrated Akhbari/Usuli controversy becomes moot, as does the theory of the closing of *bab al-ijtihad*. In other words, these notions appear as pure casuistry.

In logical terms, the controversy may be irrelevant. But there are dimensions of greater depth, which call this conclusion into question. Such questions, as is suggested by modern semiotics, show that, despite their functional vacuity, they remain essential as the locus of a superior realm of contention, only taking the form of legalism. Legalism, in the Shi'i eighteenth-century Akhbari/Usuli controversy, and in the Sunni tenth-century alleged theory of the closure of the gates of *ijtihad*, might just be a façade hiding a more significant social issue.[39]

The second caveat is related to the distinctiveness of Shi'ism. The triumph of Usulism is ultimately the triumph of the jurists. But the jurists are not so much interpreters of the law as the exclusive interpreters of religious law, of law *qua* religion. The uniqueness of modern Shi'ism lies in the autonomous body of Shi'i *mujtahid*s who are vested with the protection of the law – and religion – through their interpretative power. The fact that a lay Shi'i, a *muqallid*, must follow a living *mujtahid* in all walks of life is the most telling indication of the *mujtahid*s' importance as a compact and constantly rejuvenated body. Their significance becomes paramount on the social level, because the *mujtahid*s are established in Usuli theory as living referents for society in the most sensitive and crucial element, the law.

In the following chapters, the argument on the paramount role of the jurist will be carried further. But first, more should be said on the material circumstances of the inheritors of Usulism, particularly in the educational mechanisms which, in modern Shi'i society, streamline scholars, legitimise them, draw the intellectual configuration of their expertise, and make a relatively strict hierarchy of their leadership.

Shi'i law colleges, traditional curriculum and new concerns

Muhammad Baqer as-Sadr was intellectually precocious. But the insistence on his genius among his biographers seems disproportionate to the importance of the theme, even in the quasi-hagiographic descriptions of his students and followers who wrote about him.[40] Sadr's written work[41] speaks for itself, and there is little doubt that in the world of Islam in the twentieth century, he will rank with time as highly as the great reformists of the calibre of Jamal ad-Din al-Afghani and Muhammad 'Abduh.

But there was perhaps more to the assertion of Sadr's intellectual superiority than a biographer's laudatory inclination.

Whether for Sadr's personal life, or in the larger terms of Shi'i law, this chapter would like to suggest that intellectual superiority is not neutral in Shi'i circles. On it depends recognition, and recognition in Shi'i civil society[42] entails financial as well as social establishment, and in the State (whether as opposition or government), recognition means leadership. The crucial question in the case of Sadr was whether he could, whilst still alive, claim the highest intellectual achievement among the Shi'i jurists. As was just seen, a main point of divergence between the Usulis and the Akhbaris revolved over the imitation, *taqlid*, of a dead jurist. By establishing the necessity to choose a living jurist as the source of emulation, the Usulis had succeeded in institutionalising a pattern of active competition in the scholarship of the law.

Competition, thus, is of the essence in the legal and social structure of Shi'ism. It determines the barometer of learnedness and the subsequent number of followers in the Shi'i civil society, let alone in the State when it is, like in Iran, based on the government of the most learned *faqih*.

Two episodes of Sadr's life serve well the purpose of unveiling characteristics of the Shi'i law schools, and the consequent repercussions on the Islamic state. The first event is taken from Sadr's early life, and introduces the description of the schools of law in the Iraqi South. The second event was far more dramatic, and sheds light on the higher echelons of the Shi'i hierarchy. These episodes are used here to introduce the structure of the law schools where the jurists were assembled in a specific hierarchy, and to exemplify the ladder of this hierarchy, as well as the repercussions of these structures on the constitution of the Islamic State.

An early episode: when did Sadr stop imitating?

I asked the *ustadh* [The master, Sadr] one day if he followed sometime a *'alim*? He answered: I followed (*qalladtu*) before reaching the age of responsibility (*qabl bulughi sinn at-taklif*) the late Muhammad Rida Al Yasin. But after this age, I stopped following anyone. And I [Ha'iri] cannot recall whether he said: I worked since adulthood after my own opinion (*ra'yi*), or I used to waver between working with caution (*ihtiyat*) or after my opinion (*bir-ra'i*).[43]

Even before the 1958 Revolution, the young apprentice-*'ulama* in Najaf had come to realise that short of a renewal, their position might be irreversibly jeopardised. Sadr was among the discontented, as were Mahdi al-Hakim, Muhammad Bahr al-'Ulum, Muhammad Mahdi Shamseddin, and Muhammad Husain Fadlallah. The respect earned by 'martyrdom' of the Communist leader Fahd on the gallows in the wake of the 1948 revolt, furthered a well-grounded fear of the Shi'i *'ulama*: they were losing their audience.[44]

In the early 1950s, an intellectual renewal had already occurred at the highest hierarchical level with the publication by the great *mujtahid* Muhammad Husain Kashif al-Ghita' of *al-Muthul al-'Ulya fil-Islam la fi Bhamdun*, and of his *Muhawarat* after the visit to his home in Najaf of the British and American ambassadors.[45]

These books, which went into numerous editions, meant for the enthusiastic young Najafi *'ulama* that a door was opened to a new kind of literature. In them, as already suggested, two essential messages of Kashif al-Ghita' were charting the way ahead: (1) that a renewal of Islam was the only solution; and (2) that short of this Renaissance the two threats that had made violent inroads into Islamic society, Zionism and Communism, would remain unchecked.

The problem with opening the door widely to a new type of literature was the challenge posed to the Najaf curriculum, and it is understandable that some of the older *mujtahid*s, including Kashif al-Ghita', would have had second thoughts over the matter. It was inconceivable to overhaul the curriculum completely. But Communism was on the rise, and there was not much room to manoeuvre.

Between the slow ladder towards scholarship which put reins on the young scholars' enthusiasm, and the daunting Communist threat, a compromise had to be sought. A by-product of this compromise appears in this remembrance of Ha'iri on Muhammad Baqer as-Sadr's spirit of independence in *ijtihad* from the acknowledged pundits, quoted at the beginning of this section.

In this recollection, Sadr's independence appears in contrast to the constraints of a *ʿalim* within a relatively precise hierarchy which he could not bypass without endangering his juristic rank. It was all very well to write about the village of Fadak and the early problems of Sunni and Shiʿi legitimacy,[46] or a few years later, as he turned thirty, about an Islamic philosophical system that would put Communism in check,[47] but the traditional studies required for a *ʿalim* could not be forgotten lest the advancement of the young Sadr be jeopardised. In those early years, little in terms of his works was directly related to the teachings in the law that the Najafi schools were supposed to produce. The answer of Sadr to Ha'iri about his refusal to imitate any other *ʿalim* is therefore a testimony of rebellion, both against the received curriculum of Najaf and against the hierarchical structures, the ladder of which any *ʿalim*, however gifted, had patiently to climb.

Interestingly, the rebellious answer Muhammad Baqer as-Sadr gave his student Ha'iri was couched in the traditional language: *taqlid*, *ra'i*, *ihtiyat*. This respect for the tradition was also enhanced by the hesitation reported in the last sentence of the quote. Ha'iri could not remember whether Sadr's *ijtihad* was qualified, or whether it was total. *ʿAmal* (or *ijtihad*) *bir-ra'i* means a complete independence towards the other *ʿulama*, and the ability to issue decrees accordingly. *Ihtiyat* on the contrary suggests that Sadr was indeed independent, but that he kept his conclusions, out of caution or insecurity about their absolute correctness, to himself.

The essential dilemma facing the whole structure of the Shiʿi schools appears in the balance between tradition and renewal. In the particular case of Sadr, the Iraqi apprentice-jurist did not, for his own sake, and the promising future that awaited him, completely discard the received scholarship, and he chose to work in parallel over the most arcane areas of *usul al-fiqh*.[48]

Much as the debate appears rhetorical, it remains quite significant in terms of Sadr's legal-political development. But it is also important against the background of the teaching in Najaf, which was perceived in the Shiʿi circles themselves to have become dangerously obsolete. The genius of Sadr appears in his capacity to offer new insights both into questions at the heart of the changes rocking a troubled society, and to prove his intellectual capacity as a Shiʿi *ʿalim*.

Sadr's earliest works suggest a clear preference for matters of the law akin to such fields as economics, philosophy, or institutional and historical legitimacy. He was at the same time careful not to remain on the fringe of the hierarchy. But how was the hierarchy organised in the turbulent 1950s? How was law taught in Najaf to and by the *ʿulama*? And did Sadr exert renovation, *ijtihad* in the wider sense, on both the traditional and modern worlds of the law?

Legal studies in Najaf, or how one becomes a mujtahid

Teaching in Najaf has triggered in the past few decades an interest that stems from several concerns. Among these, which appear in the writings of several Shi'i scholars, was the longevity of the city as a centre of Shi'i learning, and the continuity of this pre-eminence,[49] along with the fact that, in the Arab world, it was for the Shi'is the equivalent of Cairo's Azhar for the Sunnis.

The Azhar, in contrast to Najaf, was a recognised centre of Islamic learning, known and celebrated worldwide. Arab Shi'is rightly thought that their city deserved no less consideration, having been founded as a place of learning (according to their history books) when Shaikh at-Ta'ifa Abu Ja'far at-Tusi emigrated from Baghdad to settle in Najaf towards the year 448/1056. This was when Cairo was barely fifty years old as a city,[50] and al-Azhar still in its infancy.[51] But if al-Azhar's history had been written and re-written, and its reputation spread worldwide, there was scant literature on Najaf.[52]

To date, no definitive history of the 'University of Najaf'[53] has been published. However, some shorter works have dwelt in one way or the other on Najaf as an educational centre, and from these scattered sources, a picture can be reconstituted of the curriculum at Najaf in the 1940s and the 1960s, the structure of the course of studies, and Najaf's link with the body of Shi'i '*ulama*.[54]

In the early 1960s, there were about 5,000 students in the religious schools of Najaf.[55] Education was free for all students. Muhammad Jawad Mughniyya, a prominent Najaf 'graduate', recorded that one of the reasons why a poor student like him was able to go to Najaf was because he could 'find, in the worst case, enough bread, a small room in the city and a learned teacher to educate him'.[56] Free education for students, of course, is not particular to Najaf. What is unique is the fact that the teachers themselves were not remunerated in Najaf, and that they even offered, in several cases, to support with their own sources of income the students who had no family resources for their studies. This changed slowly, as awareness grew for a more stable and fairer educational system (since all the '*ulama* could probably not afford to help their pupils), and as the state started to compete with the Shi'i schools for free higher education.

By 1964, this relationship was to some extent institutionalised by Muhsin al-Hakim, who organised an academic body on a more permanent basis. This body, '*al-marja'iyya ad-diniyya al-'amma*' (the general religious *marja-'iyya*), 'represents the highest *marja'* of the Shi'is [Muhsin al-Hakim] by giving out monthly stipendia to the students each according to his [social] status (*tabaqat*)'.[57] The Iraqi Government, or the governments of origin of the students (who came from the four corners of the world, Pakistan, India, some African countries, Bahrain, Syria, Lebanon, Iran), had no contact with the Najaf schools, which relied solely on the individual revenues of the '*ulama*.[58]

The non-interference of the rulers in educational matters, in this case the

Iraqi Government, is an old phenomenon which is one further sign of the relative independence of the Shi'i *'ulama*. At least since the nineteenth century, when the Ottomans controlled the South of Iraq, the Shi'i *'ulama* had retained a much cherished financial autonomy, which allowed them not only to decide on teaching and rituals (such as their celebration of non-official occasions like 'Ashura), but also secured the avoidance of the military draft. This situation was probably perceived as a bane both to Najaf and to Constantinople, since the domination of the frontier-like Iraqi Southern region had been uneasy for four centuries both for the Ottomans and the powerful Shi'i Persian empire which sometimes controlled the city.[59]

Being self-financed, the *'ulama* could also set their own course of studies in accordance with their traditions and beliefs. How far back the system (as it appeared in the 1950s and 1960s) goes is difficult to determine. But the relative laxity of the overall structure must have harkened back to times when degrees were unknown and the word *shahada* (diploma) had not yet acquired its educational connotation.

Although still somewhat hazy in terms of degrees and educational levels, a hierarchy started to crystallise towards the middle of the twentieth century in the Najaf schools. In fact, the first detailed testimony of the curriculum, written in the 1940s,[60] does not mention a first stage of studies which was related in the 1964 description of Muhammad Bahr al-'Ulum.[61] The lack of an established and precise structure indicates how the Najaf cycle of studies has gained its reputation of a '*Freie Universität*'.[62] But with the importance of Najaf both educationally and politically in later years, this vagueness left room for much abuse, especially as some of the young students who went to Najaf from far places in the Shi'i world could rely on their mere stay in the city as the basis for their social fame in their countries of origin. Legally, as will be suggested later, this hierarchical haziness was at the root of many uncertainties in the structure of political parties and public institutions which emerged prominently in the wake of the Iranian Revolution.

Before turning to the qualitative change that befell the Shi'i hierarchical and educational system with the access of the *'ulama* to state power in Iran, the hierarchy will be assessed against both the stages of education and the curriculum background.

Study cycles

Three levels, or cycles (*halaqat*), are required to complete the course of study of the would-be Shi'i *mujtahid*.[63] There are no examinations; nor is there any prescribed time for the completion of the studies. The aim of the student is clear, he must acquire enough scholarship to become a '*mujtahid*', a title 'which is only reached by the most outstanding students'.[64] On average, the two first cycles combined require a minimum of ten years of study;[65] the student starts at a young age, generally between fourteen and twenty.

The first of the three prescribed cycles, which was not mentioned in the earlier report on the schools, and appears only in Bahr al-'Ulum's text,[66] is called 'the prolegomena', *al-muqaddimat*. The student learns grammar, syntax, rhetoric and logic. The books used in this cycle are difficult, and tend not to be covered completely in the course of the cycle.

In grammar, they include Ibn Hisham's (d. 761/1360) *Qatr an-Nada* and *al-Ajrumiyya*, glosses on Ibn Malik's (d. 672/1273) *Alfiyya* by other grammarians like Ibn Hisham and Ibn an-Nazim (d. 686/1287). *Mughni al-Labib*, also by Ibn Hisham, is used at the last stage of the first cycle. In rhetorics, the books generally used are Taftazani's (d. 791/1388) *al-Mutawwal* and *al-Mukhtasar*, and al-Hashimi's (fourteenth century) *Jawahir al-Balagha*. Non-Arab-speaking students are introduced to Arabic in special books. The Iranians use for instance *Jami' al-Muqaddimat*, and go on to perfect it with the books of Suyuti and ar-Radi on Arabic. In logic, the student reads Najafi's (d. 981/1574) *Hashiya*, Qutb ad-Din ar-Razi's *Shamsiyya*, and the modern book on logic by Muhammad Rida al-Muzaffar (d. 1964). In *usul al-fiqh*, are used Hasan ibn ash-Shahid ath-Thani's (d. 966/1559) *Ma'alem*, Muzaffar's first two parts of the *Usul*, as well as Haidari's *Usul al-Istinbat*. In the early sixties, the new – and much more accessible – *al-Ma'alem al-Jadida* of Muhammad Baqer as-Sadr was also introduced.[67] In *fiqh*, al-'Allama al-Hilli's (d. 726/1325) *Tabsira* and *Mukhtasar an-Nafe'*, as well as al-Muhaqqiq al-Hilli's (d. 676/1277) *Shara'e' al-Islam* are taught, along with the more recent works by Muhammad Kazem at-Tabataba'i (d. 1337/1919) (*al-'Urwa al-Wuthqa*) and Muhsin al-Hakim (d.1970) (*Minhaj as-Salihin*).

The more able students at the prolegomena stage can try their skills at some other topics, such as *kalam* and literary disciplines. Old-style mathematics is also provided for those interested. At this stage, the student meets a teacher of his own choosing, reads (in theory) the books he prefers, and spends between half an-hour and one hour daily with his professor. All classes are held on a personal, tutorial basis. According to Bahr al-'Ulum, a student spends an average of three to five years at the prolegomena stage.[68]

The second cycle is called *sutuh*: surfaces. *Sutuh* introduces the study of the substance of deductive jurisprudence (*al-fiqh al-istidlali*), as well as *usul al-fiqh*. Generally, courses are arranged in series which are also conducted on a tutorial basis, although tutorials would involve groups of seven to ten students, rarely more than twenty. According to Faqih,[69] sessions last between half an hour and an hour. Students whose absence recurs or who seem incapable of following the class are encouraged to withdraw, or to return to easier courses.

Sutuh requires three to six years, sometimes longer. At the end of the cycle, the student gets to be considered a *murahiq*, literally adolescent. This title indicates his proximity to the maturity of *ijtihad*.

Teachers, as well as books, are also freely chosen by the student, who familiarises himself with *kalam*, philosophy, *tafsir* (Qur'anic exegesis), *hadith*, as well as law and *usul*.

The books most widely used at this stage are, in *fiqh*, ash-Shahid ath-Thani's *Sharh al-Lum'a ad-Dimashqiyya*, Ansari's (d. 1329/1911) *Makasib*, as well as ash-Shahid ath-Thani's *Masalik al-Ifham*. In *usul*, the student reads Qummi's (d. 1231/1816) *Qawanin*, Muhammad Kazem al-Khurasani's (d. 1328/1910) *Kifaya*, Ansari's *Rasa'el*, the third part of Muzaffar's *Usul*. In recent years, the comparative work on *usul* of Muhammad Taqi al-Hakim,[70] which was also used in Baghdad, has been introduced as a work of reference in Najaf.

The third and ultimate cycle is called *bahth al-kharej*, literally graduate or outside research. The system at this stage is completely different. Instead of tutorials, the student chooses to attend the important public lectures of the most prominent *mujtahid*s of Najaf, who conduct their discussions as lectures and seminars organised in series (*dawrat*), over a period of months or years. The classes, depending on the prominence of the teacher, can be heavily attended, not only by the *murahiq*s, but also by other *mujtahid*s. Discussion is free in the class, but the lectures are generally intricate, and sometimes result in books being compiled by the students and eventually published.

Muhammad Taqi al-Faqih described the studies of *bahth al-kharej* in some detail. They generally consist of lectures that dwell on a subject over several days. The lecturer must painstakingly prepare his class. Although he would not read from an already written text, he is expected to have exhausted the texts related to the topic discussed, and be ready for an intricate discussion to which students will subject him, 'as disputes are numerous':[71]

> The lecturer will differ from the authors [whose books are used in these courses] in that he might not be in agreement with the classification of themes from the perspective of their presentation or conclusion, or with the discussion or silent acknowledgment of some hypotheses. He might even contradict traditional authorities in their exposition (*naql*) or in their understanding of some questions. He can be in agreement with the conclusion or not, or could agree with it without accepting the evidence that they provide. He can realize what they have missed or undermine in part or in totality of the evidence they have constructed.
>
> If the teacher has reached such level, then he will have become a *mujtahid*.
>
> And if he has shown competence in these subjects that surpasses his colleagues, then he will be even greater (*a'zam*).[72]

It is therefore not sufficient, writes Faqih, to know the works of jurists in a given topic well, because most students who attend the lectures will have studied them beforehand. Those who can only reproduce arguments are not considered *mujtahid*s. They go under the name of *muhassil*s, and are apt to teach these works only superficially (*tadris sathi*, from *sutuh*). In contrast, a *mujtahid* is required to answer a theoretical argument by a theoretical argument, and must have reached the ability 'to bring any hypothetical argument to a definitive argument, however long the argument's chain'.[73]

Muhammad Bahr al-'Ulum mentions three levels in *bahth al-kharej*. At the first level, formed by students who have just completed the study of *sutuh*, it is usual to address the chapters of a legal treatise in a general manner, without insisting on the sequential logic of the text, and to add in some commentaries by other *'ulama*. The teacher will thus train his students with the logic of a given work, and introduce them at the same time to his own method.

At the second stage of *bahth al-kharej*, exposition is more elaborate. For instance, the second part of Khurasani's *Kifaya* can give way to lengthy analyses, which are supplemented by Murtada al-Ansari's *Rasa'el*, and the commentaries of Muhammad Husain Na'ini (d. 1936). Texts are thus presented, discussed, and choices are made by the teacher as to the most cogent interpretations.

The third stage, which is the most advanced in the curriculum, is what 'has made the glory and fame of the teaching bestowed' at Najaf, and has allowed for the great renovations and progress in Shi'i *ijtihad*, as can be noticed, suggests Muhammad Bahr al-'Ulum, from an even perfunctory comparison between present texts and works from the fourth or fifth centuries AH.[74]

The teacher at this third stage is absolutely free to arrange his own course, choose the arguments he prefers, and end up 'with a new opinion, and with a mature approach which will be very different from his predecessors''.[75]

The 'diploma'

The issue of the Najaf diploma is closely connected with the nature of the education dispensed in the Shi'i colleges.[76]

There is no formal examination at which a student would, like in the Western world, sit to answer questions and write essays. Instead, the process of the appreciation of the student takes place over a long period corresponding to the apprenticeship. This system is said to prevent 'any kind of cheating or bribery, intermediation (*wasita*), favouring for kin or friendship. The authorities (*sulta*) cannot intercede for the student. Intercession means an absolute failure for the student who seeks such protection.'[77]

Assessment of the student is based on three elements, which are in fact a process of discovering his talents and potential: '(1) the freedom of thought with the teacher and his fellow students ... (2) the various discussions with his colleagues', technically known as 'study in confrontation, *bahth muqabala*'. This confrontation is a substitution of the teacher by the students, who address their colleagues with a given topic that they discuss together. The discussion allows the refinement of the argument and the display of knowledge. The third aspect is known as '*mudhakara*'. *Mudhakara* takes place in public when a student provokes a colleague into discussing a topic. Through *mudhakara*, the students bring the debate into the open with colleagues belonging to other schools, and the various circles (*halaqa*) so discover each another. All three exchanges take place over a long period of time, and a natural distillation develops among the students who get to know their colleagues' strengths and weaknesses.

In this way also, in contrast with examinations which suggest a rigid gradation, a wide range of appreciation becomes possible. For the few students who remain in the city after 'graduating', their familiarity with the groups of scholars and students ensures that they get known better, almost intimately. For the students who leave, however, a more official form of recognition is required: the *shahada* or diploma.

The students who leave Najaf for good [as opposed to those who leave only temporarily] take their diplomas from their professors and from the religious leader (the supreme *marja'*) [*ar-ra'is ad-dini, al marja' al-a'la*]. These diplomas include formulas which express the level of achievement of their bearers. This terminology is understood only to the few initiate (*khassa*), who in turn give the diploma holder a position [recognised] by the general people (*as-sawad*).[78]

The granting of the diploma indicates the way stratification in the Shi'i learned world operates. In this stratification, only the elite is capable of recognising the importance of a given graduate from Najaf. The diploma is not however the end of the road. The student who leaves Najaf with a diploma in his hands will be tested by the *'ulama* of his home country or his new destination as soon as he arrives, and they will make sure that the content of the graduation letter matches the real ability and expertise of the young *'alim*.

The process of delivering the diploma – or rather the letter of graduation – can be lengthy. It might involve several weeks or months of reflection, and a student who does not achieve the required work is told eventually of the impossibility of his teacher vouching for him. In the case of students who are unknown to prominent teachers whose recommendation is sought, 'the paper [diploma] remains for days with the teacher'.[79] Only after an investigation among the select circles of the upper strata of the hierarchy will the diploma be drafted, redrafted, and finally handed over to the prospective *'alim*.

The nuances are infinite in the kinds of degrees which are granted upon the apprentice leaving Najaf, since the diploma is in effect no more than a letter of recommendation stamped with the seal of the high *marja'*. A *'alim* might also want to encourage a student to pursue his studies further, although 'the student might think he is abler than he really is ... or he might be young and there are worries about the danger of him drifting ... The student is then advised to stay in Najaf until his scientific abilities are strengthened.'[80]

Some students leave Najaf temporarily, often out of the necessity of supporting their family financially. They might be given in this case a special letter 'directed to the believers [the lay Shi'is], or to some of their sponsors [at home], which enjoins them to follow their preaching and guidance'.[81] This permission is known as '*waraqat khubz* [literally a paper for bread], which means that its carrier produces it for financial help, since the faithful are accustomed to support with grants the carriers of such papers'.[82]

There are therefore several types of titles that Najaf grants its students. For Faqih, this extreme flexibility is no surprise: 'Najaf supplies society to the degree needed.'[83] After all, he adds, there is no need to profess a profound scholarship just to perform rituals or dispense simple legal rules, such as supervising marriage or divorce. Too much scholarship might even be detrimental: what is the point of explaining the existence of God or the legitimacy of 'Ali's leadership to the layman by an arduous legal and logical terminology when a simple causality line will convince him better?[84] A soft-spoken and casual speaker can have a better impact than a highly theoretical *mujtahid*, and Najaf is there to embrace and cater for all social needs.

This apprenticeship of the *'ulama* of Najaf, and the graduation in the city of several layers of 'men of religion', brings the analysis to the two other levels of Najafi influence on contemporary constitutional theory. How one becomes a *mujtahid* must be supplemented with the place of *mujtahid*s in civil society and with its corollary: the sensitive issue of the pre-eminence of some *mujtahids* over others.

The structure of civil society

There are, in theory, two categories of persons who are recognised by modern Shi'i law: the *mujtahid*s and the *muqallid*s. A *mujtahid* ought 'to be capable of deduction in all fields of *fiqh*',[85] or at least in one of these fields. The *muqallid* is the layman, who is devoid of such knowledge. He or she is bound to follow the *mujtahid*'s decrees. The rule admits no exception:

> The act of a layman, *'ammi*, who proceeds without *taqlid* or without *ihtiyat* [defined as 'the act which is certain in good faith when in presence of an unknown matter'] is void, except in two cases: (1) if the *muqallid* acts in accordance with the *fatwa* of the *mujtahid* he follows; (2) if the act performed is a matter of worship, in case of an approximation of the situation [i.e. its close resemblance to rituals usually performed]. Nonetheless, in the latter occurrence, it is recommended that the act be consonant with the *fatwa* of the *mujtahid* whom the *muqallid* should have related to at the time of performing of the act.[86]

Against this description of Shi'i civil society by *Ayat Allah* Abul-Qasem al-Khu'i, the graduation process of Najaf and the schools' curriculum can now be judged. When the apprentice becomes a *mujtahid*, and chooses to leave Najaf to go to Iran, India, Afghanistan, or Lebanon, he carries with him a recommendation which might be influential for a position of judge or of religious leader at his destination. A stay in Najaf, like a stay at the Azhar for a Sunni, is a priori very prestigious. The content of the letter of recommendation, the *shahada*, will further testify to the graduate's particular abilities. The reputation of the scholar trained in Najaf, which might have been already enhanced by the network of the Shi'i *'ulama*, the visits to the shrines of Najaf by compatriots, and all the intricate contacts between the civil society and the hierarchy of *'ulama*, will put him in a position which commands respect in the society. This position is also the key to his financial survival in the city or village where he resides.

Voluntary taxation is the other aspect of the network created by the legal structure. The *sahm al-imam*, which is the tax levied for the *'alim* in his capacity as representative of the Hidden Imam, constitutes one of the two essential revenues of the *'ulama*, the other being the *khums*, which is paid to most *mujtahid*s in their capacity as *sayyed*s, or descendants of the Prophet through his daughter Fatima and the first Imam 'Ali.[87] The degree to which the tax is paid varies naturally with the relative wealth of the society where it is levied, and with the fame of the *'alim* to whom it is paid. Since the state system is completely independent from the Shi'i structure, such tax cannot be enforced with the help of coercive measures.[88] Depending on the religious commitment of the followers of a *'alim*, financial contributions will consequently be more or less forthcoming. But there is competition among the *'ulama* for the pool of financial support.

The pooling of religious taxes is obviously not structured. This is due in the first place to the impossibility of enforcing taxation without state power. It is due, further, to a combination of the international character of the Shi'i civil society system and to the absolute freedom for a *muqallid* to choose his or her own *mujtahid*.

Shi'i internationalism

Internationalism is at the heart of the Najaf network, as the description of the schools suggests. It also derives from the constant interaction between the *'ulama* of the various parts of the Shi'i world after they have graduated from Najaf, and internationalism is enhanced at the level of the population generally by the visits and pilgrimages, as well as by a mystique surrounding the burial in Najaf, the 'valley of peace'. In this context Najaf represents the most prominent pilgrimage. In Qum and in Mashhad, visitors stream to the holy places, and the structure of pilgrimages suggests a dense network of varying intensity. Political and more arcane scholarly reasons will influence the various flows of visitors. The most dramatic recent example is, of course, the barring of Najaf to Iranian visitors after the outbreak of war with Iran, but even in more relaxed times, the stream of visitors will be subject to some turbulence or other in Middle Eastern affairs.

On the scholarly level, the history of Najaf and the central Shi'i places suggests that the reputation of a particular Shi'i centre of learning will significantly affect the ebb and flow of its visitors. At the turn of the century, Karbala and Kazimiyya were more important in Iraq than Najaf, and in the thirties, the foundation of Qum as a centre of learning under the scholarship of *Ayat Allah* al-Ha'eri pushed Najaf momentarily into the background. From the mid-1940s however, until the 1970s, Najaf recovered its importance in the Shi'i world as the most respected centre of learning.[89]

Legal scholarship and religiosity are peculiarly intertwined in Shi'i civil society. The pilgrimage to Najaf or to Qum depends to a large extent on the importance of the scholars in the city. This appears in remarkable contrast to the Sunni world, where the pilgrimage to Mecca is completely independent of the reputation of the city as a centre of Islamic learning. Of course, there is, in the same way as the *hajar* in Mecca, *as-sahn ash-sharif* in Najaf, where the first Shi'i Imam is believed to be resting. But in comparison to the Sunni *mazar*s (religious places to 'visit'), there is a further dimension to the connection between the Najaf scholars and the visitors to the city. This supplementary characteristic is due to the structure of Shi'i civil society and the *mujtahid–muqallid* dichotomy.

The choice of a *muqallid* by the layman is absolutely free. In theory, it is compulsory for the *muqallid* to choose a living *mujtahid*, and this feature of Usulism figures, as suggested earlier, as the most important distinctive mark in the Usuli school in contrast to the Akhbaris. This explains the more intense dimension to the pilgrimage at Najaf: the pilgrim pays homage not only to the memory of the Imams, he also salutes those living *'ulama* who bear the flame of Imamism.

If Usulism compels *taqlid*, it does not interfere in the choice of the jurist who is imitated. As a consequence, the way a *'alim* becomes important comes not only from the superiority of his knowledge of the law as is recognised in his educational training. It is also vital that he relates to the mass of lay persons, and that they also recognise his religious leadership. Since the *muqallid*s are free to choose the *mujtahid* they prefer, a *mujtahid*'s importance will grow proportionally to the number of his *muqallid*s. This importance is not only scholarly. The *mujtahid* is also rewarded financially by his *muqallid*s as the recipient of *sahm al-Imam*.

Internationalism is decisive in this respect, since a *muqallid* can choose beyond his own limited geographical confine, and reach in his *taqlid* the far away *'ulama* whom he knows by reputation. Thus, it is common for a Shi'i in Lebanon for example to profess *taqlid* of an Iraqi *mujtahid*. Nationality in this respect is neutral. Shi'i civil society transcends state boundaries. Until his death in August 1992 it is said that the *mujtahid* who commanded the largest number of *muqallid*s was Abul-Qasem al-Khu'i in Najaf. Why this importance, and the number of *muqallid*s, is disputed now appears evident. The system is essentially oral. There is no register of *taqlid*. But were there a central register, it would be meaningless. The lay Shi'is have several ways of 'practising' their *taqlid*. Since there is no coercion at any level in the system, the gamut of *taqlid* will run from absolute passivity to hearty financial and religious commitment. The only constraint, which is the hallmark of Usulism, is the necessity of following a living *mujtahid*. This trait guarantees the smooth reproduction of the system.

'Reputation' and the new concerns

The internationalist dimension of Shi'i civil society is one of the two major characteristics of the system. The other characteristic lies in the proper hierarchical structure of the students who have 'graduated' from the Shi'i law colleges, the *mujtahid*s. It is the hierarchy of *mujtahid*s of which he is now part that counts most for the Najaf graduate. This hierarchy, in the contemporary world of Shi'ism, is the key to important political events. Naturally, education is only part of a much wider context which transcends pure knowledge, and the Shi'i hierarchy has meant much more to societies with a significant Shi'i population, both as a social weight or corrective, and as a focal organisation for popular movements that have rocked the Islamic world in recent years.[90]

As suggested earlier, the key word for understanding Najaf is reputation.

In the absence of a strict examination system and of an 'honours' diploma, it is the student's reputation in legal competence which allows him to pass from one stage to the next, and it is again his reputation, as recognised by his peers or by other *mujtahid*s, which decides ultimately his right to accede to the elite of the *marja'iyya*.

The importance of reputation does not stop with graduation. Its centrality from the early days of apprenticeship recurs throughout all the stages of the process of knowledge, and is even more important for the various degrees in the ladder towards supreme *ijtihad*.

Whether the graduate *'alim* remains in Najaf or goes to another city across the Shi'i world (traditionally in the East, including Pakistan and India, but since the late 1960s also in places like Germany, the United Kingdom, and the United States), he is part of both the educational structure and of Shi'i civil society at large.

From the educational point of view, he can start teaching at various levels, depending on the students who come to him. His circle will obviously depend on the place where he teaches. A *'alim* in Najaf and in Qum will carry more importance than his colleague in Jabal 'Amil or in Pakistan. The competition of the various schools and *hauza*s will also affect the *mujtahid*'s educational importance and *rayonnement*. To this extent, and bearing in mind the flexibility built into the system of 'registration' which will allow any Shi'i to find a teacher and means of livelihood in university towns like Najaf and Qum, the *mujtahid*s as professors function like their counterparts in Western universities to a limited degree only.

The difference from Western teachers is notable. This is true in the educational field, in the civil society at large, as well as in the fiscal dimension of the *mujtahid*s' sway. Financially, as mentioned earlier, the *mujtahid*s are independent from state support, and their revenues will vary largely according to their reputation, to the degree of religiosity in the society generally, and of course, according to the wealth and commitment of their *muqallid*s. Since the *muqallid*s' financial support cannot be constrained, the reputation of a given *mujtahid* will constitute in the final analysis the criterion for his *taqlid*.

The challenge to the law curriculum

It is in the light of the Najaf curriculum that the personality of Muhammad Baqer as-Sadr appears best, and his answer to his disciple Ha'iri, mentioned at the beginning of this section, is indicative of the intricacies of Najaf's world of learning. The contradiction inherent to scholarship which requires, on the one hand, the gradual recognition of fellow *'ulama* after long years of study, and on the other, the necessity of improving the received tradition, is at the heart of the Najaf educational structure.

The *risala 'amaliyya* (the comprehensive legal treatise mentioned earlier) comes for the most talented young scholars as the crowning of the long years of their apprenticeship. This *risala* will be produced in the form of commentaries over the accepted legal compendia written by the great *mujtahid*s of the nineteenth and twentieth centuries, or it can be a compilation according to the views of the author asserting his capacity to offer a comprehensive picture of state-of-the-art Shi'i law.

The *risala* seldom offers real novelties in legal research.[91] It represents an element in Shi'i education which preceded the turmoil of the twentieth century. The educational structure in the law schools might well have encouraged the constant renewal of glosses and commentaries over the received Shi'i *fiqh*. Yet the renewal remained constrained by the nature of the texts which were out of step with the contemporary age.

The description of the various texts of reference in the curriculum has pointed out how dated some of these works could be. Grammar texts of the twelfth century were still the basic tools followed by the colleges for language teaching, and the study of *usul*, despite improvements introduced with the simplified treatises of Muhammad Baqer as-Sadr and Muzaffar, have remained of little relevance to the modern period.

Notwithstanding the 'official' texts listed in the curriculum, there was a more fundamental adaptation under way in the law schools of Najaf. A turning point occurred in the 1940s with the writings of Muhammad Husayn Kashif al-Ghita', and a reading of his two short works mentioned earlier, *al-Muthul al-'Ulya* and *al-Muhawarat*, as well as his introduction to Shi'ism for the layman,[92] shows the distance rapidly covered in the probing of new interests around Najaf.

In view of the number of editions published in a few years,[93] these works certainly appealed to the uninitiated Shi'is, and even more to the younger *'ulama*. They opened the way to a more decided interventionism in the daily life of the city, but they cannot be considered scholarly departures from the legal tradition. Their subject-matter remained outside the legal sphere.

The new generation, which was the generation of Muhammad Baqer as-Sadr and his Najaf companions, welcomed the literature which Kashif al-Ghita' permitted in his considerations of the 1940s. From a specific legal perspective however, the renewal of Islamic law required more than just opening the door to politics. The elaborate educational system of Najaf was not being challenged in these works, and the scholarly training of Kashif al-Ghita' remained inevitably underused in books introducing Shi'ism or railing against Western colonisation or injustice. More fundamental alternatives were awaited.

The most conspicuous alternative issues, which straddled the legal tradition and the new worldly interests, were understandably undertaken in the realm of public law, and Muhammad Mahdi Shamseddin's *System of Governance and Administration in Islam*[94] is a good example of the new legal literature. But the effort was not limited to public law, and Shamseddin's work was in any case as much an overview of the way an Islamic state should conform with the tradition, as a polemical work against the Sunni legal conception. A deeper and more interesting dimension of the new juristic interests in Najaf appears in a multi-volume treatise by Muhammad Husayn

Kashif al-Ghita' on civil law, which addressed in remarkable detail the technicalities of the most influential civil code of the time, *Majallat al-Ahkam al-'Adliyya.*

The *Majalla,* Iraq's Civil Code for decades, is an Ottoman Sunni text of great repute, which had no equivalent in the Shi'i world. Kashif al-Ghita''s article-by-article four-volume commentary, *Tahrir al-Majalla,* represents the practical answer from a jurist's point of view to the dominance of Sunni law in Iraq. To date, *Tahrir al-Majalla* represents the most interesting compendium of differences between Sunnism and Shi'ism in the under-studied (from the point of view of the *shari'a*) but crucial questions of civil law. Beyond the minute details of this work, it is clear that the interest in such worldly matters came from a legitimate concern with the protection of the Shi'i message in its creative manifestation, and in its ability to address contemporary legal problems. Such awareness is spelled out in the introduction, which presents Kashif al-Ghita''s contribution as a necessity, considering that '*al-Majalla al-'Adliyya* or *Majallat al-Ahkam* is the book taught in law colleges from the times of the Turks to the present'.[95] Kashif al-Ghita' decided therefore to undertake a long and minute commentary on each of its articles and maxims: 'The main object [of the work] is twofold: (1) to explain and comment [on the *Majalla*] and solve some of its complexities and problems; (2) to show what concords in it with the Imami school and what is different.'[96]

The result of this endeavour is a remarkable compendium of practical Shi'i law, which is much closer in its relevance to the modern world than any of the traditional Shi'i works normally taught in Najaf.

Kashif al-Ghita' was disappointed with the way the book was received. *Tahrir al-Majalla* was published over a period of three years starting in 1940. In the second volume, published in 1941, the lack of serious attention to the book was ascribed by the Najaf *mujtahid* to 'the difficult circumstances of the times ... the world convulsions, and the raging wars'.[97] The reference is to the outbreak of the Second World War. Iraq, like many other Mashreq countries, was directly affected by coups and countercoups of pro-British and pro-German generals. In the longer term however, misfortune befell the commentary of Kashif al-Ghita' as the *Majalla* itself was superseded by the new Iraqi Civil Code, and the painstaking commentary of the Najaf '*alim* fell into sudden disuse.[98]

In any case, it was clear that, as a prominent Shi'i jurist of the time, Muhammad Husayn Kashif al-Ghita' was interested in a more critical say in contemporary law. *Tahrir al-Majalla* can be considered as the first scholarly endeavour for a Renaissance which culminated in the works of Muhammad Baqer as-Sadr and in the Iranian experience under the Ayatollahs. Since then, the Islamic jurists were keen to offer a key to a comprehensive understanding of critical contemporary issues, from the question of women to the articulation of Islamic banks.

Relevance to the present

So far, the analysis of the schools of law in Najaf and the juristic efforts carried out by some of the Shi'i *'ulama* has mainly touched upon the intellectual exercise undertaken against the unstable background of the Iraqi scene towards the middle of the century. Clearly, some conscious attempts were directed at revamping the approach to law in order to enhance its contemporary relevance, but Muhammad Kashif al-Ghita' had remained the exception at the time. The law curriculum offered little comfort for the daunting social problems and the obsolescence of the Shi'i schools. This is when Muhammad Baqer as-Sadr and his companions took to overhauling the legal field, until by the end of the 1970s a comprehensive alternative Islamic system was almost completed. Rooted as it was in the law colleges and their early curriculum, the importance and effective impact of the *'ulama* and of the colleges did not emerge fully until the present period.

Regardless of the educational content dispensed at Najaf, the very structure of the schools represents a unique element in the Islamic state which the *'ulama* would eventually try to build. The hierarchy which brought the apprentice up the ladder of knowledge to the position of *ijtihad* offers a constitutional blueprint which is perhaps unique in the history of modern nation-states. The way in which the apparently anodyne shell of the 'University of Najaf' turned into the most decisive element in the construction of the Islamic state in Iran, and how it succeeds in explaining the strength and weaknesses of the opposition of Islamic groups in countries like Iraq and Lebanon, as well as the structure of the 'Shi'i International' so prominent in the 1980s, is the object of the next section. As in the remarks of Sadr towards the end of his apprenticeship, an odd exchange of letters between Ruhullah al-Khumaini and Muhammad Baqer as-Sadr in 1979 provides the starting point of analysis.

A late episode: Sadr and the exchange of letters with Khumaini in 1979–80, or 'who is the most learned jurist?'

The relationship between Muhammad Baqer as-Sadr and Ruhullah al-Khumaini, in the long years that Khumaini spent in Najaf, has remained unclear. Despite the closeness in the outlook of the two leaders, the common protection of *Ayat Allah* Muhsin al-Hakim, and the physical neighbourliness, it does not seem that they met regularly. Their exchange seems to have remained sporadic. To an extent, this is the result of Khumaini's reserved attitude throughout his stay in Najaf, partly because of a shy nature and some apparent difficulty in spoken Arabic, but mainly because of a deliberately cautious political attitude. Khumaini knew the difficulty of finding a safe place of exile. In the aftermath of the Khordad Revolt, which ultimately led to his departure from Iran on 4 November 1964, he spent a few months in Bursa near Istanbul. In Turkey Khumaini was no doubt completely isolated in a society which is overwhelmingly Sunni, and which in any case is completely dominated politically by a secularist state. In October 1965, he left Bursa for Najaf. From October 1965, and until he was forced to go to France on 6 October 1978, Khumaini remained with his family in the small Iraqi city, where he was liable to immediate deportation by a wary and unfriendly government. It is in this light that his connections with the Iraqi world must be viewed. Even with the local *ʿulama*, Khumaini remained at a distance.

There are, therefore, few recorded instances of contacts with Sadr, who by 1965 had already become famous in Shiʿi circles for his scholarship.[99] In Sadr's biographies, despite great efforts to show that strong contacts and deep friendship had tied the two revolutionaries together, there is not a single significant instance of any close contact before the revolutionary days in 1979–80. Indeed, only one (unreliable) biography of Khumaini mentions familiarity and connivance, reporting that the Iranian *ʿalim*, 'who was shunned by all the clerical establishment of the Iraqi city [which in any case was incorrect, since Khumaini had been invited by Muhsin al-Hakim]', was visited in 1967 by 'Mohammad-Baqer Sadr,... who was trying to mobilise the religious leaders in view of what he called the decisive battle against Israel'.[100]

It is difficult to imagine, however, that the two men were not acutely aware of each other's existence. But in those early days, and until 1977–8, Khumaini was not an important character in Najaf. By the time of the first demonstrations against the Shah, the problems between central government and Shiʿi leadership in the city had acquired a significance and reached a level compared to which Khumaini's presence was marginal.

But things radically changed as the revolution overtook Iran. At that time, Iraq had been witnessing two major developments: the assertion of Sadr's unquestioned leadership among the militant *ʿulama* after the death of Muhsin al-Hakim in 1970, and the rapid rise of the Iraqi revolutionary Islamic tide. By then, Khumaini and Sadr had become the unchallenged heroes of the day, and they were thrown together into the realm of confrontation.

If Iran saw the decisive victory of the Islamic revolution led by Khumaini, the situation in Iraq was in 1979 more elusive. The new nickname of Sadr, 'Iraq's Khumaini' inevitably came, but in his case the confrontation with the state failed. By then, in contrast with their earlier relationship, the contacts between the two Shiʿi leaders had acquired an important public dimension, and every single word or gesture of the one towards the other was carefully observed.

In 1979, the Iraqi situation appeared to be on the verge of an explosion similar to that in Iran.[101] Two years earlier, in 1977, the riots in Najaf at ʿAshura had rocked the country, and echoed even inside the higher councils of the Baʿth party.[102] It is important to note in this respect that disturbances came *before* the success of Khumaini, who was still living in Najaf, and who was completely unknown internationally. But the demonstrations in the South of Iraq turned him into a first-hand witness of organised antigovernmental demonstrations. For fear of immediate expulsion, and also probably because his own network was directed solely towards the Iranian scene, Khumaini remained in February 1977 on the margins of Iraqi turmoil. None the less, his stay under the protection of the Najaf *'ulama* is important in the light of the subsequent negative developments.

Two years later, Tehran became in turn the model for those in Najaf to follow, and tension rose in Iraq very quickly after the victory of Khumaini. When, in 1979–80, pressure increased on Sadr, the Iraqi leader naturally considered seeking refuge in the new Iran. But Khumaini did not reciprocate the Najaf hospitality.

Khumaini sent Sadr a telegram which was broadcast on Radio Tehran:

> *Samahat* [Your grace] *Hujjat al-Islam al-hajj sayyid* Muhammad Baqer as-Sadr: we have been informed that your holiness has decided to leave Iraq because of some events [disturbances, *hawadeth*]. I do not see good [*min as-saleh*] coming from your leaving the city of Najaf, the place of Islamic sciences, and I am worried about this matter, and hope, God willing, that the worries of your holiness vanish, peace and God's mercy be on you.[103]

Sadr's answer came on the 5th of rajab 1399/1 June 1979:

> *Samahat Ayat Allah al-'uzma al-imam al-mujahid* [literally 'Your holiness the great sign of God and the fighting imam'] *sayyid* Ruhullah al-Khumaini, I have received your respectable telegram, which embodied (*jassadat*) your fatherhood (*ubuwwat*) and spiritual protection for a Holy Najaf that has kept living your grand victories since parting with you; I draw from your honouring guidance a spiritual breath, as I also feel the depth of responsibility for the protection of the scientific existence of Holy Najaf. I would like to express to you on this occasion the salutations of millions of Muslims and believers in our dear Iraq, which found in the light of Islam, now shining again thanks to you, a guiding beacon for the whole world, and a spiritual energy to strike the atheist (*kafer*) colonialism, and American colonialism in particular, and to free the world from all the forms of its crimes, foremost among which the crime of the rape of our holy land Palestine; we ask God almighty to grant us the perenniality of your precious presence, peace on you and God's blessing and mercy.[104]

Behind the flowery language and the emotional charge of the exchange, significant details appear in these telegrams. Before examining those details, it is also worth mentioning parts of the message of Khumaini when he learnt, on 22 April 1980, of the certainty of Sadr's execution:

> According to the report sent by the Foreign Minister which is based on several sources in the Islamic countries and also other sources, with utmost grief I have come to know that the martyr Ayatollah Sayyid Mohammad Baqir Sadr, and his illustrious, noble sister, who held a high station [i.e. rank] among the scholars and possessed a radiant position in the literary field, have attained martyrdom under the most heart-rendering circumstances at the hands of the perverse regime of Iraq ... It is no wonder that Sadr and his sister have attained martyrdom; what is strange is that the Islamic nations and in particular the noble nation of Iraq and the tribes of the Tigris and Euphrates, and the proud young men of the universities and all other dear youths of Iraq may pass indifferently by this great calamity that has affected Islam and the Household of the Messenger of God (S), and give their opportunity to the damned Ba'th party that it may martyr their illustrious leaders one by one in the most atrocious way ... I do not

have any hopes from the higher officials of the Iraqi Armed Forces, but I have not lost my hopes from the officials, non-commissioned officers and soldiers of the Iraqi Army. I expect them to rise courageously against this regime and overthrow the structure of crime from its very foundations – as it happened in Iran ...[105]

The striking element in these letters is of course of a political nature. It is epitomised by Khumaini's calling the Iraqi army to rise in rebellion after Sadr's assassination. It is also important in view of the deterioration of the situation between Iraq and Iran, which soon led to the bloodiest Mideastern war of the century. But politics aside, it is the legal dimension, in the light of the Najaf schools and the structure of Shiʿi civil society, which constitutes the more interesting dimension revealed by the exchange.

Sadr's initial request was an appeal for help. His situation in Najaf had become critical. After many arrests, and the rise in tension in the wake of the Iranian Revolution and the problems facing the Baʿth internally, the security deriving from his position as religious leader had been spent, and he could only think of exile as a way out of the impending confrontation with the government. He therefore appealed to Khumaini, naturally expecting a positive answer. After all, the pattern was well established since the 1920s, and many of the most prominent *ʿulama* had taken the route of exile,[106] long before Khumaini's own exile from Iran and his protracted stay in Najaf. The answer of Khumaini was therefore puzzling: it was partly rooted in the belief that the Baʿth would not dare humiliate Sadr more than it had already done. But the misjudgment of Khumaini might not have been merely caused by a political error.

There is a subtler dimension to Khumaini's telegram. In his address, Sadr acknowledged Khumaini's prominence. The maximal title appears in the Iraqi scholar's letter repeatedly. Khumaini is not only called *Ayat Allah al-ʿuzma*. He is also addressed as *imam*, an indication of Sadr's absolute deference. This appears more clearly when contrasted with *Ayat Allah* al-Khu'i's message of congratulation to Khumaini after the victory of the Revolution. Khu'i addressed Khumaini as *Hujjat al-Islam*, and not, as could have been expected, as *Ayat Allah*, a matter which was understandably shocking in Shiʿi circles,[107] since it meant that whatever Khumaini's success, he remained second in learning to all the recognised *Ayat Allah*s and to Khu'i himself.

The exchange between Sadr and Khumaini is in the same vein. Khumaini did not reciprocate the title with which he was honoured, and he addressed Sadr as *Hujjat al-Islam*. For a scholar like Sadr who, by 1979, had done more for the renewal of Islamic scholarship than any other writer in the century, this constituted a humiliating, and indeed a puzzling episode. In the countries that count the largest Shiʿi communities, the denial by Khumaini of the supreme degree of *ijtihad* to Muhammad Baqer as-Sadr reveals an uneasy strain, which is typical of the competition between *ʿulama*. As in the case of Khu'i and Khumaini, and more recently between Khumaini and Muntazeri,[108] the competition for recognition of the most learned jurist developed at the highest echelons, between the two foremost political *ʿulama* of Iran and

Iraq, with the dramatic result of trapping Muhammad Baqer as-Sadr in the deadly course of collision with the Ba'th. This is the more ironic in view of the posthumous title given to Sadr by Khumaini, when in the 22 April message, he was acknowledged as Supreme Ayatollah and as the 'prize' of Islamic learning.[109]

This episode in Sadr's life, as well as his early rejection of *taqlid* quoted at the beginning of the section, constitute the manifestations of a deeper problem in the structure of Usuli Shi'ism. Until the state became the terrain of competition between the *'ulama*, this problem never appeared as a critical question for the hierarchy, and whatever antagonisms have surfaced in the *marja'iyya* after the death of leading scholars, the fact that the lay person was ultimately free to choose his or her own *marja'* deflected the impact of competition. When, in the late 1970s, the line between leadership of the state and religious leadership became blurred upon the *'ulama*'s access to power in Iran (and the threat they represented in Iraq), the problem became a constitutional issue.

Until this level was reached, there were significant intermediary stages in which Sadr played a central role. Before turning to these developments, it will be helpful to put the Shi'i legal structure in a more general perspective.

Conclusion: the Renaissance and the *marja'iyya*

With all the Renaissantist efforts among the Shi'i *'ulama*, the renewal in the aftermath of the Iraqi Revolution of 1958 managed to take place within the traditional educational structure. There was a conscious effort to salvage the structure of learning, and the bulk of legal production remained in the hands of old-style *'ulama*. Muhammad Husayn Kashif al-Ghita' himself was wary of too much involvement in politics, and the defeat and exile of the *'ulama* in the 1920s must have been constantly on his mind.

For the new generation, threatened as it was by the Communist appeal, intervention was urgent. Its most successful paragon was, in due course, *Ayat Allah* al-Khumaini. The way he saw and legitimised political intervention by the *'ulama* will be discussed in the following chapters. But Khumaini owed a lot to the structure of the Shi'i schools, which was to be reproduced by the Iranian State. The shell offered to activism by the Shi'i educational tradition, at the level of apprenticeship, then for the hierarchy of the *mujtahid*s itself, will now be summarised.

As described earlier, it is only after a long and hard period of study, which averages some twenty years, that the apprentice-*'alim* becomes a *mujtahid*. The apprentice-*'ulama* were expected to live in difficult conditions, with scarce resources, and they were dependent on favours from their elders. Those who did not come from well-known families depended on the established *mujtahid*s, some of whom also lived in dire poverty. It is normal in this context, especially in an Iraq where the urban poor were overwhelmingly Shi'i,[110] that the appeal of social justice and revolutionary ideas from the left could prove so attractive to students and even to the *'ulama*.

In theory, the Najaf curriculum was very flexible, but this *Freie Universität* was not without any control or regulation. In fact, the *marja'iyya* oversaw the whole process of selecting material to be taught and of the students' progress. Some legal works were necessary to the studies of the young scholars, and only the mastery of these works would open up the ladder to the apprentice. This was inevitable to some extent. A young student could hardly find his way through the maze of the scholarship of Islamic law without the guidance of his tutors in the recognised legal authorities of Shi'i history.

In strictly educational terms, recognition of the apprentice's legal aptitude took place in one of two ways. Either it was an absolute recognition by his peers and students, or a formal admission by two recognised *mujtahid*s. He could then, with this prestigious achievement, go back home and start teaching and exercising as a religiously recognised expert in his country, and eventually have his own *muqallid*s. Or he could choose to stay in Najaf or move to other towns with a religious educational infrastructure in Iraq and Iran to pursue his studies and teachings. Whether he stayed or left, he was now part of the 'good companions',[111] closely interconnected by past experience and present recognition, and organised into an efficient and competitive hierarchy.

The distinguishing features of the hierarchy of the Shi'i *'ulama* appears most dramatically in the ways of their relation to their *muqallids* and in their relations to each other.

To a large extent, the hierarchy within the *mujtahids* reflects the early stages of apprenticeship. The students rise through the various stages of apprenticeship by a process which rests ultimately on various criteria acknowledging aptitude to *ijtihad* based on reputation and recognition. As with *murahiq* to *mujtahid*, so with the ascent from lesser to higher *mujtahid*: the *mujtahid*s rise through the hierarchy of the *marja'iyya* by a process combining lectures, seminars, and publications in the field of *fiqh*, as well as the growing acceptance and support of the *muqallid*s at large.

In the same way as the stages of apprenticeship were never made truly precise, but acquired gradually an unofficial mould which divided them in approximate numbers of years, a *mujtahid* was in theory no different from any other *mujtahid*. In strict law, the categories of *mujtahid* and *muqallid* are discrete. The individual is either a *mujtahid* or a *muqallid*, with no degree in between and no differentiation between various *mujtahid*s or different *muqallid*s. This derives naturally from the flexibility built into the theory of reputation.

Reputation also meant that in due course, a difference could be discerned between a successful and 'true' *mujtahid*, and between less brilliant and competent *'ulama*. This was reflected in the titles bestowed on the mujtahids, such as *Ayat Allah*, *Hujjat al-Islam*, *Thiqat Allah*, etc. At a time when the whole structure of the Shi'i schools was on the wane, as in Najaf from the 1920s to the 1960s, the differences between these degrees were not considerable. In effect, they were so fluid that one could not make a case for a precise distinction between the various titles.[112]

Within the hierarchy and the grades mentioned, there was, in effect, little difference. The structural reason for this fluidity was the absence of a criterion to differentiate between say, a *Thiqat Allah* and a *Hujjat al-Islam*. But more fundamentally, the flexibility came from the external element constituted by the cooptation by the *muqallid*s of their own *mujtahid*. The more *muqallid*s a *mujtahid* was said to have, the more important he was amongst his peers. Ultimately, a *mujtahid* with a consistent and huge number of *muqallid*s became a reference, a *marja'*, which is synonymous with *Ayat Allah* in the hierarchy.

The highest degree of *Ayat Allah*, or *marja'*, was somewhat distinct from the other appellations from two points of view.

Socially, it was not possible for a *mujtahid* to be more than a *marja'*, so the *muqallid*s would more readily follow a *marja'* than a *Thiqat Allah*. Although there was a vicious circle within the system because of the inevitable competition among the *maraji'*, this democratic process (in its *demos* literal acceptation, since the people ultimately decide whom to follow) ensured at the same time flexibility and uncertainty.

To an extent, this did not really matter. Since the whole structure of civil society was operating at the margins of the state, the uncertainty of the title was independent of any form of coercion. A *muqallid*'s willingness to contribute support and his readiness to acknowledge a particular *mujtahid* as his reference were the only elements which counted.

Legally, matters were more rigid because legal theory, although not adopting a more specific structure than the general dichotomy between *mujtahid* and *muqallid*, had built in a differentiation between a lesser *mujtahid*, and a more accomplished one. There was indeed some difference between a jurist who could operate in all fields of the law, and a jurist whose competence was limited to narrower matters.

This distinction between more competent and less competent *mujtahids* appears in Abul-Qasem al-Khu'i as between 'the absolute and the partial *mujtahid* (*al-mujtahid al-mutlaq wal-mutajazzi*')'.[113] *Ijtihad* being 'the deduction of the legal rule from its proven premises',[114] the absolute *mujtahid* is defined as 'the one who is capable of deduction in all fields of *fiqh*', whereas the partial *mujtahid* can operate 'in some branches (*furu'*) without others'.[115]

The debate will be enriched by taking a glance backward, to a time when the *mujtahid*s' arena was much less politicised. The testimony of the Lebanese Muhammad Taqi al-Faqih in the 1940s will serve once again to clarify, from the top of the hierarchy downwards, the operation of legal scholarship in the Shi'i world. The central question was formulated by Faqih thus: 'How is the leader [*ra'is*, the highest recognised leader], chosen [elected, *muntakhab*]?'[116]

The theoretical structure of Shi'i civil society depends on the answer to this question. More crucially for the present agitated state of affairs, the interface between the tradition and the constitutional model in Iran will help explain the parameters of the struggle for power in Tehran and its intricacies.

For Faqih, the answer to the question is 'extremely difficult', because the 'new leader is not chosen immediately after the loss of the first leader. He is not elected by a known, precise, body, and the leadership is not defined after the loss of the leader by [the remittance of leadership] to one single person.'[117]

The list of the traditional criteria necessary for acquiring the virtues of leadership offers no absolute clue to the process. Not only must the religious leader have *'ilm*, *'aql*, *taqwa* (piety), *idara* (administrative skills), and *hilm* (clemency), he must also prove to be superior in all these virtues.[118] But who, from those who are inevitably of a lower degree than the position which they must allocate, will designate the leadership? 'The learned non-scholar, how can he be called upon to testify to the scholarship of the *'alim*, and how can a person who does not have the skills of administration testify to the good skills of another *'alim*?' [119]

To answer these questions, one must look into the qualities of the electors (*nakhibin*):

For instance, there are a number of persons who are known for their scholarship and virtue, and they can be *mutlaq* (absolute), *mutajazzi'* (partial), or *murahiq* (apprentice) *mujtahid*s. They are called 'the people of discernment', *ahl at-tamyiz*. This means that they can discern the most learned from the less learned, for they have tested (*mumarasat*) the most reputable *'ulama* by attending their classes, by sharing their scholarship, and by *mudhakara* in the intricate questions which are the focus of interest of the great *'ulama*. Then the superior *'alim* becomes known to them, through his comprehensive scholarly scope, his faculties of induction and his ability to bring the legal branch back to its root, the usuli and fiqhi rule to its base, uncertain evidence to certainty (*dalil zanni ila dalil qat'i*), and through his ability to address [the arduous questions] which forebears and contemporaries failed to solve. If this is all ascertained, then they [the people of discernment] admit his intellectual supremacy, *al-a'lamiyya*.[120]

Another possibility of recognising who is the 'most' learned scholar can be achieved by the testimony of 'very' learned scholars. Those scholars who have proven their intellectual abilities can so qualify the person who is characterised in a way which elevates his degree beyond his peers', they will say he is *a'lam*:[121]

For example, the late *Ayat Allah* an-Na'ini testified to Isma'il as-Sadr's [Muhammad Baqer as-Sadr's grandfather] *a'lamiyya*. Then he changed his mind, and when he was asked about it, explained that he has seen his ability in [his knowledge in the law of] the traveller's prayer, but discovered afterwards that he was not so competent in other matters.[122]

The choice of the ultimate *marja'* is therefore difficult to assess. It can be described as a ladder of recognition, with three levels: (1) at the bottom of the ladder, the free choice of the *muqallid*s, who plebiscite a *mujtahid* over others by providing support, both in sheer number (the more the *muqallid*s, the greater the *mujtahid*'s reputation) and in the intensity of their *taqlid* (where intensity is evaluated by financial support and religious devotion); (2) the 'people of discernment', who, after a long practice, will elevate a *mujtahid* to *a'lamiyya*; (3) the recognition of established *Ayat Allah*s. The process is long, complicated, and uncertain. The mechanisms are, like in the case of the access to *ijtihad* of the apprentice *'alim*, dependent on the hazy notion of reputation. Faqih summed up the difficulties:

> Thus you can see that the election is not limited to a category of people, or to a limited number. It is subject neither to religious power, nor to temporal power. The religious leader himself cannot appoint a successor. If he does, his choice can only be considered as one further significant [but not decisive] testimony. On this election process is built the glory of the University of Najaf. This is a natural election, it comes from all (*majmu'*), and is under the supervision of all.[123]

Muhammad Taqi al-Faqih wrote his analysis in the 1940s. The difficulties he acknowledged in the choice of the ultimate *marja'* were to reemerge in the aftermath of the Iranian revolution, when the Islamic state had to decide whom its leader would be. The model offered by the Shi'i law colleges constituted the blueprint of the overall model of government in the new system. But it needed to be translated into a constitutional language, which Muhammad Baqer as-Sadr provided.

2 On the origins of the Iranian constitution: Muhammad Baqer as-Sadr's 1979 treatises

Introduction: on *wilayat al-faqih*

There is little doubt that the theory of *wilayat al-faqih*, as developed in Khumaini's lectures of Najaf, was most influential in the creation of the constitution passed in Iran in the wake of the Revolution. In these Najaf lectures, delivered in 1970, Khumaini developed the idea of the '*ulama*'s responsibility in the state, in the form of an institutionalised structure which should be entrusted with the country's leadership.[1]

The general thrust of the theory is not completely original. One can find the idea of the *mujtahid*s' responsibility in the state developed much earlier in the century, for example when a dispute over Parliament and the new State of Iraq broke out in 1922–3.[2] After the great revolt of Najaf against the British, which was led by the '*ulama*, the continuation of this leadership through some representation in the state could not fail to be advocated in circles close to the Shi'i jurists:

> The program of the 'Union of '*Ulama*', which was received in Kadhimain on November 7, 1926, from Shaikh Jawad al-Jawahiri and was read at the house of the '*alim* Sayyid Muhammad as-Sadr on November 13, 1926, called for the establishment of a more intimate link between the '*ulama* of Persia and Iraq; the formation of religious societies which would be charged with the welfare of Islam in general, and which would work in Persia and Iraq for the improvement of relations with Turkey and Soviet Russia; and lastly, the control of these societies by the *mujtahid*s in their capacity as religious leaders of the people.[3]

In other countries of the Arab and Muslim world, similar propositions for the protection of 'the welfare of Islam in general' by the '*ulama* were also voiced at critical junctures in the encounter with colonialism, either in a direct fashion, such as the Persian Constitution of 1906 after the 1905 popular upheaval, or indirectly, as in some of the debates in Egypt in the 1920s.[4]

In contrast to the embryonic shape of this advocacy, Khumaini had gone to great length in the call for the '*ulama* to intervene directly in all matters political, and his Najaf lectures were primarily concerned with the legitimation of this necessity. 'They [the enemies of Islam] said Islam was not concerned with the organisation of life and society, or institutions of any kind, but that it should only be concerned with rules of menstruation and parturition, and that there might be in Islam some ethical issues, beyond which it had no say on life or the ordering of society.'[5]

Islamic Government is a long diatribe against this state of affairs, and the book of the Muslim *mujtahid* develops a theory of *wilayat* along two major lines:

(1) The involvement of the *'ulama* in the affairs of government: most arguments in the first chapter, and part of the second, are devoted to Khumaini's insistence, based on the Qur'an and on Shi'i *hadith*, on the necessity for the *'ulama* to get involved in government: 'Teach [Khumaini is addressing his students in Najaf] people the truth of Islam, so that the young generation does not think that the people of learning are confined to the corners of Najaf and Qum, and that they separate religion from politics.'[6]

A minimal involvement is not unusual in Shi'i modern history, and was manifest at major historical crossroads, most prominently in Iran during the Tobacco Revolt,[7] in the 1905 constitutional revolution,[8] and in the Iraq of the First World War, when the Iraqi South rebelled against the British invasion.[9] But this involvement can be portrayed as a negative one. It came when the society the *'ulama* knew and represented was facing what they perceived as a daunting threat. In the day-to-day development of the country, they had not actively and positively taken part in the life of government, until the theoretical lectures of Khumaini in Najaf, and the Iranian Revolution of 1978 in practice.

(2) The emphasis on the role of leadership for the *'ulama* in government: it is one thing to advocate political intervention premised on the alleged fusion of *din* and *dawla* (religion and state) in Islam, another to call for the *'ulama* to assume total responsibility at the highest level of the state apparatus.

There is some ambiguity in Khumaini's exact definition of leadership. Leadership can be meant to cover a wide spectrum of measures, ranging from the lowest level, non-binding advice, to the highest level, which means effective executive and legislative power: passing legislation and implementing it through state coercion. Between these two extremes, the public responsibility entailed in the jurists' leadership crosses several thresholds. The most conspicuous manifestation is the equation of leadership and guidance which, translated constitutionally, means a form of overview of society that censures the consonance of civil servants in the state, citizens at large, and legislation, within a frame of overarching references generally embodied in the Constitution. This latter acceptation is common in modern democracies, even though it does not go under the name of 'leadership'. This is the case of the Conseil d'Etat and the Conseil Constitutionnel in France, the Supreme Court in the United States, and various similar judicial institutions in many countries in the world.[10] In Iran, this leadership was constituted by the body of jurists entrusted with supervising the respect for Islamic law in Article 2 of the Supplementary Laws of the 1906 Constitution. Even though this council rarely met, it was at least an important precedent in the country's constitutional tradition.

Where does Khumaini in *velayat-e faqih* put the responsibility (*velayat*) of the *'ulama* in this scale?

No clear answer emerges in the text of 1970, but the weight of the argument tends toward some combination between the guidance concept of 1906 and a more decided attitude towards governmental matters as they are understood in the executive-legislative mould of contemporary democracies.

On the side of Khumaini's advocacy of absolute control by the *'ulama*, are the diatribes against the importation of foreign laws, amongst which Khumaini cites the Belgian provisions which were at the heart of Persia's 1906 constitutional text: 'At the beginning of the constitutional movement, when people wanted to write laws and draw up a constitution, a copy of the Belgian legal code was borrowed from the Belgian embassy and a handful of individuals ... used it as the basis for the constitution they then wrote ... '[11] Also, Khumaini equates *wilaya* with 'the governing of people, the administration of the state and the execution of the rules of law'.[12] But there are also passages acknowledging a relative power of the *'ulama* in terms of state control. This appears a contrario when Khumaini writes: 'If the sultans have some faith, they just need to issue their actions and decisions by way of the *fuqaha*, and in this case, the true rulers are the *fuqaha*, and the sultans become mere agents for them.'[13] This last passage echoes a well-known tradition in Iran, to the effect that a country is plagued when *'ulama* are found at the doorsteps of rulers, and blessed when the rulers are at the *'ulama*'s doorstep.[14] That the *'ulama* have the final word does not alter the reality of an effective separation of powers. The supervisory function lies precisely in this nuance, and it is hard to find in Khumaini's Najaf lectures an exact balance as to the role of the *'ulama* and the rulers in the state. The final word, certainly, is the *'ulama*'s, but the substantial content of their sway remains undefined.

In 1970, Khumaini was more concerned with arguing against the quietist interpretation of the *hadith* and of the Shi'i tradition, and less with the details of the nature of the *'ulama* leadership. This is understandable in view of the declining role of the *'ulama* in society, even as a consultative body. In 1970, the 1906 Constitution, especially in the dimension specified by Article 2, was a dead letter.

When the *'ulama* took over in 1979, a gap remained, and there is to date a missing link between the generalities of the Najaf lectures and the text of the Iranian Constitution.

Thus the arguments by Khumaini and in the Persian circles around him, constituted, in effect, broad suggestions for interventionism. The scheme adumbrated in the Najaf conferences and in Mahmud Taliqani's constitutional articles[15] only offered a general framework, which lacked the necessary specification of institutional articulation. Another text may have exercised a more direct influence on the framing of Iran's present constitution. This treatise, written by Muhammad Baqer as-Sadr in 1979, was designed precisely in answer to a query by fellow Lebanese *'ulama* on Sadr's view of a *Project for a Constitution for Iran*.[16]

Before discussing the substance of this *Note*, and comparing it with the structures at work in the Iranian Constitution, there are two further, more abstract levels in the theory of the Islamic state. The first abstraction is ontological. It is based on the necessity of establishing the theory of the Islamic state, as closely as possible, on the *Urtext* (the Qur'an).

On which Qur'anic ground can the responsibility for this state, or its leadership by the *'ulama* be defended? In other words, why should the jurist be entrusted with any such kind of responsibility in the affairs of the State?

To the necessity of finding a textual basis in the Qur'an, the modern theoreticians among the *'ulama* have answered diversely. Often, it is the verse on the *shura*[17] which is put forward, but it is clearly a text that cannot be used to legitimise a leadership by the *'ulama*. Khumaini, in his Najaf lectures, also referred to the '*amr bil-ma'ruf wan-nahi 'an al-munkar*' (enjoining the good and forbidding the evil).[18] This reference is even less precise from a constitutional point of view, and cannot be construed to mean more than the necessity for the moral injunction to enter the public realm. However, the chapter on *amr bil-ma'ruf* in the major compendium of laws of Khumaini includes some interesting details on his view of the attitude of the *'ulama* towards the state from a negative point of view: but this discussion is an extension of the Shi'i jurists' classical texts.[19]

The second level of abstraction in Islamic state theory is philosophical, and looks for the significance of power in an Islamic state from the perspective of its survival through fourteen centuries of adversity. In the tradition of Ja'farism, this dimension is coupled with Shi'ism as a minority sect in the world of Islam, and the importance of its tradition of resistance as exemplified in Karbala and the Husayn paradigm. But in the modern activist texts, as in Khumaini's *Hukuma Islamiyya*, the philosophical dimension is of little concern. In Sadr's attempt to complete his constitutional view in 1979, this philosophical aspect, which carries further the tradition of *Falsafatuna*,[20] was the object of a pamphlet on *The Sources of Power in the Islamic State*.[21]

Before turning to aspects of the constitutional question dealing with the substance of the power relationship and the *'ulama*'s responsibility in the state, it is important to see how a more sophisticated position has been developed by Muhammad Baqer as-Sadr through the grounding of such a power in the Qur'anic text, and how Sadr sought to expose a philosophical thread running through the whole of Islamic history.

Stage 1: reading the Qur'an constitutionally

It is in verse 44 of the fifth *sura* (chapter) of the Qur'an that Muhammad Baqer as-Sadr finds the legitimation of the Islamic state, and of the institutionalisation of the *'ulama*'s position in it. First published in 1979, *Khilafat al-Insan wa Shahadat al-Anbiya'*[22] provides a significant insight into the Iraqi scholar's ideas and positions at the end of his life, and is one of the most sophisticated texts in the modern literature of Islam on the connection between the Qur'an and the structure of an Islamic state. This will appear more significantly in a comparative approach with some other key interpretations of verse 44 in the modern age.

Verse 44 is rendered thus in one modern translation:

> It was We Who revealed
> The Law (to Moses) [The Torah, *at-tawrat*]: therein
> Was guidance and light
> By its standard have been judged
> The Jews, by the Prophet [Prophets, *nabiyyun*]
> Who bowed (as in Islam)
> To Allah's Will, by the Rabbis [*rabbaniyyun*]
> And the Doctors of Law [*ahbar*]:
> For to them was entrusted
> The protection of Allah's Book
> And they were
> witnesses [*shuhada'*, from *shahada*] thereto.[23]

This verse could be read as a very narrow text, and this was done frequently in the past. Some of the authoritative modern *tafsir*s continue to read the verse narrowly, as will be suggested in this section. Such a narrow interpretation emphasises the received *sabab an-nuzul* (cause or occasion of revelation) associated with the verse. The case is of two Jews in a dispute over adultery. They came to the Prophet for arbitration, and the Prophet emphasised the relevance of their own law as it was revealed in the books and developed by the *ahbar* in charge of its interpretation.[24] The institutional incidence of the verse in this interpretation is obviously limited. Legally, it could be classified as a case of conflict of laws, with a relatively strict adjudicatory system.

In contrast, Sadr's interpretation is characterised by a scheme that is tinged both by a constitutional-political exegesis and a characteristically Shi'i understanding. After citing the verse, Sadr explains:

> The three categories in the light of this verse are the *nabiyyun*, the *rabbaniyyun*, and the *ahbar*. The *ahbar* are the *'ulama* of the *shari'a*, and the *rabbaniyyun* form an intermediate level between the *nabi* and the *'alim*, the level of the Imam.
>
> It is therefore possible to say that the line of the *shahada*[25] (testimony) is represented by:
>
> First – The Prophets (*anbiya'*).
>
> Second – The Imams, who are considered a divine (*rabbani*) continuation of the Prophets in this line.
>
> Third – The *marja'iyya*, which is considered the righteous (*rashid*) continuation of the Prophet and the Imam in the line of the *shahada*.[26]

In this interpretation of the Qur'anic verse, Sadr extracts a purely Shi'i institutional scheme. First, he omits the patent Judaic reference by subsuming the Torah under a 'divine book' classification. Then, by referring to the *rabbaniyyun* not as the rabbis, which the context would suggest, but as the twelve Imams of the Ja'faris, he gives a strong Shi'i ring to his interpretation. The *ahbar*s, the Doctors of the Law in the translation, are understood to mean the Shi'i *marja'iyya*, which constitutes for Sadr the last body of witnesses in the line of the *shahada*, and which, in the verse cited, is entrusted to protect the Book after the Prophet Muhammad and the Twelve Imams. Thus charged with an implication of public responsibility, Sadr's *shahada* confers on the *marja'iyya* the task of guarding the Islamic Republic in the fashion designed by Plato for the Philosopher-Kings of his ideal city.

The originality of this reading of the Qur'an appears more fully when contrasted with the leading *tafsir*s of the twentieth century.

Muhammad Rashid Rida, in his *Tafsir al-Manar*, understands the verse restrictively: 'The Prophets, Moses and the Prophets after him, rule over those who became Jews (*hadu*). [Moses and the Prophets of Israel rule over] the Jews in particular because it is a law specific to them, not a general law, and this is why the last one of them, Jesus, said: I was sent only for the lost sheep of Israel.'[27] Therefore, in the reading of this passage by Muhammad 'Abduh's disciple, the importance of the whole citation is curtailed because of the Judaic reference. In Rida's *tafsir*, no constitutional system is mentioned which could even suggest that a religious leader, and less so a *marja'*, is destined to continue the line of *shahada*.

For Sayyid Qutb also, some fifty years later, the Shi'i dimension is understandably absent. However, the political appeal of the text is strongly emphasised, and the reading into it of the need for a fully Islamic political system is determinedly underlined:

> This text, wrote the theoretician of the Egyptian Muslim Brotherhood, addresses the most crucial (dangerous, *akhtar*) issue of the Muslim way (*manhaj*), the system of governance and life in Islam ... In this *sura*, [this issue] takes a precise and assured form, that the text conveys in its wording and in its expressions, not just through its concepts and suggestions.[28]

Qutb however does not dwell on the constitutional system alluded to, as Sadr does. The importance emphasised in connection with this verse resides in its general appeal for a total and undiluted Islamic society, in which the prescriptions of the Qur'an are adopted and respected in all fields of life. Qutb uses this text, which is indeed the most explicit on the question of governance and the necessity to follow the Qur'an, to advocate a state which is completely Islamised, that is, in his world view, a state which goes, so to speak, by the Book. Furthermore, on the role of the *ahbar* (Sadr's *marja'iyya*), Qutb takes a diametrically opposed stance to Sadr's:

> Nothing is uglier than the betrayal of those who have been entrusted, ... and those who bear the name of 'religious men' (*rijal ad-din*) betray, deform, and falsify, remain silent over what should be done to rule by what God has prescribed, and strip the word from its context to please the whims of those in power, to the detriment of the Book of God.[29]

This text implies that there are two categories of religious men, those who betray, deform and falsify to serve the people in power, and the honest ones who presumably do not act 'to the detriment of the Book of God'. For Qutb, who had completely been abandoned by the Egyptian *'ulama*, and not surprisingly in view of the coyness he perceived as the characteristic of the shaykhs of the Azhar, the worst thing would have been to entrust the rule of God to the religious hierarchy. Neither he, nor most of the historical leaders of the Brethren, such as Hasan al-Banna and 'Umar Talmasani, had much political affinity with the quietist Azhar.[30]

In contrast, Muhammad Baqer as-Sadr was evolving in Najaf among a whole generation of 'religious men', who by 1979 were looking for him to be the Khumaini of Iraq. Understandably, the reservation of Qutb towards an interpretation of the Qur'an which underlines the *shahada* of the *'ulama* in the definition of the Islamic state was not shared by the Iraqi *mujtahid*s.

However, the emphasis on the political dimension of the verse, as well as on the foundation of a 'nucleus' of the Islamic state in the Qur'an renders Sadr and Qutb very close in parts of their *tafsir* of verse 44.

Sadr's exegesis is also peculiar in the Shi'i world. But its variance with the great Shi'i interpreters has a logic of its own. Tabataba'i's *Mizan*[31] and Shirazi's *Taqrib*[32] both denote Shi'i references in the explanation of the *sura*. For Shirazi, the verse means that the Torah as a divine book should be abided by, until superseded, by a Book of better guidance and greater light.[33] In so far as the text of the Holy Book has not been adulterated, it is permissible for those who believe in it to be ruled by it, and 'Ali's authority is invoked to substantiate this interpretation in reference to the Jews and the Christians.[34] Like Rida's, Shirazi's reading is restricted and non-political: he tends to limit the impact of the verse to the Judaic context. Even the Shi'i element remains general, despite the reference to the first Imam.

Not so Tabataba'i. His comment is more universal, in that like Qutb and Sadr, he reads into the text a more general statement than the reference to the Torah might suggest.[35] Unlike theirs, his universality is not political, and this political neutrality resembles Rida's and Shirazi's. But Tabataba'i introduces a notion absent from the other *tafsir*s, and this notion is expanded in Sadr's scheme to form the key to his whole constitutional system. Tabataba'i writes: 'It is certain that there is one level *(manzila)* between the levels of the *anbiya'* and the *ahbar*, which is the level of the Imams ... and the combination of prophecy and Imamat in one group does not preclude them being separated in another.'[36]

Thus a formal separation is introduced between the three categories, the Prophets, the Imams, and the *'ulama*: 'And ['Ali's] saying: "the Imams are beneath *(duna)* the Prophets", means that they are one degree below the level of the Prophets according to the gradation of the verse, in the same way as the *ahbar, who are the 'ulama,*[37] are beneath the Imams *(rabbaniyyun)*.'[38]

This exclusively Shi'i scheme,[39] it should be noted, is purely theological, and is included in the context of Tabataba'i's 'narrative analysis' *(bahth riwa'i)*.[40] It is not alluded to in the section 'on the meaning of the *shari'a*' devoted to the legal interpretation of this passage.[41] Unlike Sadr, Tabataba'i does not derive a constitutional system from verse 44, and this restriction is in accordance with his general appreciation of the Shi'i scholars' social role to be more a spiritual than a political guidance.[42]

But only Tabataba'i's categories, and the similar Shi'i tradition of *tafsir*,[43] indicate how the celestial vault of Sadr's constitutional scheme was formed. This Shi'i classification, which endows Sadr's *marja'iyya* with the function of continuing the public role of the Prophets and the Twelve Imams, ushers in an 'ideological leadership', as Sadr calls it, which is meant to offer 'the objective criterion to the community from the point of view of Islam ... not only as to the fixed elements of legislation in the Islamic society, but also to the changing temporal elements. [The *marja'*] is the supreme representative of the Islamic ideology.'[44]

Several positions emerge in the interpretation of verse 44 of the Qur'an. They are summarised in the following table:

Qur'an v:44	Quietism/ Interventionism	Relevance of '*Ulama*	Particularist (P, Shi'i)/ Universalist (U, Islamic)
Shirazi	Q	No	P
Rida	Q	No	U
Tabataba'i	Q	Yes	P
Qutb	I	No	U
Sadr	I	Yes	P

For Sadr and Qutb, this verse should be interpreted as an invitation to a determined political intervention based on the necessary application of Qur'anic rules, *qua shari'a*, in society. But Qutb, unlike Sadr, sees no overall Shi'i scheme and keeps the religious hierarchy out of the role of leadership in the city, if indeed he trusts it with any role at all. In contrast, Tabataba'i, like Sadr, considers the role of the *'ulama* to be essential in the reading of the verse. This explains also that they are both particularist in their interpretation. The *'ulama* are perceived as the followers of the Prophets and of the Shi'i Imams.

It is interesting to note that the Shi'i Shirazi is also a particularist, but his emphasis on Shi'ism does not come from any relevance he accords the *'ulama* in the reading of the verse. There is no mention of any succession of the Imams which would, as with Tabataba'i and Sadr, devolve on the *'ulama*. His Shi'ism is merely 'cultural'. In comparison, the reading of the Sunni Qutb and Rida, as would be expected, carries no trace of Shi'ism, and their interpretation becomes ipso facto universalist: their reference is to an Islam in which particularist (communitarian) beliefs are irrelevant.

Sadr and Qutb are the only interpreters who assign a political value to the verse. Shirazi, Rida and Tabataba'i read it 'apolitically'. For Shirazi, Tabataba'i and the Rida of the *Manar*,[45] the verse carries no political charge. Shirazi and Rida's readings are restricted to an interpretation that limits the impact of the verse, and confines it to its Jewish context. The *sabab an-nuzul* becomes for them the only horizon of its application. Albeit not a call for a constitutional model to be based on verse 44, Tabataba'i's *tafsir*, in contrast, introduces a Shi'i element which founds, in combination with the political advocacy of Qutb and Sadr, the latter's institutionalisation of the *marja'iyya* at the heart of the Islamic state.

The constitutional system of Sadr's *marja'iyya*, thus founded in the Qur'an, is not only distinct when compared with the interpretation of other luminaries of twentieth-century Islam. By placing a Shi'i concept at the heart of the Islamic state advocated, it marks a break with Sadr's early writings. When in *Iqtisaduna* Sadr addressed briefly the question of the leadership in the Islamic state, he avoided 'talking about the system of governance in Islam, and the question of the individual and the apparatus that should legally succeed the Prophet in his rule (*wilaya*) and prerogatives as a leader'. Instead, through his masterpiece, Sadr 'assume[d] in the analysis the presence of a legitimate ruler'.[46] Whenever the ruler's role is mentioned in the 'discretionary sphere', 'the area of vacuum', *mantaqat al-faragh*,[47] which he should regulate, the word *wali al-amr* (person in charge) or *hakim shar'i* (legal ruler) is used.[48] Thus was suggested a denotation far more universal than the Shi'i concept of *marja'iyya* prevailing in Sadr's writings at the end of his life.

Stage 2: the philosophical perspective

Khilafat al-Insan wa Shahadat al-Anbiya' provided the foundation in the Qur'an of an institutional system in which the *'ulama* continued the role of the Prophets and of the Shi'i Imams at the head of the community. In Sadr's last year, he also wrote another contribution on the state, *Manabi' al-Qudra fid-Dawla al-Islamiyya*, which was part of a series of six booklets published in 1979 in a collection entitled *Al-Islam Yaqud al-Hayat*, 'Islam guides life'.[49] Those works were clearly inspired by the victory of the Iranian Revolution, and they were meant to enhance its ideological impact. Before discussing the parallels between the constitutional *Note* which Sadr also wrote in 1979 for the collection, and which best represents his importance for the understanding of the present Iranian legal system, a presentation of the ideas advocated in *Manabi' al-Qudra* will show Sadr's philosophical perspective on power in the wake of the Iranian Revolution.

Manabi' al-Qudra is a general work on the Islamic polity, and was probably meant by Sadr as a continuation of his long awaited study on the society. 'The Islamic state is sometimes studied as a legal necessity because it institutes God's rule on earth and incorporates the role of man in the succession of God', writes Sadr at the outset of this book, in probable reference to the two other constitutional studies in the collection *Islam guides life*. 'Sometimes', he continues, 'the Islamic state is studied in the light of this same truth, but from the point of view of its great achievement as civilization and immense potential which distinguish it from any other social experience.'[50] In *Manabi' al-Qudra*, this cultural aspect of the 'Islamic necessity' is developed along two general lines, (1) 'the ideological (doctrinal, *'aqa'idi*) structure that distinguishes the Islamic state, and (2) the doctrinal and psychological structure of the individual Muslim in the reality of today's Islamic world'.[51]

As to the state, two elements constitute its connection with Islam. Like any other society, there is an aim for which the system vies. For the Islamic state, the aim is to take the way towards 'the absolute God', and the values attached to Him, 'justice, science, capacity, power, compassion, generosity, which constitute in their totality the object of the march of human society'.[52] But the other element is the one on which Sadr insists most in that year of revolution, the 'liberation of man from the attachment to the world'.[53] This, writes Sadr, is not, like in many other countries or systems of the world, just 'an imaginary conception'.[54] Equality was lived and practised by the Prophet and by the first Imam, and equality in an Islamic state should not only be a mere word on the paper of a constitution. It must be implemented in practice.

This historical experience of the effective fight against inequality, injustice, and exploitation is then discussed at the level of the individual. The Muslim individual, writes Sadr, has retained, despite all adversities, a particular attachment to his religion. 'This faded (*bahita*) Islamic doctrine has constituted, despite its quietism, a negative factor against any cultural framework or social system that does not emanate in thought and ideology from Islam'.[55] It is only by force and violence that those other systems have been sometimes able to control Muslim societies. Individuals have always shown in a spontaneous manner, as when they took up arms against an invader, or in a more consistent way, such as when they kept on paying alms to the poor as prescribed, that foreign control would always remain constrained by their attachment to their faith.

This survival of Islam is deeply rooted in history. For a Muslim, writes Sadr, there has always remained the example of the first Islamic state and the necessity to match its perfection. The dating of this state is slightly more precise than in *Iqtisaduna*: 'The Islamic state offers the Muslim individual an example as clear as the sun, close to his heart... would one find any Muslim who does not have a clear picture of Islamic rule in the times of the Prophet and the Caliphate of 'Ali and most of the period between them ... ?'[56]

In the *Sources of Power in the Islamic State*, there is actually little said on these sources. The study is mainly devoted to indicating, once more, the singularity of the Islamic state, both historically, as an experience which draws back on fourteen centuries of the attachment to Islam, and synchronically, as a constant quest for the perfection of God. Perhaps the most striking theme that emerges from this study is the insistence on 'detachment', *zuhd*, in the effort of 'clothing the earth with the frame of Heaven' (*ulbisat al-ard itar as-sama'*).[57] This theme of justice has obviously re-emerged in the Middle East of 1979 as a central tenet of the assertion of political Islam.[58]

The process that led to the narrowing of Sadr's institutional basis of leadership developed concomitantly with a historical context that bore the stigma of the confrontation with the state.[59] The constitutional grounding of his thesis clearly reflects a care for a close control, in times of stress, of the revolutionary apparatus. In Iraq, in 1979–80, the choice for Sadr was between a loose oppositional front, which his last call 'to the people of Iraq' typifies,[60] and the narrow appeal to the Shi'i *'ulama*'s leadership followed both in the practice and the theory of verse 44. Iraq is indeed a complex society grouping ethnic and confessional groups, and Islam's call faces a very difficult social terrain. In Iran, by contrast, the relative homogeneity of the religious composition of the population renders debatable the important sectarian variable. That there remains the ethnic dimension is of course important.[61] But for Sadr, in the enthusiasm that followed the victory of the Revolution, the ethnic problem mattered little. In 1979, he wrote his constitutional considerations in the *Preliminary Legal Note on the Project of a Constitution for the Islamic Republic in Iran*.[62]

Stage 3: proposing a constitution for Iran

Manabi' al-Qudra occupies the second stage of a three-level process in the adjustment of Sadr's thought to the new realities of the Iranian Revolution. In the first level, *Khilafat al-Insan* offers the celestial, theological level of the constitutional system in the peculiar Qur'anic reading of sura 5. As a second level, *Manabi' al-Qudra* constitutes a philosophical quest for the enduring significance of Islam throughout history. *Lamha Fiqhiyya Tamhidiyya* expresses the third stage of an actual, practical implementation of these theories in the process of the Islamic Revolution.

The exact date of this *Note* is important in assessing Sadr's influence in Iran and in Iraq. It was completed on the 6th of *Rabi' al-Awwal* 1399, corresponding to the 4th of February 1979.[63] That was before the final victory of the Iranian revolutionaries. The army in Iran was then still under the command of Shapur Bakhtiar, who was appointed Prime Minister just before the Shah's departure, and a tense two-powers situation prevailed in the country. Only during the night of the 10/11th February, when the army rallied the revolution, did the last bastion of the Old Regime crumble.[64] At the time of writing the *Note* therefore, the concept of an Islamic Republic did not have a precise constitutional form, and the scheme forecast in Khumaini's Najaf conferences[65] and in Taliqani's constitutional articles[66] merely offered a general framework which lacked the minutiae of institutional articulation.

It would in any case have been impolitic and premature to go into details of that sort when the final battle had not yet been won, and Khumaini had too deftly avoided commitment to a precise societal scheme during the period spent in his French exile at Neauphle-le-Château to act rashly so close to victory.[67] For all these reasons, Sadr's *Note* appears not to have been a comment on any pre-existing draft, despite its misleading title.[68] By asking Muhammad Baqer as-Sadr to express his thoughts on Khumaini's 'Islamic

Republic', the Lebanese Shi'i *'ulama*, who were anxious for more details on an eventual Islamic system, were not referring to any specific text.

The *Note*, therefore, is one of the early blueprints (probably even the earliest) of the Constitution finally adopted in Tehran. It is also remarkable in terms of its precedence over the debate on the Constitution of Iran in 1979, particularly in view of the text prepared by the first post-revolutionary Government and unveiled on June 18, which 'made no mention of the doctrine of the deputyship of the *faqih*'.[69]

Sadr's *Note* was translated immediately and was widely circulated in Iran in both the Arabic original and the Persian translation.[70] In view of the stature then held by Sadr in religious circles, its influence is beyond doubt. But there is more to it than its formal importance as the blueprint of Iranian fundamental law. The analysis of the *Note* vis-à-vis the final text of the Iranian Constitution, we would like to suggest, shows that the system adopted in Iran has incorporated almost invariably the proposals, hesitations and contradictions included, of Muhammad Baqer as-Sadr's last important contribution.

'The Qur'anic state', Sadr writes in the *Note*, is premised on an intrinsic dynamic towards the Absolute: God. It contains therefore the strength of the eternal and unfathomable character of God's words. Borrowing a metaphor from *surat al-kahf*, Sadr juxtaposes 'the march of man towards God' with the verse introducing the power of the Divine word: 'If the sea were ink to the words of my God, would it exhaust itself before God's words.'[71]

The following are for Sadr the basic principles which, in the *Note*, offer the comprehensive picture of the Islamic state.

In Islamic *fiqh*, these principles are:

(1) Original sovereignty (*al-wilaya bil-asl*) rests only with God.

(2) Public deputyship (*an-niyaba al-'amma*) pertains to the supreme jurist (*al-mujtahid al-mutlaq*) habilitated by the Imam in accordance with the saying of the Lord of the Age (The Awaited Imam, *imam al-'asr*): 'for actual events, go to the reporters of our stories, they hold evidence (*hujja*) for you as I am evidence to God'. This text shows that they are the referees (*marja'*) for all real and actual events insofar as these events are related to securing the application of the *shari'a* in life. Going to them as the reporters of stories and bearers of the law gives them the deputyship, in the sense of righteousness (*qaymuma*) in the application of the *shari'a* and the right to complete supervision (*ishraf*) from the *shari'a*'s angle.

(3) Leadership (succession, *khilafa*) of the nation (*umma*) rests on the basis of the principle of consultation (*shura*), which gives the Nation the right to self-determine its own affairs within the framework of constitutional supervision and control (*raqaba*) of the deputy of the Imam.

(4) The idea of the persons who bind and loose (*ahl al-hall wal-'aqd*), which was applied in Islamic history, and which, when developed in a mode compatible with the principle of consultation and the principle of constitutional supervision by the deputy of the Imam, leads to the establishment of a Parliament representing the nation and deriving (*yanbathiq*) from it by election.[72]

This text, which comes at the end of the *Note*, sums up Sadr's constitutional view as he applies it to Iran. From the outset, the principle of

God's sovereignty is asserted as an Islamic principle of government deliberately put forward in contrast with Western theories. This quotation is followed by a brief review of the alternative constitutional theories prevailing in the West. On the basis of his Islamic model, which obtains from a divine sovereignty combined with the amalgamation of the principle of popular representation by a Parliament-elect and the supervision of jurists, Sadr rejects 'the theory of force and domination' (in reference to Hobbes), 'the theory of God's forced mandate' (in reference to the medieval Divine Right of Kings, which he puts in contrast to his notion of a divine sovereignty actuated by Parliament and the jurists), 'the theory of the social contract' (in direct reference to Rousseau, and indirectly to Locke and other social contract theorists), and 'the theory of the development of society from the family' (in probable reference to Friedrich Engels' *Family*).[73]

In the general principles adopted by the Iranian Constitution of 1979, it is difficult not to be struck by the similarities with Sadr's work. The first principle stated by Sadr is echoed in Article 2 (1) of the Constitution, which declares that 'the Islamic Republic is a system based on the belief... in the sovereignty of God'. Article 56 repeats the principle further: 'Absolute sovereignty over the world and over man is God's. He grants man the right of sovereignty over his social destiny, and no person is allowed to usurp or exploit this right.'[74]

This principle, which looks as if it were too general to carry any consequences, is useful as a pointed contrast to the traditional vesting of ultimate power in people by modern constitutions.[75] Such divine sovereignty is emphasised by Sadr[76] in contrast 'to the divine right that the tyrants and kings have exploited for centuries',[77] and is clearly directed against the practice of the Iranian Shah. The principle is translated institutionally in two important directions. The first is the limits put on the powers of the Executive and Legislature vis-à-vis the jurists entrusted with the protection of the *shari'a*. The second consequence touches upon the absoluteness of the right of the individual to property. In Sadr's scheme, there can be no such absolute right to property, since man is at best a lessee of riches pertaining to God, in an environment over which only God can claim absoluteness.

The central role of the jurist as interpreter and protector of the *shari'a*, advocated by Khumaini in 1970 but articulated by Sadr in his contributions of 1979, appears paramount both in the *Note* and in the text of the Iranian Constitution, which states in Article 5 that 'during the Occultation of the Hidden Imam (*vali-e asr*), ... the responsibility for state affairs (*vilayat-e amr*) and the leadership of the nation are entrusted to a just (*'adel*) ..., competent (*aga be-zaman*) jurist (*faqih*)'. For Sadr, as in the text quoted earlier, the *wilaya 'amma*, which is the responsibility for the affairs of the state, rests ultimately with the supreme jurist, who must be just (*'adel*) and competent (*kafu'*).[78]

Thus, in Sadr and Khumaini's proposals, as well as in the Iranian

Constitution, final decision rests with the holder of a position which Sadr calls *marja' qa'ed* [79] or *mujtahid mutlaq*,[80] Khumaini *faqih 'alem 'adel*,[81] and the Iranian Constitution *rahbar*, Leader (Art. 5, Art. 107ff.).

If the supremacy of the jurist is final, it is not absolute. In Sadr's proposals, the system is a system of law, which is binding for all, including the *marja'*, who enjoys no particular immunity: 'Government is government of law, in that it respects law in the best way, since the *shari'a* rules over governors and governed alike.'[82] Khumaini wrote similarly in 1970, insisting in *Wilayat al-Faqih* that 'the government of Islam is not absolute. It is constitutional ... in that those who are entrusted with power are bound by the ensemble of conditions and rules revealed in the Qur'an and the *Sunna*... Islamic government is the government of divine law.'[83]

This is echoed in the description of the *rahbar* in the Iranian Constitution. Article 112 states that 'the Leader or the members of the Leadership Council are equal before the law with the other members of the country (*keshvar*)'.

It is no surprise to find mention of the equality for all, including the Leadership, before the law. But the real limitation on the power of the Leader rests in the definition of his ultimate arbitration, or supervision, against the other powers established by the Constitution.

The model of this supervision is exposed in the scheme of separation of powers which has been implemented in Iran. The blueprint of the model appears in its clearest expression in Sadr's *Note*. But it goes back, in many of its characteristics, to the Shi'i legal structure inherited since the triumph of Usulism, and later reproduced and refined in the educational system of the schools of law. This singularity, on the level of the state, transforms the system in Iran, as well as Sadr's scheme, into a two-level articulation of the separation of powers.

The two-tier separation of powers

With the sovereignty vested in God, and the *mujtahid*-leader being the mouthpiece and the ultimate guarantor of the implementation of divine law, Sadr's system (and in this the debt of Iran's constitution is much heavier to him than to Khumaini) is also premised on emanations of sovereignty which derive from the people,[84] or as appears more frequently in his constitutional treatise, in the *umma* (the Muslim community). In the text quoted earlier, these emanations of the people are vested, according to principles 3 and 4, in the establishment of a consultation and consequently of a parliament and a presidency elected directly by the people. This dual emanation of sovereignty is at the root of the double-tier separation of powers. In the *Note*, consultation and election are further developed:

> The legislative and executive powers are exercised (*usnidat mumarasatuha*) by the people (*umma*). The people are the possessors of the right to implement these two powers in ways specified by the Constitution. This right is a right of promotion

(succession, *istikhlaf*) and control (*ri'aya*) which results from the real source of powers, God Almighty.[85]

In practice, continues Sadr, the control (*ri'aya*) is exercised through the election by the people of the head of the executive power, after confirmation by the *marja'iyya*, and through the election of a parliament (called *majlis ahl al-hall wal-'aqd*), which is in charge of confirming the members of government appointed by the Executive,[86] and 'passing appropriate legislation to fill up the discretionary area'.[87]

Sadr's constitutional proposal retains a traditional feature of modern constitutionalism, the separation of powers between the Executive, the Legislature, and the Judiciary. The last power, in its traditional form, is included in the proposal as a 'supreme court to hold account on all contraventions of the aforementioned areas', and as an ombudsman, which Sadr calls the *diwan al-mazalim*, and which acts to redress the wrongs brought on citizens.[88]

At the level of the separation of powers, there is little new. Most countries in the world which are not based on the power of a single party advocate in their constitution some form of division of powers deriving from the Montesquieu model: in general, a separation between the executive, the legislative, and the judicial branches of government, with each branch checking the power of the other and protecting its own domain against the others' encroachment. The Iranian Constitution does not differ in this respect. In its broad lines, it follows Montesquieu's scheme. The Executive's structure, mode of election and prerogatives are stipulated in the Constitution's chapter 9 (Arts. 113–32 on the president, Arts. 133–42 on the Prime Minister and the Cabinet). The Legislature is governed by Arts. 62–99 in chapter 6, and the Judiciary by the rules of chapter 11 (Arts. 156–74). Some of the detailed points of the system will be further discussed in the next chapter, but it can be already noted that this aspect of the separation of powers offers no novelty in the Islamic Republic's constitutionalism.

It is the second tier of separation of powers which lends originality to Sadr's system, as well as to the Iranian Constitution. The concept of *marja'iyya*, wherein lies the originality, is at the heart of that constitutional model.

Prerogatives of the marja'/rahbar

In contrast to Khumaini's 1970 lectures, the practical concern is prominent in Sadr's *Note*, as well as in the Iranian Constitution. The power of the *faqih*, which for Khumaini was the concluding point of his argument in Islamic government, has become the starting point of Sadr and the victorious Iranian constituent actors. In 1979, the materialisation of this power and its institutionalisation were the major concern of the Iraqi leader and the Iranian followers of Khumaini.

The peculiarity of the *marja'iyya* as an institution resides in two dimensions: its prerogatives, and its internal structure in the light of history.

A major dichotomy appears in the prerogatives of the *marja'*. Though his essential function is of a judicial nature, and consists in securing the compatibility of all activities in the country within the framework offered by Islamic law, the *marja'* also retains strong executive privileges. For Sadr, 'the *marja'* is the supreme representative of the state and the highest army commander'.[89] Defence responsibilities are directly echoed in Article 110 of the Iranian Constitution, which confers on the Leadership the command of the army and of the revolutionary guards. As to the supremacy in the state, it comes indirectly in Article 113: 'The president of the republic holds the highest official position in the country after the Leadership.'

Also, Sadr's *marja'* puts the stamp of approval on the candidates for the Presidency. The wording in this case is interesting in view of the options chosen by the Iranian Constitution. In the *Note*, 'the *marja'* nominates (*yurashshih*) the candidates [to the Presidency], or approves the candidacy of the individual or individuals who seek to win [the position of] heading the Executive'.[90] In the Iranian Constitution, a similar distinction is made between the approval of the candidate-elect, which is a prerogative of the Leader after the elections (Arts. 110–14), and the screening of the candidates to the Presidency, which is the prerogative of the Council of Guardians.[91]

The *marja'* appoints the high members of the Judiciary in Sadr's system,[92] as does the Leader according to Articles 110–12 of the Iranian constitution. He also appoints the jurists who sit on the Council of Guardians of the Constitution (Arts. 110–11). In Sadr's *Note*, the *marja'iyya* 'decides on the constitutionality of the laws promulgated by the Parliament (*majlis ahl al-hall wal-'aqd*) in the discretionary area'.[93] The nuance in these prerogatives is important. In the Iranian practice of the post-revolutionary area, the Council of Guardians did in fact decide on the constitutionality of laws, and this essential task was the major cause of the institutional crisis which culminated in a major revision of the Constitution. In effect, Sadr's vesting of the direct control of constitutionality in the *marja'iyya* appears in retrospect as a wiser measure than the stipulations of the Iranian text, which separates between the *marja'/rahbar* and the Council of Guardians. This last argument will appear more clearly in the context of the crisis described in the next chapter.

Evidently, the powers of the *marja'/rahbar*, who also decides on peace and war,[94] are wide-ranging, and, to some extent, defeat the whole traditional scheme of separation of powers. The Leader is not a marginal honorific figure. He must act on several issues positively, and he appoints several high dignitaries in the government, as well as in the courts. In effect, the importance of the *marja'iyya/shuray-e rahbari* undermines the division between the Executive, the Legislature, and the Judiciary by the sole merit of its powerful existence. In theory, the three traditional branches check each other, but the presence of the *marja'iyya* creates an authority of last resort which is superior to them. The separation of powers becomes a double division, and the multi-layered combinations of checks and balances make the dialectic of the traditional system appear simple in contrast. At the same time, the *marja'iyya* under Khumaini has not developed a day-to-day smooth mechanism of implementation. This uneasy and complex system will appear even more so in the light of its internal structure.

Internal structure and historical legitimisation

The key text in Sadr's work in terms of the originality of the constitutional model for Iran relates to the internal structure of the *marja'iyya*. It derives from his observation that 'the *marja'iyya* is the legitimate expression (*mu'abbir shar'i*) of Islam, and the *marja'* is the deputy (*na'eb*) of the Imam from the legal point of view'.[95] The following mechanism is devised for the implementation of the principle:

> The *marja'* appoints a council of (*yadumm*) one hundred spiritual intellectuals (*muthaqqafin ruhiyyin*) and comprises a number of the best '*ulama* of the *hauza*, a number of the best 'delegate '*ulama*' [*wukala'*, i.e. '*ulama* charged with a specific mandate], and a number of the best Islamic orators (*khutaba'*), authors and thinkers (*mufakkirin*). The council must include not less than ten *mujtahids*. The *marja'iyya* carries out its authority through this council.[96]

Much of the uncertainty in the constitutional arrangement in Iran can be read into the equivalent provisions. The main aspect of this uncertainty derives from the vicious circle which can be detected in the arrangement. The authority of the highest power is understood to be exercised through the council of the *marja'iyya*. But the council is appointed by a sole person, who is the *marja'*. In turn, the *marja'iyya* as a collective body is in charge, as Sadr points out later, of 'nominating the *marja'* by the majority of its members'.[97] Who nominates whom, of the *marja'* as an individual, or of the *marja'iyya* as a collective body, is blurred and seemingly contradictory.

One can see the reflection of these provisions in the text of the Iranian Constitution, which solves the contradiction only in part. The three relevant articles on the *marja'* and the *marja'iyya*, Articles 5, 107 and 108, stipulate that:

> If there is no such *faqih* [as the one specified in the first lines of this article, 'whom the majority of people have accepted and followed'], to have won the majority, the Leader [*rahbar*, which is the equivalent of *marja'*] or Council of Leadership [*shura-ye rahbari*, *marja'iyya*] composed of the *fuqaha* who fulfill the qualification stipulated in Article 107 will be entrusted with that authority [of *velayat-e amr* and *imamat-e ummat*]. (Art. 5)

> Otherwise [i.e. if there is no *faqih* who has been adopted 'by a decisive majority of the people ... like *Ayat Allah* Khumaini'], the experts elected by the people shall consult about all those considered competent to be vested with such authority and leadership. If one such authority is known to be preeminent above all others, he shall be appointed

as the Leader of the nation; otherwise, three or five authorities fully qualified for Leadership shall be appointed as members of the Council of Leadership. (Art. 107)

Art. 108 presents the status and competence of 'the experts' (*khubregan*):

The law related to the number and qualification of experts, the way to elect them and the internal regulations of their session for their first assembly will be decided and approved by the majority of *fuqaha* of the first Council of Guardians, and endorsed by the Leader of the revolution [Khumaini]. Then, any alteration or revision of the law will be decided by the Assembly of Experts.

In theory then, the Iranian Constitution solved what had appeared contradictory in Sadr's text by means of a mechanism which allowed the Council of Guardians to draft legislation regulating the choice and competence of the Assembly of Experts, subject to the approval of Khumaini *qua* leader of the revolution.

In turn, this Assembly would, in its first meeting, readjust the law, and then proceed regularly with its work. But beyond this, the members of the Assembly of Experts had to be elected by the people. So far, the mechanism, though complex, seems to solve Sadr's vicious circle.

But the problem arises again from the interplay of historical legitimacy and popular election in relation to the Leader or the Council of Leadership. The text of the Iranian Constitution suggests that the Leader 'must be accepted by the majority of the people' (Art. 5), 'as has been the case'(Art. 108) with *Ayat Allah* al-Khumaini, who is specified by name. Sadr had suggested a similar scheme, which was however more elaborate than the mere reference to the persona of Khumaini as the historical model to follow: 'The *marja'iyya* is a social and objective reality of the nation (*haqiqa ijtima'iyya mawdu'iyya fil-umma*), which rests on the basis of the public legal balance (*mawazin*). In practice, it is effectively represented in the *marja'* and leader of the revolution [*inqilab*, the Persian word for revolution rather than the Arabic word *thawra*], who has led the people for twenty years and who was followed until victory by the whole nation.'[98]

Sadr, like the Iranian revolutionaries, was aware of the uncertainty of a repetition of the Khumaini phenomenon. An institutional scheme had to be devised, 'as a higher concept (*maqula 'ulya*) of the Islamic state in the long run'. The person who could be such *marja'* had to embody that concept by:

(1) Having the qualifications of a religious *marja'* who is capable of absolute *ijtihad* and justice;
(2) Exhibiting a clear intellectual line through his works and studies which proves his belief in the Islamic state and the necessity to protect it.
(3) Showing that his *marja'iyya* in effect in the *umma* has been achieved by the normal channels followed historically.[99]

The first condition mentioned in this paragraph echoes the usual requirements in the Shi'i tradition of the *'ulama* hierarchy. The second condition is a requirement which helps separate politically minded from a-political *'ulama*. The third paragraph is the most interesting, because it reveals in so many words the exact problem faced by the institutionalisation, at the level of a state, of the structure of the Shi'i colleges of Najaf.

'The normal channels followed historically' refers to what the previous chapter was trying to analyse, and explains how the *rahbar* of the Iranian Constitution corresponds to the *faqih* of Khumaini's Islamic Government, to the *ra'is* of Muhammad Taqi al-Faqih's University of Najaf, and to the *marja' qa'ed* of Sadr's *Note*. All denominations stem from these normal channels of the Shi'i hierarchy, with the uncertainty and vagueness which made it so 'extremely difficult' for Muhammad Taqi al-Faqih, back in the 1940s, to explain how the *ra'is* of the Shi'i world was elected or chosen. This uncertainty can be read into the fine lines of Art. 107 of the Iranian Constitution, which requires the Assembly of Experts to choose as Leader 'one such authority who is known to be pre-eminent above all others'. This 'knowledge' is none other than Sadr's 'normal channels followed historically', Muhammad Taqi al-Faqih's 'protracted democratic process', and beyond, the 'living *mujtahid*' of the Usuli tradition. What constituted a long and complicated process was reduced by the Iranian constitution to an ad hoc decision of the Assembly of Experts, which was entrusted with the appointment of the 'Leader'. In strict Shi'i law, however, nothing forces the lay person to accept that leader as the *mujtahid* whom he or she chooses to follow.

It is worth noting that the reason why this difficulty did not develop into a major contradiction of the Iranian system of government had to do precisely with the stature of Khumaini, and the exceptional circumstances which brought him to power in Tehran. The absence of Khumaini reopens the wound of the protracted process of choice. Even if the Assembly of Experts can choose a 'Leader', the choice will always be under threat of the re-emergence of the historical Shi'i process of choice, in which, in theory, the more knowledgeable will eclipse the less knowledgeable at the head of the community, even if the former emerges after the latter has acceded to power.

This is one of the most intricate problems faced by the system. The choice of the Leader-*marja'* is an open and repetitive process according to the theory of Shi'i law. In the Iranian Constitution in contrast, the process is constrained.

The other problem is also rooted in the discrepancy between the Shi'i legal tradition, which makes of the *marja'* a *primus inter pares*, and the mechanisms of the Iranian system. That Khumaini played since the establishment of the Islamic Republic a role of undisputed leader does not mean that the same would be true for another leader.

Before Khumaini's death, the succession problem was relatively marginalised by the unquestioned supremacy of 'the leader of the revolution'. Now that he is no more to provide a last resort to the conflicts between institutions, the Iranian constitutional system faces a situation of uncertainty on the level of Leadership, which will be reinforced by the 'normal channels' of the Shi'i *marja'iyya*.

The quietist dominant trend of the *'ulama* and the diversity of *maraji'* has traditionally rendered marginal any conflict at the top of the hierarchy. Once the system was institutionalised, the mild competition between the scholars would have easily acquired the character of a serious constitutional crisis. Khumaini's presence alleviated that danger and kept the system going. It will be interesting to see how an inevitably less charismatic Leader will react to the pressure of events.

There were other essential problems deriving from the two-tier separation of powers which characterises the intricate structure of the Iranian constitution. The decade of constitutional developments related to these problems is examined next.

3 The first decade of the Iranian constitution: problems of the least dangerous branch

In the preceding chapters, the relevance of the Shi'i schools of law for the modern constitutional debate, as well as the most direct sources at the origin of the present Iranian Constitution, primarily Muhammad Baqer as-Sadr's 1979 studies, have been presented. With these contributions in mind, this chapter will analyse some of the constitutional issues which have recently unfolded in the system. Occasionally, a comparative perspective will be introduced to shed more light on the problems that the Iranian institutions face.

In the widest acceptation of government, the quintessential constitutional question is about who ultimately holds the power to say what the law is. In view of tne centrality of the *shari'a* in the definition of an Islamic state, this issue represents the essential problem of contemporary Islamic law.

A guiding perspective to the analysis of this chapter is offered by the celebrated exchange between Humpty Dumpty and Alice: '"When I use a word," Humpty Dumpty said, in rather a scornful tone, "it means just what I choose it to mean – neither more nor less". "The question is," said Alice, "whether you can make words mean so many different things." "The question is," said Humpty Dumpty, "which is to be master – that's all" ';[1] or, as in a sermon preached two centuries ago: 'Whoever hath an absolute authority to interpret any written or spoken laws, it is he who is truly the lawgiver, to all intents and purposes, and not the person who first spoke or wrote them.'[2]

The jurists in the constitution

The Council of Guardians between legislature and executive

The problems related to the institution of Council of Guardians have developed out of the unusual system of separation of powers that regulates the Iranian state. Whereas the division between the executive, legislative and judicial branches would normally engender problems similar to the ones facing such a system in any modern democracy, the complication of the Iranian state arises from the centrality of the Leadership's position. The *marja'iyya*, which forms the peculiarity of Shi'i constitutionalism, has already been discussed in some of its forms in the preceding chapters. How it interacts in practice with other powers established in 1979 Iran will be the subject of a more thorough analysis in this section. But this aspect of the double-tiered separation of powers is not the sole distinguishing feature of Iran's present Constitution. The specificity of the Iranian system is due to the special powers entrusted with the Council of Guardians (*shuray-e negahban*), which has wielded much authority since the Revolution, and encroached on Parliament's legislative functions in a way that developed in 1988 into the most serious constitutional crisis of the Islamic Republic since its foundation.

The Council of Guardians has no British equivalent. In France, it is very similar to the Conseil Constitutionnel, which, in the system of the Fifth Republic, mainly looks to the concordance of the laws passed by Parliament with the French Constitution and 'Republican principles'.[3] Many Iranian constitutional bodies resemble institutions fashioned in Gaullist France, and the Council of Guardians, the election of the President in two turns (Iranian Constitution, Art. 117), as well as the President's prerogatives over the Prime Minister and the Assembly, are very similar in the two systems. But the Council of Guardians bears a specificity which makes it also very different from its French equivalent.

In France, the scrutiny of a law by the Conseil Constitutionnel can take place only if requested by the six persons or bodies specified by Article 61. In Iran, the scrutiny of the Council of Guardians is automatic:

> All enactments of the Majlis shall be submitted to the Council of Guardians and the Council shall examine them within ten days after the receipt thereof to see whether or not they reconcile with the tenets of Islam and constitutional law.
>
> If the Council of Guardians finds the enactments contrary to Islamic tenets and constitutional law, it shall return them to the Majlis for reconsideration. (Art. 94)

The main articles on the Council of Guardians form part of chapter 6 of the Iranian Constitution, on 'the Legislative Power', and complement the dispositions dealing with Parliament and its prerogatives. One could presume that, on the surface, the Council of Guardians is no more than a 'corrective' to possible exaggerations of Parliament, or eventual gross departures from accepted principles of the *shari'a*. But the reality is different. As appears from Article 94, the Council of Guardians was destined to play a major role in the definition of the functions of Islamic law. But important as that was, this supervision did not constitute the sole significant prerogative of this body. In other texts of the Constitution, the Council of Guardians was entrusted with the scrutiny, not only of Parliament's acts, but of the other important institutions of the country.

The executive branch in the Iranian system, which is headed by the President of the Republic, comes also under the control of the Council of Guardians. The screening process of candidates to the Presidency is a distinctive characteristic of the Iranian Constitution.

The control of the Presidency is two-fold. As mentioned in the preceding chapter, it is exercised, according to Art. 110, by the Leader, who 'signs the decree [formalising the election] of the President of the Republic after his election by the people'. But the Council of Guardians must also approve of the candidates to the Presidency: 'The suitability of candidates for the Presidency of the Republic, with respect to the qualifications specified by the Constitution, must be confirmed before elections take place by the Council of Guardians.' The Council of Guardians has therefore the effective, automatic prerogative of screening the candidacies to the highest executive position. The screening prerogative is even stronger than the power of the Leader in this respect, for it is difficult to see the Leader, except in very exceptional circumstances, refusing to institute an elected President. The preliminary screening of *candidates*, in contrast, is a measure far easier to take.

This executive screening by the Council of Guardians is, of course, a feature that distinguishes the Iranian system in a way unparalleled in modern nation-states. The fact that a candidate to the Presidency can be rejected for motives based on political grounds means that the whole devolution of the people's power is in effect checked by a decision of the Council. The Council of Guardians controls the person of the President, not simply his acts. And if the ratification of an elected President could be conceived as an *a posteriori* formality akin to the Crown in England calling a newly elected Prime Minister into office, the *a priori* control given to the Council of Guardians entails a noticeable strengthening of its already vast institutional power.

There is nothing in the Constitution that indicates how the mechanism of the Council of Guardians' screening of the presidential candidates operates. One must presume that the decision is based on the qualifications required for the Presidency in Chapter 9 of the Constitution on the executive power. Article 115 specifies that the President must be Iranian both by origin and nationality, be pious, etc., and that he must have 'a convinced belief in the fundamental principles of the Islamic Republic of Iran and the official school of thought in the country'. In other words, the President must be Shi'i, and this appears as another institutional characteristic proper to Iran. Some Arab countries have included in their constitutions a clause requiring the President to be 'Muslim',[4] but none requires him to be specifically Sunni or Shi'i.

The oath sworn by the President offers other indications of the criterion of his 'suitability' in the eyes of the Council of Guardians. Again, the Shi'i character appears in the text of the required declaration: 'I will guard the official school of thought of the country.' Also, the President must swear fidelity 'to the Islamic Republic and the Constitution of the country' (Art. 121).

In sum, these texts are too general to limit the screening power of the Council of Guardians. Unchecked, this control of the Presidency furthers the juristic hold (particularly the Council of Guardians) of the Shi'i hierarchy over all branches of the Government. That this power is not mere rhetoric appears in one famous instance of the Council of Guardians' exercise of his screening of the presidential candidates, when it rejected the candidacy of the first Prime Minister of the Islamic Republic, Mahdi Bazargan, in 1985.[5]

The composition of the Council of Guardians further betrays its hybrid character. Technically, because it comes under Chapter 6 on the legislative power, it could be considered a pure appendix of the legislative branch, which is in principle entrusted with an elected Parliament.[6] But the composition of the Council of Guardians points out the equal importance of its judicial character. Article 91 states that

> in order to protect the ordinances of Islam and the Constitution by assuring that legislation passed by the National Consultative Assembly does not conflict with them, a council to be known as the Council of Guardians is to be established with the following composition: (a) six just *fuqaha* (*fuqaha-ye adel va aga be-muqtadayat-e zaman*), conscious of current needs and the issues of the day, to be selected by the Leader or the Leadership Council; and (b) six Muslim jurists (*huquqedan*), specialising in different areas of the law, to be elected by the National Consultative Assembly from among the Muslim jurists presented to it by the Supreme Judicial Council.

It is clear from this text that the Council of Guardians, despite its formal attachment to the legislative branch, is dominated by the Judiciary in its composition. Though there seems to be a difference between the *fuqaha* chosen by the Leadership and the Muslim jurists appointed by Parliament, the screening operated by the Supreme Judicial Council leaves little doubt that jurists of classical Islamic law, as opposed for instance to lawyers or judges of the Ancien Régime, would be prominent on the Council. The Supreme Judicial Council itself is constitutionally formed of 'classical' '*ulama*. According to Article 158, the Supreme Judicial Council consists of five members, 'three judges ... possessing the quality of *mujtahid*, the Head of the Supreme Court, and the Prosecutor-General', both of whom must also be *mujtahid*s (Art. 162).

The institutionalised juristic quality of the Council of Guardians seems thus inevitable. It is difficult to imagine that the composition of the Council could escape the traditional Shi'i *ijtihad* structure. Half of its members must by law be *fuqaha*, and the rest are screened by a body which consists of *fuqaha*. Therefore, the Council of Guardians appears in its composition to bear all the qualities of a judicial body, and even though its position in the Constitution makes it technically part of the legislative branch, both in its composition and in its prerogatives, its legislative aspect fades before the judicial impact of Shi'i public law.

The dispositions in Art. 94 give an extremely wide role to the Council of Guardians in the legislative process, and these powers are further comforted by Articles 95 to 98, which allow the Council of Guardians, inter alia, to attend the sessions of the Majlis while a draft law is being debated, and for its members to express their views if an urgent bill is on the floor.

Thus, on the one hand, the Council of Guardians bears resemblance to some of the constitutional systems of the West, particularly in France and in the United States. With France, it shares the immediate scrutiny of legislation discussed in Parliament. With the United States, a similar scrutiny is carried out by the Judiciary, but it is only after a protracted process that it reaches the Supreme Court.

On the other hand, the Council of Guardians is set apart by the systematic and automatic revision power through which the Constitution empowers it to examine, and possibly undermine, all legislation. Furthermore, the Council of Guardians can allow itself ten extra days if it deems the first period insufficient for its analysis (Art. 95). With such unparalleled power, the Council of Guardians was bound to become a Super-Legislature, and its extraordinary prerogatives have been compounded by the vagueness of its mandate. The 'tenets of Islam' and the 'constitutional law' of the land are vast categories, which encompass virtually any area which the Council deems prone to its intervention, scrutiny, and possible rejection.

This unusually powerful body might have functioned smoothly as long as the divergences of its members and the majority of the deputies in Parliament were not too pronounced. But in the turbulent Iran of the post-revolutionary era, Parliament and the Council of Guardians turned out to hold different views of the law, and their differences have surfaced at several critical moments of the young Republic. Significantly, the most important disputes between the two bodies have emerged in what could generally be described as 'economic issues': foreign trade nationalisation, labour and industrial codes, and most prominently, agrarian reform.[7] Independently from the substantial dimension of these issues, it is important to describe how, from a formal perspective, the divergences in the interpretation of the law have so critically recurred between Parliament and the Council of Guardians so as to render the institutional crisis of 1988 almost inevitable.

Along with the supremacy of the *faqih*, the importance of the Council of Guardians is a decisive indication of the juristic hold over society. It is an irony of the constitution that, because the power allocated to the *'ulama* (and more specifically to the jurists *qua* Shi'i hierarchy) is so extensive, this power was difficult to sustain in practice. The example of the early American constitutional years, when the considerable power of the US Supreme Court was established by Chief Justice John Marshall in *Marbury* v. *Madison*,[8] offers an enlightening contrast. It was precisely because the US courts have been careful not to overstep the limits they assigned themselves to respect that they avoided the self-defeating course taken by the Council of Guardians. The error of the Council of Guardians resides in it not respecting the balance suggested by the Iranian constitutional emphasis on the people's electoral power (e.g. Art. 6: 'the affairs of the country must be administered on the basis of public opinion expressed by means of election', Art. 7ff.).

Yet it is true that the measure beyond which the 'government of the judges' cannot be stretched is unlikely to be established with total precision, and the continuing lively American debate on the Supreme Court is witness to this constitutional predicament. In the Iranian Constitution, there was a fundamental flaw in the phrasing of the texts on the Council of Guardians from the outset. The Council of Guardians has in fact done nothing more than stick to the powers enunciated for it in the Constitution. These powers were, from the beginning, wider than any judicial body could sustain in a Republic. By rendering all legislation automatically deferred to the Council of Guardians, there was no reason for the *'ulama* who constitute it to avoid looking into these laws according to their own understanding of the constitutional mandate. This abnormal system of separation of powers did not resist the pressure of revolutionary times, and the clash was inevitable.

Before addressing the recent turn of events, another aspect of the singularity of the Iranian institutions should be addressed, which is the role of the supreme *faqih* and the problems arising from the definition of his powers.

The jurist in the Iranian constitution: comparative perspectives

Chapter 2 emphasised the similarity between the power of the Leader in the Iranian constitution and the stipulations for the *marja'* enunciated by Muhammad Baqer as-Sadr. In this section, the Leader is appraised in the logic of the Iranian text against a wider historical and comparative perspective.

To the traditional separation between the Executive, the Legislature and the Judiciary, with the Council of Guardians straddling several government branches, has been juxtaposed the institution of the supreme jurist, the Leader.

Articles 5 and 107ff. specify the most important characteristics of the Leadership. It is helpful to quote them again in full. Article 5 states: 'During the absence of the Ruler of the Age (*vali-e asr*), may the Almighty hasten his advent, the authority to command and lead the people shall vest in an Islamic theologian and canonist, just, virtuous, abreast of the times, organiser and judicious, whom the majority of the people accept as their leader.'

In chapter 7 of the Constitution, on the Leader or Leadership Council, the composition of the Leadership and its powers are further defined. Article 107 states: 'Whenever one of the *fuqaha* possessing the qualifications specified in Article 5 of the Constitution is recognised and accepted as *marja'* and leader by a decisive majority of the people – as has been the case with the exalted *marja'-i taqlid* and leader of the Revolution *Ayat Allah al-Uzma* imam Khumaini – he is to exercise governance and all responsibilities arising therefrom.'

The necessary qualifications of the leader are therefore both moral and technical.

Morally, the Leader must be just and pious, acquainted with the circumstances of the age (*aga be-zaman*), etc. Obviously, the justice and piety qualifications cannot be fathomed with any kind of precision. They have probably been included – as in the text of Sadr quoted earlier – in the traditional manner of the Shi'i law textbooks. *Ayat Allah* al-Khu'i, in *al-Masa'el al-Muntakhaba*, *Ayat Allah* Muhsin al-Hakim in *Mustamsak al-'Urwa al-Wuthqa*, Tabataba'i in *al-'Urwa al-Wuthqa*, all introduce their major compendia with similar qualifications for the *faqih*.[9]

From a technical point of view, the 'acquaintance with the circumstances of the age' is more typical of the novelties in the Iranian Revolution and of its incidence upon Islamic state theory. It represents the *political* side of the involvement of the *'ulama*. The *faqih* must not live in an ivory tower of learning, he ought to know about the world he lives in, and prove competent and knowledgeable in all worldly matters.

This qualification for the eligible *'alim* or *faqih* excludes the non-political *faqih* from the leadership. In the Husayn-Hasan paradigm of Shi'i history,[10] that is, the paradigm of the interventionist Husayn and the non-interventionist, non-political Hasan, the Husayni aspect is clearly privileged by the Iranian constitution.

A forceful writer against the *'ulama*'s involvement in worldly matters was Ibn Khaldun. Five centuries ago, he had pondered over some of the problems connected with the jurist's involvement in running the affairs of a country. In the *Muqaddima*'s chapter 'on the *'ulama* among the people [as those who are] farthest from politics and its parties', Ibn Khaldun wrote about the logical impossibility for the *'ulama* to be 'abreast of the circumstances of the age':

> The rules and analyses of the *'ulama* remain in the mind and do not come into application. What is outside [i.e. the outside reality] differs from what is in the mind. Thus, legal rules are branches of what is left from the arguments of the Book and of the *Sunna*, and require the alignment of what is outside it. This is contrary to the analyses of rational sciences, which, to be true, require to be aligned with the outside world. So when jurists (because of what they have been used to in generalising rules and comparing things to one another) look into politics, they measure it with the model of their analysis and their type of reasoning, and frequently fall into error. They cannot be trusted.[11]

This view flies in the face of the tradition advocated by Khumaini and Sadr in their Najaf lectures. The logic presented by Ibn Khaldun is interesting in that it lifts the veil over an essential predicament of the jurist's leadership in the city and the governance of the judges, not only in Iran, but in virtually all the constitutional systems of the world which allow for an independent, protected, and separate power for the Judiciary.

In Ibn Khaldun's view, the predicament derives from the 'jurists' habit of indulging in theoretical studies and questioning meanings of words by extracting these meanings from the world of the sensible, and by abstracting them in the mind as general, total, things'.[12]

For modern specialists of constitutional law, similarly, the power to determine the law cannot be the one that directs its effective application. It is because of this essential limitation that, in Hamilton's celebrated words, the Judiciary constitutes 'the least dangerous ... and the weakest of the three departments of power ... [13] The courts must declare the sense of the law, and if they should be disposed to exercise WILL instead of JUDGMENT, the consequence would equally be the substitution of their pleasure to that of the legislative body.'[14]

For the qualifications of the faqih as a specialist of law who needs to know about the circumstances of the age in which he lives, these reflections of Hamilton and Ibn Khaldun are central to their emphasis on the inherent contradictions that cannot be escaped by the jurist who is involved in politics. Of course, the whole controversy of the juxtaposition of worldly competence and juristic function could be deflated by giving a purely moral dimension to the competence of the supreme *faqih*. This competence would then be a perfunctory figure of speech, similar to the necessity of piety or justice. But the departure from the received, dominant Shi'i tradition of the non-involvement of *'ulama* in politics, as it appears in the *leitmotiv* of Khumaini's and Sadr's works, and in the practice of the Iranian Government since the Revolution, suggests that the expression does not merely yield moral value. Worldly competence is the constitutional embodiment of the political responsibility of the *faqih*.

The problem is in part, as in the texts of the *Muqaddima* and the *Federalist*, the generality and relative impartiality of the law, in contrast to the turbulent, biased, and specific ambit of daily life. But it is more profound than that. Indeed, the argument over the generality of the laws and the case-by-case application by the Judiciary does not resist the reality of the power of the courts in any country. In his assessment of the law, Ibn Khaldun was correct about the difficulty for the *'ulama* to say what the law means, and run the affairs of a country at one and the same time. But this argument can be obviated by the fact that it is of the essential nature of a court of law to proceed from the inevitable generality of a law to its application to the narrow case at hand.

There remains however the more important Hamiltonian distinction between 'will' and 'judgment', or, in the Khaldunian equivalent, the difference between the normative nature of the law and the constrictive running of governmental business.

The *aga be-zaman* requirement of Article 5 suggests, as an essential corollary, a fundamental choice made in the constitutional practices of Iran, and this choice is an important departure from the received theory of the state. This dimension is common to the Iranian system and to the system which is probably closest to it among the constitutions of the modern age, that of the United States. This resemblance is rooted in the similarity, on the most abstract level, between the American Supreme Court and the Iranian Judiciary, understood to encompass the *faqih*-leader and the Council of Guardians of the Iranian Constitution. John Hart Ely, a most prominent constitutional specialist in the United States, puts the predicament in the following way:

> When a court invalidates an act of the political branches on constitutional grounds ..., it is overruling their judgment, and normally doing so in a way that is not subject to 'correction' by the ordinary lawmaking process. Thus the central function, and it is at the same time the central problem of judicial review: a body that is not elected or otherwise politically responsible in any significant way is telling the people's elected representatives that they cannot govern as they'd like.[15]

That problem of judicial review, in the sense of the review by jurists (be they the Council of Guardians or the supreme *faqih*), of acts of the legislative or executive branches, appears in Iran on two levels: first, as a classical separation of powers problem, when the Council of Guardians declares an act of Parliament unconstitutional, or when it censures the candidates to the Head of the executive branch. This is one aspect of the aforementioned double-tiered separation of powers. But there is a second dimension which is proper to Shi'ism and, on a state level, unique to Iran. It appears in the disproportionate role accorded to the supreme *faqih*, who is at one and the same time, the Leader of the state and the number one jurist of the Shi'i hierarchy.

In this perspective, the worldly qualifications required for the Leader reflect the political difficulties that he is bound to face. Following Articles 5 and 107, the powers of the supreme jurist, which effectively derive from the institutionalisation of this supremacy, are enumerated in detail by the Constitution. According to Article 110, the Leader is in charge of 'the supreme command of the armed forces, exercised in the following manner: (i) appointment and dismissal of the Chief of the general staff; (ii) appointment and dismissal of the Commander-in-Chief of the Corps of Guards of the Islamic Revolution; (iii) the formation of a Supreme National Defence Council;... (iv) appointment of the Supreme Commander of the branches of the armed forces; (v) the declaration of war and peace'.

The control by the Leader of the armed forces in the country, which is generally under the competence of the Head of the executive branch,[16] indicates how the position of Leadership in Iran impinges on executive branch grounds, which are specified in Chapter 9 of the Constitution. It is true that the President of the Republic is awarded in the Iranian Constitution the responsibility of 'heading the executive power' (Art. 113). However, expressly excepted are 'matters pertaining directly to the Leadership' (id.), and these include the sensitive control of the military. Under the Constitution, the President has neither direct nor indirect control over the Armed Corps. To a large extent, such limitations render executive power hollow.[17]

The supremacy of the *faqih* appears also in its power over the appointment and the dismissal of the President. As mentioned earlier, the Leader has a say in the nomination of the President, in that, according to Article 110d, he can block his accession to his post after the election. The Leader also decides ultimately on the dismissal of a President. 'The Leader dismisses the President of the Republic, with due regard for the interests of the country, after the pronouncement of a judgment by the Supreme Court convicting him of failure to fulfill his legal duties, or a vote of the National Consultative Assembly testifying to his political incompetence.' In this way, although the power of the Leadership in the appointment and dismissal of the President is limited, it is clear that the juristic-theological importance of the Leadership, in the supervision of the 'conformity' of the President with the spirit of the Iranian Constitution, is paramount. He has the final say in both processes. Considering that the screening power over Presidents and candidates to the Presidency ('who must announce their candidacy officially',

Art. 116) is shared with the Council of Guardians, the juristic-theological hold over society, as opposed to government officials acceding to power through the voting process, seems almost complete.

From a comparative perspective, examples might suggest some temperance to this conclusion. In several systems, control over the voting process is often entrusted to judicial bodies, and the activities of the Head of the Executive never go completely unchecked, as he/she is as bound by the law as any other citizen. Constitutions also suggest ways to impeach elected officials, and impeachment, although rare, is not impossible.[18] But presidential impeachment usually requires an arduous and protracted process, as well as a lengthy mobilisation to reach results and achieve constitutional dismissal.

Iran can be said to share this tradition, in that the President, once in power, cannot be easily impeached. It is true that in the short span of its life, the Iranian Constitution has already witnessed the impeachment of its first President, and it is noteworthy that the dismissal of Bani-Sadr was carefully clothed in a relatively lengthy constitutional procedure, despite the obfuscating quasi coup-de-force that accompanied the ousting.[19] In the normal course of events, however – and it could even be argued in the case of Bani-Sadr – presidential impeachment is not an easy task. But the ousting of Bani-Sadr has revealed some peculiarities of the Iranian system as to procedure, and indicated the decisive role of the Leadership even in this instance.

In the chapters of the Constitution related to the two bodies in charge of presidential impeachment, the Supreme Court (Ch. 11) and the Parliament (Ch. 6), there is no mention of the exact steps to be taken to carry out the impeachment procedure. Only in Article 110e in the chapter on the Leadership, are the competence of the Supreme Court and the Majlis mentioned in this regard. The ultimate decision on the dismissal of the President is considered to be a prerogative of the Leadership, 'with due regard for the interests of the country'.

The way to dismissal is not specified further, but one can assume, as in the case of Bani-Sadr, that the Majlis exercised the very general right mentioned in Article 76, 'to investigate and examine all the affairs of the country'. No less vague is the task of the Supreme Court in convicting a President who has 'failed to fulfill his legal duties'. Thus, it is only by gathering general rules related to the Supreme Court in the Constitution that one reaches the unusual conclusion that the grounds on which a President can be impeached in Iran are not different from the conviction of any other citizen (vide Arts. 161, 165, 166, 167, 168, 173, etc.). These general rules can be supplemented in the case of the President by Article 140: 'Accusations of common crime against the President of the Republic, the Prime Minister, and the ministers will be investigated in common courts of justice after the approval of the National Consultative Assembly has been obtained.' This vote, when juxtaposed with the vote of the Majlis on the President's 'political incompetence' (Art. 110), clearly shows the shortcomings of the Iranian Constitution on the impeachment issue. The President lacks the protection needed when political tension increases in the country, since the Majlis seems strong enough to impeach him by a mere majority vote. This is probably the reason why President Bani-Sadr was so easily evicted, and why the Presidency has since seemed particularly vulnerable.

These remarks, however, are more strictly concerned with the problems stemming from the separation of powers between the Executive and the Legislature. It is true that in the case of presidential impeachment, the legislative branch is stronger than the executive branch, especially since, out of concern for the dangers of a repetition of the old policies of the Shah, there is no provision in the Iranian Constitution allowing the president to dismiss Parliament. In this respect, the system is closer to the strict separation of powers as practised in the United States, in contrast to France where the President has the right to dissolve the National Assembly.

But there is in Iran, in all these processes, an overseer who is the Leader. The Leader, or the Leadership Council, acts as ultimate referee, even in the relations between Parliament and the Executive, as appears in the impeachment procedure of the President. In this, the normal structure of the separation of powers is different from any other model, but the drawbacks are also significant, because there is no constitutional model that could allow for a regulatory comparison. Nor can the system of the Islamic Republic rely on historical examples in the country's past for comfort. This, of course, is not necessarily negative, and it is normal that the text of a constitution be sufficient in itself for the regulation of the country's powers. The problem in Iran stems from the fact that, in the early turbulent years of the Republic, force has more than once dictated the meaning of imprecise constitutional dispositions.

The January debate and its aftermath

With no established precedent in history to guide it, the Iranian system quickly found its practice riddled with constitutional ambiguities deriving from the text, and from the complexities of the double-tiered separation of powers on which the Constitution is based. The major problem stemmed from the difficulties surrounding the two most original bodies instituted in 1979, the Leadership (with, in the background, the Assembly of Experts) and the Council of Guardians.

In early 1988, the uneasy balance between the various powers exploded. But the debate started tangentially, over the definition of *wilaya* in the theory of *wilayat al-faqih*. The controversy, as earlier indicated, had simmered for a while, mostly in the debate over agrarian laws. With Khumaini's direct intervention on 6 January 1988, the controversy turned immediately into the most critical constitutional problem in the system.

At the origins of this intervention was a declaration made on Friday 1 January, at the prayer sermon, by the President of the Republic 'Ali Khamene'i. In this sermon, Khamene'i defended an interpretation of *wilayat al-faqih* which rendered the Executive and the Legislature in an Islamic state bound by a law that was superior to them. In reality, there were more nuances in the Iranian President's text, and the general thrust was, as could be expected, an insistence on the *faqih*'s importance. Khamene'i divided legal matters into those that operated on a personal, individual (*masa'el-e shakhsi va fardi*) level, and those that were of a total, national type (*masa'el kully-e keshvar*). The first could be decided by the usual *taqlid* method, and 'the *fatwa*s of other *faqih*s [than the supreme *faqih*] are evidence to follow'. But in the second category, 'only are acceptable the *fatwa*s of the Imam'.[20]

There was little in Khamene'i's sermon that warranted the impassioned intervention of Khumaini. The President's text was within the received notion of *wilayat al-faqih*, and though the categories alluded to in the sermon did not necessarily fit within the usual amalgamation of devotional and non-devotional legal matters in the same operation of *taqlid*, they did not constitute such an important departure of the theory advocated by Khumaini in Najaf, and later institutionalised in the Iranian Constitution. None the less, Khumaini, who had so far remained silent over many of the problems related to Islamic law and its application, chose to break the controversy open, by taking a strong stand against Khamene'i. But his criticism, rather than weakening the President, completely worked to the Presidency's advantage.

Khumaini's important letter is worth quoting at length:

> It appears, [Khumaini writes to Khamene'i] from Your Excellency's remarks at the Friday prayer meeting that you do not recognise government as a supreme deputyship bestowed by God upon the Holy Prophet (S) and that it is among the most important of divine laws and has priority over all peripheral divine orders. Your interpretation of my remarks that 'the government exercises power only within the bounds of divine statutes' is completely contrary to what I have said. If the government exercises power only within the framework of peripheral divine laws, then the entrustment of divine rules and absolute deputyship to the Prophet of Islam ... would be hollow and meaningless.[21]

Whatever Khumaini's claim to the contrary, these remarks are an important variation on the accepted version of *wilayat al-faqih*. For the first time, Khumaini was suggesting that the *faqih* was not in charge of making certain that the *shari'a* is the ultimate legal reference in the country. Formally, of course, the *shari'a* remains the source from which all laws are derived. What ultimately matters, however, is the recognition that divine law needs to be interpreted, and in fact – though this is never stated so bluntly – altered. Khamene'i's remarks, as they were received and rejected by Khumaini, suggested that divine laws could not be interpreted, and that whatever the interpretation, there remained a consensus over a core meaning (total, national in Khamene'i's parlance) which was unalterable. In this, he was certainly in tune with the received interpretation of *wilayat al-faqih*: the basic principle is that the jurist-governor in his governance, in his *wilayat*, is bound by the *shari'a*. Khumaini demurred, and his remarks acquired a dynamism of their own.

The rest of his letter to the President only strengthened the Leader's departure from the received version of *wilayat al-faqih*. Khumaini followed up his arguments with 'the consequences that would make *wilayat al-faqih* inoperative' if Khamene'i's interpretation were to prevail:

> For instance, the construction of roads which may entail requisition of houses or their environs is not within the framework of peripheral injunctions. Conscription, compulsory dispatch to the front, prevention of entry or exodus of any commodity, the ban on hoarding except in two or three cases, customs duty, taxes, prevention of profiteering, price-fixing, prevention of the distribution of narcotics, ban on addiction of any kind except in the case of alcoholic drinks, the carrying of all kinds of weapons, and hundreds of similar cases which are within the prerogative of the government would be inadmissible according to your interpretation.

Khumaini's letter constitutes a major turning point in the history of the Iranian Republic, not only in terms of the political struggles that it had reinforced – for instance, by the heavy criticism of the President by the Leader – but on two central constitutional grounds: (1) the role of Islamic law in the society with regard to its interpretation and the power to bind governmental actions; and (2) the structure of the institutions in Iran and the functioning or misfunctioning of the double-tiered separation of powers.

Islamic law constrained

Two ambiguities appear in Khumaini's letter: the differentiation between what he calls divine peripheral injunctions as opposed to central injunctions, and the association between government and the power of jurists.

Khamene'i had expressed in his Friday prayer the impossibility for government to contradict divine statutes, and in the quote mentioned earlier, the President seemed to differentiate between two categories of law, one of which, public law, was definitive and unchangeable by government, because it belonged to the interpretative realm of the *faqih*. The thesis was read by Khamene'i to mean that there is a superior, central Islamic law, the injunctions of which are clear (e.g. not to eat pork or drink alcohol, fasting), and that the government can in no way act against this category of the law. However, in peripheral or secondary issues (which could be presumed to be represented by personal devotional matters or, what is more important, areas of the law where no clear injunction has been stated, such as labour law, industrial nationalisation, or even areas where there is no received single interpretation such as the absoluteness of the right to property) the *faqih* must have the last word.

Khumaini shifted the terrain of the debate. Part of the letter asserts that there is no such distinction as central or peripheral law, and he uses several examples from the register of received 'central' injunctions only to discard them as pliable to governmental injunctions: 'The government is empowered to unilaterally revoke any *shari'a* agreements which it has concluded with the people when these agreements are contrary to the interests of the country or

Islam.' The argument is stated even more strongly: 'The Government can also prevent any devotional ['*ibadi*, from '*ibadat*] or non-devotional affair if it is opposed to the interests of Islam and for so long as it is so. The government can prevent *hajj*, which is one of the important divine obligations, on a temporary basis, in cases when it is contrary to the interests of the Islamic country.'

In this text, Khumaini seems to draw no distinction between primary, central, and secondary, peripheral spheres of law, since, in any case, the government in the theory of *wilayat al-faqih* is authorised to supersede the most central of injunctions.

But there is another passage in the letter which suggests that Khumaini had not completely abandoned the distinction between different categories of the law: 'I should state', he writes to Khamene'i, 'that the government, which is part of the absolute deputyship of the Prophet, is one of the primary injunctions of Islam and has priority over all other secondary injunctions, even prayers, fasting and *hajj*.' Thus, the distinction between central and peripheral remains to some extent pertinent, although the classification of prayers and *hajj* as 'secondary' appears unusual. But the contradiction is not necessarily total. What Khumaini seems to advocate is that such central precepts as prayers or *hajj* are *secondary to the one and only central injunction*, the establishment of *wilayat al-faqih*. But *wilayat al-faqih* in this case does not mean the governance of the jurist, i.e. the governance of the Leader as head of the *mujtahid*s' hierarchy, but a government understood under its most general and abstract acceptation. Government is supreme because it has priority in setting directives, and this priority derives from the paramountcy of 'the country or Islam'.

From the text of Khumaini's letter, there follows that the distinction between categories of law is not pertinent, since all laws are superseded by the choice of government. If any such distinction exists, it must be understood as a differentiation between one central injunction to the effect of empowering the government to make any law, and the rest of the legal field, with various devotional and non-devotional matters, all of which are secondary. This probably is the crux of Khumaini's criticism of Khamene'i.

On the distinction between central laws and peripheral laws, the debate that followed indicates that, at least in one major instance, this taxonomy could not so easily be discarded. *Ayat Allah* Muntazeri, successor of Khumaini to the Leadership until his demise in March 1989, commented on the 6 January letter with an emphasis, at least from the formal point of view of their promulgation, on the existence of laws with different regimes.

Muntazeri develops a three-stage theory in law-making:

> The first stage is to elucidate the general issues which have been revealed through inspiration to the Prophet by God. All laws and ordinances, even the important laws regarding the absolute *wilayat* of the Prophet and the pure Imams and the fully qualified *faqih*s, have been revealed by God. Regarding the absolute *wilayat* of the Holy Prophet (S), the Qur'an clearly states: 'The Prophet is closer to the Believers

than their own selves.' After himself, the Prophet of Islam conferred this position on the holy Imams, and the immaculate Imams passed it on to the fully qualified *faqih*s, and the necessary conditions for it are based on the Book and on the *Sunna*. If the [leading] *faqih*, who enjoys the position of vice-regent on behalf of the immaculate Imams, issues a decree or an order, it is incumbent upon all individuals and strata, even other *faqih*s, to obey it.[22]

Muntazeri repeats here the same arguments that were presented in Sadr's *Lamha Fiqhiyya* and in *Khilafat al-Insan*, and ascribes the absolute power of the *faqih* to his succeeding the Prophet and the Imams. Thus is specified the first stage of the laws, which are the decrees and opinions of the Leader, and which, because of this chain of authority, are as binding as the Qur'an and the *Sunna*.

'The second stage', continues Muntazeri, 'is the proper understanding of the divine laws by the *faqih*s and the *mujtahid*s who express their opinion regarding peripheral laws, on the basis of the generalities which have been revealed to the Source of Revelation [i.e. the Prophet].' Here, the distinction between important or central laws (i.e. those promulgated by the Leader and supreme *mujtahid* on the basis of their being revealed in the Qur'an and the *Sunna*), and 'peripheral laws', is clearly established. The distinction seems however specious, since Muntazeri, unlike Khumaini, does not specify what these peripheral laws are from a substantial point of view. One can only infer, a contrario, that they neither belong to a sphere that is 'supreme' (the Leader's competence), nor to the 'third stage', which is defined by Muntazeri as

the stage of implementation and deciding on appropriateness, which is performed by the Islamic Consultative Assembly [Parliament] and the Council of Guardians. It is at this stage that the needs and requirements of each time and each region should be investigated and the appropriateness of the laws which have been legislated will be decided upon and clarified. The needs and requirements of various times and places have been registered in different books of jurisprudence and opinions of the faqihs, such as *Jawahir* and *Tahrir*.[23]

An example is then offered to show the difference between 'general law' and 'peripheral application'(!):

For example, the fact that one cannot confiscate the land of somebody else is a general law, and it is recorded in Risalas [*risala 'amaliyya*], and there is no need for the Majlis and the Council of Guardians to act regarding that law. What concerns the Majlis and the Council of Guardians are particular examples of its application, because a great part of the land is part of *anfal*.[24]

This example contradicts the theory that Khumaini expounded in his letter to Khamene'i. Then, Khumaini had precisely said that the prohibition of land nationalisation, which is arguably a received precept of the *shari'a*, could in no way prevent the government from proceeding to confiscate land, and there was no mention of any *anfal* justification. It is not, as is the case with Muntazeri (and possibly Khamene'i, whom Khumaini was disputing), that Khumaini was creating an exception to a legal precept, or applying the law in a peripheral matter. For Khumaini, the only general rule is that government is free to apply any law it deems fit for the circumstances. For Muntazeri, in contrast, it is up to the Majlis and the Council of Guardians to decide whether a peripheral matter could be an exception to the 'general law'.

This position is surprising. The amalgamation, if not the confusion of Muntazeri between the stages of law-making process (framework, understanding, application) and the classification of laws as general and peripheral, is reminiscent of the Khaldunian mistrust of the jurists dealing with the affairs of the city. Muntazeri brings together in the same final stage the Council of Guardians and the Majlis, adding a dimension which, in the exchanges between the Leader and the President, was not even mentioned. But the clue to the whole debate, as it unfolded in Iran, was precisely the problems of legislation between the two conflicting bodies of chapter 6 of the Iranian Constitution. Khumaini would not have had to intervene, were it not for the crippling institutional deadlock between the Council of Guardians on the one hand, and the Legislature and Executive, on the other. Perhaps there is ambiguity in Khumaini's wording of his edict. As argued earlier, he did not altogether abandon the potential distinction between central and peripheral. But the confusion rests primarily in the absence from the wording of the debate between Khumaini and Khamene'i of the underlying cause of their constitutional feud: the Council of Guardians.

What Khumaini had written on 6 January suggested that in his view, the government (small g), which includes the Executive and the Legislature, could do whatever it pleaseth without heeding the other powers of Governance (capital G) of the *faqih* in the theory of *wilayat al-faqih*. The consequence of the edict was immediately clear to all the protagonists on the Iranian scene, and the Council of Guardians, without even being named in the exchange, was eventually neutralised by foes who capitalised on Khumaini's admonition of Khamene'i. The most flabbergasting twist in the affair came from the fact that the apparent victim of the Leader's edict, Khamene'i, was the head of the institution which mostly benefited from the constitutional row.

To the credit of Muntazeri, one should add that his intervention, at least, did not obfuscate the real debate, the one between the Council of Guardians and the Executive-Legislature. In the quote mentioned, he does not differentiate between the two bodies, and they are brought together into the third stage of law-making. But in another passage of the same comment, he admonishes the blocking postures of the Council of Guardians: 'It should not be the case that the law adds a problem to other problems. The Council of Guardians should also have a wide vision and should take completely into account all the realities of the country and of the Revolution and the various requirements before rejecting or approving a law. It should not be the case that its practice is always to negate or reject.' Since the Council of Guardians has only the power to negate or reject, Muntazeri's message was clear: the supervisory power should supervise less.

Whatever the carefulness – to the point of confusion – of Muntazeri in avoiding meddling between the Council of Guardians and Parliament, and his encouragement, in the same letter, for the two bodies to hold joint sessions in order to break the deadlock, there is little by way of rapprochement that he could have done. In the first place, this suggestion is redundant, because joint sessions, in the sense of meetings over legislation in which members of the two Assemblies would attend, had already been held. The Constitution itself, in Article 97, specifies that the members of the Council of Guardians could attend parliamentary sessions, and, in the case of urgent drafts, they were even allowed to intervene in the debate. It is generally after a long process of discussions and arguments that the deadlock intervenes. Nor is this surprising, considering that the power of the Council of Guardians in the supervision of the laws, being automatic, is so large. It is a legitimate question to wonder what in these circumstances remains of the power of a parliament under permanent, immediate and total scrutiny, and what is left of the legislative power of the Legislature. With Article 96ff., Article 4 of the Iranian Constitution gives the Council of Guardians a quasi-absolute legislative mandate:

> All civil, penal, financial, economic, administrative, military and political laws, shall be based on the Islamic standards. This article shall generally govern all the articles of the Constitutional law and also other laws and regulations and this shall be at the discretion of the religious jurists who are members of the Council of Guardians.

This is indeed a very wide range, which gives the Council of Guardians the ability to destroy all legislation it deems to be outside 'Islamic standards'. Only by a tremendous exercise of self-restraint could a limit to those overwhelming prerogatives be found. The Council of Guardians could not avoid exercising this power. Had it restrained its sway, the Council of Guardians might have retained its influence; but in view of the clear dispositions of the constitutional text, it would have thereby failed to fulfil its duties under the Constitution.

Fortunately for the Majlis and for the executive branch, the separation of powers that accorded the Council of Guardians so much influence was not exclusive. It covered only one of the two tiers of the whole system, and solace was to be found in the powers of the Leader. By enlisting the Leader's support, the Council of Guardians' opponents were ultimately able to deflect the constitutional provisions.

Paradoxically, the curtailing of the Council of Guardians' power to the advantage of government came in the wake of a legal dispute between the Leader and the Head of the Executive branch. Why Khumaini chose to take sides with the President of the Republic at this particular moment is not clear, and the extraordinary positive result of what was intended to be a mere admonition, suggests that Khumaini was unaware of the full institutional consequences of his intervention. Other factors also contributed to the blowing up of the letter into a major institutional crisis. This was the time of grave setbacks for the regime, with the relative defeat on the Iran–Iraq front and economic hardships inside, and an aging leader humiliated by the constraints and violence exercised against Iranian pilgrims in Saudi Arabia (hence his explicit reference to the *hajj* in his letter). In this atmosphere of unease, the way to the weakening of the Council of Guardians was now wide open. The deadlock in Parliament and the frustration before the repeatedly quashed legislative work could at last be broken. The new interpretation of *wilayat al-faqih* offered the long awaited backdoor opportunity. The person of the President, Khamene'i, was weakened in the process, but the position he fills at the Head of the Executive, as well as the Legislature, came out victorious.

Ambiguities remained, precisely because the controversy emerged over the definition of *wilayat al-faqih* and the position of the government in relation to the Leadership. But Islamic law was further constrained, in that the apparatus of its control was taken out of the hands of the *fuqaha* of the Council of Guardians, and devolved totally to the Executive and the Legislature. In 'the interest of Islam', and – more forcefully – 'in the interest of the country', Parliament and the Cabinet could, in the logic of *Ayat Allah* Khumaini's letter, regulate any field without the threat of the Council of Guardians' sword of Damocles.

As a consequence, the central constitutional issue shifted to the relationship between Parliament and the Council of Guardians, but the whole institutional theory underlying the Iranian system was rendered more complicated by the tangentiality of the process. In Khumaini's letter to Khamene'i, the Council of Guardians was not even mentioned.

Immediately after Khumaini's declaration, the debate gripped the country at all possible levels, and pressure mounted over the Council of Guardians. The arguments and the process that built up towards its demise are analysed in the following section.

Towards the demise of the Council of Guardians

As previously argued some of the confusion in the debate over who can ultimately interpret the law, and how far government is bound by the *shari'a*, came from the paradoxical circumstances which arose between the Leader and the President. It is worth noting again how the circumstances that ultimately led to the demise of the Council of Guardians bear close resemblance to that other famous instance of constitutional theory in the history of modern nation-states, the US case of *Marbury* v. *Madison*. This case is relevant for the Iranian developments because both in the circumstances in which it took place, and in the legal arguments that were brought up, the parallels are significant.

Marbury v. *Madison* was argued in the early days of the US Supreme Court, when judicial review was still not an all encompassing accepted practice. The supremacy of the Court is not acknowledged by the Constitution, and if there is an Act of Congress the constitutionality of which is perceived to be doubtful, there is in the written American text no indication that the Court could deem it so, and that it could challenge the constitutionality of an action that the Government might have taken.

It is against this background that the jurisprudential skills of Chief Justice John Marshall were exercised in 1803 to render the Court the most powerful institution in the judiciaries of the world. By a series of arguments, John Marshall was able to introduce the notion that the best way to protect the system was to let the judiciary make certain that no other power or person in the country can impinge on rights protected by the Constitution. The Court, since Marshall's judgment, considers it should intervene to redress the situation to the advantage of the constitutional text:

> So if a law be in opposition to the constitution, if both the law and the constitution apply to a particular case, so that the court must either decide that case conforming to the law, disregarding the constitution; or conforming to the constitution, disregarding the law; the court must determine which of these conflicting rules governs the case. This is of the very essence of judicial duty.
>
> If, then, the courts are to regard the constitution, and the constitution is superior to any ordinary act of the legislature, the constitution, and not such ordinary acts, must govern the case to which they both apply.[25]

It is with *Marbury* that the establishment of a judicial body to be the ultimate interpreter of the higher law of the state has come to apply in the contemporary world. Under similar terms, the question was posed again in the Iranian Constitution.

The circumstances of *Marbury* v. *Madison* are also relevant to the Iranian case, because it is by an apparent defeat that such power was ultimately conceded to the Supreme Court. Chief Justice Marshall was in a difficult position. As a former member of the Federalist party, which had just lost the elections, his Court was the target of the recently elected President, Thomas Jefferson, the leader of the New Democratic party. Jefferson resented the fact that the Federalists had taken refuge in the Judiciary by making a number of 'midnight' appointments to several judicial positions in the country.

One such last minute appointment was John Marbury's, whose nomination had not been formally completed. Marbury sought confirmation of his job by the Supreme Court. His request was rejected on a minor procedural point. The Court, Marshall argued, could not satisfy the demand of Marbury, because it did not have authority 'to issue writs of mandamus to public officers',[26] and Marbury's appointment failed to be confirmed. But this did not mean for Marshall that the Court would be incompetent in other cases where the question of interpreting the Constitution was at hand. The US Chief Justice, on the contrary, used the case of Marbury to assert that it was the courts' primary task to look into the conformity of all rights protected by the Constitution, and make certain that these rights were respected in text and spirit.

There is a noteworthy parallel between *Marbury* v. *Madison* and the recent Iranian controversy. It is true that in terms of result, the American case was diametrically opposed to the present Iranian case, as the Supreme Court was granted absolute right to judicial review of constitutional matters, whilst the Council of Guardians was stripped of its power of judicial review under the Iranian Constitution. But the parameters of the debate were exactly the same, both in terms of the underlying theme, judicial review of legislative and executive measures, and in terms of process, the irony of defeat through apparent victory. Not only is the theme behind the *Marbury* v. *Madison* controversy, in terms of precedence of the Constitution over ordinary laws, and in terms of the jurist's responsibility to assess the conflict, similar to the Iranian January debate, but it was through the apparent defeat of Marshall and the Federalists, when the court denied its competence in the case at hand, that its overall competence as an institution was acknowledged and confirmed. In Iran, it is the apparent defeat of Khamene'i that acknowledged and confirmed the overall competence of the Presidency in matters related to executive and legislative power, and its freedom from the scrutiny of the Council of Guardians. The separation of powers, and the Humpty Dumpty question on who ultimately 'gives meaning to the word', was equally at the heart of both quarrels. Only in America, the judiciary was entrusted to ultimately determine the law. In Iran, the Council of Guardians was stripped of this power originally vested in it by the 1979 Constitution.

The circumvolutions of the Iranian debate continued, and this section will dwell on the most important developments that took place in Iran since January 1988, and on the arguments which developed into the demise of the Council of Guardians and, further, prompted the qualitative change in Sadr and Khumaini's theory of *wilayat al-faqih*.

In his letter, Khumaini had criticised Khamene'i's views in an unusually strong manner. Coming from the Leader of the Revolution, and being so *ad hominem*, the criticism was serious. Khamene'i reeled before the humiliation. A letter to Khumaini shortly followed, in which he defended himself from any misunderstanding:

> A point that I deem necessary to mention is this: on the basis of Your Holiness's religious jurisprudence opinions – which I learnt from Your Holiness many years ago, and have accepted and acted accordingly – the points and instruction raised in Your Holiness's letter are part of the certainties, and I, as your servant, accept them all. What I meant by discussing the religious limits in the Friday prayer sermon is something that I can explain in detail if necessary.[27]

There was no need for these details, as the logic of the arguments had opened the door to the shift in the debate from a discussion between the Leader and the President to engulf the Council of Guardians. But Khumaini, perhaps realising the personal blow dealt to Khamene'i, wrote back immediately to reassure his former student of the esteem in which he held him personally, and his respect before his jurisprudential competence:

> Your kind letter was received with pleasure. I was in close contact with Your Excellency in the years before the Revolution and, thanks to God, this contact has continued. I believe that Your Excellency is one of the capable arms of the Islamic Republic and I regard you as a brother familiar with issues of jurisprudence,

committed to it and a serious supporter of religious principles related to absolute *velayat-e faqih*. Among the friends and those committed to Islam and Islamic laws, you are one of the rare individuals who radiate like the sun.[28]

The psychology of Khumaini's relation to Khamene'i may appear to be of little interest in terms of constitutional law, but the use of flowery language – or scathing criticism – hides a more significant legal problem. As suggested earlier in the exchange between Muhammad Baqer as-Sadr and Khumaini, and in the structure of the Shi'i schools of law, 'reputation' and 'jurisprudential ability' are vital to the hierarchical assignment of the Shi'i jurists, and are directly echoed in the institutional structure in Iran. The acknowledgment of Khamene'i as 'a brother familiar with issues of jurisprudence' came to counterbalance 'the ignorance' lashed in the first intervention, and its repercussion on the future of *Hujjat al-Islam* 'Ali Khamene'i.[29] But this was marginal to the extent that the actual problem had more to do with the Council of Guardians and its obstructions than to Khamene'i the jurist.

In the debate over the exact rules of the separation of powers in the Islamic Republic, the conflict between Khamene'i and Khumaini served, as in the appointment of John Marbury in *Marbury* v. *Madison*, to mask the more acute problems between the Council of Guardians and government. Khumaini's edict paved the way to the institutional strengthening of the Legislative and Executive vis-à-vis other powers. But there was a further dimension, encapsulated in the Leadership's new position in the double-tiered separation of powers.

The proper reading of the debate between Khamene'i and Khumaini quickly surfaced in Iran, and although the name of the Council of Guardians was not mentioned in the exchange, the real object of the newly flared controversy was clear to all. On 13 January, the Secretary of the Council of Guardians, which was probably worried by the consequences of its prerogatives of Khumaini's 'new' reading of *wilayat al-faqih*, paid him a visit and reported that the Leader had reassured him that 'the Council of Guardians ... has not been, nor will be weakened in any way'. Despite this reassurance, the blow was recognised, as '*Ayat Allah*' Lutfallah as-Safi also declared: 'The Council of Guardians fully accepts what Your Eminence [Khumaini] has said as regards *velayat-e faqih* and governmental decrees: it is in no doubt about the matters and *considers itself subordinate to government decrees*.'[30]

Acknowledgment by the Council of Guardians of its subordination to government decrees was the first step towards the effective demise of this body. Safi's utterance, however, was not an 'official' declaration, and did not constitute the necessary long-term formalisation sought by the forces energised and emboldened by Khumaini's unusual assertiveness in these separation of power matters. Nothing could prove that once the storm was over, and the words of the Leader a matter of the past, the clear constitutional wording of the Council of Guardians' extensive powers would not reinstate the Council into its past glory. The forces opposed to the Council of Guardians were seeking the institutionalisation of the Leader's decree, in a way that would neutralise the power of the Council of Guardians as spelled out in the 1979 Constitution.

Who were these forces, what were the arguments they used to develop Khumaini's logic to its fullest, and to what extent did they succeed in curtailing the constitutional power of the Council of Guardians?

As mentioned earlier, Muntazeri was amongst the many important *'ulama* who took part in the controversy. The case of Muntazeri is peculiar, because of his position then as the successor of Khumaini to the Leadership. He was hesitant to read Khumaini's words as a complete blow to the Council of Guardians, and this hesitation is understandable in view of his position at the periphery of the debate. But these hesitations also revealed the quandary he faced on a different account, which is yet another side of the entangled scheme of separation of powers in the Iranian Constitution.

The direct parties to the controversy were therefore the Council of Guardians on the one hand, and the two branches on the other.

Traditionally, the separation of powers functions as a check and balance system between three institutions, the Legislature, the Executive and the Judiciary. In the controversy triggered by Khumaini's 6 January letter, the problems have pitted the Council of Guardians, which generally corresponds to the judicial branch, and the Government, understood in the present Iranian terminology as a combination of the Legislature and the Executive. The other 'branches' of the Judiciary, the Supreme Court, the Prosecutor-General and the courts in general have remained on the margin, and rather unconcerned, for the essential problem derives from the 'legislative' strength of the Council of Guardians, its power to render a law initiated by government inapplicable as contrary to the Constitution or the tenets of Islamic law.

The major actors were quick to take position after the issuing of Khumaini's opinion. As we have seen, Khamene'i immediately did this, as he was directly concerned because his understanding of *wilayat al-faqih* had been faulted by the Leader. Another important voice was 'Ali Rafsanjani's, the Parliament's Speaker. On 7 January, he saluted Khumaini's intervention as an issue that requires to be paid 'great attention', 'so that no longer do we assume the right in future to impose something on Islam by raising vague and ambiguous issues'.[31]

Rafsanjani also spoke of the role of the Leadership, to which he reserved a special constitutional domain. For the Speaker, the Leadership must intervene at critical instances in the life of the Islamic Republic:

> That is, the leadership should respond to the call of the people, the revolution, society and Islam at necessary moments and junctures, when a sensitive issue might create a vacuum or discord in society, and divide the people and create sedition. Otherwise, it is no duty of the leadership to supervise routine matters of life. We, the functionaries, should see to routine matters, and the leader who looks at society with a wider view, should take charge of sensitive junctures.[32]

Now, Rafsanjani continued, in reference to the general reluctance for Khumaini to intervene in the Iranian controversies, it is possible to understand the meaning and reason of Khumaini's 'silences'.

But it is mostly the role of the Council of Guardians in relation to legislation that Rafsanjani discussed in his parliamentary intervention. The arguments are raised in an indirect way, as the Council of Guardians was not officially party to the discussion between the Leader and the President. Also, Rafsanjani was careful not to reach a point of no return with any institution:

I beg the esteemed Council of Guardians, the gentlemen who were appointed by His Holiness the Imam, to pay serious heed to the Imam's guidance and not to make their own views or those of others an obstacle to implementation of the Imam's guidelines ... Of course, in my opinion, the issues were clear from the start. The day that the Imam graciously said: 'If the majority of the Majlis approves something ...'

Rafsanjani did not complete his sentence. But the rest of the speech clearly indicates that he meant his disagreement, and Khumaini's support to him in this, with the Council of Guardians' overstretching its role when it repetitively strikes down laws decided by the Majlis. 'The day that the Imam granted this permission', Rafsanjani continues, 'the issue should have become clear to everyone. However, there was some talk that His Holiness had mentioned two thirds [i.e. a majority of two thirds in the Majlis for passing a bill]. Later they raised the issue of primary and secondary injunctions and created this talk. There is no need for such talk. As the Imam has graciously said, the government's prerogative applies absolutely to most of the matters the gentlemen are talking about.' [33]

What were the issues about which the 'gentlemen' of the Council of Guardians are talking? 'For instance, some individuals might raise a particular idea, by saying for instance that "you should not touch such a large economic or social sector, because there is a saying against it somewhere", or other such issues.'

'Aye, there is the rub':[34] the substantial issues involved in most of the disagreements between the Council of Guardians and the Government were the latter's 'radical' intervention in the economy.[35]

Rafsanjani had other occasions to comment on the Leader's remarks. On 15 January 1988, his Friday sermon was devoted again to the subject of the new interpretation of *wilayat al-faqih*. After criticising the 'orientalist' approach, which in the Speaker's opinion will be set on reading into Khumaini's letter yet another sign of power struggle and factionalism in Iran, he addressed the edict's impact on 'the definition of the reality of *velayat-e faqih* and Islamic government'. Factions are not important, he continued, and it is a healthy sign of the republic that all the institutions play their role to the fullest:

In the midst of all this, the Majlis is a huge social base, it is a respected institution which should remain popular and respected. The Council of Guardians is a respected institution, which is a watchdog over the process of the Legislature, the preserver of Islamic law and of religious law, and it should be popular and respected so that it may be able to carry out its duties ... The Government is responsible for implementing regulations and shoulders the most difficult responsibilities in a state of war, and the most difficult task falls on the shoulders of the Cabinet and the Prime Minister.[36]

The Prime Minister and the Cabinet had also an important say in the matter, and they did not lose any time in drawing the favourable consequences of Khumaini's letter. In an interview on 10 January, Prime Minister Hussain Musavi acknowledged the importance of the Leader's intervention, which he qualified as 'one of Khumaini's most important decrees and guidances', enabling 'the holy system of the Islamic Republic to deal with the complexities and problems it is facing all over the world, due to superpower plots and also ambiguities imposed on society by the present century'.

In answer to a question over the rumoured resignation of ministers (which had been going on since before Khumaini's letter), the Prime Minister indicated that 'the message of the Imam was a boost to the brothers who were uncertain about whether they will stay at their posts'. This was a further indication of the paralysis of the Government before the Council of Guardians's attitude, and the Iranian Prime Minister also confirmed the hope brought to the Government in an end to the deadlock reached with the Council of Guardians: 'The bills and proposals at the Majlis could be reviewed and solutions found, using this decree [of Khumaini], especially the decree in connection with the Labour Act.'[37]

The Government did not waste any time over the revival of the bills held pending by the Council of Guardians. On 12 January 1988, the Cabinet discussed 'the bills and proposals held in abeyance in the Majlis, as well as the bills withdrawn by the Government and which now can be reviewed and resubmitted [to ratification] following the categorical opinion given by his eminence the Imam regarding the prerogatives of *velayat-e faqih*'. More specifically, the Cabinet discussed a report by cabinet committees dealing with economic and educational bills, as well as a series of proposed regulations on the formation of social councils by the Government, import-export laws, etc.[38]

The final stage

The institutional problems of the first decade of the Islamic Revolution were two-pronged. As an instance of conflicts arising from the separation of powers, was expressed the clash between the 'legislative-executive' branch of government grouping the Ministers and the majority of Members of Parliament on the one hand, and the 'judiciary' in its Council of Guardians' manifestation on the other. This was the formal dimension of the debate. The legislators, the President of the Republic and his Cabinet moved immediately forward to carry Khumaini's edict to its logical end. This meant and necessitated a constitutional Amendment.

The other dimension of the controversy was substantial. The conflict between the Council of Guardians and the majority of Parliamentarians and

Ministers had been running for years over the 'social' significance of the Revolution. The debate was anchored in the most delicate issues of economic freedom and the social balance which the State should or shouldn't establish. To that extent, the problems between the Council of Guardians and its critics was eminently social.

The importance of social issues for the determination of the nature of the Islamic Revolution carries the investigation away from the formal-constitutional domain in which it expressed itself, to the deeper background relating to complex themes like social justice, the state role in the economy, freedom of contract, property rights and duties, and land and labour reform. How the substantial debate over land reform developed in the history of the Islamic Renaissance will be examined more closely in the following chapter, from the ideological context initiated by Muhammad Baqer as-Sadr's *Iqtisaduna* through to the stifling of land reform in the last decade of Iranian revolutionary history.

The articulation of 'social justice' themes on the constitutional controversy must be made clear, for the issue was generally muted in the formal debate. In itself, the constitutional controversy was a major event in Iranian history, and led to fundamental institutional changes. The deadlock reached in 1988 was broken by the redrafting of the 1979 Iranian Constitution.

Those persons in the system who were reeling from the extraordinary powers of the Council of Guardians – the President, the Speaker, the Prime Minister, and the members of Cabinet – were eager to read into Khumaini's letter the important 'clarification' needed to break the ties imposed by the Council of Guardians as an institution. One way to achieve their means with the new Khumainist theory would possibly have been to push forward with the bills held in abeyance until then, and pass them immediately, while the effects of the new theory had not yet dissipated. As mentioned earlier, this course was started, but it was not deemed sufficient in the long run from an institutional point of view, probably because nothing prevented the Council of Guardians from regaining its former power under other circumstances. But the choice of a more drastic measure against the constitutional review was rooted also, no doubt, in the twisted way in which the weakening of the Council of Guardians had taken place.

A formal decision was needed to do away, for good, with the potential threat that the Council of Guardians represented.

On 6 February 1988, a month after Khumaini's letter and the subsequent national debate, a letter was sent to the Leader by a high-powered group comprising the President of the Republic, the Speaker, the Prime Minister, the Head of the Supreme Judicial Council, and Khumaini's son Ahmad. The full grievances of the signatories appear in this text, which reads as a legal summary of the problems of separation of powers between the Council of Guardians and the Government. In it, Khumaini is asked to solve 'the problem which remains, [i.e.] the method of implementation of the Islamic sovereign right with regard to Government ruling'.[39]

The signatories then complained about the operation of the separation of powers in the legislative field:

At present, government bills are discussed in the relevant cabinet committees and then in the cabinet itself. After being read in the Majlis, they are usually examined twice in the specialised committees. These examinations are carried out in the presence of government experts and the views of the experts are also taken into account. These views are usually communicated to the committees after having been stated and published. Usually, a single government bill is examined in several committees depending on its content. Then it has two readings in plenary session, in which all the Majlis deputies and cabinet ministers, or deputy ministers in the relevant ministries, participate. They will explain their views in line with their specialisation; in the same manner they also make amendment proposals.

If it [a piece of legislation] originates as a private member's bill, although initially it does not benefit from the expert view of the Government, in committee and in plenary session it is discussed like a government bill, and the relevant experts express their views on it. And after final ratification, the Council of Guardians announces its views in the framework of theological rulings or the Constitution. In some cases the Majlis accords with its view, but in others it cannot do so. In such a case the Majlis and the Council of Guardians fail to come to an understanding.

The deadlock, the signatories suggest, is then complete: 'It is here that the need arises for intervention by the *faqih* to clarify the subject matter of the government ruling. Though many of these examples are due to differences of view among experts, they concern the issue of Islamic rulings and the generalities of the Constitution.'[40]

The problem of the confrontation between the Council of Guardians and the other branches could not be explained in a clearer way. For the personalities who signed the letter, the question can be summarised in the following manner: what is the point of a Majlis and a Cabinet that spend years preparing bills to have them repeatedly destroyed by the Council of Guardians over generalities of the Constitution? The underlying resentment of the letter's drafters was similar to John Hart Ely's query for the American constitutional system: why should members of parliament in Iran, who are elected by the people, and who claim no less expertise and Islamic truthfulness than the Council of Guardians' members, bow to that unelected body's decisions?

Yet, Khumaini was hesitant to take the final step, and tip the balance clearly against the Council of Guardians. So the signatories tried to force the game by insisting on the urgency of breaking the deadlock. They wrote that they were 'informed that [Khumaini] has decided to appoint an authority to state the decision of the sovereign body in case of failure to solve the differences between the Majlis and the Council of Guardians'. They urged him 'speed of action ... since at present numerous issues of importance to society are left undecided'.

The answer of Khumaini can be considered to have led to the most important constitutional development since the 1979 Constitution. Along with his letter of 6 January, to which it is an almost inescapable conclusion,

Khumaini's edict of 6 February represents a significant contribution to the whole theory underlying the Iranian Constitution, *wilayat al-faqih*, and to its effective weakening. Much of the undermining of the supremacy of the jurist in the Islamic republic was channelled through the neutralisation of the Council of Guardians.

The letter however indicates that the agreement of Khumaini was far from wholehearted, and the Leader's reluctance suggests that this aspect of the separation of powers had been significantly, but not decisively, solved. Khumaini's letter starts with an important proviso: 'Though in my view there is no need for this phase since these matters have already been through all the phases under the supervision of experts who are an authority on them ...'[41]

It is clear that Khumaini was not satisfied with the creation of a new body, or the institutionalisation of a 'superior' ultimate phase. But he reluctantly assented to the signatories' suggestion:

> In case the Majlis and the Council of Guardians should fail to come to an understanding on theological and legal points, then a council must be set up consisting of the honourable theologians of the Council of Guardians and holders of the title *Hujjat al-Islam* Messrs Khamene'i, Hashemi [Rafsanjani], Ardebili, Tavasoli, Musavi, Khoiniha and His Excellency Mir Hoseyn Musavi and the relevant minister. The council is to discuss the interests of the Islamic regime. In case of need, other experts can also be invited. After the necessary consultations, the decision of the majority of those present in the Council must be complied with.[42]

Thus was born a new institution in the Islamic Republic of Iran, which came to be known as 'Majma'-e Tashkhis-e Maslahat' (Council for the discernment of [the Republic's] interest). The structure of the original *de jure* members is such that the majority 'government' members can override the decisions of the six members belonging to the Council of Guardians, to whose detriment the deadlock was broken.

But the texts lack precision in a number of major instances. Khumaini's introductory proviso, in the first place, indicates his reluctance in principle to the advent of such a new constitutional institution. The fact that the newly established council was not given an official name of its own by the Leader, as well as the designation of the government members personally rather than under their official positions, increases the sense that Khumaini's wish was not to see the new Council perpetuated as an institution. Furthermore, the Council is considered to meet on the condition that an unbridgeable dispute between the Majlis and the Council of Guardians has emerged. Thus, in theory, it is only after a repeated deadlock between Parliament and the Council of Guardians that the Council meets. Thirdly, the Council cannot be considered as a fixed institution in so far as some members can be ad hoc experts who are invited for one specific bill. Finally, a strong personal – as opposed to the institutional – sense appears in Khumaini appointing his son as a rapporteur in the Council:

> Ahmad [Khumaini's son] will take part in this council so that reports of the meeting can be brought to me faster. The gentlemen must be aware that the interest of the

regime is an important issue. Sometimes negligence towards it will lead to the defeat of dear Islam. Today the world of Islam regards the regime of the Islamic Republic of Iran as a fully reflective *tableau* [Khumaini used the French word] for the solution of their problems.[43]

The reluctance of Khumaini might also be understood against a more delicate constitutional background, which is the absence in the Iranian fundamental law of 1979 of a mechanism for constitutional change. This is a bizarre feature of the 1979 text, which was eventually remedied by the introduction of the new Article 177 in the 1989 constitutional revision. Khumaini had, according to the original Iranian text, no power to proceed to such a drastic change as the creation of a constitutional body in general, less so of a constitutional body with such an important competence as to regulate the problems of separation of powers between the Council of Guardians and the Government. Nowhere in the prerogatives of the *faqih* is there an acknowledgment of his right to modify the constitution, and less so to create a new constitutional body.

Could it then be argued that the Majma' was unconstitutional? And if the creation of this council by Khumaini were considered legal, where does its constitutionality rest? In other words, could such an appointment survive the person of the present Leader, and be considered a permanent emanation of the powers of the Leadership?

Epilogue: the opening of a new constitutional decade

All these questions were overtaken by events.

In 1989, the first decade of a rich Iranian constitutional debate came to an end. A new decade was starting with two major developments.

On 4 June 1989, Ruhullah al-Khumaini died. On 28 July, forty-six amended articles of the Iranian Constitution which had been prepared by an ad hoc revision committee, in addition to two new articles, were approved by referendum. On the same day, the new President, 'Ali Hashemi Rafsanjani, was voted in power. The absence of a formal process of constitutional revision was remedied in the new Article 177. 'Majma'-e Tashkhis-e Maslahat-e Nazam' was formally introduced to the institutions of the Islamic Republic, to 'discern the interest in matters arising between Parliament and the Council of Guardians' and not solved at the end of the various 'legal stages'. The 'fixed and temporary' members of the Majma' were to be appointed by the Leader, and report to him.[44]

The fixed members of the Majma' are the six *fuqaha* of the Council of Guardians, the President, the Head of the Judiciary (Yazdi), the Majles Speaker (Karrubi), *Ayat Allah* Mahdavi-Kani, *Ayat Allah* Yusuf Sane'i (former Prosecutor-General), Ahmad Khumaini, *Ayat Allah* Kho'eniha (also previously Prosecutor-General), *Ayat Allah* Movahedi Kermani, Hasan Sane'i (Yusuf Sane'i's brother), Mohammed Reza Tavasoli and *Ayat Allah* Abdallah Nuri (both from the office of the late *Ayat Allah* Khumaini) and Mir Hosein Musavi (former Prime Minister). They were appointed for three years in October 1989 by the new Leader, 'Ali Khamene'i. To them must be added the two 'temporary members': the relevant minister and the Chairman of the relevant Parliamentary committee.[45]

The Majma' took its task to heart immediately. Under the leadership of the new President of the Republic and Head of the Majma', 'Ali Rafsanjani (who succeeded Khamene'i in this position), a number of deadlocks were solved. This was true in particular of the legislation on agrarian reform,[46] and of Labour law. Labour legislation, which had been a major area of contention between the Council of Guardians and the Executive and Legislative branches for ten years, was finally settled. The 203 Articles of the Code were perused by the Majma', 'in several sessions', and disputes concerning half of the Articles laid to rest. The latest version of the Bill (2/7/1368, 24 September 1989) was finally approved into law by the Majma' on 28/11/1369 (17 February 1991).[47]

The second decade of the Iranian Constitution starts with an amended text and a new leader. By introducing the Majma'-e Tashkhis-e Masalahat, the recurring problems between the Council of Guardians, on one hand, and Parliament and the Presidency on the other, were solved to the advantage of the latter. Similarly, the revision did away with the position of Prime Minister in an effort to simplify the mechanisms of executive authority. Other complications of the 1979 text were reduced. This was particularly true of the Leadership Council of Articles 5 and 107, which was suppressed in the revised text to the benefit of a sole Leader. The Leader does not need anymore, like in the case of Khumaini under the original Article 5, to 'be accepted by the majority of the people'. The deletion of this requirement vests the Assembly of Experts with a straightforward choice of the Leader. In the process, the historical specificity of the choice (or election, in Muhammad Taqi Faqih's words) of the Shi'i *marja'* is relegated outside the sphere of government. But the position of the *marja'* as Leader continues in competition for the overall support of the population with those other *marja'*s of Shi'i civil society, inside and outside Iran. The complex tiers of separation of powers arising from the legacy of the Shi'i colleges remain. But the Council of Guardians' role as supreme constitutional watchdog seems to have ended, as its hold is now diluted by the new non-Council majority on the bench of the Majma'.

The dilemmas which have recurred in Shi'i constitutionalism since the Usuli–Akhbari controversy will persist: what is the exact role of the jurist in the implementation of the *shari'a* and where does the extent of his leadership in the Islamic city end? The next decade of constitutionalism in Iran should provide more original separation of powers' conflicts and schemes to the analyst.

PART II

Islamic law, 'Islamic economics', and the interest-free bank

Introduction to Part II

One can find a large body of literature on 'Islamic economics', in Arabic as well as in English.[1] But many of the works tend to dabble in generalities and to err in a lack of rigour which prevents the emergence of a serious and systematic literature. The recent 'fad' of 'Islamic economics' has impressed the production with an urgency that has kept the literature produced so far to a superficial and repetitive standard.[2]

More serious undertakings have exploited the formidable legacy of Ibn Khaldun. Thus an Egyptian scholar writing an *Encyclopaedia of Islamic Economics* would dwell heavily on the *Muqaddima*.[3] His effort is not unique,[4] nor is it new. The legal tradition had early in the century exploited the famous historian in no less important a scholar than Subhi al-Mahmasani, who wrote his thesis in the 1920s on *The Economic Ideas of Ibn Khaldun*.[5]

The reliance on Ibn Khaldun is the sign of the apparent dearth of material from which to draw an Islamic theory of economics. In contrast to the riches of constitutional law, economics appears as a non-subject in the *faqih* tradition: there is simply no general theory of economics, let alone a basis for such theory in a specialised subject like banking.

This is why the works of Muhammad Baqer as-Sadr in economics and banking are significant. Against a classical background where the discipline of economics did not exist, and an Islamic world which by 1960 had produced no consistent reflection in the field, Sadr wrote two serious and lengthy works on the subject, *Iqtisaduna*[6] and *al-Bank al-la Ribawi fil-Islam*.[7]

Surprisingly, there was more by way of precedent on the theme of banking than in the more general 'Islamic economic system', and Cairo was the scene of a long debate on the question of *riba* and the repercussions of *riba* on the legal system, especially in relation to the Civil Code in preparation in Egypt.[8] That Code has remained the archetype of most civil legislation in the Middle East, and continues to be the basis for the system of obligations and contracts in Egypt and other Arab countries.

The discussion on *riba* proper had started early in the century, and had immediately involved the Government and the Azhar. It continued with major figures of the legal and *shar'i* field. Sadr's contribution on banking starts where the debate in Egypt had stopped. Instead of arguing for or against the equation of *riba* with interest, Sadr tried to describe the way a bank could operate without any *ribawi* transaction. The result remains unique in terms of thoroughness and depth. To date in the Muslim world, and despite the fashionability of Islamic banks since the late 1970s in the Middle East and beyond, no work has to my knowledge been published which matches Sadr's contribution.

It is not possible, as in the case of constitutional law, to see how the economic ideas of a thinker like Sadr were translated into practice. In the first place, Sadr did not produce a compact work like the constitutional *Note* either in economics in general, or in banking, to which could be compared another compact document like the Iranian Constitution. Both *Iqtisaduna* (which is some 700 pages long) and *al-Bank al-la Ribawi fil-Islam* are detailed and deal with difficult issues. Economic and banking issues are mercurial by nature, and in the case of Islamic law, have little background against which they can be measured.

We have tried none the less to examine the way Sadr's production was received in the Middle East, and to compare two important issues presented in *Iqtisaduna* with post-revolutionary developments in Iran: agrarian reform and the role of the state in the economy. In banking, a similar work was not possible, as the data on the financial developments in the Iranian banking system are even scarcer than for other economic fields. Furthermore, Sadr's main work on the alternative Islamic bank was set in a non-Islamic context to which the Iranian situation is exactly opposite.

These shortcomings notwithstanding, Sadr's theories of the interest-free bank are milestones in the Islamic legal Renaissance of the Middle East. The correspondence between theory and practice might be elusive and more difficult to appreciate than in the case of constitutional law, but this is probably not unique to the attempt at understanding economics from within the Islamic tradition.

4 Law and the discovery of 'Islamic economics'

Iqtisaduna, an exposé

Iqtisaduna consists of three parts: the two first parts are critiques of the capitalist and socialist systems and operate negatively by presenting, essentially, counterarguments to classical socialist and capitalist theories ('With Socialism', *I* 17–212; 'With Capitalism', *I* 213–54). The most interesting part is the third one which deals with the conception of the Islamic economy in Sadr's mind, and is the object of our presentation (*I* 255–700).

The exposition of 'Islamic economics' is constituted, in Sadr's outline, by several sections which appear loosely connected. After an introduction which includes various methodological remarks ('Our economic system in its general features', *I* 255–356), Sadr divides the bulk of the investigation into a 'theory of distribution before production' (*I* 385–469) and a 'theory of distribution after production' (*I* 515–80). This is followed by a fourth section on the 'theory of production' (*I* 582–628), a section on 'the responsibility of the state in the Islamic economic system' (*I* 628–58) and various appendices on points of detail on some legal-economic aspects discussed in the book (*I* 659–700).

As appears in the outline, there is no underlying concept which emerges in the book, although the central unifying element seems to be a general notion of the distribution process, which is introduced by an analysis of the 'pre-production phase' and is followed by further remarks on the role of the state in the system.

Iqtisaduna is re-arranged in this presentation under three headings: Principles and method; Distribution and the factors of production; and Distribution and justice.

Principles and method

The Islamic part of *Iqtisaduna* starts with a series of remarks, which introduce 'principles' of the system, along with methodological observations on the way to discover and expound it.

Principles of Islamic economics

Sadr begins with a presentation of the three basic principles of the Islamic system: 'multifold property', 'limited economic freedom', and 'social justice'.

Multifold property. The essential difference between Islam, capitalism and socialism, resides for Sadr in the nature of property adopted by each system (*I* 257). Whereas 'a capitalist society is a society which believes in private property as its basic (unique) principle, and considers [measures like] nationalisation as the exception to the rule', and 'whereas a socialist society is a society which considers socialist (common, *ishtirakiyya*) property as its principle, and recognises private property only under special circumstances', an Islamic society will differ from both by acknowledging simultaneously different types of property, 'posing thus the principle of multifold (dual, *muzdawija*) property, a property with various forms' (*I* 258). These forms are three: 'private', 'public' (*'amma*), and 'statal' (*milkiyyat ad-dawla*). But an Islamic society is not a bicephalous entity, as if it had 'combined the traits of both Socialism and Capitalism' (*I* 259). For these various forms of property are not a mixture, however complex (*mizaj murakkab*), but the original and principled expression of the Islamic rules. They are specific, and stand in an essential conflict with their socialist and capitalist counterparts.[1]

Limited economic freedom. Two limits hamper the absoluteness of private property. The first limit is subjective, and derives from the moral values of wealth-sharing taught by Islam. These values cannot be quantified and are independent of state coercion. Each individual's generosity in sharing his wealth with others differs, but the economic element of the subjective factor is less important than its contribution to the fabric of Muslim society. Sadr suggests that these values have proved the most precious means endowed by religion to the individual. In the course of Islamic history, the strength of this subjective individual factor has permitted Islamic society to survive through the many vicissitudes that have befallen the Muslim world.

The second limit is objective, and it is carefully defined by the law. This limit functions on two levels. On the higher level, the *shari'a* has laid down 'in its general sources [i.e. the Qur'an and the *Sunna*] ... the prohibition of a set of economic and social activities ... such as the prohibition of *riba* and monopolisation (*ihtikar*)' (*I* 262). On a lower level, the *shari'a* governs 'the principle of the ruler's supervision and intervention in public life' (*id.*), which is accepted by all Muslims in accordance with Qur'anic injunctions.[2] There might be disagreement over the ruler's method of 'appointment, and over his prerogatives and qualities (*sifat*)'. But the ruler can in no case contradict the legal dispositions defined at the higher level, like 'the prohibition of *riba*, of fraud (*ghishsh*), the annulment of inheritance laws,[3] or the suppression of one of the accepted forms of property in society' (*I* 263).[4]

Social justice. Sadr is aware of the danger of inefficient generalisations: 'It is not sufficient to know in Islam that it calls (*munadatuhu*) for social justice, it is also necessary to know the detailed representations of justice, and their precise Islamic significance' (*I* 265). The principle is not laid out in full at this point. Sadr remits the discussion to a later chapter, but he brings a clarification: the concept of social justice is divided into two sub-principles, 'public solidarity, *takaful 'amm*' and 'social balance, *tawazun ijtima'i*' (*I* 265).

The attention to detail is said to be supplied by 'two basic characteristics: realism and moralism (*akhlaqiyya*)'. Realism commands that, unlike Communism, which enjoys hovering in lofty skies and imaginative economics, and wallows in the prescription of objectives drawn from 'material circumstances and natural conditions [that have nothing to do with] man', Islam retains against the temptation of illusions a dose of realism – which takes into account the egotistic yet unavoidable human traits – and against immorality a sense of ethics, which avoids the imposition of social justice without the guiding framework of religion's moral teachings. From this passage (*I* 265–6), we can derive some elements of the general legal system which emphasise the 'moral' legal quality of *zakat* and other financial precepts.[5]

From the concept of moral corrective, Sadr deduces a utilitarian economic dimension. The psychological element should not, as in Marxism, be ignored as a key component of the economy, for it bears on the law of offer and demand. The moral dimension, adds Sadr, 'plays a major role in the economic field, for it affects the occurrence of the cyclical crises that have plagued the European [i.e. industrial-capitalist] economy' (*I* 268).[6]

'*Islamic economics as part of a larger system*'

In this chapter (*I* 269–77), the methodological concern is supplemented by two cases of encounter between old *shari'a* concepts and the contemporary challenge to their relevance. Islam as a universalist atemporal ideology is confronted with other universalist bids, particularly the Western legal world view.

Sadr first prepares the ground. Systematisation is necessary, with insistence on the necessary interrelation between the basis (*turba*, *ardiyya*) and the general form (*sigha*) of social life. The basis is formed as a combination of three elements, the doctrine (*al-'aqida*), concepts (*al-mafahim*), emotions and senses (*al-'awatef wal-ahasis*). The preferred image of the Islamic society, similar to that of modern historiography,[7] is that of a building: 'For the interrelation present in the grand Islamic design (*tasmim*) of society between each of its aspects renders it comparable to a map (*kharita*) drawn by a most skilful architect of a beautiful building . It is not possible for this plan to reflect the beauty and elegance intended by the architect unless it is realised in its entirety ... Thus the Islamic design' (*I* 271).

It is however not possible, remarks Sadr, to ponder over all the elements of social life in a single book on economics. Suffice it to keep these generalities in mind. The importance of the complex background is illustrated by two specific concepts, private property and profit. Private property includes a right of protection which commands responsibility and limits absoluteness,[8] and profit is more than a mere arithmetic computation (*I* 273). Also, 'the prohibition of *riba*, if taken in isolation, can be the source of dangerous problems in economic life', and can only be grasped within a totality which includes 'the rules of *mudaraba* (commenda), of [social] balance, solidarity, and [Islamic] finance' (*I* 274).[9]

Other non-economic issues which affect economic life include the more sensitive questions of the thief's punishment and of slavery. For Sadr, these dispositions can only be appraised in the light of the totality of the Islamic building suggested earlier. Cutting the hand of the thief is cruel in a capitalist society, in which the immense majority of the individuals are left to their miserable fate. But it should not be perceived to be harsh in a pure Islamic society, when all motives for crime have been abolished. Similarly, if Islam has admitted slavery in times of war, the disposition must be appraised against the whole picture, as the best available means to a just ruler in times of legitimate war (*I* 274–7).

The question of slavery in war is important for Sadr's rare appreciation of the conditions of a just war, and sheds light on the methodology used in such sensitive questions. Understandably, the conditions for slavery and the *hudud* (penal provisions) are among the most delicate areas of the discussion on the projected Islamic state. Sadr avoids understating them, or passing them by in silence. But the way he chooses to address them is historical. In the case of slavery and just war, a perspective on the past offers the key to their legitimacy. It is true, says Sadr, that there are rules for the enslavement of prisoners as war booty. This, however, was common practice, for Muslims and their opponents alike. Among a series of three legal dispositions concerning the prisoner of war – amnesty, release against ransom, and enslavement – the third could be chosen by a just ruler if he deemed it as most appropriate. It is important to make clear that the war in the first place must be a just war, *jihad*.

For Sadr, war becomes *jihad* only if two conditions are met: (1) that all peaceful means, 'buttressed by arguments and evidence' (*I* 275), have been exhausted. Then Islam will have no other recourse but to use violence. (2) That the permission to carry out *jihad* be authorised by a just ruler. The definition of a just ruler is not discussed in *Iqtisaduna*.

Historical perspective is also the way to deal with the *hudud*. Its form however is prospective: the *hudud* are projected into the future Islamic society. When, and only when such a fair society is established, and is governed by a just ruler, the *hadd* (singular of *hudud*) will lose its harsh character and be applied.

The status of religion in the economy: *subjective impulse* v. *social interests*

Some problems, says Sadr, do not create a conflict between the individual and society. As with the encouragement to combat tuberculosis, everybody will be in agreement (*I* 279). But these topics of non-conflict are rare. Much more significant are the areas of social concern in which the subjective interest itself is at odds with the achievement of the common good. Guaranteeing for the worker his means of living in case of redundancy contradicts the interests of the wealthy, who have to pay for compensation. The nationalisation of land contradicts the interests of those who can monopolise it for their sake. The same is true of every social interest (*maslaha ijtima'iyya*) (*I* 281).

The sphere of these conflicting social interests is at the root of the social problem.[10]

Science can bring no answer to this dilemma. Science can help discover the reality, and sheds light on the effect of a new chemical product or on the iron law of wages (*I* 283–4). But this hardly solves the social problem. Only religion can provide the solution, as the 'sole energy (*taqa*) which can compensate man for [the loss] of any temporary [immediate] pleasure ... [by convincing him] that present life is but a preparation to eternal life, and by creating in his mind a new perception of his interests, and a conception of profit and loss which goes beyond [is superior to] the mere commercial or material content' (*I* 286).

Unlike historical materialism, which sees in the laws of history the solution to the social problem, in that classes are pitted against each other until the victory of the class which 'controls the means of production', Islam views the contradiction as a way to vindicate the role of religion in the social process: since a subjective interest will inevitably clash with the common good, religion can act to temper the dominance of the individual's drive by tendering him an ideal of the Good drawn from a higher perception of worldly existence, which is then perceived as a step on the way to reward – or punishment – in eternity (*I* 284–6).

'Islamic economics is not a science'

This teleological attitude which is another aspect of the premise in the building metaphor, and the emphasis on an approach to economics that subordinates it to a totality ultimately determined by religion, is substantiated by the thesis that 'Islamic economics is not a science' (*I* 290–4) and by the presentation of a critique of the Marxist correspondence between mode of production and social relations (*I* 295–305).

The first thesis is central to the methodology later followed for the development of the alternative Islamic view of economics. Unlike Marxism, Islam does not pretend to be a science:

> In that sense, Islamic economics resembles the capitalist economic doctrine, for it is a means of changing reality, and not a means of explaining it [i.e. Marxism tries both to explain and change]. The doctrinal task facing Islamic economics is the unravelling (discovery, *kashf*) of the whole picture of economic life according to Islamic legislation (*tashri'*), and the study of the general ideas and concepts that emanate from (*tashu''*) this picture (*I* 291).

The prolegomena of the method are laid out in this text: by not pretending to the scientific method, Islamic economics will start from its social goals, and conflate the economic reality with them. Science can and will be used for the assessment and clarification of the reality, but it is throughout secondary to the end sought. But how is this end discovered? In the Qur'anic precepts, of course, but also in the more precise and more comprehensive legal body that derives from the Qur'an and the *Sunna*, accumulated throughout the centuries. 'The operation of discovery of the economic doctrine' will be discussed later in more detail, and the role of the law, particularly in jurists' works, fleshed out. But the system needed a frank appraisal of Islamic economics as an ideological doctrine not subordinated to science.

Unlike Islam, Marxism claims the scientific method. Sadr proceeds to refute the dangerous claim. Marxism, he says, is a doctrine which seeks to develop its conclusions in the process of changing the world according to its own 'scientific' assessment. At best, this constitutes a logically flawed circle.

Marxism, Sadr explains, apart from the previously discussed and ill-proven assumptions that 'productive forces make history' (*I* 297 and first part), adopts as its central economic thesis the position that 'any development in the operations of production and its modes is accompanied by a necessary development in social relations in general, and in the relations of distribution in particular' (*I* 296).

This, for Islam, is incorrect. There is no necessary connection between these two elements.

Islam sees that man operates in two spheres: in the first sphere, man exercises his work on nature, and tries variously to exploit it and subdue it for the fulfilment of his needs. In the second sphere, man exercises his work over relations with other individuals in several areas of social life. The forms of production are the result of the first sphere, and the social systems (*anzima*) the result of the second sphere. Each of the two spheres – in its historical existence – was subject to many developments in the mode of production or in the social system, but Islam does not see a necessary connection between the development of the forms of production and the development of the social rules (institutions, *nuzum*). It therefore believes that it is possible to conserve the same social system, with its functions and essence through the ages, whatever the differences between the various modes of production (*I* 296–7).

The analyst, Sadr continues, must distinguish between essentially different social spheres. Man in society functions according to two types of need. The first type is constant and unchanging, and is connected with man's 'apparatuses for eating, reproduction, perception and feeling' (*I* 298). But these needs are determined on the other hand by a changing environment, and require that part of the legislation remain constantly open. In 'the main sphere' (*al-janib ar-ra'isi*), Sadr's 'Islamic social system' includes 'the basic fixed needs in man's life, like his need to living allowances, reproduction and security, and other needs that were addressed in the rules on the distribution of wealth, the rules on marriage and divorce, crime and penalty (*hudud wa qisas*), and other similar rules in the Qur'an and the *Sunna*' (*I* 299).

What is then left to the secondary (*thanawiyya*) sphere? These 'open-ended aspects' (*maftuha lit-taghyir*) Islam has allowed the ruler (*wali al-amr*) to submit to new legislation (*yajtahid*), according to the interests and needs of society. Sadr does not specify what these areas are, although he devotes a later chapter on the sway of *wali al-amr* in the 'discretionary area' (*mantaqat al-faragh*). But he acknowledges that there are also fixed rules that pertain to the main sphere, but vary in their mode of application, as in the rule of the 'rejection of *darar*',[11] and the rejection of compulsion in religion (*nafi al-haraj fid-din*) (*I* 299).

Against Marxism, Sadr proposes therefore the recognition of two types of social need, which constitute legal spheres with different regimes; and if the denial of historical materialism is not enough by way of logic, Sadr continues, it is sufficient to look at history. The historical materialists will scoff at the attempt of slaves or serfs to free themselves and to ask for equality before the modern age brought bourgeois ideals to the political arena. But did Islam not establish equality in the society of seventh-century Mecca and Medina? And has the *hadith* not established that 'no Arab will be better than a non-Arab except in piety', and that 'people are equal as the teeth of a comb (*asnan al-musht*)' (*I* 301)?

The central economic problem

Capitalism's central economic problem is, for Sadr, the scarcity of natural resources with respect to the demand imposed by civilisation. For Socialism, the central economic problem is the contradiction between the mode of production and the relations of distribution.

Islam disagrees with the capitalist outlook because it considers that nature has ample resources for mankind, and with the socialist outlook in that the problem resides not 'in the forms of production, but in man himself' (*I* 307).

> Man's injustice manifests itself in the economic field as bad distribution ... for when injustice is obliterated from the social forms of distribution, and the capacities of mankind are mobilised to exploit nature, then the real problem disappears from the economic field. (*I* 308)

Iqtisaduna's thrust is therefore based on distribution, and the ways in which Islam has organised distribution to maximise the economic wealth by man's exploitation of natural resources. The concept of distribution forms the bulk of Islamic economics analysed by Sadr and the main division of the book separates 'distribution before production' and 'distribution after production'.

Before proceeding with the description of the distributional scheme, Sadr concludes the introductory section to the Islamic economics core with some remarks on two essential concepts of the doctrine, need and labour, from the perspective of the *shari'a*.

Labour and need

Central to the legal perspective is the fact that distribution is identified as the area in which the central economic problem of society is generated. The 'apparatus of distribution' is therefore discussed by Muhammad Baqer as-Sadr by way of the two concepts which underpin it, need and labour. 'The apparatus of distribution, *jihaz at-tawzi'*, in Islam, is constituted by two essential tools: labour, *'amal*, and need, *haja*' (*I* 308).

'From the Islamic perspective, labour is the cause of the worker's ownership of the result of his labour. This private ownership based on labour is a natural drive of man to appropriate for himself the result of his work' (*I* 311). Consequently, whereas

> the communist rule is that labour is the cause for society, and not for the individual, to ownership [status]; the socialist rule is that labour is the cause of the commodity's value, and therefore the cause of the worker's appropriation of the commodity. In Islam, labour is the cause for the worker's appropriation of the commodity, and not the cause of the commodity's value. For when the labourer extracts a pearl, he does not thereby confer value to the pearl, but he possesses it by this very work [of extraction]. (*I* 312)

In Sadr's theory, the concept of need functions in a way which is specific to Islam. He explains that in socialist theory, need is precluded by the centrality of labour. Each society comprises three main strata – a group which works and earns what it needs and more, another group which works but lives beneath its basic needs, and a group which is incapable of working for various reasons. In the strict logic of socialist theory, this last group is condemned, because there is nothing that 'justifies its earning a share of the general output in the operation of distribution' (*I* 315). This stands sharply in contrast with Islam, where need is an essential component of distribution, which is regulated by the moral principle of 'general insurance and social solidarity in the Islamic society' (*I* 313).

With need and labour, a third element underpins for Sadr the Islamic theory of distribution: Islam's original view of property. 'When Islam allowed the emergence of private property on the basis of labour, it contradicted both Socialism and Capitalism in the rights granted to the proprietor' (*I* 321). In Islam, labour is the central concept from which property derives. All the forms of property must therefore be qualified. In this perspective, property becomes 'a secondary element of distribution' (*I* 321), and is always limited by a set of moral values and social interests established by religion. The general rule is that 'private property appears only in goods (*amwal*) which have been mitigated in their composition or adaptation with human labour, excluding goods and natural resources which did not mix with labour' (*I* 320). 'Land, for instance, is a commodity in [the constitution of] which labour does not enter. It cannot be owned as private property' (*id.*).

The three elements forming the basis of the distributive apparatus of Islam are summarised by Sadr as follows:

Labour is a primary tool of distribution from the standpoint of ownership. The person who works in nature reaps the fruit of his work and possesses it.

Need is a primary tool of distribution as the expression of a human right which is essential in life. Islamic society recognises and supplies essential needs.

Property is a secondary tool of distribution, by way of commercial activity which Islam permits within special conditions which do not conflict with the Islamic principles of social justice ... (*I* 322).

The essential social problem, injustice, is therefore 'explained' economically by Sadr in the context of distribution. Most of *Iqtisaduna* is devoted to the exposition of an Islamic distributive system deriving from the injunctions of Islamic law in the economic field. Before addressing the details of these legal rules, the Najaf scholar was still concerned with two further preliminary points:

First he briefly addresses the peripheral question of circulation (*tadawul*), which he discusses as another area where injustice is created, since money becomes a commodity ready for hoarding or using, not as a means to facilitate circulation, but as an object of wealth per se. Islam, in Sadr's view, was careful to prevent this predictable twist of events so typical of capitalist societies. Capitalism severs money from its circulation use, and uses it for its own sake. But the right balance is restored by three essential prescriptions of the *shari'a*: the payment of taxes (*zakat*) which directly deflects the propensity to hoarding, the prohibition of *riba*, and the discretionary intervention of the ruler (*I* 322–31).

Then he argues for the need to establish methodologically the intimate connection between law and economics, and the precise role of the *shari'a* in the discovery of the discipline of Islamic economics.

The method of Iqtisaduna: *law and economics*

The premise on which the whole method of *Iqtisaduna* is based derives from the distinction between doctrine and science, in which *madhhab* (doctrine, school)[12] is defined as the way a society pursues its economic development and addresses its practical problems; and *'ilm* (science, knowledge), is defined as the science which explains economic life and the links between economic facts and the causes and factors which determine them.

From this central distinction, Sadr draws a number of conclusions and corollaries, which we can regroup here into four theses:

Thesis 1: Islamic economics is a *madhhab*, a doctrine, not a science, *'ilm*. It shows the way to follow in the economy, and does not explain the way economic events occur.

These two areas of doctrine and science must be clearly separated in the approach to Islamic economics. It is pointless, argues Sadr, to look in Islam for a science of economics. Such a discipline simply does not exist. There is in Islam nothing resembling the writing of thinkers like Ricardo or Adam Smith (*I* 338). The epistemological mistake in pretending to the economic scientific status of Islam derives from a refusal to appreciate that what Islam offers is not the established conclusions of a science of the economy but guidelines offered by the doctrine.

Thesis 2: Islamic economics is based on the idea of justice.

The doctrine in the case of Islam is a powerful reality based on one central concept, economic justice (*al-'adala al-ijtima'iyya*). No wonder then that there exists no science of Islamic economics, since the concept of justice does not belong to the realm of science. Justice is by essence an 'ethical appreciation' (*taqdir wa taqwim khuluqi*) (*I* 339). Thus, concludes Sadr, 'the concept of private property, of economic freedom, of the prohibition (*ilgha'*) of interest, or of the nationalisation of the means of production, all of these come under the doctrine, because they are related to the idea of justice. In contrast, the law of decrease in profit,[13] the law of demand and offer, or the iron law of wages, are scientific laws' (*I* 339).

Corollary: The concepts of *halal* (the permissible), and *haram* (the prohibited) in Islam are present in all walks of life, and they help put Thesis 2 in practical perspective. Through the idea of prohibited and permissible actions, it is possible to discover the details of the doctrine of Islamic economics (*I* 341). *Halal* and *haram* being the two central concepts of Islamic law, it is necessary to turn to the law for the programme of Islamic economics.

Thesis 3: Islamic law is the preferred way to Islamic economics.

Sadr starts out by stressing the impossibility of equating law and economics, whether in Islam or in any other school of thought. Many countries have a capitalist system, but some follow laws of Germanic-Romanic origin, whereas others have adopted the Anglo-Saxon tradition.

This notwithstanding, there remains a strong connection between law and economics. In terms of civil law for example, the centrality of the notion of obligation and the contracting parties' free will are at the heart of legislation on contracts, such as sales and lease. Similarly, in the law of realty, property is the central absolute right, and the legislation will abide in its various manifestations by respecting and securing this absolute right. In both cases, if the legal notion of obligation derives essentially from the concept of free will, and if the law of realty is essentially based on the concept of free ownership, they are both rooted in the doctrine at the heart of the capitalist system, which is the belief in freedom and the individual's right freely to contract and possess (*I* 342–4).

This can be further exemplified, adds Sadr, by the fact that in the twentieth century, the absoluteness of individual rights has been undermined by the rise of collective rights. The law of obligation, and the necessary accommodation of collective contracts, as well as the law of property, and the right of the state to proceed to expropriation, followed suit.

These remarks clarify the validity of the method chosen to expound Islamic economics. In order to understand the economics of Islam, the way to proceed is to start from the law, and from the operations of the law, develop the mechanisms of the economic structure. Sadr again uses the metaphor of a building, and the familiar Marxist concepts of superstructure and infrastructure. Civil law, in this scheme, is the superstructure, the upper floor (*bina' fawqi*) resting on the economic basis (*qa'ida*) of the building (*I* 343). The way for the Islamic thinker is therefore to proceed from this legal superstructure to discover the underlying economic foundation. This represents an exercise in discovery (*iktishaf*) which constitutes the distinctiveness of the Islamic method, in contrast with the intellectual process of formation (*takwin*) which characterises Western economic theory.

Thesis 4: Islamic economics is based on discovery, not on formation.

The particular methodological course of Islamic economists sums up in Sadr's system the difference in attitude between these scholars and scholars who study any other economic system. Whilst the scholar looking into capitalist and socialist economics will directly relate to the writings of their pundits, without, as in the case of Adam Smith or David Ricardo for instance, having to worry about their legal views, the starting point for the scholar of Islam 'will have to rest on a different method'. The Islamic scholar has in fact little choice, because classical economic writings are not known to Islam, and because the methodology premised on the prohibited–permissible paradigm laid out by the Qur'an requires inferences drawn from the superstructure, the law, to the infrastructure, the economy:

> We can define this method in the light of the sequential relationship (*'ilaqat at-taba'iyya*) that we explained earlier about the doctrine and the law. So long as civil law constitutes the upper floor (*tabiq fawqi*) in relation to the doctrine, is built on the law, and draws its directives from it, it is possible to discover the doctrine by way of the law, if we know the law upon which the unknown doctrine is based. It is then necessary for the discovery process to look for the irradiations (*ish'a'at*) of the doctrine in outer circles, i.e. on its superstructures and the effects that it reflects in various fields, in order to reach through these irradiations and effects a precise appreciation of the type of ideas and theories in the economic field which hide behind these manifestations. (*I* 348)

This passage is the central epistemological tenet of Sadr's 'topsy-turvy' (*bi-shakl maqlub*)[14] economic system (*I* 349). From it derives the whole structure of Sadr's discoveries. In the civil law and the financial system as presented by the classical Islamic jurists, he reads throughout *Iqtisaduna* regulations which he then moulds into a modern economic phraseology.

But the regulations, Sadr acknowledges, are larger than the system's economics. When Islam enjoins the prohibition of *riba*, the absence of interest-bearing loans is part of a general legal superstructure which is specific to an Islamic economy. But the prohibition of fraud (*ghishsh*) carries no particular significance for the Islamic economic doctrine, since all economic systems share the prohibition. In a related distinction, the 'two taxes of balance (*tawazun*) and *jihad*' operate in a markedly different manner. Whereas the tax for social balance, as in the case of *zakat*, is part of the discovery process, and helps define the economy of the system, 'the *jihad* tax is related to the role of proselytism (*da'wa*) in an Islamic state, and is not connected with Islam's economic doctrine' (*I* 351–2).

Together with legal injunctions, the discovery can be aided by what Sadr calls concepts, *mafahim*, which are akin to elements of a *Weltanschauung*. These world view pillars tend to be generalities dealing with the Islamic perception of the universe, man, society, and nature, and do not constitute positive law. But they help clarify the mould in which the economic system operates. Such is the case of the Islamic view of the place of man in the universe, as the successor/deputy of God on Earth, and of general conceptions of ownership or circulation: 'We thus know that Islamic views of the world can constitute an intellectual framework for the economic field. This framework is essential, for it allows legal texts to manifest themselves, through it, in a comprehensive manner' (*I* 355).

These elements based on the Islamic world view are also important to understand the place of the government's intervention, which is so central to both Sadr's system and the actual economic and institutional questions that have rocked the Iranian debate since the revolution.[15]

Mantaqat al-faragh, an essential concept in Sadr's system, is the discretionary area of the ruler in society, and his interventionist role as prescribed by the law. As mentioned earlier, Sadr avoids in *Iqtisaduna* the problem of the ruler's legitimacy, and the way he is to be appointed to power. His 'just ruler' is the *hakim shar'i* of the Shi'i tradition, but he is also simply called *imam* (with a non-Shi'i connotation). The premise is the existence of an Islamic ruler who governs the society on the basis of the law, and *Iqtisaduna* offers in the last chapter some of the tasks which the ruler can and ought to perform to redress the social balance in view of the economic problem.

At this point in his study, Sadr is therefore only concerned with how to discover the economic theory of Islam and its incidence on the ruler's area of discretion. Since the *shari'a* is the preferred way to this discovery, the special 'economic' reading of the jurists must be examined in more methodological detail. Primal to the epistemology of *Iqtisaduna* is the relation between economics and the *shari'a*.

A long section is devoted to the process of reading the law. This is developed along two lines: the necessity of *ijtihad*, and problems of objectivity.

Muhammad Baqer as-Sadr's section on *ijtihad* is important because of the role of the concept in the Shi'i context. Sadr was careful to avoid the pitfalls of Shi'i sectarianism in most of his major treatises, particularly in his works on philosophy, logic, economics, and banking.[16] His success in this score in the Sunni world, where his works have been used in the universities, is testimony to the importance of the universalism of his contributions on the Islamic stage. This is particularly true of *Iqtisaduna*, where the use of the concept of *ijtihad* is similar to the one found in the understanding of Sunni reformists in the century from Muhammad 'Abduh onwards. In this understanding, *ijtihad* is a creative process in the realm of the law, where rules to be found in the Qur'an and *Sunna* are interpreted to fit the requirements of the modern age.

Sadr insists on the necessity of this creative process, and legitimises by the same token the special place of the *shari'a* in discovering the Islamic theory of economics. It is true, he writes, that it would normally be sufficient 'to bring up the texts of the Qur'an and the *Sunna* to gather enough rules and concepts, by which one will end with general doctrinal theories ... But the texts do not manifest – generally – their legal or conceptual content in a clear precise manner' (*I* 359). It is therefore inevitable to make a further effort to draw up economic rules. This is the essence of the process of *ijtihad*.

Obviously, different *mujtahid*s will explain the economic reality with various points of view. This, writes Sadr, is a normal phenomenon. The danger starts when the process gets undermined by 'subjectivism' (*dhatiyya*). In the field of economics, as opposed to areas related to rules concerning the individual, the threat of subjectivism looms larger because of the long historical separation between the setting down of the original rules and their present application.

Subjectivism is further explained as the danger of 'justifying reality'. In the case of banking for instance, it explains *riba* as usury and not interest, so that the widely practised loan for interest can be justified. Secondly, justifying reality can take the form of a text which is interpreted in a framework which is not Islamic. This is the case of private property, which is construed to be all-encompassing, when it is actually limited to a specific and narrow domain. Thirdly, Sadr warns against 'abstracting legal evidence from circumstances and conditions' surrounding it. This is called in *fiqh* terms *taqrir*, which Sadr defines as 'the silence of the Prophet or the [Shi'i] Imam over a specific act that he witnessed, a silence which reveals his allowing it and hence Islam's acceptance of it' (*I* 365). Such a silence, as a rule, is agreement. But this form of abstraction cannot work in a situation which is much more complex today than it was in the days of the Prophet, objects Sadr. For instance, many forms of industrial production are being related to a permission given to similar, much more straightforward situations of early Islam, and this is methodologically incorrect as an anachronism justifying present practices. 'Reality today is full of examples of capitalist production and extractive industries, which take the form of the work of salaried employees who extract mining resources such as salt or oil, and a capitalist who pays them wages and considers himself as the owner of the commodity extracted. The employment [lease] contract (*'aqd al-ijara*) appears today normal in its content – i.e. the employee receiving the salary and the capitalist being the owner of the commodity ... '(*I* 366–7). By way of *taqrir*, and on the face of the analogy, the silence of the *shari'a* on this type of *ijara* becomes evidence of Islam permitting it. However, Sadr remarks, there is a major flaw in the reasoning, because this form of abstraction ignores the original circumstances of permission, the fact that this practice was not widely known at the time of the Prophet. It is guilty of 'abstracting the living behaviour (*suluk mu'ash*) from objective circumstances, and projecting this behaviour backwards to legislative times', i.e. to the days of the Prophet or the Imam (*I* 364–70).

Another problem with subjectivism lies in the preconceived positions of the reader of the law who tries to apply it to the theory of Islamic economics. In other words, it is the problem of the lawyer looking into the classical texts for rules that fit what he is looking for to complement his economic system.

Subjectivism, he explains at length (*I* 370–84), is sometimes inevitable:

Ijtihad is a complex operation, which is fraught with doubts on all sides. However cogent the result may be in the opinion of a *mujtahid*, he cannot absolutely be certain of its correctness in reality so long as an error can be thought of in his reasoning. This can be caused [by a number of reasons]: the incorrectness of the text *vis-à-vis* reality (even if it seems to him correct); a misunderstanding of the text; the way the text is reconciled to other texts, or because the [conclusions drawn from] a text do not include other texts of significance for the subject-matter, which the practitioner has ignored, or which have been forgotten by the centuries. (*I* 373)

None the less, concludes Sadr, the lure of subjectivism should not deter the *mujtahid*'s effort in the realm of economics. There is a unity and a comprehensiveness in the legal world of Islam. 'The belief [in the reality of such a legal world] has made us [Sadr] consider the legal rules as a superstructure, which must be transcended to reach what is deeper and wider, and discover the bases upon which this superstructure stands and with which it accords' (*I* 374). *Ijtihad* will no doubt include mistakes, concludes Sadr, but it is a correct and necessary exercise to discover in the law the way to Islamic economics.

In a final important methodological remark addressed in this part of *Iqtisaduna*, Sadr uses the problems and difficulties faced by the *mujtahid* in his endeavour to elaborate on a topic which appears central to the concerns of the Middle East in the sixties. It is the problem of the equation of Islam and Capitalism. The example used to undermine this assumption is drawn from another aspect of the error embedded in the 'justification of the reality' approach. The mistake takes the form of what he described as 'the deceit of practical reality, *khida' al-waqe' at-tatbiqi*' (*I* 378–84).

In the same way as a theoretical study of Islamic economics is possible by way of perusing the classical legal texts, Sadr defends the idea of the study of the Islamic economy through some of its early application. Applied economics can be analysed, Sadr argues, thanks to the period, however short, of the Prophet's life (*I* 378).

Such a study of applied economics remains obviously limited, since it is harder to generalise from the few relevant instances that have reached us from that epoch. This is particularly true for the generalisation which draws together Islam and Capitalism.

'I do not deny', says Sadr, 'that the individual in the society of the Prophet's era was carrying out a free activity, and that he retained his freedom to a large extent in the economic field, and I do not deny that this reflects the capitalist aspect of Islamic economics' (*I* 379). But there is a contradiction between this practice, which is related to us in a number of cases, and the theory which reaches us from the legal rules. This contradiction can be solved by favouring the latter over the 'deceit of practical reality' because of man's limited power over nature at the time (*I* 380):

> Those who thought that the Islamic economic theory is capitalist, and that it believed in capitalist freedom, would have some excuse if they drew their conclusions [feeling] from the study of man in the time of praxis [i.e. at the time of the Prophet] and from man's extent of freedom. This is however a mistaken feeling (*ihsas khade'*), because the intuition derived from looking at the praxis cannot stand in lieu of the established facts of legal and jurisprudential texts, which disclose a non-capitalist content. (*I* 382)

This does not mean that Islam constitutes some early brand of Socialism, and Sadr hastens to add Islam's rejection of its socialist nemesis, a thesis he had defended lengthily in the first part of *Iqtisaduna*. These theories were in *Iqtisaduna*'s first part negative, in that they tended to show why Islam differed in its economic and social outlook from the two prevailing world systems. The rest of the book is devoted to a positive exercise. Through the reading of the law, in a relationship which has now been methodologically justified, Sadr sets out to unveil the structure of Islamic economics in its tradition of independence and purity by a *détour* in the jurists' works (*I* 384).

Distribution and the factors of production

Factor one. Land

As presented in Sadr's methodological remarks, the substance of Islamic economics is centred on the analysis of the distributive apparatus of Islam as can be constructed from the legal texts.

Distribution is divided in two, distribution before, and distribution after production. Under the former, four factors are identified as the natural resources for production (*masadir at-tabi'a lil-intaj*): (1) land; (2) raw materials, mostly mining resources; (3) water; and (4) the remainder of nature's resources (sea, pearls, game etc.).

For modern times, access to land is considered the most important economic factor. *Iqtisaduna* devotes its longest section to the analysis of rights attached to land.

A Land historically determined

In Sadr's reading of the classical jurists, the ownership of land cannot be separated from the way a particular land came under Islamic rule: 'The ownership of the land in Iraq is different from the ownership of the land in Indonesia because Iraq and Indonesia differ in the way they embraced Islam' (*I* 394). Three general types of land can be derived from the historical pattern: (1) land which 'became Muslim' by conquest (*fath*), such as Iraq, Egypt, Syria, Iran, and 'many parts of the Islamic world' (*I* 394); (2) land which became Muslim by persuasion (*da'wa*); and (3) land of agreement (*sulh*).

*A*1 *Land of conquest*

In the land of conquest, a distinction is made between (a) man-made prosperous land at the time of the conquest, (b) dead land at the time of conquest, and (c) land that was naturally prosperous.

*A*1*a* *Man-made prosperous land: public property*

Both Shi'i and Sunni jurists, Sadr writes, agree that the land of conquest which was cultivated at the time of the victorious drive of Islam is the property of all the Muslims. Private ownership thereof is consequently forbidden. Fruits and profits reaped by the labourers on this land are, in principle, the property of the community (*umma*), and the worker who exploits the land must pay tribute [to the state] as if he were only renting it. The price of rent is called *kharaj*, and the land consequently classified as *kharaj* land. There is no private ownership of *kharaj* land. It falls under public control. Sadr is careful to specify in this regard that control is in this case different from nationalisation. State ownership of *kharaj* land is described as 'public' (*'amma*). To clarify the distinction between nationalisation and public property, he invokes the refusal by Abu Bakr, the second Rashidi Caliph (ruled 634–44), to divide conquered land among the soldiers, because land is different from the booty of war, *ghanima*. Unlike war booty, which is distributed among the Muslims, conquered land is destined to be forever the property of the *umma*. 'Public property of land in Islam is an original device. It is not a nationalisation which occurs at a later phase, after the establishment of the principle of private ownership ... Public ownership of conquered land [attaches to it] as an original character' (*I* 339).

Public ownership of prosperous land which became Muslim by conquest bears the following legal features:

(1) It is not subject to the rules of succession and inheritance.
(2) It is not subject to alienation or to any form of contract, except for the initial lease between the labourer and the state represented by the *imam*. Sadr quotes the Shi'i jurist, Muhammad Ibn Hasan at-Tusi (d. 460/1067): 'There is no right to sell, purchase, trade off, inherit, bequeath or sublet [this type of land]' (*I* 405).
(3) The head of the state (*wali al-amr*) is considered responsible for the control of the fructification of the land, and for the *kharaj* imposed on the tenant.
(4) The *kharaj* paid by the labourer is public property.
(5) As soon as the lease ends, the land becomes independent of the former tenant.
(6) If once prosperous land withers away, it retains its public character, and its revival (reclaiming, *ihya'*), does not allow the person who revives it to become its owner.

Finally, as for all types of land, prosperous land which becomes Muslim by conquest is determined historically, and 'on this basis we need for today's practice a wealth of historical information on Muslim lands and how prosperous they were at the time of the conquest' (*I* 407), so that the proper category of each can be specified. To find whether a particular lot was prosperous requires a thorough historical investigation.

A1b Dead land at the time of the conquest: state property

Like *kharaj* land, this land is not subject to private ownership. But its status falls under the category of state property, *milkiyyat ad-dawla*. Both state property and public property appear similar, in that they suggest an ownership in common, which conflicts with individual ownership. But state property attaches to the position (*al-mansib*), i.e. to the ruler *qua* ruler, whereas public property attaches to the community, *al-umma*. The difference is important in Sadr's scheme because of the legal regime deriving from each of the two categories. The main legal differences are described as follows:

(1) The exploitation of *kharaj* land (public property) benefits the whole community. The *wali al-amr* cannot use it for the sake of a particular person or group. He must exploit it for the benefit of the community as a whole, for instance by way of using *kharaj* money to establish schools or public hospitals. In contrast, the *wali* has more leeway in dead land falling under state property since he decides whether a particular interest might benefit from its fructification. He can consecrate the land to narrower effect.
(2) The ruler (*imam*) has the right to grant an individual the property of dead land if he deems it of general interest. This is totally forbidden in the case of public property.
(3) A contract of sale or lease can affect dead land.
(4) In case dead land is revived, the *imam* can grant the labourer a special right, even though control (*raqaba* or *ruqba*) remains a state prerogative.

The main difference between dead land and prosperous land at the time of conquest appears in the consequences of their revival. In the case of prosperous land, revival does not add a single right to the reviver, even though the land might have been left barren for years. Revived dead land, on the contrary, grants the reviver a special right. A *hadith* is invoked in support of the distinction: 'Whoever revives land that belongs to nobody has a better title to it' (*I* 413).

There is a controversy as to whether land in this case changes its status from state property to become private land. Some *'ulama* consider this to be the case, but Sadr leans towards the more restrictive interpretation of Tusi, according to whom the land retains its initial status, although the labourer who revives it can benefit from his deed and prevent others from competing with him on the same land as long as he still works on it. He is however subject to a special tax, the *tasq*, which is imposed by the *imam* according to the profits he gets out of the land exploitation.

'Thus', concludes Sadr, 'the difference between the farmer who works on public property and the farmer who works on state property is that ... the former is a mere tenant, *musta'jir*.' The *imam*, as landlord, can let the land to someone else once the lease is expired: 'Whereas the latter [i.e. the farmer who works on state property] has a right over the land which entitles him to usufruct (*intifa'*), and will continue to prevent others from working the land as long as he takes care of it and makes it prosper' (*I* 422).

A1c Naturally prosperous land

This land is defined as land which had been prosperous without man's intervention at the time of conquest, such as forests.

Sadr's description of the legal regime of naturally prosperous land is confusing. In one section, he suggests that it is not any different from land which was revived, and adds that whether it came under Muslim rule by conquest or not does not affect its status: 'Naturally prosperous land is state property regardless of whether it was acquired by force' (*I* 421). This third type of land of conquest, which prospered without the intervention of human labour, is and remains state property, the fate of which is decided, like the dead land, by the *imam*.

On the other hand, he suggests also that 'forests and naturally prosperous lands which are conquered by force and taken from the hands of the heathen (*kuffar*) are the public property of the Muslims ... and when forests enter the ambit of public property ..., they become land with an owner. The owner is then the whole community' (*I* 420–1).

A2 Land of persuasion

Sadr describes this category as land whose dwellers answered the call of Islam willingly and without any pressure of either threat or violence. This was the case in Medina or Indonesia.

This land, like the land of conquest, is divided into three types:

(a) Man-made prosperous land of persuasion (i.e. which came to Islam willingly). It remains as it was before Islam. Private property thereof is absolute, and no *kharaj* can be taken from its inhabitants.

(b) Dead land of persuasion. This land is, in contrast to the previous type, similar to the dead land of conquest. It is *anfal*, which falls by definition under state property.

(c) Naturally prosperous land of persuasion. It is also state property on the basis of the legal maxim: 'Any land without an owner is *anfal*' (*I* 421). The difference between (b) and (c) in terms of legal regime is that the revival of dead land confers on the reviver a 'private right'.

A3 Land of agreement

To this category belongs the land whose inhabitants neither fought Islam as in the land of conquest, nor embraced it willingly as in the land of persuasion. It became part of the Muslim world without its inhabitants relinquishing their religion.

The status of man-made prosperous land in this category depends on the agreement by which its inhabitants became part of the Muslim world. In case the expansion occurred on condition that the land remained the property of the non-Muslim inhabitants, the agreement will be honoured. But dead land and naturally prosperous land follow the rules which govern the equivalent Muslim land by conquest: they are state property, unless there has been an initial agreement otherwise (*I* 423–4).

B The requirement of constant exploitation and the theory of land ownership

Whatever the specific category a piece of land falls into, it is subject to an important requirement: the owner, if there is one, must constantly exploit the land. When land is forsaken and turns sterile, it falls automatically outside the legal reach of its owner. Furthermore, if the person who takes care of the land dies, the rules of inheritance govern his succession, including the land, but his descendants who come into property are bound by the same requirement of constant exploitation. If they fail to do so, land which has become non-productive because of their negligence becomes public property (*I* 428).

The concept of work, as well as the concept of revival, are essential to the general theory of land ownership in Sadr's system: 'Thus we understand that the privilege over land – by derived or original right – is conditional upon the accomplishment by the individual of his social function (*wazifa*) on the land. If he abandons it and lets it wither until it dies, his relationship to it is severed. The land becomes free of any tie with him' (*I* 429).

Thus unwinds the second characteristic of the Islamic theory of land in Sadr's system. Next to the historical characteristic, which determines the original status of a piece of land, Sadr develops in *Iqtisaduna* an attachment to land ownership which indicates a strong 'radical' tendency: the exigency of labour to perpetuate and protect the right of ownership.

Sadr allows room for private ownership, as in the broad case of the land of persuasion where the owners who were initially exploiting it retain their privilege as long as they keep working the land, and as in the more exceptional case of the land of agreement, where private ownership of the non-Muslims is respected in return for a tax. But 'the [general] principle is state property of the land. Besides this principle, there exists a right of revival which grants the reviver – or the person who received [through inheritance] the land from the reviver – a privilege on the land. This privilege remains as long as revival is maintained ... ' (*I* 430).

In the case of *kharaj* land, change of status is impossible. The general right of state ownership cannot be stripped away. *Kharaj* land is said to be held in trust (*mawqufa*). The difference of the right of the state to *kharaj* land and its right in case of absolute property lies in the possibility for the *imam* to grant specific individuals or groups the right to exploit the land and pay *kharaj* in return.

Sadr concludes by recapitulating the two sources which can permit the individual's relative right to appropriate the land and its fruit. They are both expressed in the concept of 'labour': (1) revival, 'which is economic by nature', and (2) 'political work' (*I* 437), which is understood as the early effort of Muslim soldiers, who, by their military 'work', succeeded in opening the land to Islam and extending control over it.

Revival, as opposed to political work, remains relevant as a perpetual condition of ownership. It is important in the case of the dead land which is rehabilitated and thus possessed by the reviver. But it also permeates all subsequent rights because the privilege remains as long as the reviver or his heirs keep fructifying the land. If land becomes Muslim by conquest, 'political work is considered the work of the community, not the work of an individual, and therefore the community becomes the owner of the land' (*I* 438). If land becomes Muslim by adherence of its inhabitants to Islam, then room is left to private ownership. However, 'the right of private ownership is not granted in an absolute way, and [Islam] has conditioned it upon the exploitation of the land by its inhabitants. If they abandon the land, a number of scholars like Ibn al-Barraj (tenth century) and Ibn Hamza (d. after 566/1171) consider it to become again the property of the community' (*I* 439).

Summing up the theory of land property, Sadr tries also to connect it to the more general scheme of the system he proposes.

The category of property falls in this scheme within the general theory of distribution before production (*I* 430). For Sadr, it is important to strip the economic content of the Islamic rules of property from the contingencies of 'political considerations' (*I* 430), and thus to complete the description of the theory of land.

A general theory can now be sketched:

> The land, by nature, is the property of the *imam*. An individual does not possess a right of control, *ruqba*. A personal interest (security, specialisation, *ikhtisas shakhsi*) is not valid, except on the basis of the labour spent by the individual on the land to prepare it (*i'dad*) and exploit it (*istithmar*). This security, or the right gained by an individual as the result of his work does not prevent the *imam* from excising a tax (*tasq*) on the revived land, so that all of mankind can profit from it. This does not prevent [the *imam*] relieving [the labourer] from the duty of *tasq* sometimes, in exceptional circumstances. (*I* 433)

Sadr acknowledges that 'the history of private property over land is full of injustice and exploitation, as land becomes inaccessible to the masses inasmuch as it opens up to some of the privileged' (*I* 436). This adulteration of history, it is suggested, runs against Islamic principles, although the position of Sadr is not too clear on this point. He writes that 'we do not negate the elements of violence and occupation (*ightisab*) and their role in history', but in the chain of events, he sets the principle of labour at the centre of the theory of land ownership before 'the operation of occupation' (*I* 434–5).

Factor two. Minerals

The second element of wealth to be distributed in the pre-productive phase of the system is constituted by minerals. The legal question posed in the theory is whether minerals follow land, i.e. whether a mineral follows the same legal regime as the land in which it is found.

The answer is negative. For minerals 'to be in the land of an individual is not reason enough, from a jurisprudential point of view, for their ownership by this individual' (*I* 454). The theory of land ownership is based, as developed earlier, 'on one of two reasons: by revival, or by the entry of the land into the ambit of Islam by voluntary conversion. Revival creates a right vested in the reviver, and the voluntary embracing of Islam makes the convert an owner of the land. Neither of these two causes extends to the minerals found inside the earth. They are limited to the surface' (*I* 455).

There is in Sadr's reading of the classical jurists a separate theory of minerals based on their classification as 'external' or 'internal'. Internal minerals are 'any minerals which require, for the manifestation of their qualities [as useful minerals], to be worked on and developed, such as iron or gold' (*I* 444). But external minerals should not be understood, 'as the word may suggest, in the sense that they do not need excavation and work in order to reach them, but they are minerals the mineral nature of which is manifest, whether or not man requires work to reach them' (*I* 443).

The importance of work in this distinction does not lie in the difficulty to reach the internal or external minerals, but in whether, once the minerals are reached, work is necessary to develop them in order to render their mineral qualities 'operational'.

Among external minerals, following jurists such as al-'Allama al-Hilli (d. 726/1325), 'Amili (d. 1226/1811), Shafi'i (d. 204/820) and Mawardi (d. 450/1058), Sadr lists salt, oil, sulphur (*kabrit*). Among internal minerals are gold, iron, silver (*I* 445–7).

The legal status of external minerals is that of 'public property'. 'They are publicly shared among the people, and Islam does not recognize the title of anyone to them' (*I* 444). Only the state, or its representative, can exploit them. 'As to private projects by which the individuals exploit these minerals, they are absolutely forbidden' (*I* 445). The most any individual can profit from external minerals is restricted to his personal need.

Internal minerals are subdivided into two: internal minerals which are found near the surface, and 'hidden internal minerals' which require double labour: first to reach and excavate them, then to treat them in order to bring out their mineral 'quality'. The legal status is different in each case. For internal minerals near the surface, says Sadr, 'the jurists do not allow private property for the appropriation (control, *ruqba*), of the mineral, but [as in the case of external minerals], they allow the individual to take from the minerals a reasonable quantity for his needs' (*I* 449). On this issue, there is agreement among the jurists.

In contrast, hidden internal minerals have given way to a debate. Some like

Kulayni (d. 329/941), Qummi (d. 1231/1816), and Mufid (d. 413/1022), consider them as *anfal*, and *anfal* is state property. Others, like Shafi'i, consider them to be public property, shared by all the people (*I* 449).

'The question is whether the individual can own the mines of gold and iron as private property if he discovers them in his excavation' (*I* 450). Many jurists answer in the affirmative, considering excavation as a form of revival, but put limits on ownership. What is included in the property is 'the material discovered by excavation. It does not extend to the depths of the earth, to the ores of the mineral and its roots ... This is what is called in *fiqh* the mineral's contiguous area, *harim al-ma'dan*'(*I* 451).

These limits once set, Sadr concludes that even with potential privatisation, 'this kind of property is very clearly different from the ownership of natural resources in the capitalist doctrine, because it is a kind of property which does not differ from being a type of division of labour among the people. It cannot lead to the establishment of private monopolistic enterprise, in the fashion of enterprises in capitalist society' (*I* 452).

Factors three and four. Water and other natural resources

The third and fourth factors of production are water and other natural resources, which Sadr discusses briefly. The legal regime of water has two aspects. Manifest water, i.e. open resources (*masadir makshufa*), is considered public property. A person will take from it the equivalent of the effort invested in getting it, such as pumping it with a machine, or digging a hole to retain it. Hidden water, water which is not immediately available, will give the person who discovers and extracts it a priority to the extent of his needs. Any excess can be acquired by others (*I* 466–8).

Other natural resources are considered 'public domain, *mubahat 'amma*'. Amongst these are game and forestry, which 'can be appropriated to the extent of the labour necessary to achieve their acquisition' (*I* 469). A bird which falls inadvertently into someone's property does not automatically come into his possession. Only positive work (in this case going out hunting) will permit possession.

The discussion of the four factors forming part of the pre-productive stage in Sadr's system is, at this point of *Iqtisaduna*, complete. By drawing on the works of the classical jurists, Sadr introduced his own view of the legal regimes affecting the distributional system related to each of these elements. Among the critical questions addressed was the issue of oil, which Sadr solves in a 'radical' fashion. As an 'external mineral', oil is considered to be in law subject to 'public property', and private persons are not entitled to exploit oil fields. Only the state can put it to profit for the benefit of the public. But the most important source of wealth in Sadr's analysis is, not surprisingly, the issue of land ownership. A critical question in post-revolutionary Iraq, it proved to be also a major contentious point in the immediate years following the success of the Iranian Revolution.[17]

Once the empirical description is completed, Sadr proceeds to the wider stage in the analysis, and attempts to draw a picture of 'the general theory of distribution before production'.

Conclusion: *The general theory of distribution before production*

Once the legal rules on the distribution of factors of production are laid out, Sadr proceeds to the next level of abstraction, which is the theory of distribution per se. 'This is', he writes, 'the second half of the discovery process which goes from the superstructure to the basis, and from legal details to theoretical generalities' (*I* 473).

In the early methodological parts of *Iqtisaduna*, and in the efforts to describe a theory of land ownership, Sadr had at times attempted to draw some more general conclusions from the details of legal rules found in classical jurisprudence. Here he is concerned with giving a fuller picture of the whole economic system. The emphasis shifts to comprehensiveness.

For Sadr, the theory of distribution has two aspects, negative and positive. The negative aspect manifests 'the belief in the inexistence of property and primary private rights attached to raw natural wealth [which would exist separately] from labour' (*I* 474). Whether land, water resources, or hunting, 'the individual has no private right a priori, which would distinguish him legally from any other individual, unless this distinction be a reflection of a specific work' (*I* 475).

The positive side rests, conversely, in the element of labour. 'Labour is a legal basis for the acquisition of rights and private entitlements in natural resources' (*I* 476). From the principle that only labour confers private rights, derive three corollaries. The first corollary is fixed, and consists in an identification of labour and property. The two other corollaries are variable. The emergence of a right or entitlement will depend on (a) the type of labour, and (b) the type of private rights created by labour (*I* 478). The combination of the principle and the corollaries make up the whole system which, for Sadr, informs the superstructure. The most interesting examples in the system are the following (*I* 479–81):

(1) Dead land revived by the labourer will prevent the claim of any other person over it.
(2) Prosperous land farmed by the labourer will remain in the labourer's keeping, as long as he keeps working it. The difference with the dead land is that the reviver of the dead land loses his right over it only if he abandons it long enough for it to become dead again. In the case of the prosperous land, the private right ceases as soon as exploitation stops.
(3) A mine which would be discovered gives the discoverer priority on the field, but if another person reaches the mine by a different way, he would also have the right to exploit it.
(4) The person who digs a well is entitled to use it to the extent of his needs. Beyond these needs, he cannot prevent others from having access to the water.

This recapitulation allows Sadr to sum up his distributional scheme at the stage of pre-production. Labour is a primary source, but different kinds of labour entail different legal consequences. An element of opportunity is hence introduced. It is true, he notes, that there is a factor of labour both in the process of reviving a dead land and in the process of farming a land which is already prosperous. The difference, however, is that revival entitles the creation of an economic opportunity which does not pre-exist labour in the case of the prosperous land. 'The discovery of the connection between the labourer's right to natural resources and the opportunity created by labour in this resource entails that the right of the individual attached to a natural resource ceases if the opportunity created vanishes' (*I* 487). Consequently, 'the general criterion for allowing or prohibiting non-labourers from taking advantage of the natural resources which have been revived by labourers, or in which labourers have created the opportunity [for wealth] resides in the degree of influence over the opportunity that labourers have created by reviving natural resources' (*I* 490).

Sadr includes within this scheme all types of appropriation of wealth. What is true of land is also true for hunting and mining, and these rules are summarised in the following text:

> [The general theory of distribution before production] is exemplified by the revival of a mine, or a water resource hidden in the depth of the earth, in the same way in which it happens for the revival of land. The [amount of] labour which achieves the operation of revival creates the opportunity of exploiting the natural wealth which [the labourer] revives, and he owns this opportunity as the fruit of his effort. It is not permissible for another to make him lose this opportunity. The labourer has the right to prevent others from taking the resource (*marfaq*) away from him. This can be considered the right of the labourer over a land, a mine, or a water resource ... But the practice of farming in a land prosperous by nature, or the use of a land for cattle-grazing, are activities which, though being exploitation and fructification of natural resources, do not justify the existence of a right for the farmer or the shepherd in the land ... What is justified in this case is the ownership of the fruit that the farmer produces, or the animals which the shepherd takes care of. It does not justify their ownership of the land or their right over it. (*I* 486–7)

Sadr then proceeds to a further degree of abstraction in the theory. Alongside the principle of labour as a creator of rights, continuous possession is presented as the condition for the perpetuation of rights. Sadr can derive, from the study of the general principles of distribution before production, the two basic tenets of this theory:

(1) The labourer who exerts his efforts on raw natural resources owns the fruit of his labour. This is the general opportunity to profit from the wealth one creates.
(2) The perpetuation of exploitation (*mumarasat al-intifa'*) in any natural resource grants the individual exploitant a right which precludes others from taking the resources away from him, so long as he keeps taking advantage from this particular resource.

'On the first principle are based the rules which organise the rights in the operation of revival and hunting. On the second principle are based the rules of possessing removable goods, which nature has offered man the opportunity to exploit' (*I* 497–8).

Distribution and justice

A Distribution after production

The general theory of *Iqtisaduna* on distribution before production has introduced the concept of need and the central notion of labour, as well as the general theory of land distribution and other factors of production. Sadr then moves, after some general remarks on issues rapidly discussed in earlier parts,[18] to the theory of production after distribution.

Both the structure and the method of *Iqtisaduna* appear very clearly in this section, which is introduced by a caveat, in which Sadr shows his awareness that 'the two studies [distribution before and after production] interact (*tadakhala al-bahthan*)' because of the difficulty of dividing the phases of the economy into pre- and post-production. The process is particularly intertwined in the Islamic assessment of the central concept of labour. 'We had tried in the theory of distribution before production to specify the rights that individuals acquire in raw natural resources viewed as one aspect of their distribution. Since these rights are the result of labour, the analysis was focused on the role of labour in these natural resources. Natural resources developed by labour comes in this perspective under pre-production wealth' (*I* 517 n.). Thus the inevitability of some confusion, since 'the sources of production', i.e. 'land, raw materials, and the tools necessary for production' which were analysed in the section on the process of distribution before production, must be addressed again from another angle. This time the analysis aims at explaining legal rules of distribution after production, which are concerned with 'productive wealth, which is the goods made by labour exercised on nature, and results from a combination between these material sources of production'. This is 'secondary [or derivative] wealth' (*I* 387–8).

This section represents perhaps the clearest model of Sadr's method in the book. In following the argument in some detail, the reader can watch the modus operandi of *Iqtisaduna* in one of its best applications.

To find the rationale of the economic system, Sadr posits a number of rules from the superstructure which he reads in the classical texts of *fiqh*. He then offers the alternative theory from the two competitive schools, Capitalism and Socialism. Then, by way of deduction from the classical texts, and by way of contrast with Socialism and Capitalism, he draws the specific attitude of Islam towards these economic problems.

The superstructure – What the fuqaha *have to say*

Example 1. Al-Muhaqqiq al-Hilli (d. 676/1277) wrote that agency (*wikala*) is not acceptable for gathering wood (*ihtitab*) and other similar works in nature. If a person hires an agent for gathering wood, the contract is void, and the principal will not own the wood collected by the agent.

Example 2. In 'Allama Hilli's *Tadhkara,* as well as in the works of some Shafi'i scholars, agency is void in matters such as hunting, gathering wood, reviving the dead land, appropriating water, and similar activities.

Examples 3, 4. This interdiction is also forbidden in other works, such as in 'Allama Hilli's *Qawa'ed,* and Jawad al-'Amili's *Miftah al-Karama.*

Example 5. Some editions of Tusi mention his rejection of agency in land revival, and wood and grass gathering (*ihtishash*). Abu Hanifa (d. 150/767), according to Ibn Qudama (d. 620/1223), considers that the contract of partnership (*sharika*) is not permitted in such activities like *ihtishash,* because partnership cannot be without agency (*wikala*), and agency in such matters is invalid. Whoever collects the grass or the wood becomes their owner.

Example 6. 'Allama Hilli associates agency and tenancy (*ijara*) in these interdictions. 'In the same way the principal will not become the owner of what the agent gets in gathering wood, grass, or reviving dead land, so the lessor will not own [the result of] the tenant's labour in nature' (*I* 518–19). Asfahani (d. 1137/1725) and Hasan ibn ash-Shahid ath-Thani (d. 966/1559) wrote in a similar vein.

Example 7. 'Allama Hilli in the *Qawa'ed* writes that, notwithstanding the intent to share the product of gathering or hunting with a partner, the whole result of the activity is the property of the sole gatherer or hunter. Intent is immaterial.

Example 8. Tusi and the two Hillis have ruled that the intent of sharing with others is immaterial as to the ownership of 'natural wealth, *tharwa tabi'iyya*'.

Example 9. In the *Qawa'ed,* and in other *fiqh* works, it is stated that in case a person gives another person a net for fishing, the value of providing the net is independent from the product of the activity (fishing). The value is based on assessing the act of providing the net as a hire contract.

Example 10. Even when hunting (or fishing) with an illegally held tool, the result of the activity is not affected according to 'Allama Hilli. The tool will be returned and a price given on the basis of hire, independent of the resulting fish or game. This is confirmed by an-Najafi (d. 1266/1850), who further comments that the price of hire is due even when there is no result to the activity. The Sunni *faqih* Sarakhsi (d. *c.* 485/1092) develops the same idea in his *Mabsut.* 'The tool', Sadr writes, 'does not have a share (*hissa*) in the commodity produced' (*I* 520).

Example 11. In Tusi's *Mabsut,* this last rule is likened to the water peddler (*saqqa'*) in partnership. Even if there is an intent to share the result of selling the water, none of the revenue goes to the partner.

Example 12. Al-Muhaqqiq al-Hilli gives a similar example based on a partnership in which the *saqqa'* is given a draught animal for the job by a partner. The animal will simply be considered on hire, and the value of hire will be independent of the *saqqa'*'s revenue. The partnership is void. So have also ruled Ibn Qudama and Shafi'i (*I* 518–21).

These examples constitute the 'superstructure'. Sadr must now interpret them to derive his economic infrastructure. But first, a contrasting example is offered through the exposition of the capitalist theory.

Capitalism, Sadr writes, divides 'productive wealth', or what is equivalent to it, 'monetary wealth', into categories which are equal amongst each another from the capitalist school's perspective. These four categories, interest, salaries, rent, and profit, separate or combined, form the root of productive wealth in capitalist production.

Islam rejects this classification, since Islamic economic theory does not assign an equal value to these sources. 'The general theory of distribution before production considers that what is produced from raw nature is the property of the sole producer, the labourer ... Only the productive individual is the original owner of the wealth produced from raw nature' (*I* 524). If the labourer happens to use somebody else's 'tools of production' (means of production, *wasa'el al-intaj*), he remains none the less the sole owner of the goods produced. A mere compensation (prize, *mukafa'a*) is granted to the person whose productive tools are used.

The rules derived from the *fuqaha*'s works can be summarised in three principles:

(1) The principal cannot reap the fruit of his agent's work in matters of raw natural wealth. This is clear from the first eight examples.

(2) The contract of hire is similar to the contract of agency mentioned in the preceding principle. This can be read in example 6.

(3) 'The productive individual, who uses in his exploitation of nature a tool or a machine which is owned by another person ... becomes indebted to the owner of the tool with a compensation for the service rendered in the process of production. The produce is in its totality the labourer's property. This is clear in examples 9, 10 and 12' (*I* 527).

These principles have significant consequences in the industrial world. 'It is possible for capital [in the capitalist perspective] to hire labourers for cutting wood from the forest or extracting oils from wells, and to pay them salaries ... In the Islamic theory of distribution, there is no room for this kind of production. Labour is a direct condition for the appropriation of natural wealth, and gives the sole labourer the right to own the wood he cuts or the mineral he extracts' (*I* 526).

A similar process of comparison is repeated to draw further economic rules from the legal 'superstructure', and from a contrast between Islam and a competing school of thought, this time Marxism.

After a series of examples drawn again from classical *fiqh*, Sadr tries to show that unlike Marxism, which does not distinguish between the exchange value of a commodity and its property, Islam stresses the difference between the two concepts, and emphasises instead the stage in which the intervention of the worker takes place in the process of production:

The material on which the productive person applies his labour, if not owned before [the labour element intervenes], will grant the totality of the resulting wealth to that person. All other contributory productive forces are considered at the service of that person and receive a compensation from him, but they are not considered partners in the result ... But if the material was previously owned by an individual, then whatever development happens to it, it remains his property ... (*I* 535)

This, for Sadr, derives from the *fiqh* principle of the 'permanence of ownership (*thabat al-milkiyya*)', of which the best example is the wool given to a worker by its owner. Even if the worker transforms the wool into another commodity (like a garment), the commodity will remain the property of the original owner. The worker will only receive a compensation for his labour, which is independent from the garment (*I* 530–40).

The rest of the chapter, and the remarks which follow it (*I* 541–81), try to refine the principles and solve outstanding problems which derive from the distinction introduced by Islamic rules between the compensation (*ajr*, salary), which is fixed, and partnership in profit or product (*musharaka fir-ribh aw an-natej*), which is the hallmark of contracts such as *muzara'a* and *musaqat*, (sharecropping agreements), *mudaraba* and *ju'ala* (*I* 556).[19] The latter profit, which is essentially variable, attaches particularly, as in *mudaraba*, to commercial ventures. Compensation, in contrast, is relevant to a situation where a tool of production is offered by one of the parties. 'The tool of production and commercial capital are opposed as to the way to legitimise profit' (*I* 558–9). Underlying the distinction is, again, the concept of labour: 'It is not possible for an individual to guarantee for himself a profit without work. Work is the essential justification for profit in the [Islamic] theory' (*I* 562). This is where capital will be invested only in a venture where profit is not assured, since, according to Sadr, it cannot qualify like the tools of production as accumulated labour.

B *Production and the role of the state*

The remainder of *Iqtisaduna* consists of two shorter (and less interesting) chapters on the 'theory of production' (*I* 582–627), and on 'the role of the state in the economy' (*I* 628–58). These chapters, which emphasise the role of the state in the economic system as a main power for productive wealth as well as for distribution purposes, conclude Sadr's analysis on a very general level.

The chapter on production starts with the earlier mentioned differentiation between doctrine and science, and suggests that the maximisation of production, which is the only underlying common goal of all three systems, belongs to the realm of science. Islam as a *madhhab* can benefit from the other theories for a better planning of the economy of the Islamic state. The distinctiveness of the Islamic doctrine appears in the subjective side of the theory of production, which is developed in the legal framework accompanying the productive process. These rules, such as the importance of reviving and exploiting the land for its regime ownership (*I* 590), the prohibition of *riba* (*I* 591–2), the encouragement of commerce as productive activity and not as intermediation (*I* 621–2), these and the other legal rules which form part of the legal superstructure all show how Islam tries to protect the productive process from activities purely centred on 'the tyranny (*zulm*) of man in the distribution of wealth'. This tyranny, and the betrayal of divine prodigality (*kufran an-ni'ma*), 'constitute the two causes for the problem which the poor has faced since the earliest times of history' (*I* 609).

This economic problem warrants the last remarks of the book on the responsibility of the state in the economy. The Islamic state, in Sadr's theory, is an actor of the utmost importance, whose intervention is behind the 'great projects' in the economy. This is because these projects need the accumulation of capital otherwise impracticable because of the legal rules which prevent the hoarding of wealth (*I* 600). The state will intervene in the economy to guarantee the right course of social production, to distribute with equity and efficiency raw natural material, and to control extracting industries (*sina'at istikhrajiyya*) and the production of raw material (*I* 626–7).

The state, in effect, has a large role to play in the Islamic economy. This is consonant with the gist of *Iqtisaduna*, and consists of the application of those rules which have been specified in the *Sunna* and in the classical texts. This is the ambit of *mantaqat al-faragh*, which was introduced early in *Iqtisaduna* as the area of discretion for the government's activity. In this area, the *imam* as *wali al-amr* will take economic measures needed to fulfil 'social security, *daman ijtima'i*' (I 629–37) and 'social balance, *tawazun ijtima'i*' (*I* 638–51). Social security is further defined as consisting of public solidarity (*takaful 'amm*), which operates 'within the limits of extreme need' (*I* 631), and of 'the right of the group, *jama'a*, in the sources of wealth' (*I* 632). Social balance provides the state measures such as the ones described earlier, along with the right to impose taxes and create public sectors (*I* 643). This interventionism is meant to guarantee the levelling of social disparities. In the general context of *Iqtisaduna*, this will ensure that social differences will not be so acute as to allow, in the words of the Qur'an, wealth to remain exclusively in the hands of the rich (*I* 636).[20]

The area of discretion, which closes *Iqtisaduna*, is meant to be flexible enough to allow Islam to cater for social needs and solve the economic problem in all times and ages.

Iqtisaduna, Perspectives

Iqtisaduna *in the literature*

The preceding pages were an attempt to describe and reconstitute the essence of Sadr's main contribution and his claim to fame, the theory of an Islamic economic system presented in *Iqtisaduna*. *Iqtisaduna* is a relatively early work, which Sadr prepared when he was in his thirties.

Iqtisaduna is a product of the times. As in the case of *Falsafatuna*, it was written when Communism was on the rise in Iraq and in many other countries of the area, Syria and Iran in particular. Most importantly, as mentioned already, the very audience of the *'ulama* was under threat. This period, which generally corresponds to 'Abd al-Karim Qasem's rule (1958–63), necessitated answers to the troubling questions of economics and philosophy, for which Communism seemed to offer, to the great dismay of religious circles, alluring and comprehensive answers.

The earliest edition of *Iqtisaduna* which can be traced bears the date 1961,[21] and suggests that the book was the result of work undertaken in the late 1950s. This corresponds to the time of the communist challenge, and the structure of the book betrays this importance. Hence the division of the work into three parts, in which, as mentioned earlier, the first is a lengthy and significant critique of socialist economic theories (*I* 15–212). The second part is, in comparison extremely short, as it briefly deals away with 'Capitalism' (*I* 213–54). It is interesting in this regard to note that the critique of Capitalism in this section is much less rewarding than later passages of the book when 'capitalist' concepts such as risk and individual property are contrasted with their Islamic equivalents. On the whole, the anti-Marxist and anti-capitalist sections, which formed most of the first volume in the original edition, are burdened with the terminology of the early 1960s, when the works of Stalin and Politzer were still important in Marxist theory in a country like Iraq.[22] Their significance remains mostly as a testimony of the atmosphere prevailing in the Middle East of the communist intellectual ascendancy in the 1950s and early 1960s. The third part, the largest and most interesting, constitutes the most innovative effort in *Iqtisaduna*. It is the part of the book which has survived best the demise of communist ideology in the area.

To date, *Iqtisaduna* stands as the most interesting and the most comprehensive work written on Islamic economics. In the Muslim world, it has been used in Arab and Iranian circles, and translations in several languages of part or whole of the book have appeared, including two Persian translations, one of which was read in the Iranian *hauza*s (circles of scholars) before the Revolution.[23] There have also been Turkish, German and English translations. The German translation of the 'Islamic' part of the work by Andreas Rieck is the best and most scholarly effort to date on *Iqtisaduna*.[24] The English translation of the largest part of *Iqtisaduna*, published in Tehran in 1982, is poor and unreliable.[25] Another serialised translation of some chapters of the book has been more recently published in the Shi'i journal *al-Serat*.[26]

In the Arab world, a summary of *Iqtisaduna* was published in Beirut in four short books.[27] The summary adds little to the work, but the effort is indicative of the stature held by *Iqtisaduna* in Islamic circles. This is not limited to the Shi'is, and *Iqtisaduna* was used and continues to be discussed in several countries of the Arab world, including universities in the Maghreb. The then Dean of Kullyat Dar al-'Ulum at the University of Cairo, 'Ali an-

Najdi Nasef, wrote in 1976 the preface to Sadr's *al-Fatawa al-Wadiha*,[28] and Sadr's execution in 1980 was featured in major Cairene newspapers. It is difficult to assess the exact incidence of Sadr's thought in Arab and Muslim circles, but its use in Arab universities was common even before the Iranian Revolution, and the repeated references to it in any Persian and Arab work on Islamic economics suggest that its reputation is well established in the field. Considering the significant pool of classical *fiqh* sources used in *Iqtisaduna*, the interest in the book is not surprising.

Yet *Iqtisaduna* has also been subject to scathing criticism by Sunni scholars, who have put forward the Shi'i limitations of Sadr's theory.

The most detailed such criticism appears in a book published at Dar as-Sahwa in Cairo in 1987.[29] It consists of two separate critical essays on *Iqtisaduna*, contributed by 'authors who did not meet once before the writing of this introduction ... The book addresses a single subject, which concerns one of the most famous Shi'i books on Islamic economics, Muhammad Baqer as-Sadr's *Iqtisaduna*.'[30] For the publisher, bringing together these two critics was needed 'to strip bare a widely reputed book, which had been received in good faith, despite its deadly methodological mistakes, and obfuscating legal consequences'.[31]

Both essays are constructed on the same pattern: an overall presentation of the content of *Iqtisaduna*, a discussion of its methodological shortcomings, and a brief presentation of some of the book's substantive mistakes.

While Harak's essay is a serious work, Kamal tends to lose focus by easy generalisations and the use of texts taken out from later writings by Muhammad Baqer as-Sadr, including incorrect statements such as the alleged thesis that Sadr had argued for the legitimacy of *riba*,[32] and impossible quotations.[33] Harak in contrast presents a systematic and well-structured analysis. His main methodological unease relates to Sadr's permissive use of the concept of *ijtihad*,[34] 'his methodological error in the discovery of the *madhhab*',[35] and the invention of categories which have no basis in the Sunni tradition, and which he ascribes to the 'Shi'i influence' on *Iqtisaduna*'s author.[36]

On the matter of *ijtihad*, Sadr's remarks on the pitfalls which threaten the objectivity of a contemporary reader of the tradition are criticised for the relativisation of the legal rules drawn by the *fuqaha*. For Harak, casting such doubts on 'the Prophet's legislation' is tantamount to heresy. First it is anathema to separate, as Sadr does, between Muhammad's role as a Prophet and the rules he has laid down in response to particular circumstances. It is also incorrect to pretend that the jurists' writings offer such a leeway for interpretation as is suggested in *Iqtisaduna*.

The whole principle of the discovery of Islamic economics, on which *Iqtisaduna* rests, is also faulted. This is because Sadr ends up selecting in the superstructure of civil law those elements which can be of use to his own personal discovery of the infrastructure constituted by the economic *madhhab*. In the course of this intellectual activity are lost all the legal rules which do not fit the structure of the derived Sadrian *madhhab*. Furthermore, Sadr has to discard and contradict well-established rules which do not conform with his general system. A case in point, Harak submits, is Sadr's establishment, following the Shi'i *faqih* Tusi, of a general principle of the *imam*'s ownership of reclaimed land, and of its consequent imposition by *kharaj*. In that, he is in clear contradiction with the *hadith* of the Prophet on full property for whom revives a dead land. His way of dealing with it, for Harak, is simply to consider that the Prophet's saying dealt with a temporary and exceptional situation, and that the general principle was still one of state ownership.[37]

Thirdly, Sadr's methodology drives him to invent categories which have no place in Sunni *fiqh*. Most conspicuous is the concept of discretionary area, 'as if what is meant that the discovery of a discretionary area is an insistence on the validity of Islam for all times and places ... This is a good intention ... But wishes are not sufficient in such matters, and the road to hell may well be paved with good intentions.'[38] The discretionary area is a figment of Sadr's imagination, adds Harak. It allows him to give leeway to 'his' ruler where Sunni understanding is adamantly opposed to such interpretative powers; 'the validity of Islam in all times and places is the sign of a legal wealth, not of legal void [*faragh*, as in *mantaqat al-faragh*]. We can never accept that there be void in legislation. New matters, which have no text to be based on, have been ordered by God to be examined by a process of *ijtihad*, in the light of the general objectives of the *shari'a*. We have kept a huge legal tradition, thanks to the painstaking efforts of jurists who did not leave a single tool for legal *ijtihad* unused.'[39] This for Sunnis is the role of analogy, of deduction, of care for the general interest, and other such methods developed by *fiqh*. Under no circumstance can such an operation of juristic logic contradict the established rule: 'The correctness (legitimacy, *mashru'iyya*) of rules comes from the support it finds in the texts, it never comes from contradicting them.'[40]

In Harak's essay, *Iqtisaduna*'s mistakes in substantive law which derive from the flaws in the method are many. Most important is the one related to land property and to the role of labour in Islamic economics. In Sunni *fiqh*, Harak argues, the principle is the sanctity and absoluteness of private property. Sadr's theories are directly inspired from Socialist thinking adduced with a sectarianism which derives from the importance of the Twelve Imams in Shi'i law and theology. Similarly, the principle in labour law is the absolute freedom of an owner to have labourers work for him on the basis of a salary. 'Mere work cannot be considered as the sole justification to ownership.'[41]

For both Harak and Kamal, all the mistakes of *Iqtisaduna* are rooted in Shi'i influence on Sadr. But can Sadr's Shi'ism really explain his emergence as a leading scholar of Islamic economics, as both Harak and Kamal clearly recognise?

It was suggested that part of the originality of constitutional theory in the circles of Najaf was rooted in the relative independence of the Shi'i *'ulama* from the State apparatus. The Islamic state advocated by Sadr and applied in the Iranian constitution of 1979 had an essentially Shi'i character. In contrast, the explanation for the originality of Sadr's economic works cannot easily be found in an intellectual ferment traceable to Shi'ism as opposed to Sunnism.

Sadr's economic contribution was unique in the Shi'i world itself, where Muslim oppositional leadership was also eager to discover an Islamic alternative to a system which was perceived to be unjust. The closest work to *Iqtisaduna* in Iran was Mahmud Taleqani's *Islam va Malekiyyat*,[42] which came after the publication of Sadr's book, and which in any case cannot compare with *Iqtisaduna* either in depth or comprehensiveness. Nor can one find a clue in nationality. In the Iraqi holy city of Karbala, another young *'alim* wrote a book on 'Islamic economics' in the early sixties. That scholar, the scion of an important family of *'ulama*, was extremely active in the organisation of the Islamic opposition in Iraq and later in Lebanon. But his work on economics, *al-Iqtisad*, published in the early 1960s, is superficial and uninteresting.[43]

Conversely, amongst the theoreticians of 'Islamic economics' who were also prominent for the 'Islamic' form of their opposition to the state in the Sunni world, Sayyid Qutb and 'Allal al-Fasi have dominated the Egyptian and Moroccan scenes. This does not mean that the Shi'i cultural milieu was more favourable to the emergence of an Islamic system of economics. Both Fasi and Qutb dabbled with 'economics', but their best contributions in the field fall far short, in terms of quality, of Sadr's works.[44]

A more solid historical case can be built on the argument that there was a significant chasm between Sunni and Shi'i attitudes on the question of land ownership (notably for the *kharaj* category), and that Sadr did not take it into account. Indeed, classical Hanafi authors like Quduri (d. 428/1036) draw an important distinction between *kharaj* and *'ushr* land. As for *kharaj*, the element of private property, in contrast with Sadr's prohibition, is dominant: 'The main land in Iraq is *kharaj* [land] and belongs to its inhabitants (*ahl*) who can sell it and dispose of it at will.'[45] This may be so, but the immense number of authors, of historical periods and variations, and the use of words like *kharaj*, *'ushr* and *tasq* to convey a wide range of legal regimes (which in any case tend to be obscure in the classical text), suggests rather that several economic systems can and will be derived by the modern Islamic seekers of 'correct economics'. The wide spectrum covered is characteristic of the possibilities offered by the legal tradition. It is much less a function of sectarian closed models (which would favour in Sunnism private ownership and the state cum Imam in Shi'ism) than a characteristic to be found *within* both Shi'i and/or Sunni *fiqh*. As the debate in Islamic Iran between the defenders of absolute private property and those who favoured state nationalisation and redistribution of land clearly shows, the non-sectarian dimension of the divide is profound. In Iran, the tenants and opponents of absolute private property are all Shi'is.

Iqtisaduna is actually remarkable for the absence of any conspicuous Shi'i sectarianism in its analysis and sources. If, as appeared in Part I, the constitutional works of Sadr and their application in the institutions of the Iranian Revolution have been strongly impressed by a strictly Shi'i tradition, reading *Iqtisaduna*, in contrast, suggests that in matters of economics the scholarly ground for research reached beyond the Shi'i tradition. Sadr has freely drawn on Shi'i and Sunni scholars, and it is difficult to find any reference which would specifically betray sectarian leanings, even if on the whole references to Shi'i jurists prevail in *Iqtisaduna*. But Shafi'i (the eponym of the Shafi'i school), Malik (the eponym of the Maliki school), Sarakhsi (Hanafi school), Ibn Hazm (Zahiri school), as well as many of their disciples and followers, all are authoritative sources for the discovery exercise of Muhammad Baqer as-Sadr. In *Iqtisaduna*, Sadr uses abundantly Shi'i as well as Sunni scholars from all schools of law. Even the school most antagonistic to Ja'farism, the Hanbali school (in its Wahhabi-Saudi version), is drawn upon in the persons of Ahmad Ibn Hanbal and Ibn Qudama. In fact, the absence of sectarianism in *Iqtisaduna* explains the interest in Sadr beyond the strict confines of the Shi'i world. There are traces of *Iqtisaduna*'s theories in recent writings in far apart areas in the Arab world, and in as diverse quarters as the Egyptian Supreme Constitutional Court and Tunisian and Algerian Islamic militants.[46] But it may be that the atmosphere of increased sectarianism which is characteristic of the second half of the 1980s would inevitably throw suspicion on the best meaning works in the literature.

Theory and practice: **Iqtisaduna,** *land reform and state intervention in Iran*

Did Sadr succeed in rendering his discovery of Islamic economics applicable to modern times?

Unlike the case of the constitutional precepts, where an almost direct genealogy can be traced with compact texts such as Sadr's *Note* and the Iranian Constitution of 1979, *Iqtisaduna* did not generate a Persian 'compendium of Islamic economics'. Scholars have described parallels between Sadr's forays in the field and the debate on land reform in Iran, as well as parallels between Sadr and the 'economic' works of the first Iranian President, Abul-Hasan Bani Sadr.[47] In a fundamental debate where many voices were heard, Sadr's legacy was important more as a general focus for the tenants of 'social justice in the countryside' than as a recipe charting a decisive way ahead.

With all its lengthy analyses of land property and the economic system, *Iqtisaduna* did not offer mechanisms which could be applied to an economy in search of precise guidelines. But the richness of the work and its scholarly thoroughness suggest that some paradigms have been established in the field along lines first elaborated in *Iqtisaduna*. The virtues of the book may reside more in these paradigms than in the application of the ideas to the economy of the 'Islamic' state.

But the failure of a strict 'applicability' of *Iqtisaduna* is also due to methodological problems inherent to Sadr's original motivations on the one hand, and, on the other hand, to the flaws of the internal methodology which he chose to develop in the book.

As in *Falsafatuna*, the obsession with the critique of Marxism has unduly constrained the author's recourse to the tradition. Sadr, it must be emphasised, had been working on imperfect translations of books belonging to the stalest Marxist tradition. In the case of more serious original works, such as Marx's *Capital*, an authoritative translation from the original German into Arabic has yet to be undertaken, and Sadr's reading of classics of Marxism was hindered by the quality of the material at hand. He in fact did extremely well within these constraints, and Sadr's critique is unique in its thoroughness and the care in avoiding the oversimplification typical of the '*ulama*'s reading of socialist literature. As for the use of 'capitalist' material on the economy, Sadr's concern was too peripheral for a genuine attention to the works of modern economists, or even to classical writers whom he occasionally mentions, such as Ricardo and Adam Smith.

In the properly 'Islamic' part of the book, Sadr was operating from a *tabula rasa*. The systematic use of the *fiqh* compendia is therefore remarkable, but there was an inherent contradiction which surfaces in the book. When Sadr mentions the 'subjective' strength of Islam, which allowed a system to build up and develop, and to overcome various threats throughout history, the argument he used was essentially a-historical. It allows him to undermine the Marxist claim that ideologies, including religions, are dependent on the forms and relations of economic production. Hence the emphasis of *Iqtisaduna* on the concept of distribution, through which Sadr could proceed freely with the advocacy of a self-contained and different system. At the same time, the a-historical dimension also affects the *fiqh* works, which are described and used as immutable documents. Sadr avoids the stultification of these documents by a careful process of selection. As in the cases on hunting, wood gathering, or fishing, these texts are used to investigate the higher 'economic rule' which underlies them. Sadr could not however avoid the burden entailed in the historicity of these sources, and the dilemma is reflected in those passages where he admits that the history of Islam is replete with examples of poverty and exploitation, even though the juristic rules are interpreted in *Iqtisaduna* in exactly the opposite direction.

The constant resurfacing of the historical dimension in the law also leads Sadr to plainly impossible suggestions. This is the case in particular in the early presentation of the rules on land property and Sadr's conclusion on the necessary connection between the way a particular land has come into the Muslim empire and its legal regime. The works of the *fuqaha* indicate indeed that land property was originally related to its conquest, particularly in terms of taxation and succession rights.[48] But the historical link has been somewhere severed. It does not appear realistic to decide in the late twentieth century on the legal regime of a land according to the way its inhabitants have embraced or accommodated early Islam.

More interesting and of easier application is 'the general theory of land ownership'. Sadr's analysis of the concept of labour, particularly in relation to revival and constant exploitation, is reminiscent of the familiar 'agrarian question' and its emphasis on the socialistic principle advocating the devolution of land to the peasants. This indeed constitutes the important dilemma of post-revolutionary Iran.

For Sadr, revival, with its close connection with the concept of labour, is at the root of the general theory of land ownership. With the waning of property rights deriving from 'work by conquest', legitimation of the right to the fruit of land had to be based on the principle of revival and constant exploitation. In the arguments of the advocates of land reform in post-revolutionary Iran, the concept of labour for the exploitation of land and the ownership of its fruit has also been introduced under the more general heading of 'social justice'. Alongside revival, Sadr also developed a number of legal concepts which put the ruler of the Islamic state, individually as well as institutionally, at the heart of a legal order which is centralised and *dirigiste*. Whenever possible, Sadr seems to advocate the necessary intervention of the state as the owner of 'strategic' resources and as the provider of the lines of economic development and redistribution of wealth. This is mainly true of his theory of land ownership, which was (and remains) a sensitive element in the discussions over the nature and function of the 'Islamic state'.

The formal debate in the Islamic Republic of Iran over the separation of institutional powers has been discussed within the context of constitutional law. Here, substantive law relating to land property and land reform is presented.

There have been in practice several attempts by the advocates of land reform in Iran to enforce redistribution of agrarian property. They have been systematically undermined by the Council of Guardians. In the first decade of the Revolution, no less than seven such bills, drawn first by the Revolutionary Council (1979–81), then by Parliament, have been passed, then immediately frozen as anti-constitutional. Only in 1986 was a limited bill on 'temporary cultivation agricultural land' passed, which survived the opposition of the Council of Guardians. But even in this case, several constitutional hurdles were brought up in the Majlis by the opponents of the bill.

Thus, since the early days of the Revolution, several laws on land reform have been repeatedly struck down by the Council of Guardians, which has acted as a conservative watchdog for the opponents of reform. The debate is actually more complicated than a mere opposition between the branches of Government (the decisions of the Council of Guardians do not indicate the majority from the eventual dissenters, but it can be assumed that in a council of twelve jurists, some dissent must have taken place).[49] Within the Majlis itself, a pro-private property faction has emerged against the majority of reformers. The hesitations on the level of institutions is also not surprising. The non-committal position of *Ayat Allah* Khumaini himself, who had been sitting on the fence, was instrumental in the use of his utterances, as well as of his silence, by both groups.[50]

A brief survey of the land reform bills will show the extent of the controversy. As soon as the new regime came to power, the concern for 'social justice' which had provided a key ideological tenet in the revolutionary process, and the combination of this theme with land property in the works of the Shi'i jurists like Sadr (d. April 1980), Taliqani (d. September 1979) and Beheshti (d. June 1981), meant that agrarian reform was high on the agenda. In the summer of 1979, even before the legislative institutions came into being, a committee formed by *Ayat Allahs* Muntazeri, Beheshti and Mishkini produced a law which divided lands into three categories: *anfal* land, which was the property of the Islamic state; confiscated lands from pro-Shah landlords; and large estates owned privately. This last category was the most important and most controversial. It came to be known, following its place in the bill, as the question of *band-e jim* (clause c).[51]

Band-e jim divided private holdings into uncultivated (*ba'ir*, Persian *bayer*) and cultivated (*da'ir*, Persian *dayer*) lands. *Ba'ir* lands were subject to immediate confiscation for distribution among peasants. *Da'ir* lands were to be redistributed if the owner held a surface of land three times larger or more than was needed for him and his family according to local custom. This was clearly a radical legislative step, which precipitated the opposition of high-ranking *'ulama*. Despite his insistence on 'social justice' and the advent of a new, fairer, Islamic era, Khumaini himself suspended the bill on 3 November 1980.[52]

Another attempt, this time by the newly elected Majlis, to introduce land reform was initiated in 1981, and resulted in a more comprehensive piece of legislation on the agrarian question. After two years of discussion, the bill on 'revival and transfer of agricultural land' was approved by Parliament on 28 December 1982. This bill was more detailed than the earlier proposals of the Revolutionary Council which were suspended for being presumably too vague. Its eventual defeat after the Council of Guardians' determined veto marked a significant setback for land reform advocates.

The bill of 28 December 1982 divided land into five categories, of which the two critical ones were the *da'ir* and *ba'ir* lands.[53] *Ba'ir*, uncultivated, land (now under *band dal*, clause d) would have to be cultivated within one year, otherwise the state could reassign it to landless peasants. If the uncultivated land had been completely abandoned by its owners, it automatically became state property. But *ba'ir* land would have in any case to be exploited in a limit not exceeding three times the local custom (*seh baraber 'urf-e mahall*). The surplus would be bought 'at a just price after deduction of legal debts incurred' and reassigned by the state (Art. 5).

Article 6 of the bill dealt with *da'ir* (cultivated) land, also introducing radical measures. The owner who is engaged directly in the cultivation could retain up to three times the amount of land which is customary. If he is not engaged directly, he can keep up to twice the local use amount of land. The surplus amount would be bought by the state and redistributed, 'after deduction of debts'. There were several exceptions, including fully mechanised farms (Art. 6.8), land which came under sharecropping agreement between the owner and the tiller (*muzara'a*, Art. 6.1), as well as rented land (*ijara*, Art. 6.1). Also included in the exceptions was land held in trust (*mawqufe*, Art. 6.3).

The rejection of the Council of Guardians came on 18 January 1983.[54] The Council invalidated the bill on two grounds: it contradicted the principles of Islamic law (*mavazin-e shar'i*) and it was unconstitutional.

Article 2 of the bill, which laid down the headings for the law (*'anavin*), was considered too general. Article 2 mentions the principles of economic independence, the suppression of poverty, and the checking of rural migration, embodied in Articles 3, 43 and 44 of the Constitution; the Council of Guardians deemed these references in the bill under consideration to be 'wider than the necessity required in their application'. For the Council of Guardians, the references in the law to the confiscation by the state of *ba'ir* and *da'ir* land were not rooted in any compelling necessity, and the purchase and transfer of these lands by 'persons who were not entitled legally to intervene' were contrary to Islamic law. The Council of Guardians pointed out also that the dispositions of the law were 'outside the limited secondary sphere (*heyte-ye ahkam-e thanawiyye va mahdude*)' mentioned in Imam Khumaini's decree (*farman*).[55]

The dispositions on *da'ir* and *ba'ir* land were singled out by the Council of Guardians as opposed to the *shari'a*:

> Article 5 and 6, relating to clauses *dal* and *ha'* (*ba'ir* and *da'ir* land) in conjunction with Article 10 [which develops the mechanisms of state redistribution according to a strict list of priorities with state and barren land at the top and *ba'ir* and *da'ir* land to be redistributed afterwards] do not constitute [do not rest on] compelling necessity (*darura fi'lyya*) and the remainder of the articles of the law associated with these two categories are not covered by the decree of Imam Khumaini. They are contrary to Islamic law (*mavazin-e shar'i*).[56]

The Council of Guardians also found fault with the general principle of necessity under which Parliament had presumably introduced agrarian legislation. This 'necessity must be based', said the Council, on the 'country's state (*awda' wa ahwal-e maujud dar sath-e keshvar*)'. In other words, the objective situation giving rise to 'land reassignment' legislation must be exceptional enough to warrant state intervention. In this context, the necessity considered by Parliament was deemed unfounded: for the Council of Guardians, Parliament could not 'put a limitation on the power of the land owners from a legal point of view'.

Article 44 of the Iranian Constitution had mentioned land generally under the category of private property (the two other categories being state and cooperative property). So the bill was also deemed contrary to several dispositions of the Constitution. The indictment of the Council of Guardians was general and blunt: 'The totality of the bill on revival and transfer of agricultural land, insofar as it renders agriculture ultimately statal (*dawlati*), is contrary to Article 44 of the Constitution.'[57]

Legislative work on land reform had to be taken up again, and consultations among the deputies resulted in a bill passed on 19 May 1985.[58] In the new law, many of the previous dispositions had remained, but the critical *da'ir* land category was significantly altered.

In the bill of 19 May 1985, land was again divided into five categories. The three first categories were dead (*mavvat*) land, *milli* (common) land (which comprise pastures, forests, and reclaimed land), and state (*dawlati*) land, which was defined as land whose ownership 'has legitimately been transferred, or will legitimately come, to the state' or one of its organs.[59] The controversial *ba'ir* and *da'ir* lands appeared as *band-e dal* and *ha'* (Art. 3).

Article 4 allowed the state to use the lands in the three first categories as it saw fit. For the *ba'ir* category (private land 'left uncultivated for more than five years without legitimate excuse'), the seven-person committee of the Ministry of Agriculture in charge of applying the law could re-assign the land, within one year, to other caretakers. These would preferentially be peasants who live on the land.

Da'ir land, defined as 'prosperous land under exploitation', was now untouched: '*Da'ir* land, which at the time of approval of this law [by the Majlis] is at the disposal of the owner, will remain so'(Art. 7). There was however one exception, which dealt with land which had been 'temporarily occupied' at the beginning of the Revolution (*kesht-e movaqqat*). Article 6 specified that such land would remain in the property of those peasants who had occupied it 'provided they had continued its exploitation, were making their livelihood from that land, and were completely or almost completely landless themselves'. The state would compensate the owners at 'a just price after deduction of legal fees', and the new owners would receive a title to property from the committee.

The Council of Guardians struck down the law on 2 June 1985.[60] Article 6 was dismissed as 'outside the subject. It was added to the bill but has no relation to the question of land reform.' If the dispositions it contains were to be discussed, the Council of Guardians added, they ought to be returned to Parliament for full review and an eventual passing of separate legislation.

Several other dispositions were also deemed contrary to the Constitution and to Islamic law by the Council of Guardians. Article 8 of the law, 'which forced an owner to sell or rent [his land], is contrary to the *mavazin shar'iyya* and also to Article 47 of the Constitution'. The Council of Guardians was particularly insistent on the wrong use of the concept of necessity by Parliament in devising, yet again, the dispositions in the reform ruling the *da'ir* and *ba'ir* lands.

The opinion of the Council of Guardians of 2 June 1985 was largely devoted to the 'two items' of *da'ir* and *ba'ir* land, and this time, the Council made the sanctity of private property absolutely clear: 'The land reform bill which was ratified by Parliament, and which was rejected by the Council of Guardians because of *da'ir* and *ba'ir* lands, was so [rejected] because the bill mentioned these two items without regard to compelling necessity, and was consequently outside the range of the Imam's message.'

The Council of Guardians reiterated in this passage, in more straightforward language, the principal reason why the first land reform bill of December 1982 had been rejected: the dispositions on *ba'ir* and *da'ir* land had been taken without regard to a compelling necessity which would justify the confiscation entailed in the statute.

It is not enough, continued the Council of Guardians, to include the word necessity in the new draft:

On this basis, and with consideration to what the Council of Guardians had sanctioned ... it was necessary to correct the points objected to by the Council of Guardians ... It is not possible, in those bills rejected by the Council of Guardians because they contradicted Islamic law, [for Parliament] to ratify them under the heading of necessity ... when the law itself admits that there is no necessity.

Ignoring the principles of the *shari'a*, continued the Council of Guardians, is clearly opposed to the Imam's views.

Surely the Imam did not mean in his repeated sermons and his righteous guidance which insist on the protection of divine rules and legal (*shar'i*) dispositions, when he said: 'Nobody should think that helping the dispossessed (*mahrumin*) and providing them with services is free of illegality, when it is achieved through illegal means. For this would be a deviation and a betrayal of Islam and the Islamic Republic, as well as of the *mahrumin* themselves. It paves the way to hell even to the *mahrumin*, because of what they would have received in illegal (*haram*) money or in the usurpation of money belonging to others'; ... [surely the Imam did not mean] that the bills and articles which have been rejected by the Council of Guardians on the basis of their opposition to Islamic law can be returned by the Parliament under the heading of necessity.

In the 1985 bill, as was just seen, the Council of Guardians had scolded Parliament for including the 'outside the subject' question of 'temporarily occupied land' in a comprehensive land reform system. Soon after its repeated defeat, Parliament set out to devise a more limited law which would tackle only this type of land.

The 'temporarily cultivated' category consisted of land which had been occupied by peasants in the immediate aftermath of the Revolution: some 700,000 to 750,000 hectares of land, representing five per cent of the total arable land in the country, and concerning 120,000 families of peasants and 5–6,000 landowners. The main dispositions of Article 6 of the 1985 bill were adopted again. With the cut-off date for the occupation of lands set at 20 March 1981 (except in Kurdistan where the date was extended two years because of more persistent troubles than in the rest of the countryside), the land would be tranferred to the peasants occupying it after a 'just price' was paid to the original owners.[61]

It was noted in Chapter 3 that the power of the Council of Guardians was enormous because of the automatic legislative veto it held according to Article 94 of the Iranian Constitution. The repeated undermining of 'revolutionary' legislation, particularly in matters of land reform, had frustrated the operations of Parliament so much that the only recourse left was, again, in the supreme faqih, *Ayat Allah* Khumaini. Parliament used a declaration of Khumaini, allegedly uttered in 1983, to the effect that if a law was passed in the Majlis with a two-thirds majority, it would not require to be scrutinised by the Council of Guardians.[62]

In a troubled session in late October 1986, this declaration of Khumaini was used to frustrate the threat of the Council of Guardians. Under hasty procedural arrangements, the then Speaker Hashemi Rafsanjani declared that a majority of two-thirds had been reached, and the bill was passed into law.[63] None the less, the 'temporary cultivation land' final status had to wait until its approval by the Majma'-e Tashkhis-e Maslahat, one constitutional revision and five years later.

The attempt to protect the peasants who had occupied land in the aftermath of the Revolution from its ownership reverting to the former landlords was the last battle of the advocates of land reform before the Constitutional Revision. The fact that they seem to have won it should not obscure their defeat in the overall war. Not only did the percentage of the land concerned constitute a minimal part of the agricultural land available, but its denomination and the legal categorisation under which it fell rendered it the odd and uncertain exception to firmly established principles on the absoluteness of the right of property.

This absoluteness was now clearly embedded in the 'jurisprudence' (in its French meaning) of the Council of Guardians. The Council of Guardians had succeeded in frittering away the attempts of the advocates of land reform to provide any legal argument in favour of landless peasantry. Land reform proponents were cornered into a vague and weak advocacy of the exception to the rule, on the basis of necessity. In the arguments of the defenders of the 1986 bill, it was out of necessity to the protection of the Revolution, or of landless peasant families' allegiance to the Islamic Republic, or to the impracticality of evacuating the peasants on the 'temporarily cultivated land', that ownership had to remain with these families.[64] Necessity was indeed the only rationale left, and it included very little argument in terms of law. The advocacy of necessity meant a contrario that the principle was indeed that legitimately acquired property could not be touched, and that only total urgency could conceivably offer an exception to the rule.

The theme of necessity had by 1985 become the last refuge of Parliament to try organising land reform. Its use meant also that Parliament was fighting a rearguard battle. Lest the whole field of the law would be ultimately undermined, the concept of necessity could hardly be used every time the dispositions of Islamic law were in contradiction with the legislation of Parliament.

The Council of Guardians was relentless. It reserved for itself the right to define each of the terms used by the legislator. 'Legitimately acquired property' was extended to mean practically any property (short, perhaps, of that of the Shah and his entourage). Necessity was restricted to mean that it could not blunt Islamic law or the Constitution as the Council of Guardians intended to interpret them. The only way for Parliament to save its last and limited bill on land reform was to avoid the Council of Guardians altogether.

Even when, in its decision of June 1985, the Council of Guardians asked Parliament to prepare a separate bill dealing only with temporarily cultivated land, the warning it gave was clear. As it declared Article 6 on temporarily cultivated land 'out of the subject', it took the occasion to opine that Article 6 was, in any case, 'contrary to Article 47 of the Constitution'.[65] Article 47 simply states that 'private [personal, *shakhsi*] property which is legitimately acquired must be respected. The regulation of private property will be decided by law.' In the Council of Guardians' view, restriction could not apply to this statement, which must be read narrowly. The category of temporarily cultivated land, which under the law deprived the owners of legitimately acquired property, was tantamount to illegal occupation. There was little doubt left on the fate of the Bill if it were presented again to the Council of Guardians, and the Majlis sought to avoid the Council of Guardians by reverting to the new 'qualified majority' device, the constitutionality of which was doubtful.

The pro-reform advocates in Parliament had been slowly cornered into the evasive concept of necessity. From the early reforms of 1979–81, which were put to an end by Khumaini, through to 1988, when the Council of Guardians used its power as super-legislator to undermine all Parliamentary bills on land reform, a pattern was slowly established to vindicate the rules of Islamic law as safeguards to private property, however extensive (and unfair) they might seem to be. The opponents of land reform, particularly in the Council of Guardians, slowly asserted the sanctity of private property in Islamic law. Even the advocates of land reform in Parliament had fallen in the legislative grid in which the Council of Guardians ensnared them. When in 1986 they tried to salvage the de facto occupation of 'temporary cultivation' land, the only argument left was the weak and unconvincing concept of necessity.

The powerful interests of land owners in Iran, who had by the time Khumaini suspended the first bill prepared by the Revolutionary Council in 1981 regrouped and organised, made certain that *dirigiste* and distributionist theories such as could be found in *Iqtisaduna* would not be applied by the Council of Guardians, which upheld effectively the torch of the sanctity of private property. The rejection of the land reform bill by the Council of Guardians in 1983 and 1985 meant the death of Parliament's attempts to draw comprehensive land legislation. It was clear that the Council of Guardians would not let through any law entailing the confiscation of *ba'ir* and *da'ir* land. Until the constitutional developments of 1988, and the emergence of the Majma'-e Tashkhis-e Maslahat, Parliament was completely paralysed in its attempt to introduce 'social justice' in the countryside. Sadr's theory had been defeated, although many of the concepts which he discussed in *Iqtisaduna* offered the language of the background polemic and the general paradigms which will continue to impress on the debate.

The constitutional crisis of 1988 revived the defeated philosophy, and the demise of the Council of Guardians put into question again the relevance of the philosophy of Sadr and those who, like him, understood the state of Islamic law in an interventionist and 'socialistic' manner.

In the year following the birth of the Majma', efforts were established to reactivate the bills which had 'fallen in abeyance' or had not survived the axe of the Council of Guardians. Under the leadership of Rafsanjani, the Majma' was able, in a few concise words, to legitimate the 'temporarily cultivated land' bill, by giving its stamp of approval to the Executive Order (*a'innameh*) which consecrated the rights of the new owners. The Majma' simply established that the law stood as it was, and that the controversial decision-making process of the Executive Order would be tempered by an eventual intervention of a representative of the Leader.[66]

A wider effort was also directed to reviving the *ba'ir* and *da'ir* reform. The cue given by the Council of Guardians in its 1985 rejection of the comprehensive land bill was taken up. Instead of dealing with land in the countryside as one comprehensive category, several pieces of legislation addressed more limited categories, as in the case of temporarily cultivated land. While Parliament seems to have shied away from directly tackling *da'ir* land (which in any case had been left untouched by the Bills of 1985), legislation was passed on *ba'ir* land, and was in fact approved soon after the establishment of the Majma' in 1988. The decision of the Majma' reporting the text of the law consists of one article and a note (*tazakkur*) including four clauses (*tabsereh*). The final text defines *ba'ir* land as 'land which was left without cultivation and without a valid reason for more than five years'. The radical provision entitling the government (through the representatives of the Agriculture Ministry 'directly, or through the seven-men agricultural Commission') to 'sell that land at a just price after deduction of debts' was watered down significantly by a combination of procedural review measures opened to the original owners, and by the possibility mentioned by the law to sell these properties or convert them into 'rented' or *muzara'a* land within one year of the approval of the law by the Majma'.[67]

So there was finally a legal framework for land distribution. But even at that stage, it is clear that the debate in Iran was not over, as the *da'ir* land remained outside of the purview of the reform. In the case of abandoned arable land, the reform was toned down significantly by the various aforementioned procedural and substantive restrictions. Furthermore, it took two years for the government to prepare the Executive Order requested for implementing approved law, even though the law itself had stipulated that the Executive Order would have to be prepared within two months of approval.[68] By the end of 1369 of the Persian calendar (early 1991), some mechanisms for a timid land reform had finally been established.

Against the Iranian developments in agrarian reform, *Iqtisaduna* stands as a work favouring a significant interventionist role by the state.[69] The area of discretion of the ruler can be considered large enough to accommodate the advocacy of land reform in Sadr's theory. On the basis of the thrust of Sadr's arguments, advocates of land reform in Iran were able to find comfort in a possible distribution of land by the state to landless and needy peasants in the name of social balance.

Sadr's work deals also with 'primary rules' which cannot be changed by government, and the strength of *Iqtisaduna* lay precisely in a general theory of land distribution which should not be simply altered by the ability of the ruler or the government to legislate in the discretionary area. In this case, the key thesis, which was also at the heart of the thrust of the legislation elaborated by the Iranian Parliament, introduced the property of land as a function of revival and constant exploitation. Revival (Arabic *ihya'*, Persian *vagozari*), and continuous labour, were central both to *Iqtisaduna* and to Iranian legislation on *ba'ir* land. As for *da'ir* land (man-made prosperous land in *Iqtisaduna*), its legal regime depended for Sadr on whether it was historically part of the law of conquest, or whether it was land of persuasion or agreement. In the latter case, it could remain private property. As law of conquest, it would in contrast become 'public property'. It was then not subject to the rules of inheritance, could not be leased out another time by the labourer who was working on it, and control would revert to the community as its original owner at the end of the lease.

Sadr's interventionist rules of *Iqtisaduna* became more acute at the beginning of the Iranian Revolution. In 1979, he wrote a little pamphlet in the series of 'Islam as a guide to life', where the 'radical' positions which surface at times in *Iqtisaduna* were bolstered. In his *Detailed Guidelines to the Economy of the Islamic Society*, the nuances in *Iqtisaduna* deriving from historical conquest of the land or sharecropping contracts like *muzara'a* had given way to a more firmly established role of the state than the uncertain discretionary area of the ruler. 'Rule one' of the *Guidelines* stated: 'All the sources of natural wealth are part of the public sector. Individuals have a right of usufruct (*intifa'*) on one single basis, which is the labour represented in *ihya'* meaning solely direct work.'[70] In other words, contracts like *muzara'a* or lease (*ijara*), which were tolerated in *Iqtisaduna*, were now looked at suspiciously:

> There is one single situation in which the operation of capitalist production has not been completely abolished in the *shari'a* according to some schools of law; this is the contract of *muzara'a*, in which the owner of the land agrees with the farmer who has the seeds on the basis that [the owner] offers the land and shares the fruit of labour with the farmer. If this case has not been abolished completely by law, as some *fuqaha* see it, there are discretionary elements (*'anasir mutaharrika*) in the Islamic economy which call for the abolition of this type of contract.[71]

The picture in Iran as it emerges ten years after the Revolution does not lend itself to this radical dimension of Sadr's 1979 writings. *Muzara'a*, *ijara*, *waqf* land, all these legal devices remain as an important panoply of defences against state expropriation. But the spirit of *Iqtisaduna*, which is summarised in a short study published by Sadr in 1973, remains an important element for the understanding of the social philosophy behind the advocacy of Iranian reformism:

When Islam said to the people, forsake injustice and establish equity, it offered concurrently the explication of injustice and equity, and put forth the equitable way for distribution, exchange, and production, as opposed to the unjust way. For instance, Islam mentioned that appropriation of land by force, without reviving it (*ihya'*), was injustice; that land property, on the basis of labour and *ihya'* is equity... It is true that Islam urges the rich to help their poor brothers and neighbours, but it was not satisified with the mere urging of the rich and their moral education. It imposed on the State to secure the needy, and to grant them a respectable life.[72]

The first decade of the Revolution undermined Parliamentary attempts to introduce any change to the situation of land ownership, except for the temporarily cultivated category from which it would have been difficult to expel the peasants in effective occupation. The developments in the theory introduced by Sadr and like-minded scholars were thwarted by the Council of Guardians, and private property in its most absolute manifestation turned out to be the departing point of the Council of Guardians' opinions.

Yet the influence of the logic at work in *Iqtisaduna* has been revived by Khumaini's edict of 6 January 1988 and the constitutional revision of the following year. The Amended Constitutional of 1989 has brought to life again, through the Majma', the economic philosophy of Sadr. But the consolidation of this trend will depend on a combined and domestic atmosphere which, in Iran, does not seem in the 1990s so inclined towards the radical fervour which was the hallmark of many of the jurist-leaders of earlier revolutionary days.

The difficulty of steering a clear course in the economic affairs of Iran has proved insuperable. This is true also in the constitutional field, but there are even less signposts in the Islamic tradition than in a theory of government which has always ranked high in the interests of Muslim scholars. For scholars who claim that Islam can provide the answer to the economic problems in any society, a special effort is required in a field for which the tradition is not equipped. But there now exists a rich Islamic law jurisprudence in Iran, which has taken the form of a separation of powers dispute between the Council of Guardians and Parliament, then between the Council of Guardians and the Majma'. It is hoped that the full publication of the discussions within these bodies will further enrich the Renaissance of the *shari'a*, which started with *Iqtisaduna* and continues through the Majma'-e Tashkhis-e Maslahat.

5 Muhammad Baqer as-Sadr and Islamic banking

At the heart of any legal debate over an alternative Islamic banking system lies the definition of the word *riba*. The word is mentioned several times in the Qur'an. In a concise form, the rule can be stated thus: 'God has forbidden *riba*' (Q :II, 275). Depending on the domain subsumed under the word, a number of financial, commercial and legal transactions will be included in, or excluded from, the Qur'anic prohibition. The issue is complicated by the distinction, which appears in the *hadith*, between *riba an-nasi'a* and *riba al-fadl*.

Riba an-nasi'a is the classical form of *riba*, which entails – as in a loan – a fixed increase (*riba* comes from the root verb *raba*, *yarbu*, to increase) in the amount of money over a time period. *Riba al-fadl*, which occurs in a contract of sales when there is an increase in the terms of exchange themselves, is also prohibited following the Prophet's injunction. A *hadith* mentions six commodities which constitute the object of *riba al-fadl* (the exchange *riba*): 'Gold for gold, silver for silver, wheat for wheat, barley for barley, dates for dates, salt for salt, each kind for each kind, in hand: he who increases or asks for an increase commits *riba* (*arba*), alike whether he gives or takes.'[1]

In the modern banking world, it is the first *riba*, *riba an-nasi'a*, which is the main source of contention. If *riba* is defined as usury, then there is little problem in charging interest on transactions in the way of conventional banking. As long as interest rates do not hit unusual ceilings, which in any case are not quantified, the conventional banking system passes muster for the *shari'a*. If on the contrary *riba* is strictly defined as interest, then most operations by conventional banks are tainted with illegality. Between these two definitional poles the secular debate on *riba* has been built.[2]

In the twentieth century, the re-emergence of the debate started in Egypt with the '*Sunduq at-Tawfir*' affair and culminated in the discussions on the Civil Code. As capitalist penetration had developed in *fin-de-siècle* Cairo, a number of small-scale financial institutions had been created alongside the major foreign banks, following an imported model that had little concern for the religious sensitivities of the population. One of these small money-houses, the Administration of the Posts, established in the early twentieth century a 'Savings Fund' (Caisse d'Epargne, *Sunduq at-Tawfir*), which yielded to the depositors-savers a return in the form of a fixed interest. 'Over 3,000 from among the depositors refused, out of religious conviction (*tadayyunan*), to take their interest fixed by the decree of the Khedive'. Consequently, 'some men in government, including the director of the Administration of the Posts, asked the Mufti informally ... if there was a legal way that would authorise Muslims to take the profit earned by their monies in the Savings Fund'.[3]

In the account of Muhammad Rashid Rida (d. 1935), who was relating events that took place in 1903, the Mufti, Muhammad 'Abduh (d. 1905), was dissatisfied with the system introduced by the Savings Fund: 'He [Muhammad 'Abduh] said: in no way can the mentioned *riba* be accepted, and since the Posts' administration exploits the monies which it takes from the people [the depositors] and does not borrow from them out of necessity, it is possible for these monies to be put to use (*istighlal*) on the basis of the commenda partnership (*sharikat al-mudaraba*).'[4]

The polemic over *riba* in the Posts Savings Fund involved important personalities in the Azhar and in government. The question of *riba* never subsided, and its circumvoluted history involved the best lawyers in Egypt, including the most famous jurist in the Arab world, 'Abd al-Razzaq as-Sanhuri[5] and, more recently, the Egyptian Supreme Constitutional Court. Sanhuri, who presided over the drafting of the Egyptian Civil Code, was keen on excluding rulings which were in contradiction to the *shari'a*. Avoiding *riba* was central to Sanhuri's concern, and he went to great length in explaining how the Egyptian Civil Code (as well as most other Arab Codes which were modelled after it in Syria, Libya, Kuwait, and Iraq) was consonent with the *shari'a* in this respect.

Until the establishment of the new Civil Code, the civil laws of Egypt had been constituted in the main by a mixed system partly inherited from French laws, and partly fashioned by Qadri Basha's *Murshid al-Hayran*.[6] In the mid-1930s, a committee was established for the drafting of the new laws, and 'Abd ar-Razzaq as-Sanhuri was entrusted with bringing the project into a full Code. The work took more than a decade, and in 1949, the new Egyptian Civil Code was passed into law.[7]

Among the rules which had been thoroughly studied were the dispositions on interest. In the former Civil Code, the article related to loans and interests permitted, in the fashion of the European Civil Codes of the time, interest limited by a maximum rate. Article 125/185 read:

'It is absolutely forbidden for the contracting parties to agree on interests that exceed eight per cent per annum ... Any agreement stipulating an interest rate that exceeds this limit will be reduced to the maximum interest rate allowed [by this law] in the contract.'[8]

When the door was opened to redraft the old rules, the place of the *shari'a* in the Code was obviously a matter for long discussions, and the introductory articles placed it as one of the major sources in the Egyptian legal system. The debate between 'Abduh and the Khedive rebounded, and acquired wider importance because of its crucial area of application, Egypt's civil laws sphere. The question was whether a fixed interest over a contractual loan would remain possible.

On the whole, the old principles remained, but some measures were retained to keep the disposition under check:

(1) Article 232 stipulates that 'interest on interest is prohibited (*la yajuz taqadi fawa'ed 'ala mutajammid al-fawa'ed*)'. Under the previous Code this type of interest was permitted under two conditions (a) that accrued interests (*al-fawa'ed al-mutajammida*) would be running for no less than a year and (b) that an express stipulation in the contract between lender and borrower would permit an interest accrual. In the absence of such contract, the creditor-lender would have to bring the matter before the court for a decision.

(2) If borrower and lender do not agree on an interest on the loan, Article 542 considers that 'the loan will be deemed interest-free'.

(3) In case of delay after the payment is due, an interest of four per cent in civil and five per cent in commercial transactions will eventually be owed by the defaulting borrower (Art. 226). In this case, procedural rules are favourable to the debtor. A summons by the creditor, even if official, would not be sufficient for the legal interest to start running. The lender-creditor must file the complaint with the court, and specify in the writ brought to the tribunal that his right is not limited to the principal (*ra's al-mal*), but extends to the interest arising from the delay.

(4) The totality of interest due will not be superior to the principal. But this disposition, adopted probably from the Qur'anic injunction,[9] is not taken into account for long-term productive investments (Art.232).

(5) If the creditor proves bad faith in claiming the debt, the judge is allowed to reduce the legal interest, and even completely dispense with it (Art.229).

(6) If the borrower decides to repay the loan before it is due, Article 544 allows him to proceed without requiring the lender's agreement. Accelerated repayment cannot be precluded in the contract. But the borrower can exercise his right only six months after the contract, and he has six months, after the declaration of his intent to repay, to accelerate the payment of the debt to do so. The debtor incurs the interest on the debt for the full six months.

Despite all these stipulations in favour of the debtor, the most important principle adopted by the Civil Code is posited in Article 227:

> The contracting parties can agree on a different rate of interest, whether in return for a delay in the payment [this is related to Art. 226] or in any other situation [which includes the loan for interest], on condition that this rate does not exceed seven per cent. If they agree on an interest that exceeds this rate, this interest will be reduced to seven per cent, and any surplus already paid must be returned [to the borrower].

It is at the end of a long debate that the architects of the Egyptian Civil Code reached these conclusions which, except for some constraints on the creditor's stronger position, do not put into question the legitimacy of lending for a fixed interest. In his *Masadir al-Haqq fil-Fiqh al-Islami*,[10] which were developed in a series of lectures given in Cairo between 1954 and 1959, Sanhuri offers a lengthy analysis of *riba*.

Riba, in the general system of obligations and contracts, is classified along with other 'vices of consent' which (in French legal terminology) nullify a contract. In this perspective, *riba* is considered to be a major constraining factor behind the freedom of contract.

Because of the acceptance by the Egyptian Civil Code of interest arising from various contracts, and mainly loans, Sanhuri's understanding of *riba* is qualified by the necessity to abide by the dispositions written in the Code.

The whole defence of Article 227 is based on a double syllogism.

The starting point of the syllogism is that '*riba* is forbidden', and that there are three main reasons for the prohibition: '(1) To prevent the hoarding of people's foodstuffs; (2) To prevent speculating on currency, so that currency does not become itself a commodity; (3) To avoid unfairness and exploitation when the deal is related to a single commodity.'[11]

The two first reasons derive from simple public policy considerations. The third reason sheds light on the question of *riba al-fadl*, which, according to the *hadith*, is defined as the prohibition of the sale with an increase (*riba*) of two commodities of the same kind. For Sanhuri, this classification is an important element in the articulation of the syllogism.

This form of *riba*, *riba al-fadl*, writes Sanhuri, is forbidden in classical Islamic law as a prohibition of means (*saddan lidh-dhari'a*). It is not forbidden *per se*, because it is meant to stand in the way of the more fundamental *riba* of the *Jahiliyya* (pre-Islamic era of 'ignorance'), *riba an-nasi'a*. *Riba an-nasi'a*, however, is absolutely prohibited. It is prohibited *per se*. There are consequently different degrees of prohibition, and some are less absolute than others. The forms of *riba* that are prohibited for themselves can only be excused in case of absolute necessity. But those forms of *riba* which are prohibited because they can constitute a first step towards the original *riba an-nasi'a* do not fall under the same prohibitive regime. They, unlike *riba an-nasi'a*, can be tolerated in a situation of need.

For Sanhuri *riba an-nasi'a* merely means anatocism. It is the combined (*murakkab*) interest, which makes money deriving from interest as important as the original capital. This, he adds, has been forbidden by the Egyptian legislator in Article 232 of the Civil Code.

In Sanhuri's second part of the syllogism, the original ban on *riba* falls in the category of sales. It is in sales that the vice of *riba* operates, as is testified in the juxtaposition of the good sale, allowed by the scripture, and the bad *riba*, forbidden in the same verse 275 of the second *sura*. 'Loan', writes Sanhuri, 'is not in Islamic jurisprudence one of the root (*asl*) *ribawi* contracts. It is the contract of sale which is the root, and a loan will be measured against a sale.'[12] But the opposite is not true. The sale contract, as root, cannot be measured against the derivative category of loans.

Following the syllogism, the root and the derivative cannot be addressed legally in the same manner, and the prohibition attached to a root contract is more absolute than the prohibition attached to a derivative transaction.

Consequently, what is forbidden *per se* will yield, as in the case of *riba al-fadl*, to need. Need, and not necessity as in the root contract, will open the way to the alleviation of the prohibition, and in a capitalist society like Egypt, the need for loans is overwhelming, and common. It is at the heart of the economic system. As long as it does not become anatocism, as in Article 232, it must be tolerated by the legislator in accordance with the *shari'a*.

Thus is the Egyptian system vindicated.[13] By a series of syllogisms, Sanhuri shows that Article 227 is founded in the *shari'a*. It is clear that the avoidance of the concept of loan in the article was helpful in avoiding confronting the debate head-on, but it is true that Sanhuri also produced a sophisticated if unduly complex, legitimisation of the loan for interest.

This did not prevent the polemic over *riba* from continuing, until the challenge of the Civil Code provisions on interest (particularly Art. 226 and Art. 227) before the Supreme Constitutional Court of Egypt in 1985. The Court was able to avoid dealing with the issue on a technicality, but it is clear that the cyclical resurgence of *riba* would remain.[14]

A similar process took place in Iran. The Iranian Civil Code, which was passed in stages between 1928 and 1935, originally stipulated: 'The debtor can give a power of attorney to the lender, in binding form, providing that during the time that the debt is incumbent upon him, the lender may transfer to himself, from the property of the debtor, a specified quantity of things gratis' (Art. 653). Behind the cryptic formulation lurked, as in the elliptic words of Art. 227 of the Egyptian Civil Code, the underlying permission for charging interest, for this indeed is what is meant by 'the specified quantity of things to be transferred to the lender every month or every year, in binding form'. But, as could be expected, the reaction of the followers of Khumaini would be more radical than in Egypt. Whilst most of the Code has been retained, the caption '*hazf shodeh*' (deleted) has been appended to Art. 653 in the present editions of the Iranian Civil Code. But it is true that loans for interest were not specifically forbidden.

While the exact definition of *riba* is still widely debated, the advocacy of an economic and financial Islamic system has given way more recently to conceiving and setting up alternative *non-ribawi* (interest-free) banks. Before the development of this phenomenon across the Muslim world in the mid-1970s, Sadr had written extensively on *riba* and the conceptual framework of an Islamic bank.

Iqtisaduna on *riba* and Islamic economics

The concern with *riba* was not confined to Egypt, and in the early 1960s, the issue also surfaced in Iraq.[15] *Iqtisaduna*, inevitably, had a word to say on such an important matter, and Sadr discussed in it the prohibition of *riba* as a rule of considerable effect on the system of Islamic economics.

On the definition of *riba* proper, Sadr's departing point appears simple in contrast with the lengthy elaborations of the Egyptian jurists. He gives little consideration for the subtleties between *riba al-fadl* and *riba an-nasi'a*, avoids discussing the exceptional circumstances warranted by need or necessity, and starts with an outright condemnation of loan with interest.

> *Riba* in loan is *haram* (forbidden) in Islam, which means that you lend somebody money to an [agreed] time against interest (*fa'ida*), which the debtor (borrower) pays you when returning the money at the agreed time. Loan is forbidden except when free (*mujarrad*) from interest. The creditor is only entitled to a return of his money without supplement (increase, *ziyada*), however small the supplement may be. This legal disposition is considered, in its clarity under Islam, among the necessary rules (*daruriyyat*) of Islamic legislation. (*I* 544)

In *Iqtisaduna*, there is scarce mention of the banking system. The issue briefly surfaces on the occasion of the discussion on production. In that, Sadr adds little to the arguments expounded earlier by modern jurists like Muhammad 'Abduh or Rashid Rida.[16] The essential argument is based on the encouragement under the scheme of *mudaraba* of long-term projects as opposed to the short-term focus of capitalists lured by fixed, risk-free interest, in which, unlike in the *mudaraba*, they are not directly affected by the viability and soundness of productive investments (*I* 591–2).

More interestingly, the issue of *riba* in *Iqtisaduna* is analysed from the various angles of its impact on the distribution system. It comes for instance, as mentioned in chapter 4, at the origins of the distinction between compensation (salary, wage, *ajr*), which is allowed as financial reward not involving participation in the result of economic ventures, and profit, which is based on participation in the final result. In Sadr's system, for the tools (*adawat*) of production defined as 'the things and machines (*ashya' wa alat*) used in the [productive] operation, like the spinning machine (*maghzal*) and the plough..., the reward is legally limited to only one type (*uslub*): compensation (*ajr*)' (*I* 556). Tools of production and capital are opposed (*muta'akisan*):

> Commercial capital stands in contrast with tools of production. It is not permitted for capital to expand on the basis of compensation (salaries, *ujur*, plural of *ajr*). It is not permitted for the owner of capital to lend his money for interest, i.e. that he gives it to the entrepreneur (worker, *'amel*) to trade with and earn compensation for his work, because compensation is characterised by certainty (*daman*) and independence from the practical results as to profit and loss. It would otherwise be *riba*... It is however possible for the owner of capital or of a commodity to make available his property to the entrepreneur to trade with and be solely responsible for losses, and in case of profit, to share the profits on a percentage basis. Participation in profit as well as loss is the only way (*uslub*) legally open to commercial capital. (*I* 557)

The contrast between the legal regime of land and tools of production on the one hand and money as capital on the other hand appears as one of the major 'irradiations' of the legal system on the structure of distribution. From the prohibition of *riba* derive also other rules in *Iqtisaduna* (e.g. *I* 544, 556, 564, 575, 592), of which the most important is 'the linkage of the prohibition of *riba* with the negative side' of another rule, the prohibition in Islam of earning money without investing work in a venture (*I* 558, 564). Then the essential question of *riba* in the distributive process is formulated in the following manner: 'Why is it possible for labour to earn money on the basis of participation in profit, and not possible for such a participation on the basis of production? Why have the tools of production been prevented from this way of making money when the owner of commercial capital or of land can earn money in this very way?' (*I* 568).

The answer must be sought in the Islamic scheme of pre-production distribution. 'The owner of land in a contract of *muzara'a*, the owner of capital in the contract of *mudaraba* ... who are allowed a share in the profit [on capital or on land], are in reality the owners of the material that the worker uses (*mumarasa*)' (*I* 570). Under the principle of 'permanence of ownership',[17] labour in the case of land or capital is considered to be stored (*mukhtazan*). It is not so stored, Sadr explains, in the case of the tools of production. The owner of the tool has merely the right to let it. Like the person who gives another his net to fish with, the jurists have allowed no right to a share in the product of the owner of the tools of production. The only right of the owner of the fishing net or of the tool of production is immediate (*mubashar*), and takes the legal form of compensation (*ajr*) on the work resulting from the use of the productive tool (*I* 570).

Clearly, Sadr's use of *riba* in *Iqtisaduna* was not significant in financial or banking terms. The rules on the prohibition of *riba* were introduced to bolster the scheme of ownership of land and of the tools of production. *Riba* was important as a contrasting point to the agricultural and industrial sectors of the Islamic economy. But this was not the Najaf jurist's last word on the subject.

Riba in *al-Bank al-la Ribawi fil-Islam*

Complex as it may have been, the previous debate on *riba* was impressed with one major characteristic. It operated in a negative manner. The thrust of the discussions was centred on the definition of *riba*, and included little by way of a positive construction of a viable alternative in the contemporary financial world.

This attitude was understandable, and reflected an economic situation which was not concerned with the mobilisation of a vast surplus of liquidities. The oil boom changed the picture of money flow radically, and one urgent problem facing the Arab and Islamic world was how to utilise effectively the petrodollars without openly flouting the *shari'a*. The debate shifted to the Arabian peninsula and to the oil-rich countries of the Gulf.

The question of *riba* emerged again, but the context was different. For those concerned, the premise was that *riba* simply meant interest, and loans for interest – the backbone of banking operations – could consequently not be accepted. The question revolved on the possibility for a bank, as it is known in Western capitalist countries, to lend its money and make profits without charging interest on these loans, and to attract deposits from its clients without rewarding them with a fixed interest.

In theory, the answer was simple. The key concept was *mudaraba*, and the contract of *mudaraba* was to replace the loan and deposit for interest. This had already been the answer of Muhammad 'Abduh at the turn of the century.

In view of the complexities of the banking world, more was however needed, and the Egyptian financial forays were no more than intellectual skirmishes. In the late 1960s, the urgency of investing oil money prompted some circles in the Gulf to look into the *riba* prohibition from a positive angle. It was not any more a question of simple obligations as in Articles 226 and 227 of the Egyptian Civil Code, but the whole set-up of 'money-houses', their internal structure as well as the exact form of their various operations. To date, the most original work on the subject remains Muhammad Baqer as-Sadr's.[18]

A sign of the new platform of concerns was the relegation of Sadr's discussion of the problems connected with the definition of *riba* to the book's appendix. In this appendix (*IFB* 164–83), Sadr tries 'to tackle, from the jurisprudential (*fiqh*) point of view, the various legal arguments (*takhrijat*) which aim at transforming interest (*fa'ida*) into a legitimate profit and at developing it in an acceptable (*mashru'*) way' (*IFB* 164).

Sadr was manifestly disturbed with the various excuses which work towards justifying charging interest on transactions, and he sets out to undermine the arguments systematically. Several such justifications are discussed. For our purposes, the presentation of two main arguments is sufficient.

One legal justification is based on a distinction made in the loan operation, between the money on which the contract is made and the operation of lending itself. Under this justification, if interest is charged on the money as the object of the loan, it is *riba*. If, however, it is attached to the operation itself, it becomes *ju'ala* under the law.

A definition of *ju'ala* was already given in *Iqtisaduna*: '*Ju'ala*', Sadr then wrote, 'is permitted by the *shari'a*. *Ju'ala* is the undertaking (*iltizam*) by a person to offer a reward for another person's purposeful legitimate action (*mukafa'a 'ala 'amal sa'egh maqsud*)' (*I* 546). The example given is of a person who offers a reward for another who looks for his lost book, or weaves him a cloth. In *al-Bank al-la Ribawi fil Islam*, the justification of interest is exemplified by the 'person who sets up a *ju'ala* in which he establishes a fee (*ju'l*) on a loan, e.g. who says: he who lends me a dinar gets a dirham' (*IFB* 165). In this way, interest would be charged as fee on the operation of lending, and not on the money lent.

Sadr offers two reasons to invalidate this justification: from a 'minor' point of view (*min jihat as-sughra*), this can be considered as a pure artifice of the language. In reality, the concept of *ju'ala* is misplaced. *Ju'ala* operates only in matters 'involving labour, and not money'(*IFB* 166). From a major point of view (*min jihat al-kubra*), even if we suppose that the intent of the reward was indeed the lending operation, an essential element of the *ju'ala* is undermined, which is its intimate connection with the concept of '*ujrat al-*

mithl'.[19] The money to which a *ju'ala* is 'equivalent' can only be the money rewarding work. It cannot be money rewarding money, since this would logically mean that compensation is duplicated, as the price would be both in the activity carried out (in a normal *ju'ala*, e.g. weaving the cloth; in the *ju'ala* of lending, the operation of lending) *and* in the object of the activity (the cloth, the money lent). This is unacceptable under the *shari'a* (*IFB* 166–8).

Another legal justification for the charging of interest can be found in qualifying the lending operation in a different form, for instance as a sale. This is the classical example of A selling X to B for a sum of money Y, with the understanding that B would resell X back to A at an agreed time with an increase y on Y. With X just a token, the operation of sales would be in effect a loan in which A is the lender, B the borrower, Y the capital lent and returned, and y the interest.[20] This, and the variations on the theme,[21] are discarded following '*as-sayyed al-ustadh dama zilluhu*',[22] because they are simply 'loans which have been disguised under sales'. This rejection, from a minor point of view, is based on 'the representation of the parties' real intent (*tashkhis al-murad al-jaddi lil-muta'amilayn*)'. Clearly real intent is here the loan not the sales. From a major point of view, the rejection is based on 'the extension of the ambit of loan on customary basis (*bi hasab al-irtikaz al-'urfi*)... The sale of [money against more money] on credit is a customary loan (*qard 'urfi*)' (*IFB* 176–7).

The whole debate in this section remains, in the vein of the Egyptian discussion, negative, and this is peripheral to Sadr's purposes, which, in the text of *al-Bank al-la Ribawi*, were mainly directed at convincing the reader of the viability of an interest-free bank in its full operational capacity.

An Islamic bank in an adverse economic environment

The context in which Sadr wrote his scheme of an interest-free bank was quite different from both the time of *Iqtisaduna* and the later period of revolutionary fervour in Iran and Iraq.

The difference with the early 1960s was in the new emphasis in presenting Islam as an alternative to Capitalism. In *Iqtisaduna*, the concern with Capitalism was inversely proportional to the fear of Communism. But with the new flow of money, Islam had now to appear as a convincing alternative to the seemingly boundless capitalist energy released by oil.

Sadr took advantage of a query addressed to him by a committee based in the Kuwaiti Ministry for *awqaf* (endowments), to bring this project to fruition (*IFB* vi).

From the outset of *al-Bank al-la Ribawi*, a distinction was made between a bank established 'within a comprehensive planning of the society, i.e. after [Islam] has taken over the leadership in all sectors (*marafiq*) of society', and between 'an interest-free bank established regardless of other aspects of society, i.e. with the supposition that the bad (*fased*) state of things in place continues, as well as the un-Islamic framework of society, the persistence of the other various institutions, banks and others, and the domination (*tafashshi*) of the capitalist system in letter and spirit on the economic, mental, and ethical (*khulqi*) life of man' (*IFB* 5).

Sadr acknowledges the difficulty in forming an institution which, within the system, would be operating against the stream. 'The fragmentation of practice' and 'the partial application of the idea of the prohibition of *riba*' entail that the principle 'will not come to total fruition'. This should however not 'constitute an excuse for shying away from the [proper] legal application wherever possible' (*IFB* 6). It is absolutely necessary that, within these constraints, the interest-free bank, through abiding by the dominant law, 'remains able to function and prosper within the frame of the surrounding reality, as a commercial enterprise aiming at profit'; in other words, as a bank 'which has the same role as other banks in the economy, ... a vanguard role in developing countries, ... and the effective participation in the development of industry' (*IFB* 9).

The interest-free bank: introductory remarks

The prototype of the interest-free bank is vital for the ideological battle of Islam. Some sacrifices will be made 'to carry the burden of the [Islamic] message and the preparation to save the community and its institutions from their state of disbelief, *kufr*' (*IFB* 12). In order to rid the world of *riba*, the first principle is the necessary 'emphasis on the element of human labour as the source of revenue (*dakhl*), as opposed to the element of capital in banking activities ... Whereas the *ribawi* bank exercises its activities in its quality of capitalist person, the interest-free bank insists on its quality of labourer'. This appears, on the one hand, in 'the emphasis of the interest-free bank on revenue (*'umula*) as a salary for work (*ujrat 'amal*), and the increase in profits on the basis of these revenues (*'umulat*)'. On the other hand, it appears 'in the interest-free bank's refusal (*ta'affuf*) to take interest on loans, because this interest is revenue on capital and represents capital's *ribawi* power' (*IFB* 11).

Within this setting, Sadr admits one exception, when the interest-free bank deals with conventional institutions working on the basis of interest. While refraining from lending against interest, the interest-free bank can 'indulge in placing deposits bearing interest in the banks that belong to people who do not believe in Islam, or in banks of states that do not adopt Islam as a system of government' (*IFB* 13). Two arguments are advocated by Sadr to defend this position:

(1) One argument is based on realism. It is because of the mere existence of such conventional banks that the interest-free bank is forced to find itself in unfair competitive practices.
(2) Legally, several jurists, both among the Shi'is and the Sunnis, like Abu Hanifa himself, have permitted the practice of *riba* with non-believers (*dhimmis*), and allowed taking profit (*ziyada*) from them (*IFB* 13–14).

After these preliminary remarks, Sadr introduces his discussion of an Islamic bank by setting some of the parameters chosen for his study.

In the first place, he posits the distinction between an Islamic bank operating in an 'Islamic' environment, where all *riba* is prohibited, and an Islamic bank operating in competition with interest-bearing capitalist institutions. In his 1969 scheme of the Islamic bank, the discussion deals only with the latter category.

Secondly, Sadr underlines the general principle which underlies the whole system proposed in *Iqtisaduna*, and which establishes as well all profit-making in an Islamic bank: the emphasis is not on the revenue-generating power of capital, but on the wealth-creating power of human labour.[23]

Thirdly, a dose of realism is said to be necessary. An Islamic bank, Sadr writes, cannot avoid dealing with conventional banks on a fixed interest basis.[24] This realism is well-founded in Islam, both from a historical-economic and from a legal point of view.

There follows that, from an economic point of view, the prototype of a bank is based on its role as mediator (intermediary, *wasit*), between depositors and investors-entrepreneurs. From the legal point of view, the bank's operations are generally constituted by two independent legal relationships: the bank is a debtor of the depositors, and a creditor for the entrepreneurs. In conventional banking therefore, the bank does not operate legally as an intermediary, but as a full party to the transactions: the link between, on the one hand, the pool of funds constituted by capital and deposits, and loans for business on the other hand, is completely severed.

'As a debtor of the depositors, the [conventional] bank pays them interest if their deposits are not under demand [i.e. fixed], and as a creditor to the investors, the bank receives a higher interest... It is in this way that the regime of deposits and lending associated with the *riba* forbidden by Islam' can be established (*IFB* 20–1).

Sadr's alternative is based on the following reasoning:

> The basic idea that I am trying to expose in order for a bank to develop on an Islamic basis which would protect it from dealing with *riba* is premised on the separation in the deposits the bank receives between fixed (time, term) deposits and mobile (current, demand) deposits (*wada'e' thabita wa ukhra mutaharrika, jariya*). (*IFB* 21)

Instead of the fiction necessary to conventional banking, which ignores the economic role of the bank as an intermediary and severs the connection between deposits and loans, the theory of Islamic banking proposed by Sadr enhances this role, and establishes a correspondence between the bank's resources (Capital + Deposits) and the bank's investments in loans. By classifying deposits as fixed and mobile, the theory is mainly directed towards the positioning of the bank as an intermediary for long-term deposits and loans.[25]

Before addressing the main theme of Sadr's work, the bank in its activities as the intermediary party between depositors and investors for long-term deposits, the analysis will turn to Sadr's conception of the regime of fixed and mobile deposits.

The interest-free bank between depositors and investors

A The regime of term (fixed) deposits

The central operative contract in the bank's intermediation between investors and depositors is the *mudaraba*, the commenda (also translated in the literature as 'partnership for profit and loss').

Sadr defines the *mudaraba* as

> a nominate [special, *khass*] contract between the owner of capital [lender, *mudarib*] and the investor-entrepreneur [borrower, *mustathmir*] to establish a trade [or enterprise] with the capital of the former and the labour of the latter, whereby they specify the share of each in the profit on a percentage basis. If the enterprise is profitable, they will share the profit according to the agreed percentage; if the capital remains as it was, the owner of capital will receive his capital back, and the worker will get nothing. If the enterprise makes a loss, and the capital is consequently diminished, the owner of capital only will bear the loss. (*IFB* 25)[26]

The three parties to the *mudaraba* are therefore the depositor (*mudarib*), the entrepreneur-investor (*mudarab*, *mustathmir*) or agent ('*amel*), and the bank which is the intermediary between the depositor and the entrepreneur, as well as the agent (*wakil*) of the owner of capital deposited in its safes.

Rights and duties of the depositor. Among the duties of the depositor in the interest-free bank, two are important: (1) The depositor cannot withdraw his money before six months; (2) The depositor must agree to the principle of *mudaraba*. The deposit need not be tied to a special transaction. Small deposits will also be accepted to enlarge the overall operational pool of the banks.

As for rights, once the money is deposited in the bank, the depositor retains his ownership of the amount deposited, but this amount is added to the pool of deposits which constitutes the capital invested in the business projects.

The deposit is beneficial for the depositor in three ways:

(1) It is guaranteed by the bank. The investor must not be asked to guarantee the deposit under the terms of the *mudaraba*, but there is no rule preventing the bank, as third party, from offering its own safeguards to the depositor (*IFB* 32–3).[27]

(2) Instead of a fixed return on his money, like in conventional banking, and as an owner of a share in the investment, the depositor receives a percentage of the profits made by the investment. In this way, the return is proportionate to the investment profitability. Loss, adds Sadr, is unlikely, since the deposit is tied not to a particular project, which might be independently unsuccessful, but to the totality of the bank's investment activities. How is this share calculated?

Sadr offers an arithmetical example to develop his argument (*IFB* 34–6). The argument is not easy to follow, but it is interesting as an example of Sadr's concern for practicality. The example is here reproduced according to the three lines along which it operates:

(a) Total deposits: 100,000
Profit: 20%
Interest paid by a conventional bank: 5%

In this case, the Islamic bank ought to pay twenty-five per cent of the profit, so that its rate does not get below the rate offered by a competing conventional bank.

(b) Consequently, the share of depositor = Interest + interest × risk (of non-profit, i.e. not having enough profit because of general circumstances) + interest × incomplete use of deposits.

(c) If interest rate = 5% and
risk of non-profit = 10%,
then, increase = average interest rate × risk of non-profit of the *mudaraba*. The equation will then be increase = $5/100 \times 10/100 = 1/200$ and total share of depositor = $5/100 + 1/200 = 55/1000$.

This last rate is called by Sadr 'share of profit' on the *mudaraba*. If the expectation of profit is twenty per cent on a capital of 1000 dinar,
then profit = 200 dinar,
but the share of profit = 55 dinar
and the percentage of the depositor's share of profit = $55/200 \times 100$ = 27,5% of profit.[28]

(3) The third advantage to the depositor is his ability to withdraw his deposit. Since these deposits are 'time', 'fixed' deposits, the bank can regulate them in such a way as to give more flexibility to the depositors' right of withdrawal. The depositors in this scheme should be able to withdraw some of their monies almost at will, since all the depositors will not be expected to withdraw their monies simultaneously. Sadr offers several ways to enhance the flexibility of the withdrawal process (*IFB* 38–9).

Rights and duties of the bank. The bank is not properly a full party to the *mudaraba* transaction. As an intermediary between the two fundamental parties, the investor and the depositor, it enjoys however special rights and obligations.

The bank receives a *ju'ala* (fee, commission, remuneration) for its intermediation in two ways. The first is a fixed salary (*ajr thabet*) on its work. In conventional banking, this work is rewarded by the difference between the interest given to depositors and the interest earned on the loans. The Islamic bank operates differently, since it cannot relegate, as conventional banks do, the ultimate loss to the entrepreneur-borrower. 'Therefore', concludes Sadr, 'the salary of the Islamic bank should be higher than the interest differential of the conventional bank' (*IFB* 42).

The second aspect of the *ju'ala* is the share of the bank in the entrepreneur's profit. Sadr proceeds by comparing (in a rather confused way) the approach of conventional and Islamic banks to capital, and notes that the Islamic banks, although they do not share in principle the idea of 'the salary of capital' (*ujrat ra's al-mal*), will be compelled to develop such an idea under conditions of competition with conventional banks.

In conclusion, he states that 'the Islamic bank will subtract from the profits (on the *mudaraba* project) what is over the agreed share of the agent of the *mudaraba*, and this part of the profits from several *mudaraba* operations is the total amount of the profit that should be distributed between the bank and the depositors' (*IFB* 47).

The bank will also enlarge the pool of money available for investment with parts of its own capital and with what it considers feasible to invest from the deposits on current accounts. In this case, the bank becomes the *mudarib* itself, and will be entitled to the full share of the money guaranteed and the returns constituted by the value of the risk of capital. However, the bank will invest the money of its depositors before using its own money.

Rights and duties of the agent-entrepreneur. The entrepreneur, whether dealing with a conventional bank or an Islamic one, is the 'absolute possessor of the right' on the profits of the enterprise in which he or she is engaged. The interest paid by the borrower-entrepreneur to the lending conventional bank is equivalent to the total amount paid by the entrepreneur to the Islamic bank in terms of fixed money + percentage of the profit to the depositor. 'But the Islamic bank earns in addition to this [sum] a share of the profit realised by the agent, which amounts to the difference between the price of guaranteed capital and the price of capital the value of which has been at risk' (*IFB* 49). This increase stems from the guarantee that the bank offers to capital in case of loss.

Since the bank covers the loss of capital in the Islamic system, the survival of the Islamic bank is obviously premised on the profitability of the project. How can the bank protect itself from unscrupulous borrowers who know that the loss of their projects will ultimately affect the bank, as these borrowers would stand to lose nothing except the time involved in the project?

Sadr's answer is of a more psychological than economic-legal nature, as he insists on the necessity for the bank to deal with honest and capable entrepreneurs, and to scrutinise every project. This, says Sadr, should help projects which involve specific and punctual commercial deals. For long-term economic projects based on the establishment of a commercial institution, the bank can supervise the company directly.

B *Profit and the Islamic bank*

Sadr introduces the discussion on the profits of an Islamic bank as an accounting problem. He reviews the situations in which the projects sponsored by the bank do not correspond in the accounting of their revenues with the bank's annual reports, then devises a number of simple ways to assess the profits in view of an eventual return for the bank's depositors.

More interesting however is the analysis of the profits distribution for the proposed Islamic bank.

The answer to the question would be easy, Sadr suggests, if all the fixed deposits were to be exploited at once. That would render the factor of time equal in all situations, and the arithmetics of the distribution of profits would be as simple as dividing the total amount of profits by the ratio of deposits.

In reality, deposits do not enter the bank all at the same time, and they do not get the same type of return. It would be extremely difficult for the bank to trace each return to each deposit. On the other hand, if only the factor of time is taken into account for the distribution of profits, one would return to a manifest *ribawi* situation, where a deposit-loan in the bank would be automatically rewarded according to its quantity and the amount of time it has been sitting with the bank. 'This is why we suggest that the bank establishes its accounts on the supposition that each fixed deposit which enters its safes will start being exploited two months (for example) after the deposits (this calculation varies according to the conditions of commerce, and to the degree of general demand for capital), and that it would not start being exploited before' (*IFB* 58).

There remains the point that one deposit might be more profitable than another deposit. The way out for the bank is to equalise all deposits by asking the depositor to agree to a general rate of return on the whole pool of deposits, and not to a specified rate on his own deposit.[29] In effect, Sadr's proposed system transforms the classical two-party *mudaraba* contract into a multi-party system epitomised by the pooling of the totality of deposits.

C *The regime of mobile deposits* (*IFB* 65–8)

The legal status of mobile deposits, 'which generally constitute the current account', is much simpler than the one which characterises fixed deposits. Because of the uncertainty and instability of these deposits, which can be withdrawn on the depositor's demand, *mudaraba* is more difficult to carry out on their basis. In turn, no interest or compensation will generally be paid on mobile deposits.

The bank can, however, differentiate between several types of such deposits. Part of the mobile deposits will be kept by the bank to cater for the liquidity necessitated by the nature of the deposits to repay depositors on demand. Another part will be used in *mudaraba* operations. This time, however, the bank will act as entrepreneur, and not as intermediary. A third part will be used by the banks to help cover the needs, other than in *mudaraba* projects, of its best clients. This should not, adds Sadr, relegate *mudaraba* to a second place. After all, the importance of an interest-free bank in a conventional environment is to encourage a climate in which *mudaraba* becomes the norm rather than the exception.

In the use of mobile deposits, the bank will pay attention to a number of conditions. The borrower must have a good established reputation, and the bank must be able to assess the validity of the operation undertaken. To this effect, collateral may be required from the borrower as security. Repayment of the loan must not exceed three months. This will guarantee that borrowing for longer-term operations will take the normal form of *mudaraba*.

The interest-free bank's activities

From the general regulation of the relationship between the bank, the depositors and the borrowers, Sadr moves to the second part of his thesis, which discusses various financial transactions of the interest-free bank permitted under the *shari'a*.

A Deposits, loans, and the compensation theory

In traditional banks, one finds, says Sadr, three types of accounts for customers, which correspond to two kinds of deposits: current accounts (*hisab jari*) corresponding to imperfect deposits, which are deposits under immediate demand (*wada'e' naqisa, tahta at-talab*); deposit accounts (*iddikhar*); and saving accounts (*tawfir*). The latter two correspond to perfect (or complete) deposits, which are time deposits.

In Islamic banking, such a concept of deposit is unknown. In its stead, all the monies deposited in the bank are considered 'loans always due or due at a particular moment' (*qurud mustahaqqat al-wafa' aw fi ajal muhaddad*) (*IFB* 84).

The legal concepts which underlie transactions carried out by Islamic banks and by traditional banks are different, even though the practice may indicate that Islamic banks take the same position vis-à-vis deposits under immediate demand. Islamic banks consider these deposits as loans by the depositors to the bank. Such deposits yield no interest.

In the West, adds Sadr, the deposit in the current account has slowly developed from a contract of compensation (*muqassa*) that was first decided by the courts, then was increasingly adopted as an autonomous transaction. The current account was therefore a 'contract between the bank and the depositor (*'amil*), in which the personal [subjective] rights lose their personalisation' (*sic*, *IFB* 86). Slowly, these rights are lost in the developing contract, and the idea of compensation between the rights of the bank – as a substitute to the borrower taking a loan from the bank – recede in proportion to the degree of autonomy achieved by the 'current account' contract.

Under Islamic law in contrast, the theory of virtual compensation that at one time underlay the early banking system of the West is not necessary.

'Then there is no need for current accounts. The virtuality of the subjective personality of the rights vanishing in *vis-à-vis* [because of the compensation theory] (*dhawaban al-fardiyya adh-dhatiyya lil-huquq al-mutaqabila*)', makes it feasible for a nominate contract, the *mudaraba*, to emerge. If one considers the borrower's withdrawal of funds from the bank as the expression of a loan from the bank in return for him lending to the bank (i.e. when he deposited his money in the account), it follows that two obligations are 'in *vis-à-vis*' (*mutaqabila*), and mandatory compensation, *muqassa jabriyya*, takes place without the necessity for any transaction or for a formal agreement between the bank and the '*amel*, the agent (borrower-depositor).

This mandatory compensation is accepted by most jurists in the *shari'a*, particularly, adds Sadr, the Hanafis and the Imamis. In their writings, the *muqassa jabriyya* has also been known as *tahatur* (*IFB* 87).

B *The cheque as transaction*

There are in Sadr's theory, two ways to explain the cheque as a legal operation when the drawer of the cheque has a creditor account in the bank. The first possibility is the concept of *istifa'*.[30] In the theory of *istifa'*, the cheque is considered as 'a bill of exchange-assignment[31] from the debtor to his creditor, drawn on the bank where the debtor (drawer) owns his mobile deposits (*wada'e' mutaharrika*)' (*IFB* 93). This operation of *istifa'* is legal.

If, on the other hand, the operation of the cheque is considered a new loan from the bank on which the cheque is drawn, whereby two obligations are created, the Islamic rules on lending must be respected. 'It is not possible to draw on the [bank] account by way of cheques, if they are considered as loans, unless the drawer, the bank employee or the drawee themselves receive (*qabada*) the amount drawn ... The reception (*qabd*) by the debtor [i.e the cheque drawer] or his agent-proxy [i.e. the bank employee or the creditor] is considered a basic condition for the validity of the loan under Islamic law' (*IFB* 93).[32]

It follows, concludes Sadr, that in order to avoid the necessity to perform the act of receiving the money required by the cheque theory as combination of loans, it is preferable to resort to the first, and simpler theory, legitimating the transactions on cheques of interest-free banking through the theory of *istifa'*.

These two theories presuppose that the drawer has a positive credit account with the bank. In the situation in which the drawer does not have enough funds to cover such a cheque, a problem arises. Where the theory underlying the transaction is based on the concept of loan, the formal conditions necessary for the loan must be present. However, the assignment (*hawala*) theory is more convenient in this case, 'for the assignee is not a debtor of the assignor, and the jurists agree on this [i.e on this way to legitimise the transaction] as *hawala 'alal-bari'*, assignment to the third party,[33] and I consider it a correct assignment which can be executed by acceptance from the bank' (*IFB* 94).

In this situation, there are liabilities which the accepting bank charges the cheque drawer for, such as 'postage fees, periodical fees for checking on accounts ... These are all valid' (*IFB* 95).

C Theory of deposits

In the first part of *al-Bank al-la Ribawi*, Sadr had addressed the question of deposits from the point of view of the relationship between the bank, the depositor and the borrower. Here the emphasis is on the legal theory of deposits as he derives it from the *shari'a*.

Deposits in traditional banks operate as interest-bearing funds. As such, they are unacceptable for Islamic banking, which ought to reconvert them into legally admitted operations such as *mudaraba*.

(a) Savings Deposits, *wada'e' at-tawfir*. These deposits are understood to be 'accounts in a register (*daftar*) which must be produced every time a deposit or a withdrawal is undertaken'. Like fixed deposits, they should operate in an Islamic bank on the basis of *mudaraba*.

There are two important differences in the regime of savings deposits in an interest-free bank: (1) The saver should be allowed to withdraw his money at will, whereas fixed deposits must remain with the bank for a term of no less than six months; (2) The Islamic bank can reserve a percentage of the savings deposit to be considered as a loan, and kept as fiduciary money which will not go into exploitation (*IFB* 97).

(b) Real Deposits, *al-wada'e' al-haqiqiyya*. These funds, which the depositor keeps with the bank for safety and storage, do not differ in any way from their regime under traditional banking. A fee on the keeping of real deposits is valid.

The economic role of bank deposits, says Sadr, has traditionally been threefold:

(1) Deposits are a means of multiplying funds, through 'the strong guarantees deriving from the element of trust in banks. Thus, the means of payment [i.e. circulation] expand in the commercial and economic ambits' (*IFB* 98–9).

(2) Deposits represent monies that were, until kept with the banks, economically idle. By joining the economic markets, these deposits contribute to the activation (*in'ash*) of the country's economy, and of its industrial and economic growth.

(3) Deposits contribute to an increased fiduciary relationship (*i'timan*),[34] and have an inherent capacity to multiply through business.

These three points are discussed in turn by Sadr from the point of view of the *shari'a*.

(1) As a means of payment, through the issuance of cheques, deposits become 'debts towards the depositors with the bank' (*IFB* 100). But as for all debts, they are bound by two prescriptions of the law.

One debt can be used to offset another debt by way of transfer (*hawala*) and the cheque can be used as a means of payment, i.e. as a tool of debt redemption (*adat wafa'*).

The debt can be used 'as the means of payment in which the contract vests immediately, as when the creditor buys with the debt he has with the debtor some merchandise, or when he donates this debt to another person' (*IFB* 100).

Under Islamic law, the last alternative can be accepted only if certain conditions are fulfilled: (1) As long as the merchandise purchased is not a future (*mu'ajjal*) commodity, for in that case, debt would be bought against debt, and such a transaction is prohibited; (2) If the creditor donates his debt to another person, the donee can only be the debtor himself. Otherwise the donation is considered null, for 'the reception by the donee of the money donated is a condition of validity in the donation' (*IFB* 100).

In conclusion, Sadr suggests excluding the complications of the second theory, and simply retaining the first one. Cheques should be seen as means of payment used as tools of redemption. Under this legal theory, they are valid under the *shari'a*.

(2) Sadr sees no problem with the second view of deposits as a way to accumulate capital for economic use. But the traditional theory is acceptable only if the utilisation of the monies is achieved by way of the *mudaraba*.

(3) The theory of creation by deposits of a more extensive fiduciary circulation (*i'timan*) in banking prompts the following legal question:

'Is it possible for the Islamic bank to create *i'timan*, and therefore a larger state of indebtedness than the amount of deposits kept in its possession?'(*IFB* 102).

Three hypotheses (*IFB* 102–5) are used to illustrate the problem, and the way Sadr views its accordance with the law:

(a) The bank has 1,000 dinars on deposit. Two prospective borrowers come for a loan each, and the bank commits itself (*yaltazim*), knowing that the two borrowers would be depositing the money borrowed from it, and that they would not withdraw it at the same time.

(b) The bank has 1,000 dinars on deposit. One prospective borrower gets a loan of 1,000 dinars from the bank, and pays it to his creditor, who in turn deposits the money with the bank. Another borrower appears who gets a 1,000 dinars loan from the bank. The bank will have, again, lent 2,000 dinars when it only had 1,000 in its coffers.

(c) The bank has 1,000 dinars on deposit. Two drafts are written on the bank, 1,000 dinars each, by persons who have no account with the bank. The bank accepts both drafts as loans and receives interest on them, even though it has only 1,000 dinars on deposit, because the creditors of the two drawers will not, in the bank's calculation, withdraw their monies simultaneously.

These three hypotheses, which illustrate the ability of the bank to capitalise on its deposits, are used by Sadr to show how current banking transactions may or may not be acceptable to the law.

Cases (b) and (c) offer an example of the validity of modern transactions in the light of the *shari'a*. Case (b) is, for Sadr, constituted by two separate loans, in which the receipt (*tasallum*) of money is immediate. Both loans are therefore valid.

In case (c), the bank's indebtedness stems from its acceptance of the two drafts as guarantee of the loan transaction. The bank will be duly considered a creditor for 2,000 dinars to the drafters and a debtor for 2,000 dinars to the draftees.

In both cases, the legal cause exists and is valid. In case (b), the receipt (*qabd*) by the borrower of the money lent is the underlying legal cause. In case (c), the cause is the acceptance of the draft by the bank.

In case (a), however, Sadr does not seem to find sufficient legal grounding to legitimise the bank's loans to the borrowers. The problem in the legal theory resides in that the bank merely promises to secure the loan of 1,000 dinars for each prospective borrower, at a time when it does not possess the money in its safes. This engagement, or promise to lend (*iltizam*), is not acceptable under Islamic law, because 'the element of receipt (*qabd*), which is necessary by law for the loan', is absent from the transaction.

There follows an important precision. In case (a), Sadr suggests that the transaction is void because the formal act of receipt has not taken place. But this 'receipt' does not mean that the money lent should actually be severed definitively from the lender, the bank, and enter the formal possession of the borrower. The borrower could take the money and deposit it in his current account with the bank. But would that not constitute the elements that define mandatory compensation (*muqassa jabriyya*) which was earlier depicted as an obligatory mechanism operating inevitably when two obligations are in *vis-à-vis*? In this case, would that automatic operation not undermine the whole transaction by voiding automatically both loans – the loan from the bank to the borrowers, and the loan from the borrower-depositor to the bank?

The answer is no. There is in this case no compensation, because the two loans have fundamentally different terms. The borrower in the first loan has contracted an obligation that has a more or less long term. But when the borrower turned depositor opens a current account with the loan just received, no time terms are attached to the transaction, and the mandatory compensation does not operate.

D *Other transactions*

Al-Bank al-la Ribawi devotes a long section to a number of current financial transactions that are traditionally performed in a banking system. These transactions are discussed by Sadr, again, from the point of view of their conformity with the *shari'a* precepts. These transactions are divided into three categories.

First category: Services to customers

The first category is related to the services that the bank renders to its customers, and the interest-commission that it culls for its services. The basic question which determines whether this or that service is valid depends on a number of variables, which are then methodically discussed.

Under the heading 'the first part of the bank's activities' (*IFB* 106–52), a long section is devoted to various services in modern banking, which are also discussed in some detail with a view to their conformity with the policy of an interest-free bank.

There are several such services, which Sadr lists as 'the collection of cheques, the collection of drafts, the documentary collection, the acceptance of cheques, and drafts' (*IFB* 106). The guiding thesis for the enquiry into all these transactions is derived from the question posed about the cheque: 'Can the bank, from a legal point of view, receive a fee, *'umula, ujra*, on the collection of a cheque?' (*IFB* 108).

Many sections and subsections are devoted to these banking operations. For the purpose of our analysis however, only some of Sadr's most significant analyses will be presented.

Cheques. Sadr had already addressed the legality of cheques viewed as transactions between parties through the bank. He offered two juristic justifications (the theory of *istifa'*, and the theory of loan combination), and suggested that the first theory was more encompassing and simpler. Here the issue is the validity of charging a fee for the role of the bank in the clearing operation.

Sadr is aware that in practice, a bank will not generally take a fee on its clients' drawing a cheque, except in some cases where the transaction is international and involves services abroad (*IFB* 108n.). But he is none the less interested in the validity of the principle of charging a fee from the point of view of Islamic jurisprudence.

Sadr examines two legal arguments bearing on the operation. It is, he writes, either a matter of a single or double transfer, or a transfer combined with a sale. The transaction is a single transfer if the cheque is drawn in the same place and by the same bank where it will be collected by the beneficiary-drawee, i.e. by the creditor whose debt is requited by the cheque. But the transaction would be a double transfer if a different bank is involved. In this case, there is a transfer from the drawer of the cheque on the bank where the cheque is drawn, but the collector of the cheque deals with a different bank, which credits the amount of the cheque on its accounts with the first bank. This means, adds Sadr, that the first bank has passed the cheque of the drawer onto the second bank. The collection will have been constituted by two successive transfers.

But the cheque can also be conceived as an operation combining a transfer and a sale. The drawer endorses the cheque for the benefit of the drawee through the bank, and the drawee becomes the owner of the value of the cheque. Then the sales transaction operates when the drawer-owner sells the share he possesses with the bank, and this will be a sale of debt.

Whether the first or the second justifications are adopted, Sadr continues, the operation of the cheque is valid under Islamic law. However, in terms of the fee collected on the drawing of a cheque, it is acceptable in Sadr's opinion only if the cheque is drawn on a bank other than the clearing bank, or if the clearing bank does not hold an account for the creditor-drawee. If the bank does hold an account for the drawee, the bank can charge a fee only if there is a pre-existing agreement to that effect with its creditors. The distinction here is rooted in the fact that the operation in the latter case will transfer the property of the debt only with the formal acceptance of the substituted debtor, the bank (*IFB* 109).

There remains that if the bank has branches in different locations in the same country, such as Baghdad and Mosul, it can ask for a fee for drawing the cheque in a place other than where the drawer has deposited his account.

Other activities: underwriting, transfers, etc. Alongside cheques, Sadr discusses several other activities carried out by banks, such as transfers, especially when they involve significant distances, and considers the imposition of fees on these operations to be legal. The bank can also charge fees when underwriting newly formed companies, emitting shares, keeping financial letters, guaranteeing credit and documentary papers, storing merchandise, etc. All these activities are generally considered to be legal, and one finds little dissimilarity between the way they are carried out by traditional banks and the way they ought to be performed by an Islamic institution.

There is, however, in the discussion of the charging of fees in collecting drafts, an instance where Sadr insists on preventing the imposition of fees by the Islamic bank, unless the bank can justify the fee by proper legal consideration for the service against which the fee is rendered.

The bank is entitled, says Sadr, to charge a fee on a draft that it collects for the benefit of its customers, 'whether the collection takes place by receiving the money in cash, or by transferring the value of the draft from the creditor account of the draft's drawer in the bank to the debtor account of the beneficiary. This transfer is but an assignment by the drawer of the draft of his debtor on the bank' (*IFB* 120).

There is, however, a difference between a situation in which the drawee comes to the bank with a draft which was not initially drawn on the bank, and asks the bank then to collect it, and a situation in which the drawee comes to the bank with a draft on the bank by his creditor.

In the first case, the bank can charge a fee in return for getting in touch with the debtor and asking him for an execution that will be completed either by delivering the money in cash or by transferring the money into the account. In the second situation, however, the bank becomes by way of the transfer to its order of the drawer of the draft, indebted to the beneficiary (*mustafid*) with the value of the draft, without need for the beneficiary's consent; for the drawer has a creditor account in the bank and the transfer from the creditor to his debtor is executed without need for the debtor's consent. When the bank becomes the debtor, there is no justification for its charging a fee on the remittance of its own debt. It therefore appears that the collecting of the draft can allow the bank to charge a fee if the draft is not endorsed onto the bank (*IFB* 120–1).[35]

Foreign currency, gold and bank fees. A more significant difference between conventional and Islamic banking, at least in the legal theory underlying these activities, relates in Sadr's opinion to the regime of currency in the operations of change.

'The rules on change vary in Islamic law according to the nature of the currency used' (*IFB* 146). As long as the currency involved is paper money, the basis on which this paper money is created determines the way the law will ultimately govern operations with and in that currency.

In the case of gold and silver, the classical jurists have generally allowed, writes Sadr, transacting with them on two conditions: the equivalence in quantity between the price and the commodity when both are made of gold or silver; and the complete and immediate execution of the transaction at the place of contract (*fi majlis al-'aqd*).

Sadr disputes this division, and contends that in fact, only one condition is required in transactions involving gold and silver. Equivalence is necessary, but the exchange should not be instantaneous. The second condition, immediate completion of the transaction, 'is required for the exchange of gold against silver, or silver against gold. When gold is traded against gold, or silver against silver, the exchange (*taqabud*) is not necessary at the place of contract. The sale is valid regardless'(*IFB* 147–8). Sadr argues that in the case of an exchange of gold for gold, the condition of equivalence is the only one stated in the *hadith*. There is therefore no need to add another condition. Furthermore, since an increase in the exchange, i.e. the purchase of more gold for less gold, is prohibited *riba*, an equivalent exchange is sufficient to secure a valid transaction. The formal exchange can be completed in a place other than the place of contract without prejudice to the validity of the transaction.

Finally, the purchase and sale of foreign currency should be allowed for the bank, and the profit made over such transaction is valid. Similarly, a merchant can ask his bank for a fee, to guarantee that the price for a merchandise in foreign currency does not increase in case of devaluation, and that his present payment in the local currency will be adequate for the time of delivery of the merchandise.

> This is valid also from the legal point of view as long as the price for which the bank has purchased the foreign currency to be used on term (*ajila*) is not itself a future sale (*mu'ajjal*) in the same contract of purchase. If it were, the transaction would be a sale of a debt against a debt, and this is legally void. If the price is to be agreed on in the future, an agreement can be passed outside the purchase contract. (*IFB* 139)

Second category: loans and facilities

The second category is represented by 'loans and facilities' that the bank offers. Into this section fall three major activities: (1) The loans proper; (2) Commercial papers, and related operations of discount; and (3) Letters of credit (*IFB* 153–5).

Loans proper. Loans generically understood also encompass other banking services which might end up being loans. The basic analysis of loans by the *shari'a* must be 'developed into a general policy' which will avoid *riba*. This policy, following the presentation of the first part of the book, is summed up along the following guidelines:

First: The transformation of loans and advances (*taslifat*) into *mudaraba* transactions.

Second: When *mudaraba* is not possible, lending must be done according to the rules presented earlier.[36]

Third: Conditional upon the acceptance of a loan project should be for the borrower 'the payment of a fair fee (*ujrat al-mithl*) in return for the [under]writing of the loan' (*IFB* 155).

Fourth: The payment of the remainder of the interest fee (*fa'ida*) at the time of settlement.

Fifth: If the borrower pays this fee as a grant (donation, *hubwa*) to the bank, he could be considered as a first-class client, and be privileged in later loans over other borrowers who treated the fee as loan and not as *hubwa*.

The discounting of commercial papers. Such discount operations could be perceived as another form of *riba*, says Sadr, since the discount operates for the bank as an increase of the value of the paper discounted in return for a longer term granted to the seller of the paper.

However, the discount can avoid being *riba*, as long as the fee for the bank can be construed as a service rendered for 'receiving the money that is paid elsewhere' (*IFB* 156–7).

This may not be enough incentive for the bank that has substituted itself to the beneficiary of the discount.

> Between the bank and the drawer (*muharrir*) of the commercial paper (*al-kimbiyala*), no contract arises that sets any terms between them ... Therefore I see the necessity to develop the discount operation from a legal point of view. In other examples, the discount operation was constituted by three elements: the loan, the assignment (*hawala*), and the engagement (*ta'ahhud*) [i.e. here in contrast, legitimisation does not apply, since these elements are absent from the relationship between the drawer and the bank]. The operation could [on the other hand] be construed on a different basis, as a loan which consists of the amount that the beneficiary [drawee] receives at the time of the discount, and an agency by this beneficiary to the drawer at the time of the paper's realisation. The drawer of the paper will remain the debtor of the beneficiary, not the debtor of the bank, and the bank is the creditor of the beneficiary and [operates as the beneficiary's] agent for the realisation of the value of the paper when it becomes due. (*IFB* 158)

There is another legal justification of the discount operation, based upon the theory of sales. Some jurists accept it on the basis of the legality of the sales of a loan, if the loan is not in gold or silver or some other weighable commodity. However, Sadr does not seem to support this theory, 'on the basis of some reports (*riwayat*) which show that when the creditor sells his debt for a smaller amount, the buyer can receive from the debtor only the amount he paid to the buyer. The remainder is considered to have been automatically suppressed' (*IFB* 159).[37]

Letters of credit, (*khitabat al-i'timad*). After he explains the general mechanisms of letters of credit, Sadr explains that the fee (*'umula*) charged on issuing and clearing the operations entailed is valid and legally acceptable. The *'umula*, to which the Islamic bank is entitled when issuing a letter of credit, is justified legally in one of three ways:

The bank is considered the debtor of the bearer of the letter, and is entitled to a fee whenever the letter is cleared in another location.

If the letter of credit is a loan of the bank to the bearer, a fee can be charged if the letter is cleared elsewhere. The fee is a compensation for the bearer of the letter receiving the value of the loan in a different location. This fee would be further validated if the value of the letter is paid in foreign currency, which entails extra expenses for the bank.

If, finally, the letter of credit is considered as a delegation (*tafwid*) to the bearer to receive the value of the letter in a foreign currency, the bank can ask 'for a fee as a *ju'ala* on the delegation' (*IFB* 146, 247–8).

Third category: purchase of commercial papers

The third category of transactions is constituted by what Sadr classifies as 'exploitation, *istithmar*' (*IFB* 161–3). Exploitation means 'the investment by a bank of part of its own monies, or of monies deposited with it in the purchase of commercial papers'. The norms of practice with these papers in traditional banking is 'from the jurisprudential point of view no different from any other person who buys and sells these papers' (*IFB* 161). The trade of commercial papers by the bank is legally justifiable in two ways:

As a loan: the party that emits the obligation at a value of 1,000 dinars and sells it at 950 is in fact taking a loan from the purchaser of the obligation, with the understanding that the seller will pay back the buyer's obligation with a 50 dinar surplus at the end of the year.

As a sale: the party emitting the obligation at 1,000 dinars is in fact selling it for 1,000 under a year-term against 950 payable immediately. This, however, is only 'an artificial cover, *taghtiya lafziyya*' for an operation which ought to be described as a loan.

Whatever justification, however, 'the difference between the nominal value of the obligation and the real value paid by the bank is *riba*' (*IFB* 163). The bank can only indulge in such activity if the obligations have been issued by the government, or by a private party according to the rules laid out in the first part of the book. 'Outside these limits, the bank cannot buy and sell obligations' (*IFB* 163).

Banks in an Islamic environment

Iqtisaduna and *al-Bank al-la Ribawi* were set, as indicated earlier, against very different social and financial backgrounds. *Iqtisaduna* insisted on the role of the state in the economy, as well as on the necessity to establish 'social justice'. The Islamic rules of *riba* were then part of the tempering role of an interventionist state. In 1969, the issue had shifted to the periphery, and the new work on banking was meant to introduce an Islamic order within a capitalist environment. Ten years later, when the Islamic revolution was on the agenda of both Iran and Iraq, another dimension of Islamic banking resurfaced. In the series on 'Islam guiding life',[38] Muhammad Baqer as-Sadr wrote a booklet on the principles of a bank that would function without *riba within* an Islamic economy. This essay was an attempt to sketch the background for a banking system in a state that has succeeded in establishing itself in the wake of an Islamic revolution. As in his essays on *Khilafat al-Insan* and *Lamha Fiqhiyya*,[39] Iran, and potentially Iraq, were the evident target of his work.

Sadr refers briefly to his earlier work on banking, on the occasion of a remembrance of the remarks of 'a Muslim person – who, in the deviations of our Muslim world, was appointed minister in his country – who told me personally in all simplicity and innocence that he was as disconcerted by the name of a non-*ribawi* bank as he would be on hearing someone speaking of a square circle'.[40]

Al-Usus al-'Amma lil-Bank fil-Mujtama' al-Islami was meant as an introduction to a more comprehensive work (*Usus* 24), and the separate first edition of the pamphlet bore the notice 'part one'. The 'details' promised were probably never written, but the *Usus* gives a good picture of Sadr's approach to the problem of Islamic state banking. There is little by way of comparison with the minute analysis of *al-Bank al-la Ribawi*, and the exact formulae for the operations of the bank in a favourable Islamic environment are not spelled out. But the general philosophy of the system is.

The contrast was, not surprisingly for the populist background of the Iranian revolution, with the capitalist system. As in *Iqtisaduna*, the bank was one element in 'a comprehensive Islamic system with intertwined parts, and the application in each part prepares the ground for the success of the other part and helps in turn the projected Islamic role' (*Usus* 13).

Under Capitalism, says Sadr, the role of the banks can be divided into two: an objective role, which is the mobilisation of funds for industrial and commercial ventures, and a subjective role, which is the concentration of capital in the hands of the few who control the economy, and who will use this capital to reproduce and reinforce the system.

The bank in an Islamic environment shares with Capitalism the objective role of fund mobilisation. But it is evident that the subjective role is completely different. The essential contrast is based on the primacy of labour in the creation of wealth in the Islamic system, and the role of risk.[41] In Capitalism, the banks allow the capitalist 'fixed earnings which are separate not only from the concept of labour but also from risk' (*Usus* 10). In the Islamic system, both concepts are central to the financial setting.

This is where the role of the state, which was completely absent from the essay on the Islamic bank in 1969, is so important. The state, through its responsibility towards social justice and help of the downtrodden and poor,[42] will use the means at its disposal in the *mantaqat al-faragh* (discretionary area) (*Usus* 17) to prevent hoarding, establish *zakat* on non-productive funds, and encourage free loans to the needy (*Usus* 15–18). These are matters of public policy which are consonant with the role of the state as regulator of the distribution of wealth.

From the narrower financial point of view, banking will take two forms. The bank will naturally welcome deposits, and the first form of the use of the funds deposited will be a 'guaranteed loan' (*qard madmun*) to the depositor, who becomes the creditor of the bank with restricted rights. The depositor will be able to withdraw his deposits at will. He could earmark them for specific philanthropic projects towards the poor, and the bank would open a special account for the purpose. Most importantly in Sadr's remarks, the depositor should be able to conserve the 'real value' (*qima haqiqiyya*) of his money, and have it protected from inflation: 'That the bank pays upon restitution what represents the value [of the deposits] does not constitute *riba*. The real value is calculated on the basis of gold and the price of gold exchange' (*Usus* 19).

The second form of banking is based on *mudaraba*. If the *mudaraba* is carried out directly by the bank undertaking an economic project, the profit will be split with the depositor on the pre-agreed basis of the *mudaraba* contract. If the bank merely plays an intermediary role, the *mudaraba* will be between the depositor and the borrower, and the bank will simply charge a fee (*'umula*) on its intermediation. But then, 'the depositor will not be guaranteed his money back' (*Usus* 20). The rejection of any guarantee appears to be at odds with the bank's guarantee to its fixed-term depositors in the scheme defended in *al-Bank al-la Ribawi*. It is not clear whether Sadr has overlooked the contradiction between the rules presented in the two texts, or whether he considered that such guarantee would only function in a non-Islamic environment where conventional banks are competing with interest-free institutions.

The system portrayed by Sadr does not otherwise significantly differ from the scheme presented in his 1969 work. One important difference appears, however, in the overall control of the banks in an Islamic system. In 1969, the underlying principle was the banks' independence from the adverse non-Islamic state. In 1979, the picture was quite different: 'The operation of mobilising funds and exploiting them is undertaken in the Islamic society by the state through an official bank. Banking operations (*istithmarat masrafiyya*) in the private sector are not permitted' (*Usus* 15). The *dirigiste* measures were thus consecrated.

Conclusion: new financial horizons for the *shari'a*

When, in the late 1960s, Muhammad Baqer as-Sadr set out to write a treatise on an interest-free bank in answer to a query by the Kuwaiti Ministry of *awqaf*, the territory had remained uncharted but for the debate on *riba* in Egypt.

Interest-free transactions in the banking system, as well as the rejection of *riba* in the simplest transactions ruled by Islamic law, were destined to remain an important concern for the search of an Islamic alternative by way of the *shari'a*.

Two significant practical developments ensued. In the first place, a number of Islamic banks were established, especially since the mid-1970s. Secondly, some Muslim countries have started examining the possibility of replacing their whole banking system by interest-free institutions. Yet again, the *shari'a* must adapt.[43]

The gulf between theory and practice remains significant, but it would be difficult for institutions and countries which are concerned either with the civil legislation or the establishment of Islamic financial 'money-houses' to ignore the contributions of the jurists to the field.

Epilogue: the economics of lawyers and historians

It may appear strange that the parallels with Sadr's work are mostly to be found in the writings of modern historians. The convergence can be explained by the heavy recourse, both for the *'ulama* and the historians, to the testimony of classical *fiqh*. Economic historians of the world of Islam,[44] and scholars who have more specifically written on its systems of credit and finance,[45] have questioned legal treatises for what they could express on the economics of the Islamic classical age. Similarly, the *'ulama* had to turn for their economic theories to the closest materials offered by the tradition. The Qur'an and the *hadith* could be telescoped to offer prescriptions for the economic model, but the injunctions drawn from these early sources were doubly flawed for an economic use: they were essentially of an injunctive moral nature, and they were not specific enough.

Alternatively, there had built up a body of *Khalduniana*, which took the *Muqaddima*'s economic hints as the basis for investigation. But with all the brilliant remarks of the *Muqaddima*, Ibn Khaldun remains primarily a historian. For the legal scholars in search of sources to complement the Qur'anic and *hadith* injunctions, vast riches had to be uncovered from their own background, the pure *shari'a* background. Early legal texts are extremely difficult to question. The efforts needed a systematic and highly synthetical mind, who could make concepts of modern economics drawn from Western tradition fuse with early abstruse non-economic material.

The parallel between economic historians and Sadr must however not be overemphasised. Unlike the work of historians, the efforts of contemporary jurists must be oriented to be made proficient, not merely descriptive. What the economic historian looks for in his reading of a legal treatise is confined by the method to reflecting the state of the economic situation at a given and limited time in history and for the role and working of credit institutions.

When reading the same legal treatise, the modern *'alim* seeks proficient arguments for immediate use in the system he tries to sketch as an answer to contemporary challenge. The material drawn from the text cannot be merely descriptive or explanatory, it must be able to *perform* in practice, whether in the state or in a bank. It comes then as no surprise that the task has proved complex and difficult.

The methodological hurdles of the contemporary economist in search of a synchronic Islamic theory of economics and banking (as opposed to the diachronic work of the historian) can be summed up as a pyramid of constraints.

There is no tradition of economics in Islam. Other texts of the *turath* (the classical tradition) must be questioned 'economically'. The operation is perforce highly selective, and the criticism of Sadr by some Sunni scholars described his operation of *ijtihad* correctly. But it is this particular imaginative effort which makes for Sadr's originality. The logic of the original text had to be dismantled for the sake of the new discipline.

Nor can the texts exploited be restricted to the Qur'an and *Sunna*. There is not enough material in the two sacred sources for an economic theory. The investigation must extend to the much richer resources offered by legal texts. The seriousness of 'Islamic economics' can only come from the rich and unique tradition of Islamic law. This is the only tradition which can offer conceptual tools which are properly 'Islamic'. If the contemporary Islamic scholar delves into sophisticated economic models without the prerequisite of the classical legal apprenticeship, the Islamic specificity of the model loses its sole intellectually systematic basis.

This creates a problem of expertise. Legal texts are obscure for non-lawyers. Only a jurist abreast of the legal methods and terminology can feel at relative ease in classical legal treatises. Furthermore, the performance required by the legal text is not historical. It is not directed towards understanding the past, however glorious. It is prospective, and deals with a 'programme'. The question of 'what happened?' must be supplemented with the question 'what to do?' To that prospective concern, is added the problem of terminology. The language of the discipline of 'economics' is moulded in capitalist and/or socialist categories. The Islamic economist must write his text with a language which is still in the formative process, and the attempt at being different is encumbered by terms-of-art which are alien to his or her tradition.

All these combinations require the fusing of several specialities. The Islamic economist needs proficiency in classical legal texts, a practical and performing methodology, synthesis to bring about a comprehensive system, and innovation with the terminology. No wonder that few scholars have been able to meet all the requirements, and Islamic economics is still at an early formative stage. This explains why a phenomenon like Muhammad Baqer as-Sadr is so noteworthy. He was the only scholar able to produce a comprehensive text which could draw on the 'economic' texts of the classical *fiqh* treatises as well as on the sources of Marxist and capitalist traditions available in Arabic, and surmount that pyramid of constraints with some measure of success.

It remains that Sadr was neither an economist nor a banker. Evident mistakes will be found by those who peruse his system with the tools of modern economic and financial theories.

Muhammad Baqer as-Sadr's contribution is none the less remarkable. How and why Sadr differs in this respect can be perhaps sought in the ways he has overcome two basic hurdles.

The first hurdle can be generally described in terms of sources. The most interesting side of Sadr's research appears in his emphasis on *fiqh*. In the absence of a discipline of economics in classical Islam, the complexities and riches of the *shari'a as elaborated in the works of the jurists*, and not as a direct extrapolation from a *hadith* or a Qur'anic verse, render Sadr's exercise different from most of the other endeavours in the field.

The second essential hurdle can be detected in the method. When Sadr writes that Islamic economics is not a science, he weakens perhaps some of the 'legitimacy' of the field, but he does not set as a goal an impossible Holy Grail of truth for a nascent and uncertain discipline.

Conclusion: The costs of renewal

At the outset of this work was posed the question of the advances of thought in the Islamic Renaissance. Was there anything 'new' in the theses elaborated in the Shi'i colleges, in comparison with the Middle Eastern intellectual scene, and beyond, in the *longue durée* course of the history of ideas?

We have discovered in the works of Muhammad Baqer as-Sadr a system. As in all systems, its strength comes from the avenues it opens, rather than from the specific answers it is able to provide. Sadr was confronted with several challenges, which he tried to address with the tools of the tradition available to him. In economics and banking, he was operating from difficult uncharted territory, and whilst he sometimes erred, the way he proceeded and the seriousness of his work remain unmatched in Islamic literature. As argued in this research, the détour through the *shari'a* allowed Sadr to elaborate on economic and banking issues with far more depth than his immediate contemporaries. Even in the works of the great reformists of the twentieth century, contributions in the field have been rare and unalluring.

In the longer perspective of the history of ideas, a distinguishing feature of the Najaf Renaissance has been the immediacy with which the proposed ideas have found a terrain of application. In the European Renaissance of the fifteenth and sixteenth centuries, as well as during the Enlightenment, the protagonists in the debate of ideas were relatively sheltered from the immediate impact of the application of their world view. In Najaf in contrast, Sadr and Khumaini's ideas came suddenly as the guidance of a large and powerful Iran. This unique development has prevented the analysis from seeing behind the 'Islamic phenomenon' witnessed in the 1980s the deeper renewal that had been shaped in the Iraqi South from Muhammad Husain Kashif al-Ghita' to Sadr and his companions. On the other hand, the research undertaken in Najaf in a difficult field such as economics and banking could not offer clear and decisive guidelines to action in government. The hesitations in agrarian reform in Iran, as well as the difficulty of devising a sound Islamic financial and economic system, are testimony to the problems inherent to application.

Developments in the constitutional field were different. The Iranian institutions, which were fashioned in the shape of the legal blueprint, have taken root. A decade of constitutionalism in Iran has offered, in matters of separation of powers and in judicial review *lato sensu*, a rich and lively terrain for analysis and debate. Some areas, of course, were not part of the picture, and the record on human rights is a dismal failure of revolutionary Iran. But as a peculiar and challenging answer to Juvenal's question of 'who watches the watchmen?', the old Platonic issue of the philosopher-king was being answered in effect by way of scholarship in the law. The Leader in Iran, the *marja'* in Sadr's constitutional project, Khumaini's *faqih*, are all variations on the theme of leadership in the (Shi'i) community on the basis of legal knowledge. In this, these ideas and their application offer a unique contrast to the Western tradition.

The renewal of Islamic law lost in the person of Muhammad Baqer as-Sadr its most brilliant thinker. With his execution on 8 April 1980 a page in the intellectual life of Iraq was turned. Soon the confrontation would take an international turn. The onset of the Iran–Iraq war in September of that year and the occupation of Kuwait by Iraq in August 1990 started a new era in the Middle East, the deeper consequences of which are yet to be assessed. For Najaf, the wars and revolts have brought unmitigated disaster.

The protagonists of the Renaissance in Iraq, Iran and Lebanon were the first victims of the propagation of their reading of the Islamic tradition. A decade after the death of Sadr and his sister Bint al-Huda, many of the 'good companions' of Najaf met with violence, if not with brutal death. As with Sadr and Bint al-Huda, Mahdi al-Hakim and Hasan ash-Shirazi were assassinated. Ragheb Harb was killed in South Lebanon in 1984. Muhammad Mahdi Shamseddin and Muhammad Husain Fadlallah narrowly escaped assassination attempts and were caught in a network of terror in which they were soon *dépassés*. In Iran, the long list of 'martyrs' of the Revolution includes many of the companions of Ruhullah al-Khumaini at Najaf. Amongst the Shi'i international of Najaf graduates, one can even find a leader of the Islamic movement in Pakistan, 'Aref Husaini, who was killed in 1988. As to the other militant Iraqis in Najaf, they live almost without exception scattered in European, Lebanese or Iranian exile, where they carry the torch of the Holy Cities' rebellion. These include Muhammad Bahr al-'Ulum, Muhammad Baqer al-Hakim, Muhammad Mahdi al-Asifi, Mahmud al-Hashimi and Muhammad ash-Shirazi.

Some of these names were encountered in the course of this research as the respectable authors of Islamic law treatises. Others were road companions who firmly believed that their version of the *shari'a* would in Sadr's words, 'clothe the earth with the frame of heaven'. But as in Goya's painting, Saturn has brutally claimed his children. Sadr had, in his very first publication of *Fadak in History*, warned that 'words would be the soldiers of revolution'. Revolution, as in Karbala for Husain, had failed him. But it had been successful for Khumaini, whose taking over the state had started a new institutionalised episode for Islamic law.

Beyond the political tragedies which the legal renewal has triggered, a watershed has occurred in the intellectual realm of the *shari'a*. No longer is family law the last precinct of the jurists. Islamic law has regained the high ground in disciplines which had seemed only a few decades ago beyond its pale: constitution, economics and banking.

Notes

The law in the Islamic Renaissance and the role of Muhammad Baqer as-Sadr

1 In the vast literature on the subject, some telling titles: D. Pipes, *In the Path of God: Islam and Political Power*, New York, 1983; E. Sivan, *Radical Islam*, New Haven, Conn., 1985; A. Hyman, *Muslim Fundamentalism*, London, 1985; J. Esposito ed., *Voices of Resurgent Islam*, Oxford, 1983; S. Hunter ed., *The Politics of Islamic Revivalism*, Bloomington, 1987; 'Islam and Politics', *Third World Quarterly*, (Special Issue) 10:2, April 1988; B. Etienne, *L'Islamisme Radical*, Paris, 1987; *Sou'al* ed., *L'Islamisme Aujourd'hui*, Paris, 1985; M. Ayoob, *The Politics of Islamic Reassertion*, London, 1981; O. Carré and P. Dumont eds., *Radicalismes Islamiques*, 2 vols., Paris, 1986; G.H. Jansen, *Militant Islam*, London, 1979; S. Irfani, *Revolutionary Islam in Iran*, London, 1983; M.S. 'Ashmawi, *Al-Islam as-Siyasi* (*Political Islam*), Cairo, 1987; S. Abu Habib, *Dirasa fi Minhaj al-Islam as-Siyasi* (*Study in the Method of Political Islam*), Cairo, 1985. Among the best introductions remains E. Mortimer, *Faith and Power*, London, 1982. Ironically, disparaging as the word fundamentalism may sound, it does correspond to the way some of these movements identify themselves. Among the designations, '*Usuli*' Islam can be translated literally as 'fundamentalist', in reference to *usul*, roots, fundaments. The Arabic word however has more connotations, particularly in Shi'ism. See this volume, chapter one. More neutral is 'political Islam', *al-islam as-siyasi*. Another generic designation is *haraka islamiyya*, Islamic movement. The term *salafi* (Islam of the forebears), which curried favour at the beginning of the century, especially in Wahhabi Arabia, has fallen into disuse.

2 Interesting works include, from an anthropological perspective, M. Gilsenan, *Recognizing Islam*, London, 1982; L. Caplan ed., *Studies in Religious Fundamentalism*, London, 1987; J.P. Digard ed., *Le Cuisinier et le Mangeur d'Hommes–Etudes d'Ethnographie Historique du Proche-Orient*, Paris, 1982; from a sociological perspective, e.g. Saad Eddin Ibrahim, 'Anatomy of Egypt's militant groups: methodological note and preliminary findings', *International Journal of Middle Eastern Studies*, 12, 1980, 423–53; from an historical angle, I. Lapidus, *Contemporary Islamic Movements in Historical Perspective*, Berkeley, 1983; from a broader political-cultural sense, P. Bannermann, *Islam in Perspective*, London, 1988; J. Berque, *L'Islam au Défi*, Paris, 1980.

3 See the legal thrust of the thesis of the 'Islamic engineer' Muhammad 'Abd as-Salam Faraj legitimising Egyptian President Sadat's killing, in Muhammad 'Amara ed., *al-Farida al-Gha'iba* (*The Neglected Duty*), Cairo, 1982; J.J.G.

Jansen, *The Neglected Duty; the Creed of Sadat's Assassins and Islamic Resurgence in the Middle East*, New York, 1986.

4 The word is Louis Althusser's. See e.g. his 'Avertissement aux lecteurs du Livre I du *Capital*', in K. Marx, *Le Capital*, Paris, 1969, p. 6; *Lénine et la Philosophie-Marx et Lénine devant Hegel*, Paris, 1972.

5 On Ibn Khaldun, see A. al-Azmeh, *Ibn Khaldun in Modern Scholarship*, Beirut, 1981, esp. 'Bibliography', pp. 229–318; on long waves (*longue durée*) in history, the masterpiece of F. Braudel, *La Méditerranée et le Monde Méditerranéen à l'Epoque de Philippe II*, 2 vols., Paris, new edn 1966, and his theoretical essay, 'Histoire et sciences sociales: la longue durée', *Annales ESC*, 4, Oct.–Dec. 1958, 725–53, reprinted in *Ecrits sur l'Histoire*, Paris, 1969, pp. 41–83. Attempts to look at the contemporary turmoil in Islam have not yet displayed a concern for a *longue durée* approach, but inspiration can be drawn from the study of 'salvation history' introduced into the field by John Wansbrough. See his *Qur'anic Studies: Sources and Methods of Interpretation*, Oxford, 1977 and *The Sectarian Milieu. Content and Composition of Islamic Salvation History*, Oxford, 1978; on Wansbrough, see A. Rippin, 'Literary analysis of Qur'an, *Tafsir*, and *Sira*: the methodologies of John Wansbrough', in R. Martin ed., *Approaches to Islam in Religious Studies*, Tucson, 1985, pp. 151–63; and my 'Contemporary Qur'anic exegesis between London and Najaf; a view from the law', unpublished communication, SOAS, 21 October 1987. For an approach to classical Shi'i texts inspired by Wansbrough, see Norman Calder, *The Structure of Authority in Imami Shi'i Jurisprudence*, Ph.D. thesis, London, 1980.

6 On the concept of 'breaks' in scientific disciplines, Thomas Kühn, *The Structure of Scientific Revolutions*, Chicago, 1962, new edn, 1970; Gaston Bachelard, *Le Rationalisme Appliqué*, Paris, 1975 (1st edn, 1949), pp. 104–5. On the birth and formation of Arab historiography, see A. Duri, *Bahth fi Nash'at 'ilm at-Tarikh 'ind al-'arab*, Beirut, 1960, translated by L. Conrad as *The Rise of Historical Writing among the Arabs*, Princeton, 1983.

7 Relative only, see our use of Ibn Khaldun in chapter 3 on constitutional law.

8 Ibn Manzur, *Lisan al-'Arab*, Beirut, 1959, vol. 3, pp. 175ff.

9 Az-Zubaydi (d. 1205/1790), *Taj al-'Arus*, n.d., Benghazi, vol.5, pp. 394ff. See also Schacht, s.v. *shari'a*, in *Encyclopaedia of Islam I*: 'the road to the watering place, the clear path to be followed, the path which the believer has to tread, the religion of Islam, as a technical term, the canon law of Islam.'

10 N. Coulson, *Succession in the Muslim Family*, Cambridge, 1971, pp. 2–4. This view has been seriously challenged recently by D. Powers and M. Mundy. By way of an exegetical analysis, Powers has suggested that there was an intermediary 'proto-law of succession' before the crystallisation of the system of succession. See his *Studies in Qur'an and Hadith*, Berkeley, 1986; and 'The historical evolution of Islamic inheritance law', in C. Mallat and J. Connors eds., *Islamic Family Law*, London, 1990, pp. 11–29. Mundy has studied the development and changes of succession law in the wider historical and social context, 'The family, inheritance, and Islam: a re-examination of the sociology of *fara'id* law', in A. Azmeh ed., *Islamic Law: Social and Historical Contexts*, London, 1988, pp. 1–123.

11 On slaves and slave law, see e.g. Mundy, 'The family', pp. 31–2, 38–40, 107, 109–12; P. Crone, *Slaves on Horses: the Evolution of the Islamic Polity*, Cambridge, 1980; see also the methodological use of slave law by Y. Linant de Bellefonds, *Traité de Droit Musulman Comparé*, 1, Paris, 1965, p. 9.

12 Martin Kramer, 'Tragedy in Mecca', *Orbis* (Philadelphia), 32:2, 1988, 231–47. See recently, the recriminations against Wahhabism in *Ayat Allah* Ruhullah al-Khumaini's testament, published in *Keyhan Hava'i*, '*Matn-e kamel-e wasiy-yatname-ye ilahi-siayasi Imam Khumaini*' (*Complete Text of the Divine-Political Will of Imam Khumaini*), 14 June 1989, p. 2.

13 See literature mentioned in the Introduction to Part I.

14 Exceptions can be found in Islamic Iran, Pakistan, Saudi Arabia, and the Sudan.

15 Norman Anderson has closely followed these developments, see e.g. his 'Recent developments in *shari'a* law' (i–x), published between 1950 and 1952 in *The Muslim World*; 'The Syrian law of personal status', *Bulletin of the School of Oriental and African Studies*, 1955, 34–49; 'A law of personal status for Iraq' and 'Changes in the law of personal status in Iraq', *International and Comparative Law Quarterly*, 1960, 542–63 and 1963, 1026–31; 'Reforms in family law in Morocco', *Journal of African Law*, 1958, 146–59. See also my 'Introduction' to Mallat and Connors eds., *Islamic Family Law*, pp. 1–7.

16 Wahbe az-Zuhaili, *Nazariyyat ad-Daman fil-Fiqh al-Islami* (*Theory of Responsibility in Islamic Law*), Damascus, 1970.

17 Muhammad Bahr al-'Ulum, '*Uyub al-Irada fish-Shari'a al-Islamiyya* (*Vices of Consent in Islamic Law*), Beirut, 1984.

18 This is the familiar story among specialists of Iran where even as perceptive an analyst as Fred Halliday published just before the Revolution a book which was sceptical on the solidity of the Shah's system, but failed to mention the Islamic movement which would soon topple him. F. Halliday, *Iran: Dictatorship and Development*, London, 1979. An exception was Hamid Algar, whose personal interest and friendship with the revolutionaries allowed him to discern the strongest organised element in the tidal wave that shook Iran in 1978–9. H. Algar, 'The oppositional role of the ulama in twentieth-century Iran', in N. Keddie ed., *Scholars, Saints and Sufis*, Berkeley, 1972, pp. 231–55 (original communication delivered in 1969).

19 Beyond these, there were naturally further dimensions of 'Islamicity', the most prominent of which was cultural: the referents to Islam in the culture were institutionalised. Such is the case of 'martyrdom' in the Karbala paradigmatic form, most strikingly at work in the war with Iraq. But there were other aspects as well, such as the education and the restructuring of the universities, women's issues, etc. All these topics, however, fall beyond the strict legal sphere, although the law will say an occasional word in terms of prohibitions and encouragement. In the area of family law, this probably appears best in the example of the *mut'a*. The *mut'a* however had never been forbidden by the Ancien Régime, and its enhancement under the new system has taken a purely cultural form. See the remarkable studies of Shahla Haeri, 'The institution of *mut'a* marriage in Iran: a formal and historical perspective', in G. Nashat ed., *Women and Revolution in Iran*, Boulder, Co., 1983, pp. 231–51; 'Power of ambiguity: cultural improvisation on the theme of temporary marriage', *Iranian Studies*, 19:2, 1986, 123–54, and her *Law of Desire: Temporary Marriage in Shi'i Iran*, London, 1989. On the idealised prototype of the new 'Islamic' woman, see my 'Le féminisme islamique de Bint al-Houdâ', *Maghreb-Machrek*, 116, 1987, 45–58.

20 On Shari'ati, see N. Yavari d'Hellencourt, 'Le radicalisme shi'ite de 'Ali Shari'ati', in O. Carré and P. Dumont eds., *Radicalismes Islamiques*, Paris, 1986, vol. 1; S. Akhavi, 'Shari'ati's social thought', in N. Keddie ed., *Religion and Politics in Iran*, New Haven, 1983, pp. 125–43.

21 Two books published in English cover the field of Islamic thought in a comprehensive way. Albert Hourani's *Arabic Thought in the Liberal Age*, Cambridge, 1962, and Hamid Enayat's *Modern Islamic Political Thought*, Austin, Texas, 1982, span the century with accuracy, comprehensiveness and method. See also the good study in Arabic of Ahmad Amin, *Zu'ama' al-Islah* (*Leaders of Reform*), Cairo, 1948.

22 E. Rabbath, *La Constitution Libanaise, Origines, Textes et Commentaires*, Beirut, 1982, p. 3.

23 The classic work on the first Iranian constitution is A. Kasravi, *Tarikh-e Mashruta-ye Iran* (*History of the Constitution of Iran*), 5th ed. Tehran, 1961. Kasravi was assassinated in 1946.

24 Why the Shi'i world had suddenly become the locomotive of Islamic thought will probably remain not completely answered. In a sense, an answer to a negative question must be sought, and such answers are never completely satisfactory. Perhaps some explanation lay in the absence of an independent Sunni educational machine after the taming of the Azhar at the turn of the century, whereas the Shi'i *'ulama* had retained the independence which rendered their thought and contributions much more active. The connection between a radical Islamic movement and the state also offers a partial answer: there is no equivalent to Iran as an Islamic revolutionary state in the rest of the Muslim world. The 'underdog' cultural tradition of Shi'ism might have also contributed to fuel the subsequent revolutionary message. In any case, and apart from the radical groups in the Sunni world in Syria, Saudi Arabia, Egypt, etc., which disturbed all these governments in the 1980s, it is not suggested that 'new' thought was limited to Shi'is. On the issue of *riba* (interest, usury) for example, the debate in Egyptian legal and clerical circles had no match in terms of intensity and quality.

25 On *wilayat al-faqih*, see this volume, chapter 2.

26 '*Je suis tombé par terre, c'est la faute à Voltaire,*
Le nez dans le ruisseau, c'est la faute à Rousseau.'

27 See e.g. Shari'ati, *Husayn, Varith-e Adam* (*Husayn, Heir of Adam*), Tehran, n.d.; *Tashayyu'-e 'Alavi va Tashayyu'-e Safavi* (*'Alid Shi'ism and Safavid Shi'ism*), Tehran, 2nd edn, 1350/1971.

28 On the Shi'i international, see this volume, pp. 15–19 and Part I, and literature cited.

29 'Imam Khomeini's message on hearing of the martyrdom of Ayatollah Sayyid Baqir Sadr at the hands of the American puppet Saddam Husain', in *The Selected Messages of Imam Khomeini Concerning Iraq and the War Iraq Imposed upon Iran*, Tehran, 1981, p. 47.

30 H. Batatu, 'Iraq's underground Shi'a movements: characteristics, causes and prospects', *Middle East Journal*, 35:4, Spring 1981, 577–94; published also with slight alterations as 'Shi'i organizations in Iraq: *al-da'wah al-islamiyya* and *al-mujahidin*', in J. Cole and N. Keddie eds., *Shi'ism and Social Protest*, New Haven, 1986, p. 182.

31 Muhammad Baqer as-Sadr, *Unsere Wirtschaft, Eine Gekürzte Kommentierte Ubersetzung des Buches Iqtisaduna*, Translation and Comments by Andreas Rieck, Berlin, 1984. See for various translations this volume, chapter 4, p. 142.

32 R. Dekmejian, *Islam in Revolution*, Syracuse, 1985, pp. 127–36.

33 A. Bar'am, 'The shi'ite opposition in Iraq under the Ba'th, 1968–1984', in *Colloquium on Religious Radicalism and Politics in the Middle East*, Hebrew University, Jerusalem, 13–15 May 1985.

34 Dossier: Aux sources de l'islamisme chiite- Muhammad Baqer as-Sadr', *Cahiers de l'Orient*, issue 8–9, 1987–8, 115–202.

35 The most comprehensive and authoritative biography of Sadr appears in K. Ha'iri, '*Tarjamat hayat as-sayyid ash-shahid*' (*Life of the Martyred Sayyed* [*Sadr*]), in Muhammad Baqer as-Sadr, *Mabaheth al-Usul* (Studies in *usul*), Ha'iri ed., Qum, 1407/1987, pp. 11–168. The birthdate is mentioned at p. 33. Other biographies consulted include, in order of importance, Ghaleb Hasan Abu 'Ammar, *Ash-Shahid as-Sadr Ra'ed ath-Thawra al-Islamiyya fil-'Iraq* (*Martyr as-Sadr, Leader of the Islamic Revolution in Iraq*), Tehran, 1401/1981 (published under the auspices of the Iranian Ministry of Islamic Guidance); '*Al-imam ash-shahid as-sayyid Muhammad Baqer as-Sadr*' (The martyred imam Muhammad Baqer as-Sadr), *Tariq al-Haqq* (London), 2:12, Feb. 1982, pp. 5–20. In European languages, the most comprehensive biography is Rieck's 'Introduction of the translator', in Sadr, *Unsere Wirtschaft*, pp. 39–68. See also the remarks of Batatu, 'Underground', pp. 578–81; P. Martin, 'Une grande figure de l'islamisme en Irak', *Cahiers de l'Orient*, 8–9, 1987–8, 117–35. The birthdates vary between 1930 and 1934. The late Mahdi al-Hakim told me that Sadr, like his older brother Isma'il, died a year before reaching fifty. If Sadr died at forty-nine, he would have been born in 1931. Conversations with Mahdi al-Hakim, London, Summer–Autumn 1987. (Mahdi al-Hakim was assassinated in the Sudan in February 1988.)

36 Ha'iri, '*Tarjamat*', p. 28.

37 Muhammad Baqer as-Sadr was then three years old according to Ha'iri and Abu 'Ammar. His sister Bint al-Huda was his junior, born according to Ha'iri in 1356/1937, the year of their father's death.

38 The name of his mother is not mentioned in the sources. She was the daughter of *Ayat Allah* Shaykh 'Abd al-Husayn Al Yasin, who is said to have been an important religious figure of Baghdad after the death of Murtada al-Ansari. Sadr's mother was the sister of Murtada Al Yasin.

39 Murtada was a well-established scholar when he issued a famous *fatwa* against the Communists on 3 April 1960. The *fatwa* is reported in H. Batatu, *The Old Social Classes and the Revolutionary Movements of Iraq*, Princeton, 1978, p. 954. (This important work, along with Samir al-Khalil's *Republic of Fear*, London, 1989, provide the most challenging studies of twentieth-century Iraq. See further this volume, p. 9 and my article on 'Obstacles to democratization in Iraq', which is a critical reading of modern Iraqi history in the light of Batatu and Khalil's theses, to be published at University of Washington Press, forthcoming, 1993.) Isma'il is said to have written several books, two of which, a commentary on Islamic penal legislation and a first volume of Qur'anic exegesis, were published. Ha'iri, '*Tarjamat*', p. 29.

40 Ha'iri, '*Tarjamat*', p. 44, relating a recollection by a classmate of Sadr, Muhammad 'Ali al-Khalili.

41 Ha'iri, '*Tarjamat*', p. 42; also Abu 'Ali, 'A glimpse of the life of the martyred imam Muhammad Baqir al-Sadr', n.p. n.d., p. 7.

42 Muhammad Baqer as-Sadr, *Fadak fit-Tarikh* (*Fadak in History*), 1st edn, Najaf, 1955. A reference to this first edition, which was published care of Muhammad Kazem al-Kubti, is mentioned s.v. in F. Abdulrazak ed., *Catalog of the Arabic Collection*, Harvard University, Boston, 1983. A second edition was published at al-Haydariyya Press, also in Najaf, in 1970. Several Beirut reprints followed. 'Dr Abu 'Ali' states that Sadr wrote *Fadak fit-Tarikh* when

he was seventeen. 'A glimpse', p. 7. This is corroborated in Ha'iri, '*Tarjamat*', p. 64.

43 See on Fadak within the Shi'i-Sunni communitarian background, my 'Religious militancy in contemporary Iraq: Muhammad Baqer as-Sadr and the Sunni-Shi'a paradigm', *Third World Quarterly*, 10:2, April 1988, 714–5.

44 There is a large literature on the 1920 Revolt and on the role of the *'ulama* leadership. See e.g. R. al-Khattab, *Al-'Iraq bayna 1921 wa 1927 (Iraq between 1921 and 1929)*, Najaf, 1976; A. al-Fayyad, *Ath-Thawra al-'Iraqiyya al-Kubra (The great Iraqi revolt)*, Baghdad, 1963. An excellent account is 'Ali al-Wardi, *Tarikh al-'Iraq al-Hadith (History of Modern Iraq)*, vol.6, *Min 'Am* 1920 *ila 'Am* 1924 (from 1920 to 1924), Baghdad, 1976, pp. 201–67. See also the telling testimony of Amin ar-Rihani, an eye-witness visitor, *Muluk al-'Arab* (The *Arab Kings*), Beirut, 2nd edn, 1929, vol.2.

45 The 'Communist threat' was in the 1950s a common phenomenon in the Middle East, particularly in Iran and Iraq. See generally Batatu, *The Old Social Classes*, Book II, pp. 365–705. On the impact on Sadr's writings, see this volume, pp. 11–12.

46 M. H. Kashif al-Ghita', *Muhawarat al-Imam al-Muslih ash-Shaykh Muhammad al-Husayn ma' as-Safirayn al-Baritani wal-Amriki (Conversations Between the Reformist Imam Shaykh Muhammad Husayn and the British and American Ambassadors)*, 4th edn, Najaf, 1954, p. 21. The leitmotiv on the Palestine question started early: 'There is nothing now but friendship, [Kashif al-Ghita'] said, between us and the English, if it were not for the wrongs of our Arab brothers in Palestine, and while those last, there can be neither peace nor love between us from the Mediterranean to India.' Freya Stark, *Baghdad Sketches*, London, 1947 (1st ed. 1937), p. 172. It is to be noted, however, that much as the question of Palestine was central to the *'ulama* of Iraq and Iran, the issue did not emerge in post-1967 Iraq as it did in Iran. This is due to the fact that the successive governments which were in power in Baghdad after the demise of the King and Nuri as-Sa'id (who were perceived, especially after the Baghdad Pact, to be closely aligned with Western powers and by implication with Israel) in 1958 were consistently opposed, at least in their rhetoric, to the West. This was obviously not the case with the Shah of Iran.

47 Muhammad Baqer as-Sadr, *Falsafatuna (Our Philosophy)*, 10th ed. Beirut, 1980, pp. 11–53.

48 Muhammad Baqer as-Sadr, *Al-Ma'alim al-Jadida fil-Usul (The New Configuration of usul)*, Beirut, 1385/1964.

49 *Usul al-fiqh* is the most arcane discipline in Islamic law. For a recent introduction in English, see M. H. Kamali, *Principles of Islamic Jurisprudence*, Malaysia, 1989, rpt Cambridge, 1991. On classical Sunni *usul*, see recently W. Hallaq, 'The development of logical structure in Sunni legal theory', *Der Islam*, 64, 1987, 42–67. On early Shi'i *usul*, R. Brunschvig, 'Les *usul al-fiqh* imamites à leur stade ancien', in *Le Shi'isme Imamite*, Paris, 1970, pp. 201–14.

50 Muhammad Baqer as-Sadr, *Durus fi 'Ilm al-Usul (Lessons in the Discipline of usul)*, 3 parts in 4 vols, Beirut, 1978–80. On *bahth al-kharej* and the Najaf curriculum, see this volume, chapter 1.

51 '*Daght fil-'ibara*', Sadr, *Durus*, 1, p. 9.

52 The four Shi'i books mentioned are: the *Ma'alim* of ash-Shahid ath-Thani (d. 966/1559), Qummi's (d. 1231/1816) *Qawanin*, al-Khurasani's (d. 1328/1910) *Kifaya*, and Ansari's (d. 1329/1911) *Rasa'el*. See also Muhammad Baqer as-

Sadr, *Durus*, Introduction, 1, pp. 19–29; Muhammad Bahr al-'Ulum, '*Ad-dirasa wa tarikhuha fin-Najaf*' (*Teaching and its history in Najaf*), in J. Khalili ed., *Mausu'at al-'Atabat al-Muqaddasa, Qism an-Najaf* (*Encyclopaedia of the Holy Places: section on Najaf*), vol. 2, Beirut, 1964, pp. 95, 96. See further on these jurists and the curriculum, this volume, chapter 1, p. 39.

53 Sadr, *Mabaheth al-Usul*, quoted above n. 35. According to Ha'iri, this book is only the compilation of Volume 1 of Part 2 in a series of lectures by Sadr.

54 Mahmud al-Hashimi, *Ta'arud al-Adilla ash-Shar'iyya Taqriran li-Abhath as-Sayyid Muhammad Baqer as-Sadr* (*Contradictions of Legal Evidence, a Report on the Research of Muhammad Baqer as-Sadr*), Beirut, 2nd edn, 1980. Introduction in Sadr's hand, dated 1394/1974.

55 Ha'iri, '*Tajribat*', p. 67. In his introduction to the translation of *Iqtisaduna*, p. 67, Rieck mentions ten volumes printed in Najaf since 1955.

56 Ha'iri, '*Tajribat*', p. 44.

57 Muhammad Baqer as-Sadr, *Al-Usus al-Mantiqiyya lil-Istiqra'* (*The Logical Bases of Induction*), Beirut, 1972.

58 Sadr, *Al-Usus al-Mantiqiyya*, p. 507.

59 Muhammad Baqer as-Sadr, '*Al-yaqin ar-riyadi wal-mantiq al-wad'i*' (*Mathematical Certainty and Positive Logic*), in *Ikhtarnalak* (*Choice of Works*), Beirut, 1975, pp. 9–21.

60 Muhammad Baqer as-Sadr, *Falsafatuna*, 1st edn, Najaf, 1959. Translated by Shams Inati, London, 1987.

61 Ha'iri, '*Tajribat*', p. 63. Conversations with Mahdi al-Hakim, summer 1987.

62 See Sadr's Introduction to *Falsafatuna*. Y. Muhammad, '*Nazarat falsafiyya fi fikr ash-shahid as-Sadr*' (*Philosophical Enquiries into the Thought of Martyr as-Sadr*), *Dirasat wa Buhuth* (Tehran), 2:6, 1983, 173. The debate has persisted to date. See H. Haidar, *Madha Ja'a Hawla Kitab Falsafatuna?* (*What Has been Written about Falsafatuna?*), Qum, 1403/1983.

63 The Appendix was prepared by Muhammad Rida al-Ja'fari, *Falsafatuna*, 1st edition, pp. 348–9. It was omitted in later editions. The list includes classics in Arabic by Marx, Engels, Stalin, Mao Tse-Tung, Plekhanov, a fair number of French communists popular in the 1950s, Henri Lefebvre, Roger Garaudy, Georges Politzer, as well as some 'local' Arab and Iranian Marxists such as Georges Hanna and Taqi Arani.

64 Sadr, *Falsafatuna*, pp. 227–53.

65 *Ibid.*, p. 229.

66 *Ibid.*, p. 233. See also note p. 233 n. 1.

67 *Ibid.*, p. 236.

68 In contemporary Shi'i law, see e.g. the treatises of Muhsin al-Hakim (d. 1970), *Minhaj as-Salihin* (*The Path of the Righteous*), 2 vols., Beirut, 1976, 1980; Ruhullah al-Khumaini (d.1989), *Tahrir al-Wasila* (*Clearing the way*), 2 vols., Beirut, 1985 [Original published in Najaf, 1387/1967]; Abul-Qasem al-Khu'i, *Minhaj as-Salihin*, 10th edn, Beirut, n.d., 2 vols.; summary in *al-Masa'el al-Muntakhaba* (*Chosen Questions*), 22nd edn, Beirut, 1985.

69 Muhammad Baqer as-Sadr's comments on Muhsin al-Hakim's *Minhaj as-Salihin* appear in the edition mentioned in the previous note. They were written in 1974.

70 Muhammad Baqer as-Sadr, *Buhuth fi Sharh al-'Urwa al-Wuthqa* (*Studies on al-'Urwa al-Wuthqa*), 3 vols., Najaf, 1971 ff. Another *fiqh* work is Muhammad Baqer as-Sadr, *Mujaz Ahkam al-Hajj* (*Compendium of Pilgrimage Rules*), Beirut,

n.d. (Introduction dated 1395/1975). Sadr also wrote an Introduction to the Shi'i Imam Zayn al-'Abidin's book of prayers *As-Sahifa as-Sajjadiyya*, Beirut, n.d..

71 Muhammad Baqer as-Sadr, *al-Fatawa* [or *Fatawi*, plural of *fatwa*] *al-Wadiha Wifqan li-Madhhab Ahl al-Bayt* (*The Clear Decrees According to the Rite of the Household of the Prophet*), Beirut, 1976. But see a critique of the *risala* as genre in *al-Fatawa al-Wadiha*, pp. 11–12.

72 In the 1976 edition of *al-Fatawa al-Wadiha*, there is a separately paginated pamphlet, *al-Mursil, ar-Rasul, ar-Risala* (*The Sender, the Messenger, and the Message*), which is not very original. It is independent of the proper chapter introducing *al-Fatawa al-Wadiha*, which, in contrast, includes interesting and novel remarks.

73 Sadr, *al-Fatawa al-Wadiha*, pp. 46–7. For property law and legal concepts like *zakat*, *khums*, etc., see this volume, chapters 4 and 5. See also this passage in the context of the history of Shi'i law, H. M. Tabataba'i, *Introduction to Shi'i Law*, London, 1984, p. 16.

74 Comments of Muhammad Baqer as-Sadr on Hakim's *Minhaj as-Salihin*, quoted above n. 65. Part one, *'Ibadat*; Part two, *Mu'amalat*.

75 Muhammad Baqer as-Sadr, *al-Bank al-la Ribawi fil-Islam* (*The Interest-free Bank in Islam*), Kuwait, 1969, discussed in this volume, chapter 5.

76 Muhammad Baqer as-Sadr, *Lamha Fiqhiyya Tamhidiyya 'an Mashru' Dustur al-Jumhuriyya al-Islamiyya fi Iran* (*A Preliminary Legal Note on the Project of a Constitution for the Islamic Republic of Iran*), Beirut, 1979; *Khilafat al-Insan wa Shahadat al-Anbiya'* (*Succession of Man and Testimony of the Prophets*), Beirut, 1979; *Manabi' al-Qudra fid-Dawla al-Islamiyya* (*The Sources of Power in the Islamic State*), Beirut, 1979. See this volume, chapter 2.

77 Muhammad Baqer as-Sadr, *al-Madrasa al-Qur'aniyya* (*The Qur'anic School*), Beirut, 2nd edn, 1981. (Lectures on the Qur'an given in 1979–80.)

78 For a complete list of Sadr's works see s.v. in the bibliography. An edition of the 'Collected Works' of Muhammad Baqer as-Sadr, of which fifteen large volumes have now appeared, was started in 1980 by Sadr's traditional Lebanese publishing house, Ta'aruf. It includes in volume 13 a medium-sized booklet called *al-Mihna*. Other pamphlets on Shi'ism, *Bahth hawlal-Wilaya* (*Studies on the Wilaya*) and *Bahth hawlal-Mahdi* (*Study on the Mahdi*), were published separately in Beirut in 1977, but they were written earlier, and perhaps published as prefaces to other authors' works (see the introduction of Sadr to 'Abdallah Fayyad's *Tarikh al-Imamiyya wa Aslafuhum*, Beirut, 4th ed., 1973). The contributions on Shi'i history, *Dawr al-A'imma fil-Hayat al-Islamiyya* (*The Role of the Imams in Islamic Life*), and *Ahl al-Bayt, Tanawwu' Adwar wa Wahdat Hadaf* (*The Household of the Prophet, Diversity of Roles and Unity of Goal*) were lectures given between 1966 and 1969 and posthumously published. Muhammad Baqer as-Sadr wrote also several articles published in various journals. On all these works, see generally my 'Religious militancy'. Two other collections can be found in *Ikhtarnalak*, mentioned above, n. 59, and *al-Madrasa al-Islamiyya* (*The Islamic School*), Beirut, 1973. *Al-Islam Yaqud al-Hayat* (*Islam Guides Life*) is the title of a series published in 1979, which is a collection of six pamphlets (Beirut, 1980). Three pamphlets deal with the constitution (above, n. 76), and the three others are on economics and banking: *Sura 'an Iqtisad al-Mujtama' al-Islami* (*Picture of the Economics of the Islamic Society*); *Khutut Tafsiliyya 'an Iqtisad al-Mujtama' al-Islami* (*Detailed Guidelines to the Economy of the Islamic*

Society); and *Al-Usus al-'Amma lil-Bank fil-Mujtama' al-Islami* (*General Bases of a Bank in the Islamic Society*), discussed in this volume, chapters 2 and 5.

79 A fuller analysis of the political dimensions and implications of the Najaf Renaissance can be found in various articles which I published in recent years. The following topics related to the Najaf Renaissance are addressed in some detail: the reaction of Najaf to the unification of personal status law by the government of 'Abd al-Karim Qasem ('Shi'ism and Sunnism in Iraq: revisiting the Codes', in Mallat and Connors eds., *Islamic Family Law*, pp. 71–91); the causes of the Iran–Iraq war from the vantage-point of the Najaf–Tehran axis ('A l'Origine de la Guerre Iran-Irak: l'axe Najaf-Teheran', *Les Cahiers de l'Orient*, Paris, Autumn 1986, 119–36); the works of Muhammad Baqer as-Sadr in the mirror of the delicate Sunni–Shi'i controversy in Iraq ('Religious militancy in contemporary Iraq'); the general rise of political Islam and the role of Sadr and his companions, as well as the development of the Islamic movement after Sadr's death ('Iraq', in Shireen Hunter ed., *The Politics of Islamic Revivalism*, pp. 71–87. This is a shortened version of a fuller unpublished study, 'Political Islam and the 'Ulama in Iraq', Berkeley, October 1986); the world view of Sadr's sister ('Le Féminisme Islamique de Bint al-Houdâ'); and the role in Lebanese politics of three graduates from Najaf, Muhammad Jawad Mughniyya, Muhammad Mahdi Shamseddin, and Muhammad Husayn Fadlallah ('Shi'i thought from the South of Lebanon', Centre for Lebanese Studies Papers, Oxford, April 1988). The reader can also consult a recent study on the larger scene of the Iraqi opposition, of which the Islamic movement is of course part. (*The Iraqi Opposition: a Dossier*, SOAS, London, 1991. This includes a short article on 'Démocratie à Bagdad', *Le Monde*, 12 February 1991.) For a fuller bibliography on an increasingly well-documented phenomenon, the reader is referred to the works cited in these articles.

80 The *fatwa* of Muhsin al-Hakim, which was issued in February 1960, is reported in O. Spies, 'Urteil des Gross-Mujtahids über den Kommunismus', *Die Welt des Islam*, 6, 1959–1961, pp. 264–5; Murtada Al Yasin's *fatwa* was mentioned above n.39.

81 See this volume, chapter 1. I worked with Mahdi al-Hakim on the rather unclear picture of the early confrontation between Najaf and Baghdad, but his assassination in February 1988 prevented the completion of fascinating interviews started in the summer of 1987. The present remarks are also the result of close collaboration with Muhammad Bahr al-'Ulum, who has tirelessly given me his time and documentation to lift the veil on modern Iraqi history.

82 Muhammad Baqer as-Sadr, *Iqtisaduna*, p. 5; *Falsafatuna*, p. 400.

83 Muhammad Baqer as-Sadr, *Risalatuna* (*Our Message*), Tehran, 1982. Original said to have been published fourteen years earlier (1967–8).

84 Bint al-Huda, *al-Majmu'a al-Qasasiyya al-Kamila* (*The Complete Fiction Collection*), 3 vols., Beirut, n.d. (early 1980s). This collection includes also non-fiction works, like her articles in *al-Adwa'*.

85 *Al-Majmu'a al-Qasasiyya al-Kamila*, vol. 3, p. 181.

86 Ja'far Husayn Nizar, *'Adhra' al-'Aqida wal-Madhhab: ash-Shahida Bint al-Huda* (*The Virgin of Principles: the Martyr Bint al-Huda*), Beirut, 1985, p. 33, quoting the article which is published in *al-Majmu'a al-Qasasiyya al-Kamila*, vol. 3, pp. 137–9.

87 This information appears in '*as-Sayyed yu'arrif nafsah* (*as-Sayyed* [Fadlalah] introduces himself)', *al-'Alam*, London, 13 September 1987, p. 34.

88 See these articles in M. H. Fadlallah, *Afaq Islamiyya wa Mawadi' Ukhra* (*Islamic Horizons and other Issues*), Beirut, 1980.

89 Muhammad Husayn Fadlallah, '*Adwa' 'alal-Adwa'* (Lights on *al-Adwa'*), in *al-Adwa'*, 5:2, 1984, p. 168. The new *Adwa'* journal, which is printed in Qum, has obviously been named after its illustrious predecessor. Fadlallah's article was also published as a preface to Sadr's *Risalatuna*, pp. 16–17.

90 For details on the collection *Min Hadi an-Najaf*, see my 'Religious militancy', pp. 719–23; for Hashimi and Hakim, 'Political Islam', pp. 23–40; for Shamseddin, 'Shi'i thought', pp. 25 ff.

91 Conversations with Dr Ahmad Chalabi, a prominent Iraqi businessman, now living in exile in London, winter 1990, and with Dr Muhammad Bahr al-'Ulum.

92 See Nizar az-Zein, '*Hadith ash-Shahr* (Talk of the month), *al-'Irfan* (Sidon), 57:6, October 1969, pp. 888–9; quoted in 'Shi'i thought', p. 14.

93 Muhsin al-Hakim recalled the shouts of the mourners, '*Sayyed Mahdi mu jasus, isma' ya rayyes* (Sayyed Mahdi is no Spy, Listen O President [Bakr]', and was still afflicted two decades later for not having been able to attend the funeral of his father. Conversations with Mahdi al-Hakim, London, summer 1987.

Introduction to Part I

1 There were also attempts to carve up smaller or different entities from the existing ones. Israel-Palestine is an example of the brutal coming to existence of a nation-state, and has its own exceptional logic. In the case of some Christian groups in Lebanon vying for a smaller Lebanese 'Marunistan', the concept was so circumstantially limited that it must be read into the fine print of the declarations of the most extremist leaders. On the concept of Marunistan, see J. Randal, *The Tragedy of Lebanon*, London, 1983. In the case of the Kurds, the favouring of a Kurdish entity against the fragmentation of the Kurdish people across five nations has been time and again militarily subdued. See a good public law analysis in L. C. Buchheit, *Secession: the Legitimacy of Self-Determination*, New Haven, 1978, pp. 153–62.

2 On the early forms, M. Kramer, *Islam Assembled: the Advent of the Muslim Congresses*, New York, 1986; A. Sanhoury [Sanhuri], *Le Califat*, Paris, 1926. On the later forms, Saudi style, see R. Schulze, *Islamischer Internationalismus in 20. Jahrhundert; Untersuchungen zur Geschichte der Islamischen Weltliga (Mekka)*, Leiden, 1990; G. Salamé, *As-Siyasa al-Kharijiyya as-Sa'udiyya mundhu 'am* 1945 (Saudi Foreign Policy since 1945), Beirut, 1980; (Post-revolutionary) Iranian style, F. Halliday, 'Iranian foreign policy since 1979: internationalism and nationalism in the Islamic revolution', in Cole and Keddie eds., *Shi'ism and Social Protest*, pp. 88–107. Generally on the modern period, A. Dawisha ed., *Islam in Foreign Policy*, Cambridge, 1983; J. Piscatori, *Islam in a World of Nation-States*, Cambridge, 1986.

3 Shaybani (d.189/804), *Sharh Kitab as-Siyar al-Kabir*, with comments by Sarakhsi (d. *c.* 485/1092), S. Munajjid ed., 3 vols., Cairo, 1971. See also S. Mahmassani [Mahmasani], 'Les principes de droit international à la lumière de la doctrine islamique', *Académie de Droit International, Recueil des Cours* (The Hague), 117, 1966, 205–328; M. Khadduri, *War and Peace in the Law of Islam*, Baltimore, 1955.

4 Sadr, *Lamha Fiqhiyya*, quoted this volume, General introduction, n. 76.

5 'Dossier', in *Cahiers de l'Orient*, 1988, quoted this volume, General introduction, n. 34.

1 Archetypes of Shi'i law

1 In this work, Ja'farism, Twelver or Ithna'ashari Shi'ism, and Imamism are used interchangeably. Technically, the term Ja'farism, after the 6th Imam and most renowned early jurist Ja'far as-Sadeq (d.148/765), emphasises the legal side of the sect. Imamism is more general, as it may include the Isma'ilis, who believe in the specificity of seven, as opposed to the Twelve Imams of the largest Shi'i sect, and the Zaydis. Ithna'asharism is predominant among Shi'is in Iran, Iraq, Lebanon, Pakistan, India, and parts of East Africa. For all these terms, see q.v. *Encyclopaedia of Islam*, Leiden, 1st edn, 1913–38, 2nd edn, 1960 ff.; also E. Kohlberg, 'From Imamiyya to Ithna'ashariyya', *Bulletin of the School of Oriental and African Studies*, 39, 1976, 521–34. See on sects generally, H. Laoust, *Les Schismes dans l'Islam*, Paris, 1965.

2 A. Newman, *The Development and Political Significance of the Rationalist (Usuli) and Traditionalist (Akhbari) School in Imami Shi'i History from the third/ninth to the tenth/sixteenth Century A.D.*, Ph.D. thesis, 2 vols., University of California at Los Angeles, 1986.

3 J. Cole, 'Shi'i clerics in Iraq and Iran 1722–1780: the Akhbari-Usuli controversy reconsidered', *Iranian Studies*, 18:1, 1985, 3–34.

4 Muhammad Baqir Ibn Muhammad Akmal al-Behbehani, known as al-Wahid al-Behbehani (d. 1205/1791), author of *al-Fawa'ed al-Ha'iriyya*, MS mentioned in Agha Buzurg at-Tihrani, *adh-Dhari'a ila Tasanif ash-Shi'a*, 3rd edn, Beirut, n.d., vol. 16, p. 331. See also H. M. Mudarrisi, *An Introduction to Shi'i Law*, pp. 55–7; G. Scarcia, 'Intorno alle controversie tra ahbari e usuli presso gli imamiti di Persia', *Rivista degli Studi Orientali*, 33, 1958, 211–50.

5 Faraj al-'Umrani, *al-Usuliyyun wal-Akhbariyyun Firqa Wahida* (*Usulis and Akhbaris are One and the Same* [*Sect*]), quoted in Muhammad Bahr al-'Ulum, *al-Akhbariyya, Usuluha wa Tatawwuruha*, (*The Akhbariyya, Principles and Development*), MS kindly provided by the author, 1988. [Hereinafter quoted as Bahr al-'Ulum, MS 1988], p. 1 n. 3; see also n. 9, below; Muhammad Baqer as-Sadr, *al-Ma'alim al-Jadida*, pp. 76–89.

6 The scholarship of the Bahr al-'Ulum family goes back several generations. Among the most famous *'ulama* was Muhammad ibn Taqi ibn Rida ibn Mahdi at-Tabataba'i, known as Bahr al-'Ulum, author of *Bulghat al-Faqih* (The *faqih*'s summum), who died in 1326/1908. Further see references in Agha Buzurg at-Tihrani, *adh-Dhari'a*, vol. 3, p. 148.

7 See this volume General introduction, p. 16 and note 79.

8 Muhammad Bahr al-'Ulum, '*Uyub al-Irada*; The thesis was submitted at Cairo University in 1980.

9 Muhammad Bahr al-'Ulum, '*ad-dirasa fin-najaf wa tatawwuruha*' (Studies in Najaf and their development), in J. Khalili ed., *Mausu'at al-'Atabat al-Muqaddasa*, vol.2, Beirut, 1964 [hereinafter *Dirasa* 1964]; Bahr al-'Ulum, *al-Ijtihad*, Beirut, 1977 [hereinafter *Ijtihad* 1977]; Bahr al-'Ulum, MS 1988, above n.5.

10 According to some reports, Astarabadi died in Mecca in 1026/1617, in 1033/1623 in others. Muhammad Bahr al-'Ulum, *Dirasa* 1964, p. 64. Yusuf al-Bahrani (d. 1186/1772), *Lu'lu'at al-Bahrayn*, Najaf, 1966, p. 119.

11 '*Akhbari salb*', Bahrani, *Lu'lu'at*, p. 117.
12 See now W. Hallaq, 'The development of logical structure'.
13 Bahr al-'Ulum, *Dirasa* 1964, p. 65.
14 *Ibid.* This account also suggests that the emergence and early rise of Akhbarism is rooted in the more general debate between Sunnism and Shi'ism. Akhbarism was a reaction to the imitation in Shi'i *usul* of the earlier and by then established Sunni discipline. The Akhbari school came to reinstitute the distinctiveness of Shi'ism by introducing literalism in the Shi'i legal system through a narrow and exclusive interpretation of the Shi'i *hadith*.
15 'The four books' of Shi'i *hadith* (which are *hadith* of the Prophet as well as of the Twelve Imams) are Kulayni's (d. 329/941) *Kafi*; Ibn Babawayh al-Qummi, known as as-Saduq (d. 381/991), *Man la-Yahdaruhu al-Faqih*; Muhammad Ibn Hasan at-Tusi, known as Shaykh at-Ta'ifa (the community's shaykh), d. 460/1067, *Tahdhib al-Ahkam*; and by Tusi also, *al-Istibsar*.
16 Kulayni (d. 329/941) presents *'aql* in the following passage of his *Kitab al-'aql wal-Jahl* (*Book of Reason and Ignorance*): '[The angel] Gabriel came to Adam and said to him: O Adam, I was ordered to offer you a choice of one of three. Adam said: what are the three? Gabriel said: reason (*'aql*), circumspection (*haya'*) and religion (*din*). Adam said: I choose reason', *al-Usul minal-Jami' al-Kafi* (*Rules of the Sufficient Compendium*), I, n.p., n.d., pp. 6–7.
17 The general differences and the more detailed twenty-nine legal differences presented by the Shi'i jurist appear in charts. See details in Bahr al-'Ulum, *Dirasa* 1964, pp. 64–71; Yusuf al-Bahrani, in *al-Hada'eq an-Nadira*, 2nd ed. Beirut, 1405/1985, I, p. 167, mentions that 'Abdallah ibn Saleh al-Bahrani listed up to forty-three differences in his book *Munyat al-Mumarisin*. See also charts drawn after Khwansari's *Rawdat al-Jannat*, in M. Momen, *An Introduction to Shi'i Islam*, New Haven, 1985, pp. 222–5.
18 Sunni *hadith* has been categorised by S. Mahmasani as *sahih*, *hasan*, *da'if*, (strong, good, weak), as well as *sahih*, *hasan*, *gharib* (strange). See respectively his *Al-Awda' at-Tashri'iyya fid-Duwal al-'arabiyya Madiha wa Hadiruha* (*Legal Systems in the Arab States, Past and Present*), Beirut, 1957, p. 128; *Falsafat at-Tashri' fil-Islam* (*Philosophy of Jurisprudence in Islam*), Beirut, 1946, p. 123. The late Subhi as-Saleh has adopted a general division between *sahih* and *da'if*, although he recognised, following Ibn as-Salah (d. 676/1277), the possibility of 'more than sixty-five categories of *hadith*'. *'Ulum al-Hadith wa Mustalahuhu* (*The Sciences and Terminology of hadith*), 2nd edn, Damascus, 1963.
19 *Al-Ijtihad*, quoted above n.9.
20 Muhammad Bahr al-'Ulum, *Ijtihad* 1977, pp. 168–83.
21 *Ibid.*, p. 170.
22 On the importance of this distinction see in comparison the present debate in Iran, this volume, chapter 3, as well as the comments related to the discretionary area of the Islamic ruler in Muhammad Baqer as-Sadr, *Iqtisaduna*, this volume, chapter 4.
23 Astarabadi, *al-Fawa'ed al-Madaniyya*, pp. 47–8, quoted in Muhammad Bahr al-'Ulum, *Ijtihad* 1977, p. 172. See on *al-Fawa'ed al-Madaniyya* Agha Buzurg at-Tihrani, *adh-Dhari'a*, vol. 16, p. 358.
24 Bahr al-'Ulum, *Ijtihad* 1977, p. 173.
25 Yusuf al-Bahrani's moderation is best expressed in the 'twelfth introduction' to his compendium, *al-Hada'eq an-Nadira*, above n.17, pp. 167–70, in which he admits having first been closer to the Akhbaris: however, 'what [the polemists in

the two schools] have mentioned in terms of differences is in the most, if not in totality, unfruitful (*la yuthmir farqan fil-maqam*)', p. 167.

26 Bahr al-'Ulum, *Ijtihad* 1977, pp. 173–81.

27 Bahr al-'Ulum, MS 1988, quoted above n. 5.

28 *Ibid.*, p. 18; see also *Ijtihad* 1977, p. 183.

29 Bahr al-'Ulum, MS 1988, p. 17.

30 Muhammad Rida al-Muzaffar, *Usul al-Fiqh*, rpt al-Qutayf, n.d., vol. II, p. 105.

31 Bahr al-'Ulum, MS 1988, p. 17.

32 The implications of this reading of *ijma'* are far-reaching both for the general approach to Islamic law and for the received idea on the Usuli school. In terms of general Islamic law, it tends to undermine the idea of the 'four sources of the law' by simply subsuming *ijma'* under the *Sunna*. With the imprecision of the concept of *Sunna*, this means that the whole system generally attributed as a specificity of the *shari'a* should come under new scrutiny. It is perhaps time to start questioning such received ideas as 'the sources of Islamic law', which reinforce the premises of 'stagnation' as a characteristic of the *shari'a*.

33 Muhammad Taqi al-Hakim, *al-Usul al-'Amma lil-Fiqh al-Muqaran* (*The General Bases of Comparative Jurisprudence*), Beirut, 1963, p. 299.

34 Bahr al-'Ulum, MS 1988, p. 17.

35 Vide especially Bahr al-'Ulum, *Ijtihad* 1977, p. 177.

36 Bahr al-'Ulum, MS 1988, p. 17.

37 '*Inna al-faqih al-akhbari mujtahid duna an yusarrih bi-dhalik*', *Ijtihad* 1977, p. 182.

38 See now the criticism of W. Hallaq, 'Was the Gate of Ijtihad ever closed?', *International Journal of Middle Eastern Studies*, 1984, 1–33; (originally as Ph.D. Thesis, University of Washington, Seattle, 1983); 'On the origins of the controversy about the existence of *mujtahid*s and the gate of *ijtihad*', *Studia Islamica*, 63, 1986, 129–42.

39 The works of Cole and Newman have unveiled some social dimensions concerning the controversy between Akhbarism and Usulism, but the evidence is understandably elusive. I am not aware of any work that carried the contribution of Hallaq on the myth of the closing of *bab al-ijtihad* further. There is a telltale absence of such a concept in the masterly works of Goldziher (esp. *Muhammadenische Studien*, 2 vols., Halle, 1889–90, and *Vorlesungen über den Islam*, Heidelberg, 1910). This absence suggests that the concept took root in the West sometime after the death of the great scholar. It is probable that the myth also started being established in the Muslim world at the same period. More research in the field might cast new light on interesting strands in Islamic law and Orientalism on the one hand: why was it convenient for Western scholarship to insist that the *shari'a* had been static since the tenth century?; and, on the other hand, Islamic law and *gharbzadegi* (the 'Occidentosis' portrayed by Jalal Al-e Ahmad): why have Muslim jurists found it convenient to accept and repeat the idea?

It is noteworthy that the idea of an *ijtihad* being barred at some point in history was never invoked in the case of Ja'fari law.

40 The young Sadr was often chosen to deliver sermons and prayers on the occasion of the *husayni* pageants at the celebrations of Karbala. Ha'iri, '*Tarjamat*', p. 41.

41 See this volume, pp. 7–19 and bibliography.

42 The concept of civil society has increasingly been used in the Middle East to

depict that part of social organization(s) which is not directly associated with state authorities, and for which some spaces of democratic processes seem to operate by default. The more the state apparatus tends to be authoritarian and generally disrespectful of human rights or proper electoral representation, the more 'mechanisms' of civil society seem to offer a democratic counterpoint. 'Civil society' appeared as a developed concept first in the 1830s in Hegel's *Philosophy of Right*. The concept is helpful in the Middle East contemporary context to depict '*a new reflection of what resists in society*, on the reserves of inertia and opacity which a society in crisis opposes to the actions – and acquired knowledge – of these actors'. This definition appears in the sophisticated Summa of Robert Fossaert, *La Société*, (six volumes published in Paris since 1977). In its peculiar independence from state power, 'Shi'i civil society' in twentieth-century Iraq fits well the characteristics Fossaert gives in volume 5 (*Les Etats*) on 'Les formes de la Société Civile': 'A contrario, will be considered as pertaining to Civil Society all the elements of social organization which are or seem *independent* from the State, and even those which seem to enjoy sufficient *autonomy* vis à vis the State ... ' (R. Fossaert, *Les Etats*, Paris, 1981, p. 137 and pp. 152–3. Emphasis in original.)

43 Ha'iri, '*Tarjamat*', p. 52.

44 On the 1948 revolt (the *wathba*) and the execution of Fahd, see Batatu, *The Old Social Classes*, pp. 545–71; the rise of the Communists at the expense of the Shi'i *mujtahid*s was manifest in the last great revolt against the monarchy before the 1958 coup, which took place in Najaf in 1956. On this revolt, Batatu, pp. 749–57, esp. p. 752: 'A number of factors contributed to the strength of the Communists at Najaf, the holiest city of the Shi'ah. For one thing, Najaf was still, as it had been for centuries, the seat of oppressive wealth and dire poverty. For another, Najaf was and remains at one and the same time a center for the most stubborn religious traditionalism and a ferment for the most advanced of revolutionary ideas.'

45 See this volume, General introduction, n. 46 and accompanying text. *Al- Muthul al-'Ulya fil-Islam la fi Bhamdun* (*The Supreme Values are in Islam, not in Bhamdun*) was written in answer to an invitation organised by an American proselytiser to a number of religious dignitaries to counter the 'materialist' message disseminated by Communism in the Middle East. The pamphlet, which dates from 1954, was republished in Tehran in 1983.

46 Sadr, *Fadak fit-Tarikh* (1955). See General introduction, and 'Religious militancy', pp. 712–15.

47 Sadr, *Falsafatuna* (1959). See General introduction.

48 Details on Sadr's works in *usul* in General introduction.

49 See generally E. Honigmann, 'al-Nadjaf', *Encyclopaedia of Islam*, 1st ed., Leiden 1936, III, pp. 815–16; J. Mahbuba, *Madi an-Najaf wa Hadiruha* (*Najaf Past and Present*), Najaf, 3 vols., 1955–8, especially vol. 1; Khalili ed., *Mausu'at*, quoted this volume, General introduction n. 52.

50 J. Abu Lughod, *Cairo*: 1001 *Years of the City Victorious*, Princeton, 1971.

51 On the history of al-Azhar, see e.g. *Al-Azhar, Tarikhuhu wa Tatawwuruhu* (*The Azhar: its History and Development*), Cairo, 1964; B. Dodge, *A Millennium of Muslim Learning*, Washington, 1961; A. Chris Eccel, *Egypt, Islam and Social Change: al-Azhar in Conflict and Accommodation*, Berlin, 1984.

52 See the complaints of another Lebanese graduate from Najaf, Muhammad Jawad Mughniyya, '*An-najaf fi alf 'am*' (*Najaf over a Millennium*), in *Min Huna wa*

Hunak (*From Here and There*), Beirut, n.d., pp. 48–50 (originally published in Najaf in 1957).

53 The difference between learning at Najaf and at a Western University will appear more evident in this section. It is interesting however to note that Najaf graduates, like Muhammad Mahdi Shamseddin, presented themselves as part of 'the University of Najaf' (*jami'at an-najaf*). See Shamseddin, *Nazam al-Hukm wal-Idara fil-Islam* (*The System of Governance and Administration in Islam*), Beirut, 1955, cover page. See also in next footnote the texts of Muzaffar and Faqih.

54 Descriptions of Najaf and its curriculum can be found in F. Jamali, 'The theological colleges of Najaf', *The Muslim World*, 50, 1960, pp. 15–22. (This outsider account was written by an erstwhile Shi'i Prime Minister of Iraq) [hereinafter Jamali]; Muhammad Rida al-Muzaffar (d. 1964), '*Jami'at an-najaf al-ashraf wa jami'iat al-qarawiyyin*' (The University of Holy Najaf and the University at Qarawiyyin [Fes, Morocco]), *Majallat al-Majma' al-'Ilmi* (Baghdad), 1964, pp. 293–301 (this report by a scholar versed in *usul* was read to a Moroccan audience) [hereinafter Muzaffar]; Muhammad Mahdi al-Asifi (one of the leaders of the Islamic opposition), *Madrasat an-Najaf wa Tatawwur al-Haraka al-Islamiyya fiha* (*The School of Najaf and the Development of the Islamic Movement*), Najaf, 1964; Mughniyya, '*An-najaf fi alf 'am*'; but the two most detailed analyses are Muhammad Taqi al-Faqih, *Jami'at an-Najaf fi 'Asriha al-Hadir* (*The University of Najaf in the Present Era*), Tyre, Lebanon, n.d. [hereinafter Faqih. This work is difficult to date with precision, because parts of it were written at different periods. The bulk dates probably from the 1940s]; and Muhammad Bahr al-'Ulum, *Dirasa* 1964, quoted above n. 9.
Traces of criticism of old-fashioned style and content in the Najaf system can be detected in the description of Jamali, but there is a remarkable instance of such criticism as late as 1970. See 'Ali az-Zein, '*Adwa' 'alal-madares ad-diniyya fin-najaf*' (*Lights on the Religious Schools of Najaf*), *al-'Irfan* (Sidon), 58:3–4, 1970, pp. 307–17. For the curriculum and the colleges in Iran, compare the remarkable study of an apprentice-*mujtahid*'s upbringing in R. Mottahedeh, *The Mantle of the Prophet: Learning and Power in Modern Iran*, London, 1986; M. Fisher, *Iran: From Religious Dispute to Revolution*, Cambridge, Mass., 1980, pp. 12–104.

55 Muzaffar, p. 296, Bahr al-'Ulum, *Dirasa* 1964, p. 83; but contrast Jamali, p. 15, who puts the figure at 1954 students, of whom 326 Iraqis only, 896 Iranians, 47 from Lebanon and Syria, 665 from South Asia. In contrast, Batatu notes, there were some 6,000 students at Najaf in 1918. Batatu, 'Iraq's underground Shi'a movements', p. 582. Since the definition of a 'student' of Najaf is rather mercurial, as will be seen in this section, the precision of any census cannot be ascertained.

56 Muhammad Jawad Mughniyya, *Tajarib* (*Trials*), Beirut, 1980, p. 61.

57 Bahr al-'Ulum, *Dirasa* 1964, p. 83.

58 For revenues of the '*ulama* in Shi'i law, see this volume, p. 44; the poverty of many mujtahids is related in Jamali, p. 18; at the highest echelons of the Shi'i hierarchy, however, money does not seem to have been a serious problem, especially since the 1960s and the support of many merchants for the '*ulama*'s role in containing communism. Mahdi al-Hakim told me how ridiculous the charge of his embezzlement with CIA funds had appeared in 1969, in view of the means at the disposal of his father *Ayat Allah* Muhsin al-Hakim. The charge for embezzlement was for a paltry 50,000 Lebanese pounds (then the equivalent of

some 20,000 US dollars)! This remark gives an idea, a contrario, of the scale of cash revenues available to the great *mujtahids*.

59 A remarkable case history of the turbulences in eighteenth-century Iraq can be found in R. Olson, *The Siege of Mosul and Ottoman-Persian Relations* 1718–1843, Bloomington, Indiana, 1975.

60 Faqih, above, n. 54.

61 Bahr al-'Ulum, *Dirasa* 1964, p. 92.

62 See Jamali, p. 16.

63 The following section is based on Bahr al-'Ulum, *Dirasa* 1964, pp. 92–100; Muzaffar, pp. 297–300; Faqih, pp. 105–18.

64 Muzaffar, p. 297.

65 *Ibid.*, p. 299.

66 Bahr al-'Ulum, *Dirasa* 1964, p. 92.

67 Sadr, *al-Ma'alem al-Jadida*, quoted in General Introduction, n. 48.

68 Bahr al-'Ulum, *Dirasa* 1964, p. 95.

69 Faqih, p. 107.

70 Muhammad Taqi al-Hakim, *al-Usul al-'Amma*, quoted above, n. 33.

71 Faqih, p. 111.

72 *Ibid.*, p. 114.

73 *Ibid.*, p. 115.

74 Bahr al-'Ulum, *Dirasa* 1964, p. 98.

75 *Ibid.*, p. 99; Faqih, pp. 116–17.

76 See Faqih, section entitled '*shahadat jami'at an-najaf*' (*The Diploma of the University of Najaf*), pp. 119–30, 146–54.

77 *Ibid.*, p. 120.

78 *Ibid.*, p. 146.

79 *Ibid.*, p. 147.

80 *Ibid.*, p. 148.

81 *Ibid.*, p. 147.

82 *Ibid.*, p. 149.

83 *Ibid.*, p. 150.

84 *Ibid.*, pp. 151–4.

85 Abul-Qasem al-Khu'i, *al-Masa'el al-Muntakhaba*, p. 2 [hereinafter *Masa'el*]. This work is an abridged version authorised by *Ayat Allah* al-Khu'i, who resides in Najaf to date. Khu'i has always steered away from politics, and his testimony shows the degree of consensus on the institutional structure of Shi'i civil society among both activist and quietist *mujtahids*.

86 Khu'i, *Masa'el*, pp. 2–3. On a case of *ihtyat*, see an example in the quotation of Sadr, n. 43 above.

87 On *khums*, see the treatise of Muhammad Hadi al-Milani, *Muhadarat fi-Fiqh al-Imamiyya, Kitab al-Khums* (*Lectures in Imami Jurisprudence, the Book of khums*), F. Milani ed., n.p., 1400/1800; N. Calder, '*Khums* in Imami Shi'i jurisprudence, from the tenth to the sixteenth century AD', *BSOAS*, 45, 1982, pp. 39–47.

88 H. Algar mentions that in nineteenth-century Iran 'prominent mujtahids did not hesitate to use coercion' for the collection of taxes, *Religion and State in Iran, 1785–1906*, Berkeley, 1969, p. 12.

89 With the constraints of Ba'thist rule in Baghdad, the pendulum has shifted again towards Qum and Mashhad, but more perspective is needed to judge the rise and fall of the standards of legal scholarship in Iran and Iraq. Political events will no

doubt have a decisive impact on the curriculum and role of the educational institutions in both countries.

90 In his general theory of society, Fossaert writes quite pointedly about this phenomenon in Iran. To 'understand the complexities of the relationship between the State and Civil Society ... it is important to avoid identifying at all times and in all places religious order and established political order. The Shi'i mullahs have once again demonstrated this point, in Iran between 1976 and 1979, even if they would thereafter try to convert their religious order into a new political order.' R. Fossaert, *La Société*, vol.5, p. 167.

91 See a veiled criticism by Muhammad Baqer as-Sadr of the limits of the *risala 'amaliyya*, in *Khutut Tafsilyya 'an Iqtisad al-Mujtama' al-Islami* (*Detailed Guidelines of the Economy of an Islamic Society*), Beirut, 1979, p. 12; see also this volume, General introduction, p. 13.

92 Muhammad Husayn Kashif al-Ghita', *Asl ash-Shi'a wa Usuluha* (*The Origin and Principles of Shi'ism*), original edition in the 1930s, translated in Pakistan in 1982 as *Shi'a: Origin and Faith*.

93 All three books of Kashif al-Ghita' were printed several times in Iraq, Lebanon, Iran and Pakistan.

94 Quoted above, n. 53.

95 Muhammad Husayn Kashif al-Ghita', *Tahrir al-Majalla*, (*Comment on the Majalla*), Najaf, *c.* 1940, I, p. 3.

96 *Ibid.*, p. 4.

97 *Ibid.*, II, p. 326.

98 The fact that *Tahrir al-Majalla* was disregarded by the Iraqi codifiers is surprising. No doubt the sojourn of 'Abd ar-Razzaq as-Sanhuri as Dean of the Baghdad law school and the dominant pan-Arabist trend at the time made the Egyptian influence prevalent.

99 In the most richly documented biography of Khumaini, there is only one mention of Muhammad Baqer as-Sadr, and the context is one of rivalry over the supreme *marja'iyya*. This is when Khumaini wrote a particularly disheartening letter to his son Ahmad. The text of the letter appears in H. Ruhani, *Nehzat-e Imam Khumaini* (*The Movement of Imam Khumaini*), Tehran, 1364/1985 (earlier ed., Qum, 1977), II, pp. 568–9. This letter is dated 28 Shawwal 1390 (27 December 1970).

100 A. Taheri, *Khomeiny*, Paris, 1985, p. 163.

101 For details on this period, see Mallat, 'Religious militancy' and 'Political Islam'.

102 O. Bengio, 'Shi's and politics in Ba'thi Iraq', *Middle Eastern Studies*, 1985, p. 2. Also P. Marr, *The Modern History of Iraq*, Boulder, Co, 1985, pp. 228–30; P. Sluglett and M. Farouk-Sluglett, *Iraq since 1958: from Revolution to Dictatorship*, London, 1987, pp. 198, 208.

103 Ha'iri, '*Tarjamat*', p. 117. I was not able to find the exact date of the telegram, which was aired on the Arabic program of Radio Tehran. There is also no record of Sadr's request to seek refuge in Iran. This gap has fuelled several rumours as to the exact sequence of events.

104 Ha'iri, '*Tarjamat*', p. 123.

105 'Imam Khomeini's message', quoted this volume, General introduction, n. 29.

106 See 'Ali al-Wardi, *Tarikh al-'Iraq al-Hadith* (*History of Modern Iraq*), vol.6, *Min 'Am* 1920 *ila 'Am* 1924 (from 1920 to 1924), Baghdad, 1976, p. 251. See also P. Sluglett, *Britain in Iraq* 1914–1932, London, 1976, pp. 300–16.

107 This is a well-known episode in the Shi'i hierarchy. It was matched recently by the 'downgrading' of Husain Muntazeri from *Ayat Allah* to *Hujjat al-Islam*.
108 To this could be added other examples of the 'war of the titles', such as the sudden upgrading of the (relatively) young *Hujjat al-Islam* Khamene'i to the rank of *Ayat Allah* by the Iranian Assembly of Experts in June 1989.
109 It is not a wanton speculation to trace part of Khumaini's obduracy to continue the war beyond the liberation of Iranian territory in 1982 in terms of a posthumous debt to Muhammad Baqer as-Sadr. On the connection in general between the war and the Shi'i International from a Clausewitzian perspective, see my 'Aux Origines'.
110 Batatu, *The Old Social Classes*, p. 49.
111 Compare the superb description of a similar phenomenon in the European Renaissance in Lucien Febvre, *Le Problème de l'Incroyance au Seizième Siècle*, Paris, 1947, pp. 19–104: 'Les bons camarades'.
112 Muhammad Jawad Mughniyya, *al-Islam wal-'aql* (*Islam and Reason*), Beirut, 1967, p. 230.
113 Khu'i, *Masa'el*, p. 3.
114 *Ibid.*, p. 2.
115 *Ibid.*, p. 3. In Khumaini's *Tahrir al-Wasila*, I, pp. 3–8, there is no mention of this difference, but a hierarchy is established at the top of the pyramid, with the definition of the *marja'* as the 'most competent *mujtahid*'.
116 Faqih, pp. 130–40.
117 *Ibid.*, p. 131.
118 The list is traditional. See e.g. Mawardi (d. 450/1058), *al-Ahkam as-Sultaniyya* (*Sultanic Rules*), Cairo, 2nd edn, 1966, pp. 5–6, quoted in A. Lambton, *State and Government in Medieval Islam*, London, 1981, pp. 89–90.
119 Faqih, p. 131.
120 *Ibid.*, p. 132.
121 *Ibid.*, p. 133.
122 *Ibid.*
123 *Ibid.*, p. 136.

2 On the origins of the Iranian constitution: Muhammad Baqer as-Sadr's 1979 treatises

1 There is now an important literature on these lectures. Among the best studies are G. Rose, '*Velayat-e Faqih* and the recovery of Islamic identity in the thought of Ayatollah Khomeini', in N. Keddie ed., *Religion and Politics in Iran*, New Haven, 1983, pp. 166–88; H. Enayat, 'Iran: Khumayni's concept of the "Guardianship of the Jurisconsult"', in J. Piscatori ed., *Islam and the Political Process*, Cambridge, 1982, pp. 160–80; S. Zubaida, 'The ideological conditions for Khomeini's doctrine of government', *Economy and Society*, 11:2, 1982; see also Zubaida, *Islam, the People and the State*, London, 1989, and my review in *Middle East Reports*, 21:3, May/June 1991, 46; K. H. Göbel, *Moderne Shiitische Politik und Staatsidee*, Leske, 1984. Norman Calder has published a study comparing Khumaini's thought on the '*ulama* and the state in his jurisprudential work *Kitab al-Buyu'* with classical works in Shi'i law, particularly Murtada Ansari's (d. 1281/1864) *Kitab al-Makasib*. N. Calder, 'Accommodation and revolution in Imami Shi'i jurisprudence: Khumayni and the classical tradition',

Middle East Studies, 18, 1982. Khumaini's lectures were delivered in Najaf between 21 January and 8 February, 1970 and collected from student notes to be published in Persian in 1971. This collection was translated by H. Algar as 'Islam and Government', and published in Imam Khomeini, *Islam and Revolution*, Berkeley, 1981, pp. 27–151. There are two Arabic editions, published in Beirut in 1979. According to Rose, mentioning Ahmad Khumaini, the original was in Arabic. We have used here *al-Hukuma al-Islamiyya* (*Islamic Government*), published by Dar at-Tali'a in Beirut, *Velayat-e Faqih* (Persian version), Tehran, 1357/1979, as well as Algar's English version. They are respectively quoted hereafter as Khumaini, *Hukuma*, Khumaini, *Velayat*, and Khumaini, *Government*.

2 On the early Iraqi parliament, see Muhammad Muzaffar al-Adhami, *Political Aspects of the Iraqi Parliament and Election Processes* 1920–1932, Ph.D. Thesis, London, 1978; see also E. Kedourie, 'The Kingdom of Iraq: a retrospect', in *The Chatham House Version*, London, 1970, pp. 250, 265.

3 Batatu, *Old Social Classes*, p. 1146.

4 See Muhammad Rashid Rida on the role of the *'ulama* at the time of the collapse of the Caliphate in the early 1920s, in his *al-Khilafa wal-Imama al-'Uzma* (*The Caliphate and the Great Leadership*), Cairo, 1923. An early example in Egypt of the opposition of some *'ulama* to Napoleon's invasion is documented in A. Loutfi el-Sayed, 'The role of the *'ulama* in Egypt during the early nineteenth century', in P. M. Holt ed., *Political and Social Change in Modern Egypt*, London, 1968, pp. 270–4. Compare E. Said on the accommodationist *'ulama*, *Orientalism*, London, 1978, p. 82.

5 Khumaini, *Hukuma*, pp. 8–9; *Velayat*, p. 8; *Government*, p. 28.

6 Khumaini, *Hukuma*, p. 20; *Velayat*, p. 23; *Government*, p. 37.

7 H. Algar, *Religion and State*, pp. 205–21; N. Keddie, *Religion and Rebellion in Iran: the Tobacco Protest of* 1891–1892, London, 1966.

8 See the recent book by Vanessa Martin, *Islam and Modernism: the Iranian Revolution of* 1906, London, 1989.

9 This volume, books mentioned in the General introduction, n .41; see also 'Abd ar-Razzaq al-Hasani, *ath-Thawra al-'Iraqiyya al-Kubra* (*The Great Iraqi Revolt*), 3rd edn, Saida, 1972; A. Rihani, *Muluk al-'Arab* (*The Kings of the Arabs*), Beirut, 2nd edn, 1929, vol. 2, p. 329.

10 There is a vast literature on these constitutional bodies. The best comparative work is Mauro Cappelletti's. See e.g. his 'Who watches the watchmen', *American Journal of Comparative Law*, 31, 1983, p. 1. This article, and other studies, were collected recently in M. Cappelletti, *The Judicial Process in Comparative Perspective*, Oxford, 1989. Compare A. Lambton, 'Quis custodiet custodes? some reflections on the Persian theory of government', *Studia Islamica*, 5, 1955, 125–48; 6, 1956, 125–46. See further chapter 3, this volume.

11 Khumaini, *Hukuma*, p. 10; *Velayat*, p. 11; *Government*, p. 31.

12 Khumaini, *Hukuma*, p. 50; *Velayat*, p. 64; *Government*, p. 62.

13 Khumaini, *Hukuma*, p. 46. The Persian and English versions are slightly different. See Khumaini, *Velayat*, p. 60. Algar's translation reads: 'If the ruler adheres to Islam, he must necessarily submit to the *faqih*, asking him about the laws and ordinances of Islam in order to implement them. This being the case, the true rulers are the *fuqaha* themselves, and rulership ought officially to be theirs, to apply to them, not to those who are obliged to follow the guidance of the *fuqaha* on account of their own ignorance of the law.' *Government*, p. 60.

14 '*Idha ra'ayta al-fuqaha' 'ala abwab as-salatin, fa-bi'sa la-fuqaha' wa bi'sa as-salatin; wa idha ra'ayta as-salatin 'ala abwab al-fuqaha' fa-ni'ma al-fuqaha' wa-ni'ma as-salatin*', aphorism attributed to Mirza Muhammad Hasan ash-Shirazi, the leader of the Tobacco Revolt.

15 Ayat Allah Mahmud Taliqani (d. 1979), who was second in political prominence only to Khumaini, wrote two significant contributions to the constitutional debate in Iran. The first contribution was in the form of the publication of *Ayat Allah* Muhammad Husayn Na'ini, *Tanbih al-Umma wa Tanzih al-Milla: Hukumat az Nazar-i Islam*, Tehran, 1955 (original 1909). On this work by Na'ini, see the detailed study of A. Hairi, *Shi'ism and Constitutionalism in Iran*, Leiden, 1977. The second contribution appears in his article in the important collective *Bahthi dar Baray-e Marja'iyyat va Ruhaniyyat* (*Studies on Marja'iyya and Spirituality*), Tehran, 1963, pp. 199–211. On *Bahthi*, see A. Lambton, 'a reconsideration of the position of the *marja' al-taqlid* and the religious institution', *Studia Islamica*, 20, 1964, 115–35. On Taliqani in general, see M. Bayat, 'Mahmud Taleqani and the Iranian revolution', in M. Kramer ed., *Shi'ism, Resistance and Revolution*, Boulder Co., 1987, pp. 67–94.

16 Muhammad Baqer as-Sadr, *Lamha Fiqhiyya*, quoted this volume, General introduction, n. 76.

17 Qur'an, 42:38: *wa amrukum shura baynakum* (*your affairs must be decided amongst yourselves by consultation*).

18 Khumaini, *Hukuma*, pp. 103–4. The quote is in Arabic in *Velayat*, p. 146; *Government*, p. 109.

19 See '*Kitab al-amr bil-ma'ruf wan-nahi 'an al-munkar*' (*The Book of Enjoining Good and Forbidding Evil*) [in reference to Qur'an, 3:104,114; 7:157; 22:41; 31:17], in Ruhullah al-Khumaini, *Tahrir al-Wasila*, 2nd ed., Beirut, 1985, I, pp. 424–44; and the line by line commentary by A. Mutahhari, *Mustanad Tahrir al-Wasila*, Qum, 1403/1983.

20 There is a gap in our knowledge of the development of Sadr's constitutional thought. The work on *Mujtama'una* (*Our Society*), promised as a sequel to *Iqtisaduna* and *Falsafatuna*, was probably never written. Until 1979, the strictly political-constitutional thought of Sadr must be collated from his works on history (*Fadak*, *Ahl al-Bayt*, *Dawr al-A'imma*), and on *fiqh* (*al-Fatawa al-Wadiha*). The articles published as editorials in the journal *al-Adwa'* and collected in *Risalatuna* do not give a systematic view on his thought. (All references mentioned this volume, General introduction, pp. 7–19). There is no doubt, however, that Sadr must have devoted considerable reflection to the constitutional structure of the Islamic state, and traces of it can be found in 'Izz ad-Din Salim, '*Ash-shahid as-Sadr, ra'ed harakat at-taghyir fil-umma*' (Martyr as-Sadr, leader of the movement for change in the nation), *Tawhid*, 27, 1407/1987, pp. 25–39. The late Mahdi al-Hakim told me of constitutional blueprints by Sadr in the early 1960s, but his untimely death has prevented any further elaboration on the formation of young Sadr's constitutional thought.

21 Muhammad Baqer as-Sadr, *Manabi' al-Qudra*, quoted in General introduction, n. 76.

22 Muhammad Baqer as-Sadr, *Khilafat al-Insan*, quoted in General introduction, n. 76. [hereinafter *Khilafat*]

23 Translation of A. Yusuf Ali, *The Holy Qur'an*, Lahore, 1934.

24 The cause of revelation of Qur'an 5:44 is related in early *tafsirs*. See e.g. Tabari (d. 310/923), *Tafsir*, Cairo, n.d., vol. 10, pp. 338–40. On the 'cause of revelation'

genre, see A. Rippin, 'The exegetical genre *Asbab al-Nuzul*: a bibliographical and terminological survey', *BSOAS*, 48, 1985, 1–15.

25 The word *shahada* carries several meanings. It is both testimony and martyrdom (and it means also, as discussed in chapter 1, diploma). For a 'revolutionary' elaboration, see Mahmud Taliqani, *Jihad va Shahadat* (*Jihad and shahada*), Tehran, 1963, translated by R. Campbell, and annotated by H. Algar, in Mahmud Taleghani, *Society and Economics in Islam*, Berkeley, 1982, pp. 75–105, especially at p. 99.

26 Sadr, *Khilafat*, p. 24.

27 Muhammad Rashid Rida, *Tafsir al-Qur'an al-Karim ash-Shahir bi-Tafsir al-Manar* (*Interpretation of the Qur'an known as the Interpretation of the Manar*), Cairo, 3rd edn 1367/1947, VI, pp. 397–8.

28 Sayyid Qutb, *Fi Zilal al-Qur'an* (*In the Shades of the Qur'an*), Beirut, new edn, 1973, II, p. 887. For a recent analysis of the *Zilal*, and a comparison with the *Manar*, O. Carré, *Mystique et Politique, Lecture Révolutionnaire du Coran par Sayyid Qutb, Frère Musulman Radical*, Paris, 1984.

29 Qutb, II, p. 897.

30 On these characters, see the studies of R. Mitchell, *The Society of the Muslim Brothers*, Oxford, 1969; G. Kepel, *Le Prophète et le Pharaon*, Paris, 1984.

31 Muhammad Husayn Tabataba'i, *al-Mizan fi Tafsir al-Qur'an* (*The Balance in the Interpretation of the Qur'an*), Beirut, 1970.

32 Muhammad al-Husayni ash-Shirazi, *Taqrib al-Qur'an ilal-Adhhan* (*Bringing the Qur'an Closer to the Mind*), Beirut, 1980.

33 Shirazi, VI, p. 91.

34 *Ibid.*, p. 92.

35 Tabataba'i, VI, p. 366.

36 *Ibid.*, p. 363.

37 Emphasis supplied.

38 Tabataba'i, VI, p. 362.

39 See also his reference to the Shi'i concept of *'ismat*, infallibility, *id.*, p. 362. Muhammad Baqer as-Sadr has an interesting definition of *'ismat*, which differs from the classical equation of the word with the Twelve Imams' sanctity from sin and error. It is metaphorically depicted in his *Ahl al-Bayt* as 'the expression of [the Imams'] total permeation by the Message [of Islam], and their embodiment of all the elements of this Message in the spiritual, intellectual, and mental [realms]', *Ahl-al-Bayt*, quoted at n. 78 of General introduction, p. 74.

40 Tabataba'i, VI, pp. 356–366.

41 *Ibid.*, pp. 350–6.

42 Tabataba'i's political concern was generally limited. Until he died in 1983, he had remained aloof from the world of politics, although not antagonistic to the institutions of higher learning sponsored by the Shah. In his writings, as in Henry Corbin's (who was very close to him), the esoteric and spiritual aspects of Shi'ism receive the strongest emphasis. See Tabataba'i's '*Ijtihad va taqlid dar Islam va shi'a*' (*Ijtihad and taqlid in Islam and Shi'ism*), and '*vilayat va za'amat*' (*Wilaya and Leadership*), both in *Bahthi*, above n. 15. On Tabataba'i in the Iranian context and his study of the gnostic aspects of Islam, see S. Akhavi, *Religion and Politics in Contemporary Iran*, Albany, NY, 1980, p. 138, and the introduction by H. Nasr to Tabataba'i's *Shi'ite Islam*, Albany, NY, 1975.

43 There is no trace in early Shi'i *tafsir* of the distinction made by Sadr. His reference to *rabbaniyyun* as the Imams and to the *ahbar* as the *'ulama* is not found

in the two classic Shi'i *tafsirs*: Abu Ja'far at-Tusi (d. 460/1067), *at-Tibyan*, Najaf, n.d., vol.3, pp. 526–9; Abu 'Ali at-Tabarsi (sixth/twelfth century), *Majma' al-Bayan fi Tafsir al-Qur'an*, Beirut, n.d., vol. 6–7, pp. 101–4. The *sabab an-nuzul* they mention is similar to Sunni exegesis. Both interpreters wonder about the universality of the verse or its restriction to the 'Jewish' occasion. Compare Tusi, pp. 528–9 and Tabarsi, pp. 103–4 with Tabari, above, n. 24.

44 Sadr, *Khilafat*, p. 50.

45 There is an overall correlation between the *tafsir* of verse 44 of sura 5 and the political world views and role of the five interpreters. This correspondence should however not be over-emphasised. Tabataba'i said his word on social and political issues, and occasionally criticised the laws in Iran (Akhavi, *Religion and Politics*, p. 127). The Karbala scholar Muhammad al-Husayni ash-Shirazi has been directly involved in Caesar's realm and his brother Hasan was extremely active in the Shi'i international until he was killed in Beirut in 1980; his other son Muhammad has remained involved to date in Iraqi politics, from his basis in Qum. Rida's political role, of course, notwithstanding his *tafsir* of the verse, was important. See in particular his theses on the Islamic state in *al-Khilafa wal-Imama al-'Uzma*, quoted above, n. 4.

46 Sadr, *Iqtisaduna*, pp. 359–60.

47 For further details, this volume, chapter 4.

48 Sadr, *Iqtisaduna*, pp. 331, 656.

49 See General introduction, nn. 73, 75. *Manabi' al-Qudra fid-Dawla al-Islamiyya* (*The Sources of Power in the Islamic State*) will be referred to henceforth as *Manabi'*.

50 Sadr, *Manabi'*, p. 9.

51 *Ibid.*

52 *Ibid.*, pp. 12, 13.

53 *Ibid.*, pp. 14–24.

54 *Ibid.*, p. 17.

55 *Ibid.*

56 *Ibid.*, p. 32.

57 *Ibid.*, pp. 40, 41.

58 In the 1979 Constitution of Iran, it appears as an important concern of the new 'Bill of Rights'; see especially the preliminary section on 'the economy as means and not end' and art. 3, para. 12. See generally Hamid Algar, 'Social justice in the ideology and legislation of the Islamic revolution of Iran', in L. Michalak and J. Salacuse eds, *Social Legislation in the Contemporary Middle East*, Berkeley, 1986, pp. 17–60; S. Bakhash, 'Islam and social justice in Iran', in M. Kramer ed., *Shi'ism, Resistance and Revolution*, pp. 95–116.

59 This is discussed in more detail in my 'Religious militancy' and 'Political Islam'.

60 This message appears often in the literature of the Iraqi Islamic opposition. See e.g. the back cover of *al-Hiwar al-Fikri was-Siyasi* (Tehran), 30–1, 1985; Ha'iri, '*Tarjamat*', p. 151–2. In English, the message is reproduced as 'Baqir al-Sadr's last message on the unity of the Ummah', in K. Siddiqui ed., *Issues in the Islamic Movement*, London, 1981, p. 57.

61 See Yann Richard, 'Du nationalisme à l'islamisme: dimensions de l'identité ethnique en Iran', in *Le Fait Ethnique en Iran et en Afghanistan*, Paris, 1988, pp. 267–75.

62 The *Lamha* will be quoted hereinafter as *Note*. The *Note* was translated into French by Abbas al-Bostani at Ahl el-Beit Press in 1983. It appeared again with an introduction by Pierre Martin in *Les Cahiers de l'Orient*, 8–9, 1987–8, pp. 164–78.

63 Sadr, *Note*, p. 27.

64 For good accounts of these days, see Gary Sick, *All Fall Down*, London, 1985, pp. 154–6; Dilip Hiro, *Iran under the Ayatollahs*, London, 1985, pp. 91–3; E. Abrahamian, *Iran Between Two Revolutions*, Princeton, 1982, pp. 527–9; F. Hoveyda, *The Fall of the Shah*, London, 1980, pp. 149–51.

65 See this volume, Part I, Introduction.

66 Above, n. 15.

67 It was reported in the newspapers that an aide to Khumaini mentioned 'privately' on 3 February 'that 'the main outlines' of the Constitution of the proposed Islamic Republic have been written, but not the entire document', *New York Times*, 4 Feb. 1979. But in his press conference on that day, Khumaini only alluded to a council which would eventually be formed to write a new constitution. See Foreign Broadcast Information Service, *Daily Report: Middle East and Africa* (Washington), 5 Feb. 1979. The Constitution was indeed drafted by the council a few months later.

68 A confusion of significant importance originates in the ambiguity of the Arabic title of the *Note*. There is a notion of certainty which, if included in the translation as 'a preliminary legal note on *the* project of a constitution for the Islamic Republic of Iran', might suggest that such a project existed already, and that Sadr was commenting on it in the form of the *Note*. The thrust of our argument, however, is that this element of certainty did not exist, as there was *no* document of a constitutional nature at the time of Sadr's writing of his *Note*. Sadr was not working on any pre-existing text. His *Note* was an answer to a query which was 'in the air' at the time, and it is significant, both in terms of Shi'i internationalism, and in terms of his intellectual leadership in the whole community, that the *Note* has come in answer to a question put to him by the Lebanese *mujtahid*s, most prominent among whom were relatives of Muhammad Mahdi Shamseddin, the present leader of the Lebanese Shi'i council and Ragheb Harb, who would be assassinated by the Israelis in 1984 because of his role in the Resistance in South Lebanon.

Another significant dimension is the role of the *Note* as a constitutional blueprint for the first Islamic Republic of Iran. Our argument is based on the conviction that the *Note* was of utmost importance for the Iranian Constitution adopted in 1979, because the similarities – sometimes *verbatim* – of the institutions adopted in two texts are too significant to be due to chance (see also the following footnotes). In my conversations with Iranian scholars, there has appeared some reluctance to admit that the relevance of the *Note* is as strong as I am suggesting. More light will come from the work presently undertaken at Oxford by Ahmad Jalali on the genesis of the Iranian Constitution.

69 S. Bakhash, *The Reign of the Ayatollahs*, New York, 1984, p. 74. This is confirmed by M. Bayat, quoting M. Bazargan, the first Prime Minister of the Islamic Republic: 'Neither in the preliminary working paper on the Constitution written while Khumaini was still in Paris, nor in the draft written in collaboration with the Provisional Government and the Revolutionary Council with Khumaini's and other *'ulama*'s approval, was there the slightest reference to it [the rule of the *faqih*]. It was only invented later, in the final draft of the Constitution

drawn by the Council of Experts under Khumaini's direction.' Bayat, 'Mahmud Taleqani', pp. 79–80.

70 I am grateful for this piece of information to Professor Hamid Algar.

71 Qur'an, 18 (*al-kahf*): 109; Sadr, *Note*, p. 23.

72 Sadr, *Note*, p. 24.

73 Friedrich Engels, *The Origin of the Family, Private Property and the State*, London, 1940 (original German 1884).

74 The text of the Constitution is quoted after M. Watani ed., *Majmu'e-ye Kamel-e Qavanin-e Madani-Asasi* (*Collection of Civil and Constitutional Laws*), Tehran, 1364/1985.

75 For instance, relevant to this context is art. 2 of the Iraqi interim Constitution of 1970. Text in the journal *al-Haqq*, (Cairo), September 1972, pp. 134–49.

76 This is of course true of other Islamic thinkers, such as Khumaini and the Pakistani Mawdudi. See an interesting discussion on the Constitution of Pakistan, in N. Anderson, *Law Reform in the Muslim World*, London, 1976, pp. 173–83.

77 Sadr, *Note*, p. 17.

78 *Ibid.*, p. 24.

79 *Ibid.*, p. 21.

80 *Ibid.*, p. 24.

81 Khumaini, *Hukuma*, p. 49; *Velayat*, p. 63; *Government*, p. 62. It must be noted that Khumaini did not advocate the necessity of *one* faqih to lead the government. In his 1970 lectures, he insisted on the cooperation in power of several *fuqaha*: 'The government of the *faqih* over the other *fuqaha* does not allow him to discharge them or appoint them, because all the *fuqaha* are equal in terms of capacity (*ahliyya*)… the *fuqaha* should work alone or together to establish a legal government', *Hukuma*, p. 51.

82 Sadr, *Note*, p. 25.

83 Khumaini, *Hukuma*, p. 41; *Velayat*, pp. 52–3; *Government*, p. 55.

84 'The people, *ash-sha'b*', Sadr, *Note*, p. 15.

85 *Ibid.*, p. 19.

86 This is similar to the separation of powers in the French system.

87 Sadr, *Note*, p. 20. The discretionary area (or area of vacuum, *faragh*) is a concept carried forward from Sadr's *Iqtisaduna*, see Part II. It refers in his 1979 parlance to the areas of the law which must be addressed without the guidance of precedent. The lack of precision of the concept is, not surprisingly, at the root of most of the difficult parliamentary debates in post-revolutionary Iran. See chapter 4.

88 Sadr, *Note*, p. 21.

89 *Ibid.*, p. 20.

90 *Ibid.*

91 See on the Council of Guardians, chapter 3.

92 Sadr, *Note*, p. 21.

93 *Ibid.*, pp. 20–1.

94 Through his command of the army. See supra n. 89 and accompanying text.

95 Sadr, *Note*, p. 20.

96 *Ibid.*, p. 21.

97 *Ibid.*, p. 22.

98 *Ibid.*, p. 21.

99 *Ibid.*, p. 21. For further parallels between Sadr's *Note* and the Iranian

Constitution, see the good analysis of Muhammad 'Abdallah, '*Dawlat wilayat al-faqih*' (*The State in wilayat al-faqih*), *Dirasat wa Buhuth* (Tehran), 2:8, 1403/1983, pp. 97–127.

3 The first decade of the Iranian constitution: problems of the least dangerous branch

1 L. Carroll, *Through the Looking Glass*, in *Complete Works*, London, 1939, p. 196.

2 'Bishop Hoadly's sermon preached before the King, March 31, 1717', quoted in W. Lockhart, Y. Kamisar and J. Choper eds., *Constitutional Law, Cases, Comments, Questions*, Chicago, 3rd edn, 1970 (1st edn, 1964), p. 1. This collection of cases is widely used in American law schools.

3 Article 61, mod. 1974, of the French Constitution states: 'Les lois organiques avant leur promulgation, et les règlements des assemblées parlementaires, avant leur mise en application, doivent être soumis au Conseil Constitutionnel qui se prononce sur leur conformité à la Constitution. Aux mêmes fins, les lois peuvent être déférées au Conseil Constitutionnel, avant leur promulgation, par le Président de la République, le Premier Ministre, le Président de l'Assemblée Nationale, le Président du Sénat ou soixante députés ou soixante sénateurs. Dans les cas prévus aux deux articles précédents, le Conseil Constitutionnel doit statuer dans le délai d'un mois. Toutefois, à la demande du Gouvernement, s'il y a urgence, ce délai est ramené à huit jours.' There is a large literature on the Conseil Constitutionnel. Its main decisions are collected and discussed in L. Philip and L. Favoreu, *Les Grandes Décisions du Conseil Constitutionnel*, Paris, 4th ed., 1986; see also François Luchaire, *Le Conseil Constitutionnel*, Paris, 1980; L. Hamon, *Les Juges de la Loi*, Paris, 1987. Recently, an amendment has been proposed by the French President to allow private citizens direct access to the Conseil, but the opposition did not rally around the proposal in a way that would allow its endorsement by the qualified majority needed for a constitutional revision.

4 E.g. the Syrian constitution of 1973, art. 3(1): 'The religion of the President of the Republic shall be Islam.' Text in A. Blaustein and G. Flanz eds., *Constitutions of the Countries of the World*, Vol.16, New York (issued June 1974).

5 On 29 July 1985, the Council of Guardians accepted the candidacy of only three presidential candidates. Bazargan's candidacy was rejected. In the presidential elections of July 1989, out of some eighty names, two candidacies were retained by the Council.

6 Art. 71: 'Parliament has the power to legislate in all matters, within the boundaries set by the Constitution.'

7 Discussed in chapter 4, this volume.

8 *Marbury* v. *Madison*, 1 Cranch 137 (1803).

9 Khu'i, *al-Masa'el al-Muntakhaba*, p. 8. Khumaini, *Tahrir al-Wasila*, I, p. 3. (Note an interesting detail in Khumaini's development. In the introductory section on *ijtihad*, Khumaini writes that 'the *marja' at-taqlid* must be a scholar ('*alim*), *mujtahid*, just ('*adil*), pious (*wari' fi din allah*), *and* uninvolved in worldly affairs (*ghayr mukibb 'alad-dunia*).' This is different from the thrust of the Najaf lectures on *wilayat al-faqih*.) Other traditional qualifications are attached to the person of the judge, and included in '*kitab al-qada'*' (chapter on the judiciary), *Tahrir al-Wasila*, II, pp. 366–8.

10 Khumaini was known to repeat that he was 'a Husayni, not a Hasani'.

11 Ibn Khaldun (d. 808/1406), *al-Muqaddima*, Cairo, n.d. (edition of the Matba'a Tijariyya), chapter 34, p. 542.

12 *Ibid.*

13 Also Montesquieu, *L'Esprit des Lois*: 'The power (*puissance*) of judging... becomes, so to speak, invisible and null', in *Oeuvres Complètes*, Paris, 1964, p. 587.

14 *The Federalist Papers* (1787–8), New York, 1961, paper 78 (A. Hamilton), p. 469.

15 John Hart Ely, *Democracy and Distrust*, Cambridge, Mass., 1980, p. 4–5. See also J. Choper, *Judicial Review and the National Political Process*, Chicago, 1980, p. 10. These two books, especially Ely's, are much celebrated in the United States for their theories on judicial review in the American system. For this debate, see my '*al-mahkama al-'ulya al-amirkiyya fin-niqash al-qanuni al-mu'asir*' (*The American Supreme Court in the Contemporary Legal Debate*), *Proche-Orient Etudes Juridiques*, 1987, pp. 9–26, and the literature cited.

16 E.g. in France, the President of the Republic, art. 15; in the USA, the President, Article II Section 2.

17 The principle (already quoted in chapter 2) in the opening article of the chapter on the Executive power further establishes the secondary importance of the Presidency, which 'is the highest official position of the country' only 'after the leadership'.

18 In the United States, impeachment was used only once, against President Andrew Johnson in 1868. In 1974, President Nixon chose to resign after the Judiciary Committee of the House of Representatives voted to recommend three articles of impeachment. See generally J. Labovitz, *Presidential Impeachment*, New Haven, 1978.

19 Hiro, *Iran Under the Ayatollahs*, pp. 181–2; S. Bakhash, *The Reign*, pp. 125–65, especially at pp. 159–62.

20 Sermon reproduced in *Keyhan Hava'i*, 6 Jan. 1988.

21 Khumaini's letter was published in *Keyhan Hava'i*, 13 Jan. 1988. A translation appears in *Summary of World Broadcasts*: *Middle East and Africa* [hereinafter *SWB*], (London), 8 Jan., 1988, p. A/7. See now on the letter, J. Reissner, 'Der Imam und die Verfassung; zur politischen und staatsrechtlichen Bedeutung der Direktive Imam Khomeinis vom 7. Januar 1988', *Orient*, 29:2, 1988, pp. 213–36. The date of the letter is 6 January, but its public release took place on the 7th.

22 Muntazeri, commenting on Khumaini's 6 January letter, *SWB*, 11 Jan. 1988, p. A/6.

23 This is in reference to Muhammad Baqer an-Najafi, d. 1266/1850, known as *Sahib al-Jawahir*, and to al-'Allama al-Hilli's (d. 726/1325) *Tahrir al-Ahkam ash-Shar'iyya*.

24 On *anfal*, which is associated in Sadr's economic theory with 'state property' (*Iqtisaduna*, p. 421), see chapter 4.

25 *Marbury*, at 178.

26 *Ibid.*, at 176.

27 Letter from Khamene'i to Khumaini, in *Ettela'at* (Tehran), 12 Jan. 1988; *SWB*, 13 Jan. 1988.

28 Letter from Khumaini to Khamene'i, in *Ettela'at*, 12 Jan. 1988; *SWB*, 13 Jan. 1988.

29 In June 1989, Khamene'i was appointed second *rahbar* of the Islamic Republic of

Iran, and 'upgraded' with the title of *Ayat Allah*. Without the reassurance of Khumaini's support after his initial admonition of Khamene'i's interpretation of *wilayat al-faqih*, it would hardly be conceivable for his candidacy to be retained by the Assembly of Experts. The demise of *Ayat Allah* Muntazeri itself is a significant and yet to be fully documented event in Iran. It is hoped that Professor Mottahedeh's communication on the subject (SOAS Middle East Forum, 17 May 1991) will be published soon.

30 *SWB*, 16 Jan. 1988, p. A/6. Emphasis added.

31 *SWB*, 8 Jan. 1988, p. A/8.

32 *Ibid.* Even in his letter of 6 Jan., Khumaini was reluctant to intervene: 'After greetings and salutations, I did not wish that any controversy should arise at this sensitive juncture, and I believe that in such circumstances, silence is the best attitude.' Compare constitutional silence in the American context, see L. Tribe, 'Towards a syntax of the unsaid: construing the sounds of congressional and constitutional silence', *Indiana Law Journal*, 57, 1982, 515, published also as Chapter 4 of his *Constitutional Choices*, Cambridge, Mass., 1985.

33 *SWB*, 8 Jan. 1988, p. A/8.

34 Shakespeare, *Hamlet*, III, i, 66 (G. Hibbard ed., Oxford, 1987).

35 It is again interesting to draw a parallel with the US Supreme Court at the time of the New Deal, when the majority of the judges would not let President Roosevelt's new laws pass constitutional muster, on ground that intervention in economic matters was against the 'commerce' and 'due process' clauses of the Constitution. See e.g. *Schlechter Poultry Corp.* v. *US*, 295 *US* 495 (1935), invalidating the National Industrial Recovery Act of 1933 because 'the attempt through the provisions of he Code to fix the hours and wages of employes [sic] of defendants in their intrastate business was not a valid exercise of federal power', at 550; *Carter* v. *Carter Coal Co.*, 298 US 238 (1936), invalidating an act regulating maximum hours and minimum wages in coal mines; and the formulation in *Railroad Retirement Board* v. *Alton Railroad Co.*, 295 US 330 (1935) at 338: 'It is apparent that [the new legal regulations] are really and essentially related solely to the social welfare of the worker and therefore remote from any regulation of commerce as such.' The issue was ultimately solved to the advantage of the Presidency after several changes in the membership of the Supreme Court. By 1937, *National Labor Relations Board* v. *Jones Steel Corp.*, 301 US 57, started the reversal trend by upholding the constitutionality of the National Labor Relations Act of 1935.

36 *SWB*, 18 Jan. 1988, p. A/1.

37 *SWB*, 12 Jan. 1988, p. A/5.

38 *SWB*, 16 Jan. 1988, p. A/6.

39 The letter to Khumaini, as well as Khumaini's message in response, can be found in *SWB*, 8 Feb. 1988, p. A/6. The message of Khumaini is dated 6 Feb. 1988.

40 *Ibid.*

41 *Ibid.*

42 *Ibid.* This is again reminiscent of the threat introduced by the 'Court-packing' plan of President Roosevelt. Khumaini has in effect undermined the blocking power of the Council of Guardians by increasing the number of constitutional watchdogs to a new majority.

43 *Ibid.*

44 Article 112 as amended. I am grateful to my colleague Ja'far Delshad for providing me with the original text of the constitutional amendments. The text

can now be found in the yearly publication of laws by the Ministry of Justice, *Majmu'e-ye Qavanin (Collection of Laws)*, Year 1368 (1989–90), Tehran, 1369 (1990–1), pp. 455–68.

45 These details were gracefully provided by Chris Rundle, an outstanding scholar of Iran with the British Foreign Office.

46 See details on the substantive details related to agrarian law, this volume, chapter 4.

47 See text of the Bill and its approval into law by the Majma' in Ministry of Justice, *Majmu'e-ye Qavanin*, Year 1369 (1990–1), Tehran, 1370 (1991–2), pp. 731–75.

Introduction to Part II

1 In Arabic, 'Abd al-Jabbar ar-Rifa'i, '*Fihrist al-Iqtisad al-Islami I-VII*' (*Index of Islamic Economics*), *at-Tawhid*, issue 20 (1986) to issue 27 (1987); in German and English, V. Nienhaus, *Literature on Islamic Economics in English and in German*, Cologne, 1982.

2 An overview of the literature can be found in T. Kuran, 'On the notion of economic justice in contemporary Islamic thought', *IJMES*, 21, 1989, 171–91; 'The economic system in contemporary Islamic thought: interpretation and assessment', *IJMES*, 18, 1980, 135–64. Kuran's criticism is based mainly on the literature produced in English. An interesting analysis can be found in Biancamaria Amoretti, 'Pour une analyse politique de l'économie islamique', *La Pensée*, 229, 1982, 62–70.

3 Muhammad 'Abd al-Mun'im al-Jamal, *Mausu'at al-Iqtisad al-Islami* (*Encyclopaedia of Islamic Economics*), Cairo, 1980, 2 vols.

4 See e.g. Pedro Chalmeta, 'Au sujet des théories économiques d'Ibn Khaldun', *Rivista degli Studi Orientali*, 1983, 93–120; J. Spengler, 'Economic thought in Islam: Ibn Khaldun', *Comparative Studies in Society and History*, 1963–4, 268–306.

5 S. Mahmassani, *Les Idées Economiques d'Ibn Khaldoun. Essai Historique, Analytique et Critique*, Lyon, 1932. Originally a doctoral thesis at the University of Lyon.

6 Muhammad Baqer as-Sadr, *Iqtisaduna* (Our economic system), first edition in two volumes, 1961. See this volume chapter 4, n. 21 and *passim*. For easier reference, *Iqtisaduna* will be henceforth quoted in the text as *I*, followed by the page. There have been more than ten reprints of *Iqtisaduna*. The edition used here is the 1977 one, published in one volume by Dar al-Kitab al-Lubnani (Beirut) and Dar al-Kitab al-Masri (Cairo).

7 Muhammad Baqer as-Sadr, *al-Bank al-la Ribawi fil-Islam* (*The Interest-Free Bank in Islam*), first edition, Kuwait, *c.* 1969. The reference will be henceforth to *IFB* (*Interest-Free Bank*), followed by the page number. Reference is to the eighth edition, Beirut, 1983.

8 See for details my '*Riba* and interest in twentieth century jurisprudence', in C. Mallat ed., *Islamic Law and Finance*, London, 1988, pp. 71–87.

4 Law and the discovery of 'Islamic economics'

1 For Sadr, by allowing the existence of various forms of property simultaneously, Islam did not have to provide for exceptions to the social norm, as did Capitalism

long ago by tolerating forms of nationalisation and public service; or when Socialism and Communism admitted private property, as in Articles 7 and 9 on kolkhoze private property schemes in the 1936 Constitution of the USSR (*I* 259–60).

2 *Ati'u allah wa ati'u ar-rasul wa uli al-amr minkum* (*Obey God, the Prophet and those amongst you who are in charge*), Q: IV, 58. This verse is often quoted in Sunni literature in support of obedience to the ruler, however unjust he may be. See Mawardi (d. 450/1058), *al-Ahkam as-Sultaniyya*, p. 6, quoted in Lambton, *State and Government*, p. 86. An earlier authority can be found in Abu Yusuf (d. 182/798), *Kitab al-Kharaj*, ed. Beirut, 1979, pp. 8–10; on the attitude of early Shi'i *'ulama*, see generally Lambton, pp. 242–63.

3 The reference to inheritance must be seen in the Iraqi context. See my 'Sunnism and Shi'ism in Iraqi Islamic family law – Revisiting the codes', in Mallat and Connors eds., *Islamic Family Law*; Y. Linant de Bellefonds, 'Le code du statut personnel irakien du 30 décembre 1959', *Studia Islamica*, 13, 1960, 79–135; N. Anderson, 'A law of personal status for Iraq', and 'Changes in the law of personal status in Iraq', *International and Comparative Law Quarterly*, 9, 1960, 542–63; 12, 1963, 1026–31.

4 As frequently appears in the Islamic theory of government, Sadr refers to the Prophet's rule in Medina as the ideal period in the history of Islam (*I* 263–4). In terms of Islamic economics, however, he introduced some qualifications to this depiction, particularly as to the relevance of the capitalist atmosphere prevailing at the time in relation to the present, more complex social relations.

5 This is generally consonant with the tradition. Sadr, however, introduces *zakat* in a different taxonomic framework in his *Fatawa Wadiha* (1976). See text quoted this volume, General introduction, n. 73; compare N. Calder, '*Zakat* in Imami Shi'i jurisprudence, from the tenth to the sixteenth century', *BSOAS*, 64, 1981, 468–80.

6 No explanation is given for this bizarre assertion.

7 The image of the society as a building with a basis and a superstructure often recurs in *Iqtisaduna*. This idea was current in the Marxism of the 1950s as a metaphor for society. For famous formulations, see K. Marx, 'Preface' to *A Contribution to the Critique of Political Economy* (translation of the *Grundrisse*, 1859), reproduced e.g. in T. Bottomore and P. Goode, *Readings in Marxist Sociology*, Oxford, 1983, pp. 49–50; F. Engels, 'Letter to J. Bloch, 21–22 September 1890', in K. Marx and F. Engels, *Selected Works*, Moscow, 1951, vol. 2, pp. 443–4. This was one of the editions prepared by the foreign languages department in Moscow, and was also available in Arabic. On the idea of infrastructure in the 1950s, compare L. Febvre, quoted in H. D. Mann, *Lucien Febvre: la Pensée Vivante d'un Historien*, Paris, 1971, p. 126: '[Infrastructure], mot que je n'aime guère, on me le pardonnera. Métaphore statique de maître-maçon, de cimentier prudent.'

8 Compare C. Chehata, 'La théorie de l'abus des droits chez les jurisconsultes musulmans', *Revue Marocaine de Droit*, 1953, 105–13.

9 *Mudaraba* (contract of commenda) is discussed in detail in Sadr's works on banking. See this volume, chapter 5.

10 Sadr also addresses 'the social problem' as a central philosophical question in *Falsafatuna*, pp. 11–53.

11 *Nafi ad-darar*. This is the torts principle suggested in the *hadith*, *la darar wa la darar*, see W. Zuhaili, *Nazariyyat ad-Daman*, pp. 18–19.

12 *Madhhab* denotes either an ideological school (as in 'socialist *madhhab*') or a classical school in Sunni law. On legal *madhhabs*, see G. Makdisi, 'The significance of the Sunni schools of law in Islamic religious history', *IJMES*, 11, 1979, 1–8. Sadr uses the word in both senses. See also J. Donohue, 'Notre économie', *Cahiers de l'Orient*, 8–9, 1987–8, 179–80, 192.
13 *Tanaqus al-ghilla*. This is probably a reference to Marx's laws on the fall of production, or of the tendency of the rate of profit to fall.
14 The concept of the topsy-turvy image is current in Marxist language, especially in relation to the reading of Hegel by Marx.
15 See this volume, chapter 3, 'Islamic law constrained'.
16 See further my 'Religious militancy', pp. 705–9.
17 Chapter 3 and pp. 146–57.
18 For details on *tasq*, defined after Tusi as the imposition of land for the benefit of the community, *I* 504–6; and details on the concept of property in Islam in contrast with Socialism, and on the rules of inheritance and the economy, *I* 499–514.
19 For *ju'ala* (compensation), see this volume, chapter 5.
20 *Kay la yakun dulatan minal-aghniya' minkum*, Q: 59,7.
21 I was not able to find a copy of the original edition of *Iqtisaduna*. There is reference to a first volume, published in Najaf in 1961 (the original was apparently in two volumes) in the catalogue of the British Library Oriental section in London, but the volume is missing from the shelf. The editions of *Iqtisaduna* since 1970 have been incorporated in one volume, but one can find an edition consisting of two volumes in one, published in Beirut in 1968.
22 See General introduction, n. 60.
23 *Iqtisaduna* was published in Persian in 1971 (*Iqtisadima*, vol. 1, tr. by Muhammad Kazim Musavi) and 1978 (*Iqtisadima*, vol. 2, tr. by Abdol-Ali Ispahbudi). The book was used in the Shi'i colleges in Iran, but the first translation is said to have been poor. See M. Fisher, *From Religious Dispute to Revolution*, p. 157. A new Persian translation appeared in 1981.
24 For the German translation, see this volume, General introduction, n. 28. The Turkish translation of *Iqtisaduna* was undertaken by Mehmet Keskin and Sadettin Ergün, Istanbul, 1978.
25 *Iqtisaduna* was translated in English in Tehran in 4 vols., 1982–4.
26 Translation, in part, by I. Howard in successive articles which appeared in *al-Serat* as 'The Islamic Economy I–VII' (March 1981 to Spring 1985).
27 Muhammad Ja'far Shamseddin, *Iqtisaduna, Talkhis wa Tawdih* (*Iqtisaduna, Summary and Clarification*), 4 vols., Beirut, 1986–7.
28 General introduction, n. 68.
29 Yusuf Kamal and Abul-Majd Harak, *Al-Iqtisad al-Islami bayna Fiqh ash-Shi'a wa Fiqh as-Sunna: Qira'a Naqdiyya fi Kitab Iqtisaduna* (*Islamic Economics between Shi'i and Sunni Fiqh: a Critical Reading of Iqtisaduna*), Cairo, 1987/1408. The book will be quoted here following each of the two authors' separate essay, as 'Kamal' and, alternatively, 'Harak', followed by the page number.
30 Introduction by the publisher, p. 5.
31 *Ibid.* See for similar statements, Harak, p. 91; Kamal, p. 95.
32 Kamal, p. 123.
33 On the note of page 124, Kamal quotes p. 417 of a book which is 200 pages long.
34 See especially Harak, pp. 62–3.
35 *Ibid.*, chapter 2, pp. 40–54.

36 *Ibid.*, pp. 26 ff.
37 Harak, pp. 50–1.
38 *Ibid.*, p. 65.
39 *Ibid.*
40 *Ibid.*, p. 70.
41 *Ibid.*, pp. 85–90. quote at p. 89.
42 Mahmud Taleqani, *Islam va Malekiyyat* (*Islam and property*), Tehran, 10th edn, 1965. On Taleqani, see this volume, chapter 2.
43 Hasan ash-Shirazi, *al-Iqtisad* (the economy), Beirut, 1980, originally published in 1960. Shirazi was the brother of Muhammad al-Husayni ash-Shirazi, the author of the *Taqrib* quoted in chapter 2.
44 Qutb's main 'economic' contribution is his *al-'Adala al-Ijtima'iyya fil-Islam* (*Social Justice in Islam*), Cairo, 1949; Qutb was executed by Naser in 1966. On Qutb, see also this volume, chapter 2. 'Allal al-Fasi, who was a major figure in Moroccan Islamism, wrote a short economic study entitled *Fil-Madhahib al-Iqtisadiyya* (*On Economic Doctrines*) in 1971. Muhammad Baqer as-Sadr is quoted in this book several times. See the Rabat edition at Dar ar-Risala, 1978, pp. 146–8, 166–8. To those can be added Mawdudi, who was an important Pakistani activist, but a less interesting intellectual figure.
45 Quduri, *Al-Mukhtasar*, India edn, 1847, p. 228. For Kasani (d.587/1191), the main division in his book of land (*kitab al-aradi*) lies between '*amer* (prosperous) and *mawwat* (dead) land. *Bada'e' as-Sana'e' fi Tartib ash-Shara'e'*, Cairo, 1910, vi, pp. 192–6. I am grateful to Dr Norman Calder for having drawn my attention to some of these dimensions.
46 In a decision of the Egyptian Supreme Constitutional Court, the idea of *wali al-amr* as the predecessor of the interventionist modern state was put forward to defend economic measures adopted 'in conformity with the *shari'a*'. (Decision of the Supreme Constitutional Court, 4 May 1991, published in the Egyptian Official Journal, 16 May 1991, at p. 972.) In Tunis, Salahaddin al-Jurayshi has recently published social and economic texts by Sadr, which were collected in *Jawanib min al-Mas'ala al-Ijtima'iyya* (*Aspects of the Social Question*), Tunis, n.d. (late 1980s). The commentator went to great lengths in explaining how free from sectarianism Sadr's work remains despite its general methodological setbacks (see esp. pp. 15, 23, 25, 35, and 88–93). In Algeria, *Iqtisaduna*'s distinction between state and public property featured in texts which appeared in newspapers close to the Front Islamique du Salut. See the text in M. al-Ahnaf, B. Botiveau and F. Frégosi, *L'Algérie par ses Islamistes*, Paris, 1991, pp. 175–8.
47 On Muhammad Baqer as-Sadr and Abul-Hasan Bani Sadr, who published in 1978 his *Iqtisad-e Tawhidi* (*The Unitary Economy*), see H. Katouzian, 'Shi'ism and Islamic Economics', in N. Keddie ed., *Religion and Politics in Iran*, pp. 145–65. See also S. Bakhash, *The Reign of the Ayatollahs*, pp. 166–75.
48 See a case study of Iraq in the early conquest in M. Morony, 'Landholding in seventh-century Iraq: late Sasanian and early Islamic patterns', in A. Udovitch ed., *The Islamic Middle East 700–1900. Studies in Economic and Social History*, Princeton, 1981; 'Landholding and social change: lower al-'Iraq in the early Islamic period', in T. Khalidi ed., *Land Tenure and Social Transformation in the Middle East*, Beirut, 1984. Early patterns of Islamic law and land tenure can be found in Abu Yusuf's *Kitab al-Kharaj*.
49 The Council of Guardians' debates preceding its final decision (where no dissent is reported) have not been published, but the present head of the Council,

Muhamad Muhammadi Gilani, has expressed his wish to see the minutes eventually in print. Information supplied by Mr M. Ansari-Poor, an official of the Iranian Ministry of Justice, who is currently preparing a Ph.D. at SOAS.

50 See chapter 3, n. 32.

51 On this period, see the well-informed and insightful study of H. Algar, 'Social justice in the ideology and legislation of the Islamic Revolution of Iran', in L. Michalak and J. Salacuse eds., *Social Legislation in the Contemporary Middle East*, Berkeley, 1986, pp. 18–60 (and my review in *Third World Quarterly*, 10:2, 1988, pp. 1095–8), and S. Bakhash, *The Reign*, pp. 195–216. There is a steadily growing literature on land and agriculture in post-revolutionary Iran. See especially A. Schirazi, *The Problem of the Land Reform in the Islamic Republic of Iran*, Berlin, 1987; S. Bakhash, 'The politics of land, law and social justice in Iran', *Middle East Journal*, 43:2, pp. 186–201; J. Koorooshy, 'Agrarverfassung der Islamischen Republik Iran', *Orient*, 28, 1987, 229–43; A good overview of land problems within a more comprehensive study of Iranian agriculture is K. MacLachlan, *The Neglected Garden*, London, 1988. Hooglund's *Land and Revolution in Iran*, Austin, Texas, 1982, pp. 138–52, briefly covers the revolutionary period. The classic work on land reform under the Shah is A. Lambton, *The Persian Land Reform* 1962–1966, Oxford, 1969.

52 See Algar, 'Social justice', pp. 41, 43.

53 The bill of 28 December 1982 was published in the Tehran dailies of the following day. Excerpts of the law can be found in an important reference book on constitutional law, written by a non-faqih member of the Council of Guardians: Jalaladdin Madani, *Huquq-e Asasi dar Jumhuri-ye Islami-ye Iran* (*Fundamental Law in the Islamic Republic of Iran*), Tehran, 1366/1987–8, vol. 4: *Quwwe-ye Muqannene-ye Shura-ye Negahban* (*Legislative Power – The Council of Guardians*). Access to recent legislative texts in Iran is difficult. Laws which are struck down by the Council of Guardians do not necessarily get published in the *Official Journal*. Newspapers sometimes reproduce the text of the laws, but the decisions of the Council of Guardians are more difficult to find. The appendix to Madani's book, which reproduces 'all [?] the corrective decisions' of the Council, is unique in this respect. In the case of the bill of 28 December 1982, the main articles of disagreement between the Council of Guardians and Parliament have been appended to the Council's decision. See Madani, pp. 275–7. But the Council of Guardians has recently undertaken to publish all its decisions in a facsimile edition. Two volumes covering the Council's decisions over the first decade of the Islamic Republic have appeared in Presidency of the Republic, *Majmu'e-ye Nazariyyat-e Shura-ye Negahban*, Tehran, 1369/1990–1 (kindly drawn to my attention by Mr Ansari-Poor). See now the text of the 1982 Bill in *Majmu'e-ye Nazariyyat-e Shura-ye Negahban*, vol. 1, pp. 309–14. A. Schirazi has collected and translated into German several texts on land reform in *Texte zur Agrargesetzgebung in der Islamischen Republik Iran*, Berlin, 1988. The bill of 28 December 1982 is translated in full at pp. 234–46.

54 The full text of the Council of Guardians' decision of 18 January 1983 can be found in Madani, pp. 274–5, and in *Majmu'e-ye Nazariyyat-e Shura-ye Negahban*, vol.1, pp. 307–8.

55 The date of Khumaini's declaration is mentioned as 19/7/1360 (11 October 1981). This *farman* was also quoted by the Council of Guardians in its second rejection of the land reform bill of 1985. See this volume, p. 152. In this declaration, Khumaini vests Parliament with the 'right to adopt and implement

any measure which guarantees the interests of the Islamic Republic, and the neglect of which would result in a disturbance of order... The majority in Parliament determines the existence of such a case... when it is clear that the decision is only temporarily valid and will be automatically annulled when the cause disappears.' The Council of Guardians made clear that the question of land would not be affected by the decree. See A. Schirazi, *The Problem*, p. 32.

56 Council of Guardians, decision of 18 January 1983, Madani, p. 274. *Majmu'e-ye Nazariyyat-e Shura-ye Negahban*, vol. 1, p. 307.

57 The Council of Guardians found other less significant faults in the bill. See details in Madani, p. 275; *Majmu'e-ye Nazariyyat-e Shura-ye Negahban*, vol. 1, pp. 308; Koorooshy, 'Agrarverfassung', pp. 237–8.

58 The full text of the bill of 19 May 1985 is reproduced in Madani, pp. 278–85, and is followed by the rejection of the Council of Guardians. I was unable to find this decision in *Majmu'e-ye Nazariyyat-e Shura-ye Negahban*.

59 Bill of 19 May 1985, chapter 1: definitions. Madani, p. 278.

60 Council of Guardians, decision of 2 June 1985, reproduced in Madani, pp. 285–6.

61 On the whole issue of the bill on 'temporary cultivation land', see Bakhash, 'The Politics'. For details of the breakdown of structure of land in Iran, *Ibid.*, pp. 186, 189; A. Schirazi, *The Problem*, pp. 8, 18.

62 The question of the two-thirds majority in the vote of Parliament as a device that would dispense with Council of Guardians scrutiny is an obscure development in Iranian constitutionalism. There is nothing in the Constitution of 1979 which would warrant this mechanism, introduced by Khumaini in 1984 according to Schirazi, *The Problem*, p. 17 and n. 35. Bakhash however dates this declaration in January 1983, 'The politics', p. 197. This might explain why the Council of Guardians never handed down a rejection of the bill of October 1986, despite the clear rejection it had stated in its 1985 decision. An alternative explanation might be that Parliament never sent up the bill to the Council of Guardians, and so avoided any danger of the Council's scrutiny. Four important procedural matters are worth mentioning here: (1) The process of the Council of Guardians' scrutiny is generally activated by the Speaker, who sends a letter to the secretary of the Council of Guardians once a bill is voted. If, as probably was the case in the bill on temporary land, the Speaker does not send the bill up to the Council of Guardians, he might be infringing his constitutional duty, but could have explained it under the item of the two-thirds majority. (2) The second remark is related to the position of the Leader in the controversy on land. The Leader might want to break an impasse between the Council of Guardians and Parliament by deciding on the effective substance of the law, when it is as controversial as the land reform. He is not however technically able to introduce such a radical change as dispensing a bill from the scrutiny of the Council of Guardians. Khumaini might have made a declaration to that effect. This does not preclude the anti-constitutionality of the move. Only Khumaini's unquestioned authority could have allowed it temporarily. (3) The dubious nature of such a constitutional change appears even more clearly in the fact that the Speaker himself, Hashemi Rafsanjani, declared at the time of the constitutional crisis of 1988 that the whole question of the two-thirds majority was superfluous. See this volume, chapter 3, quotation at n. 33. (4) It is also worth noting that the amendments to the Constitution which came into effect in July 1989 did not mention any two-thirds or otherwise qualified majority in relation to legislation.

The Amended Art. 89 introduces the two-thirds majority of Parliamentarians only in the new impeachment procedure of the President.

63 The description of the voting episode is well documented in Bakhash, 'The politics', pp. 198–9.

64 *Ibid.*, pp. 192–6.

65 Council of Guardians, decision of 2 June 1985, reproduced in Madani, p. 286.

66 Decision of the Majma'-e Tashkhis-e Maslahat, 7/12/1369 (26 February 1991), in Ministry of Justice, *Majmu'e-ye Qavanin*, 1369/1990–1, p. 971.

67 Decision of the Majma'-e Tashkhis-e Maslahat '*dar khusus-e hall meshkel-e arazi bayer*, for the solving of the problems of abandoned land', 25/5/1367 (16 August 1988), in Ministry of Justice, *Majmu'e-ye Qavanin*, 1367/1988–9, pp. 604–5.

68 Clause 3 of the Note to the Decision of the Majma'-e Tashkhis-e Maslahat of 25/5/1367, mentioned the two-month implementation. The Executive Order was actually published in the *Official Journal* on 28/12/1369 (18 March 1991) and reproduced in 'Executive Order for the Decision of the Majma'-e Tashkhis-e Maslahat on the solving of the problems of abandoned land', *Majmu'e-ye Qavanin*, 1369/1990–1, pp. 928–31.

69 *Contra* A. Rieck, for instance, who writes that Sadr's system includes 'a series of elements which belong to the repertory of the present system of modified Capitalism'. 'Introduction' of the translator, p. 101.

70 Muhammad Baqer as-Sadr, *Khutut Tafsiliyya 'an Iqtisad al-Mujtama' al-Islami*, quoted in General introduction, n. 75, p. 36.

71 *Ibid.*, p. 46.

72 Muhammad Baqer as-Sadr, *al-Madrasa al-Islamiyya* (the Islamic school), Beirut, 1973, p. 192. The two texts which constitute the *Madrasa* were written soon after Sadr completed *Iqtisaduna*.

5 Muhammad Baqer as-Sadr and Islamic banking

1 On this *hadith* and variations, see e.g. Tirmidhi's (d. 279/892) *al-Jame' as-Sahih*, ed. by M. 'Abd al-Baqi, vol.3, Cairo, 1937, p. 541; Zaruq al-Fasi (d. 899/1493), *Sharh Sahih al-Bukhari* (*Comments on the Compilation of Bukhari*, d. 256/870), vol. 4, Beirut, 1973, pp. 416–19.

2 Documented precedents in the Ottoman Empire have been discussed in J. Mandaville, 'Usurious piety: the cash *waqf* controversy in the Ottoman Empire', *International Journal of Middle Eastern Studies*, 10, 1979, pp. 289–308; O. Turan, 'A legal document concerning money-lending for interest in Seljukian Turkey', *Professor Muhammad Shafi Presentation Volume*, Lahore, 1955, pp. 255–65; Nesh'et Cagatay, '*Riba* and interest concept and banking in the Ottoman empire', *Studia Islamica*, 32, 1970, pp. 53–68; an early discussion on the negative impact of *ribawi* practice on the Egyptian countryside can be found in an article written in Egypt in 1895. 'Ali 'Abdal-Futuh, '*Al-ajnabi wal-'iqarat az-zira'iyya wal-bank az-zira'i*' (*Foreigners, Agricultural Land and the Agricultural Bank*), in his *Ash-Shari'a al-Islamiyya, al-Qawanin al-Wad'iyya wal-Qada' wal-Iqtisad wal-Ijtima'* (*Islamic Law, Positive Laws, the Judiciary, Economics, and the Society*), Cairo, n.d. (*c.* 1913), pp. 161–70.

3 Muhammad Rashid Rida, '*Ribh sunduq at-tawfir*' (*The Profit of Sunduq at-Tawfir*), *Manar*, 1917, p. 529.

4 *Ibid.*, p. 528.

5 An important debate over *riba* and the Egyptian Civil Code took place between

'Abd ar-Razzaq as-Sanhuri and Ibrahim al-Badawi. See Sanhuri, *Masadir al-Haqq fil-Fiqh al-Islami (The Sources of Law in Islamic Jurisprudence)*, Cairo 1954–9. Ibrahim Zaki al-Badawi, *Nazariyyat ar-Riba al-Muharram (The Theory of Forbidden riba)*, Cairo, 1964. On Sanhuri, the best work is by Enid Hill, *Sanhuri and Islamic Law*, Cairo, 1987; see also her 'Islamic law as a source for the development of a comparative jurisprudence: theory and practice in the life and work of Sanhuri', in A. Azmeh ed., *Islamic Law: Social and Historical Contexts*, London, 1988, pp. 146–97.

6 Muhammad Qadri Basha undertook in the late nineteenth century to codify privately several areas of Islamic law. This resulted in codes of family law, *al-Ahkam ash-Shar'iyya fil-Ahwal ash-Shakhsiyya*, Alexandria, 1875; of *waqf* law, *Qanun al-'Adl wal-Insaf lil-Qada' 'ala Mushkilat al-Awqaf*, Cairo, 1896; and most relevant to the Civil Code, *Murshid al-Hayran ila Ma'rifat Ahwal al-Insan fil-Mu'amalat ash-Shar'iyya*, Cairo, 1891.

7 The Egyptian Civil Code has served as a close model for similar legislation in Syria (1949), Iraq (1953) and Libya (1954). See generally S. Mahmasani, *al-Awda' at-Tashri'iyya*, pp. 266–7, 308–10.

8 The text of the Civil Code was published, along with the text of previous relevant legislation and the various debates in the Senate and in Parliament, by the Egyptian Ministry of Justice as *al-Qanun al-Madani*: *Majmu'at al-A'mal at-Tahdiriyya (The Civil Code: The Complete Preparatory Works)*, in several volumes. The quote here is from Vol. 2, at p. 581.

9 *La ta'kulu amwalakum ad'afan muda'afatan* (literally, do not eat your monies times over), Qur'an: III, 130.

10 Quoted above, n. 5.

11 Sanhuri, *Masadir al-Haqq*, p. 236.

12 *Ibid.*, p. 239.

13 More details in *Ibid.*, pp. 237–44.

14 The decision is reported in English as Supreme Constitutional Court of Egypt, 'Decision on *shari'a* and *riba*', *Arab Law Quarterly*, 1:1, 1985, pp. 100–8.

15 See 'Ala' ad-Din Kharufa, *ar-Riba wal-Fa'ida* (*riba* and interest), Baghdad, 1962.

16 See 'Abduh, per Rida, note 3 above; Muhammad Abu Zahra, *Tahrim ar-Riba Tanzim Iqtisadi* (The prohibition of *riba* as economic organisation), n.p., n.d. This work was produced originally in the 1950s; it was republished in Cairo in 1986 as *Buhuth fir-Riba* (studies in *riba*).

17 '*Thabat al-milkiyya*', see this volume, chapter 4.

18 Muhammad Baqer as-Sadr, *al-Bank al-la Ribawi fil-Islam*, Kuwait, first edn, *c.* 1969 [*IFB* quoted after the Beirut edition of Dar at-Ta'aruf, 1983]. It is important to note that in Egypt, there were practical attempts at setting 'Islamic' banks as early as the 1960s. See generally A. Mayer, 'Islamic banking and credit policies in the Sadat era: the social origins of Islamic banking in Egypt', *Arab Law Quarterly*, 1:1, 1985, 32–50, at 36–40. But there was in Egypt no systematic attempt to go beyond the negative theories of the debate on *riba* in order to reach the developments attained in Sadr's work on the mechanisms of an Islamic bank. But see the efforts of the founder of the Mit Ghamr Savings Bank, Ahmad an-Najjar, *Bunuk Bila Fa'ida lit-Tanmiya al-Iqtisadiyya wal-Ijtima'iyya fid-Duwal al-Islamiyya (Banks Without Interest for Economic and Social Development in Muslim Countries)*, Cairo, 1972.

19 *Ujrat al-mithl* can be loosely translated as fair or equivalent price.

20 For instances of such activity, see E. Ashtor, 'Le taux d'intérêt dans l'orient médiéval', in *The Medieval Near East: Social and Economic History*, London, 1978, pp. 197–213; *Levant Trade in the Later Middle Ages*, Princeton, 1983, esp. pp. 367–432; M. Khan, 'Mohamedan Laws against usury and how they are evaded', *Journal of Comparative Law*, 1929, 233–44.

21 For interest disguised under foreign currency schemes, *IFB* 177–9, for credit instalment sales, *IFB* 175.

22 Literal translation: 'the *sayyed* master, may his shadow persist'. *IFB* 175. Is that a reference to *Ayat Allah* Abul-Qasem al-Khu'i or to *Ayat Allah* Muhsin al-Hakim, who died in 1970?

23 This philosophy resembles, and might be drawn from, Marx' critique of mercantilist economists. In an Islamic bank, the *shari'a* also forbids 'money which begets money', in the formula of K. Marx, *Capital*, vol. 1, section 2, ch. 4, *in fine*.

24 As in the remark of Muhammad Faisal as-Sa'ud, who has in the past decade been the most active propounder of the Islamic banking system, both as a member of the ruling family in Saudi Arabia, and as the head of a number of Islamic financial houses: 'I didn't say that the conventional banks are going to disappear. On the contrary, I think they will remain, and I think that the two systems are going to be there in parallel ... [T]here is no conflict between the two. The two systems can exist parallel to each other without having problems. As a matter of fact, today our institutions deal, I know that our group deals with 180 *riba* banks'. 'Luncheon Address', in *Proceedings* of the First International Meeting, Islamic banking conference, New York, 1985, pp. 111, 109.

25 Sadr points up also to the existence of a third, hybrid category of deposits, savings deposits (*wada'e' at-tawfir*). Like fixed deposits, savings deposits bear a return for the depositors. But they share with mobile deposits the entitlement to withdrawal by the depositors at any time. The hybrid character of these deposits determines their regime, which is also hybrid. A bank, says Sadr, will calculate approximately how much of the savings deposits might be withdrawn at any one time. If the average is, say, ten per cent, the remaining ninety per cent will be treated as fixed deposits, whereas ten per cent will be used as if they were mobile deposits (*IFB* 64–5).

26 This definition suggests that there is little difference with the classical definitions of Muslim jurists. On *mudaraba*, compare Sarakhsi (Hanafi school, d. 1092), *Mabsut*, 30 vols., Cairo, 1906–12, vol. 22, pp. 18–19; Muhammad Kazim at-Tabataba'i al-Yazdi (Ja'fari school, d. 1919), *al-'Urwa al-Wuthqa*, chapter on *mudaraba*, pp. 594–632; Ibn Hazm (Zahiri school, d. 1065), *al-Muhalla*, vol. 8, pp. 247–50. See also the well-documented works of N. Saleh, *Unlawful Gain and Legitimate Profit in Islamic Law*, Cambridge, 1986, pp. 101–14; S. D. Goitein, *A Mediterranean Society*, vol. 1, *Economic Foundations*, Berkeley, 1967, pp. 170 ff., 250–8; A. Udovitch, *Partnership and Profit in Medieval Islam*, Princeton, 1970, pp. 170–248.

27 This is further developed in Appendix 2 of the *IFB*, pp. 184–204.

28 I am indebted to Jad Swidane for helping me to see more clearly in this section. An explanation can be presented in the following manner: The interest-free bank is competing with a conventional bank for funds. It must therefore offer at the outset a rate of return which is higher than the interest rate offered in a conventional bank. The example Sadr takes is of a conventional deposit of 100,000 dinar, with an interest rate of five per cent, and profit at twenty per cent.

Return for the depositor is therefore 5,000 per annum, and the profits stand at 20,000. The return of the share in the interest-free bank must therefore be *more* than 5,000.

How would the interest-free bank calculate this share? Sadr suggests it takes into account two elements: the risk of loss entailed generally, as well as the possibility that all the funds deposited will not be invested. This would, in Sadr's assumptions, be equivalent to some five per cent of the total deposits, i.e. 500 dinars. The return in the interest-free bank would therefore be equivalent to the interest rate in a conventional bank (here 5,000) + [interest × risk of non-profit + interest × incomplete use of deposits] (here 500) = 5,500. This amount is then expressed by Sadr in relation to the overall profits of the bank, in this case twenty per cent or 20,000 dinar. This explains the last ratio offered: share of the depositor in the interest-free bank = 5,500/20,000 = 55/1,000 = 27.5% of profit.

29 For details, see the arithmetic example offered given by Sadr, *IFB* 59–62.

30 *Istifa'* is translated by Schacht as 'receiving, taking possession', *Introduction to Islamic Law*, Oxford, 1964, pp. 138, 298.

31 The term used is *hawala*, literally transfer. See Schacht, *Introduction*, pp. 148–9; Udovitch translates *hawala* as 'bill of exchange', and as 'transfer of credit or debts'. *Partnership and Profit*, pp. 207–8.

32 This is related to the *hadith* on *riba al-fadl* stipulating the simultaneous exchange, '*yadan bi-yad*'.

33 Literally 'innocent' from obligation, see Schacht on *bara'a* in contract of sale, *Introduction*, p. 153.

34 Schacht translates *amana* as 'trust, deposit, fiduciary relationship', *Introduction*, q.v..; see also the comparison of Udovitch with the contract of *mufawada*, *Partnership and Profit*, pp. 104–7.

35 This is further developed in *IFB* Appendix 8.

36 See this volume, pp. 173–7.

37 The two reports mentioned are taken from the Twelve Imams Muhammad ibn 'Ali al-Baqer, and 'Ali ibn Musa ar-Rida, *IFB* 160.

38 *Al-Islam Yaqud al-Hayat*, see General introduction, nn. 73 and 75.

39 Discussed this volume, chapter 2.

40 Muhammad Baqer as-Sadr, *al-Usus al-'Amma lil-Bank fil-Mujtama' al-Islami* (*General Bases of a Bank in the Islamic Society*), p. 11. [henceforth *Usus*]

41 See discussion of *Iqtisaduna* this volume, chapter 4, p. 131–2. On risk in the economy, there are more details in the section of *Iqtisaduna* entitled 'the role of risk in the economy', pp. 572–5.

42 The word appears several times in the pamphlet, *signe des temps*. *Usus*, pp. 18, 21, 24.

43 See generally C. Mallat ed., *Islamic Law and Finance*, London, 1988, and the literature cited; on Islamic financial institutions, V. Nienhaus, 'The performances of Islamic banks: trends and cases', in *Ibid.*, pp. 129–70; on Islamic state banking, A. Mirakhor, 'The progress of Islamic banking: the case of Iran and Pakistan', in *Ibid.*, pp. 91–116; J. Connors, 'Towards a system of Islamic finance in Malaysia', in *Ibid.*, pp. 57–68.

44 Two prominent examples are Claude Cahen and 'Abd al-Aziz ad-Duri. See in the large bibliography of their contributions: Claude Cahen, 'L'histoire économique et sociale de l'Orient musulman médiéval', *Studia Islamica*, 3, 1955, 93–115; 'Réflexions sur l'usage du mot "féodalité"', *Journal of the Economic and*

Social History of the Orient, 3, 1960, 2–20; *Introduction à l'histoire du monde musulman médiéval*, Paris, 1982; *Jean Sauvaget's Introduction to the History of the Muslim East*, Berkeley, 1965; *Makhzumiyyat. Etudes sur l'Histoire Economique et Financière de l'Egypte Médiévale*, Leiden, 1977; 'Abd al-Aziz ad-Duri, *Tarikh al-'Iraq al-Iqtisadi fil-Qarn ar-Rabi' al-Hijri* (*Economic History of Iraq in 10th Century Iraq*), Baghdad, 1948; *Muqaddima fit-Tarikh al-Iqtisadi al-'Arabi* (*Introduction to Arab Economic History*), Beirut, 1969. In this tradition, see recently, B. Johansen, *The Islamic Law on Land Tax and Rent*, London, 1988. For the methodological relationship between law and history in Islamic studies, see the remarks of Claude Cahen in 'Considérations sur l'utilisation des ouvrages de droit musulman par l'historien', in *Atti del Terzo Congresso di Studi Arabi e Islamici*, Rome, 1967, p. 246.

45 E.g. S. Goitein and A. Udovitch.

Bibliography

Books and pamphlets

'Abdal-Futūh, 'Alī. *Ash-Sharī'a al-Islāmiyya, al-Qawānin al-Waḍ'iyya wal-Qaḍā' wal-Iqtiṣād wal-Ijtimā'*. Cairo, n.d.

Abdulrazak, F., ed. *Catalog of the Arabic Collection*, Harvard University. Vol. 3, Boston, 1983.

Abrahamian, Ervand. *Iran between Two Revolutions*. Princeton, 1982.

Abū 'Ammār, Ghāleb Ḥasan. *Ash-Shahīd aṣ-Ṣadr Rā'id ath-Thawra al-Islāmiyya fil-'Irāq*. Tehran, 1401/1981.

Abū Ḥabīb, S. *Dirāsa fī Minhāj al-Islām as-Siyāsī*. Cairo, 1985.

Abu Lughod, Janet. *Cairo*: 1001 *Years of the City Victorious*. Princeton, 1971.

Abū Yūsuf, *Kitāb al-Kharāj*. ed. Beirut, 1979.

Abū Zahra, Muḥammad. *Tahrīm ar-Ribā Tanẓīm Iqtiṣādī*. n.p., n.d. Republished as *Buḥūth fir-Ribā*. Cairo, 1986.

Abū Zahū, Muḥammad. *Al-Ḥadīth wal-Muḥaddithūn*. Beirut, 1404/1984.

Al-Adhamī, Muḥammad Muẓaffar. *Political Aspects of the Iraqi Parliament and Election Processes* 1920–1932. Ph.D. Thesis, London, 1978.

Ahmad, Mahmud. *Economics of Islam*. Lahore, 1952. 1st ed. 1947.

Al-Ahnaf, M., Botiveau, B., and Frégosi, F. *L'Algérie par ses Islamistes*. Paris, 1991.

Ajami, Fouad. *The Arab Predicament*: *Arab Political Thought and Practice Since* 1967. Cambridge, 1967.

The Vanished Imam. London, 1986.

Akhavi, Shahrough. *Religion and Politics in Contemporary Iran*. Albany, New York, 1980.

Al-'Alawiyyūn Shī'at Ahl al-Bayt: *Bayān 'an 'Aqīdat al-'Alawiyyīn*. Beirut, 1973.

Algar, Hamid. *Religion and State in Iran* 1785–1906. Berkeley, 1969.

The Roots of the Islamic Revolution. London, 1983.

Ali, A. Yusuf, tr. *The Holy Qur'ān*. Lahore, 1934.

Althusser, Louis. *Lénine et la Philosophie*. Paris, 1972.

Amīn, Aḥmad. *Zu'amā' al-Iṣlāḥ*. Cairo, 1948.

Amnesty International. *Iran*: *Violation of Human Rights*. London, 1987.

Anderson, Norman. *Law Reform in the Muslim World*. London, 1976.

Anṣārī, 'Alī, ed. *'Ahd al-Imām 'Alī ilā Mālik al-Ashtar*. Tehran, 1403/1983.

Arjomand, Said Amir. *The Shadow of God and the Hidden Imam*. Chicago, 1984.

Ashtor, E. *The Medieval Near East*: *Social and Economic History*. London, 1978.

Levant Trade in the Later Middle Ages. Princeton, 1983.

Al-Āṣifī, Muḥammad Mahdī. *Al-Ittijāhāt wal-Malāmiḥ al-'Āmma lin-Niẓām al-Islāmī*. Beirut, 1397/1977.

Madrasat an-Najaf wa Taṭawwur al-Ḥaraka al-Islāmiyya fīhā. Najaf, 1964.

An-Niẓām al-Mālī wa Tadāwul ath-Tharwa fil-Islām. Beirut, 3rd edn, 1393/1973.
Ayoob, M. *The Politics of Islamic Reassertion*. London, 1981.
Al-Azhar, Tārīkhuhu wa Taṭawwuruhu. Cairo, 1964.
Al-Azmeh, Aziz. *Ibn Khaldūn in Modern Scholarship*. Beirut, 1981.
ed. *Islamic Law: Social and Historical Contexts*. London, 1988.
'Amāra, Muḥammad, ed. *al-Farīḍa al-Ghā'iba*. Cairo, 1982.
'Ashmāwī, M.S. *Al-Islām as-Siyāsī*. Cairo, 1987.
Bābillī, Maḥmūd Muḥammad. *Al-Iqtiṣād fī Ḍaw' ash-Sharī'a al-Islāmiyya*. Beirut, 2nd edn, 1980.
Bachelard, Gaston. *Le Rationalisme Appliqué*. Paris, 1975, 1st edn, 1949.
Al-Badawī, Ibrāhīm Zakī. *Naẓariyyat ar-Ribā al-Muḥarram*. Cairo, 1964.
Baḥr al-'Ulūm, Muḥammad. *Aḍwā' 'alā Qānūn al-Aḥwāl ash-Shakhṣiyya al-'Irāqī*. Najaf, 1963.
Al-Akhbāriyya, Uṣūluhā wa Taṭawwuruhā. MS, provided by the author, 1988.
Al-Ijtihād. Beirut, 1977.
Maṣdar at-Tashrī' li-Niẓām al-Ḥukm fil-Islām. Beirut, 1397/1977.
'Uyūb al-Irāda fish-Sharī'a al-Islāmiyya. Beirut, 1984.
Al-Baḥrānī, Yūsuf. *Al-Ḥadā'eq an-Naḍira*. Beirut, 2nd edn, 1405/1985.
Lu'lu'at al-Baḥrayn. Najaf, 1966.
Baḥthī Dar Barāy-e Marja'iyyat va Rūḥāniyyat. Tehran, 1963.
Bakhash, Shaul. *The Reign of the Ayatollahs*. New York, 1984.
Balta, Paul. *Iran–Iraq: Une Guerre de 5000 ans*. Paris, 1987.
Banī Ṣadr, Abul-Ḥasan. *Iqtiṣād-e Tawḥīdī*. n.p., 1978.
Bannermann, Patrick. *Islam in Perspective*. London, 1988.
Batatu, Hanna. *The Old Social Classes and the Revolutionary Movements of Iraq*. Princeton, 1978.
Bāz, Salīm. *Kitāb Sharḥ al-Majalla*. Beirut, 1888.
Berger, Raoul. *Government by Judiciary*. Cambridge, 1977.
Berque, Jacques. *L'Islam au Défi*. Paris, 1980.
Blaustein and Flanz, eds. *Constitutions of the Countries of the World*. New York, updated 1989. Vol. VII.
Bottomore, T. and Goode, P. *Readings in Marxist Sociology*. Oxford, 1983.
Braudel, Fernand. *La Méditerranée et le Monde Méditerranéen à l'Epoque de Philippe II*. 2 vols., Paris, new edn 1966.
Brinton, J.Y. *Mixed Courts of Egypt*. New Haven, 1968.
Buḥairī, Marwān, ed. *Intellectual Life in the Arab East* 1890–1939. Beirut, 1981.
Al-Ḥayāt al Fikriyya fil-Mashriq al-'Arabī 1890–1939. Beirut, 1983.
Cahen, Claude. *Introduction à l'Histoire du Monde Musulman Médiéval*. Paris, 1982.
Jean Sauvaget's Introduction to the History of the Muslim East. Berkeley, 1965.
Makhzumiyyāt. Etudes sur l'Histoire Economique et Financière de l'Egypte Médiévale. Leiden, 1977.
Calder, Norman. *The Structure of Authority in Imāmī Shī'ī Jurisprudence*. Ph.D. thesis, London, 1980.
Caplan, Lionel ed. *Studies in Religious Fundamentalism*. London, 1987.
Cappelletti, Mauro. *The Judicial Process in Comparative Perspective*. Oxford, 1989.
Carré, Olivier. *Mystique et Politique*. Paris, 1984.
Carré, Olivier and Dumont, Paul eds. *Radicalismes Islamiques*. 2 vols., Paris, 1986.
Carroll, Lewis. *Through the Looking Glass*, in *Complete Works*. London, 1939.
Choper, Jesse H. *Judicial Review and the National Political Process*. Chicago, 1980.
Cole, Juan and Keddie, Nikkie eds. *Shi'ism and Social Protest*. New Haven, 1986.

Connors, Jane and Mallat, Chibli eds. *Islamic Family Law*. London, 1990.
Contemporary Aspects of Economic Thinking in Islam. n.p., 1980. 1st edn, 1970.
Corbin, Henry. *En Islam Iranien*. 4 vols., Paris, 1971–2.
Coulson, Noel. *A History of Islamic Law*. Edinburgh, 1964.
Succession in the Muslim Family. Cambridge, 1971.
Crone, Patricia. *Slaves on Horses: the Evolution of the Islamic Polity*. Cambridge, 1980.
Dawisha, Adeed ed. *Islam in Foreign Policy*. Cambridge, 1983.
Dekmejian, Richard. *Islam in Revolution*. Syracuse, 1985.
Digard, J. P. ed. *Le Cuisinier et le Mangeur d'Hommes– Etudes d'Ethnographie Historique du Proche-Orient*. Paris, 1982.
Dodge, Bayard. *A Millennium of Muslim Learning*. Washington, 1961.
Donohue, John J. and Esposito, John L. eds. *Islam in Transition*. New York, 1982.
Ad-Dūrī, 'Abd al-'Azīz. *Baḥth fi Nash'at 'ilm at-Tārīkh 'ind al-'Arab*. Beirut, 1960. Translated by L. Conrad as *The Rise of Historical Writing among the Arabs*. Princeton, 1983.
Muqaddima fit-Tārīkh al-Iqtiṣādī al-'Arabī. Beirut, 1969.
Tārīkh al-'Irāq al-Iqtiṣādī fil-Qarn ar-Rābi' al-Hijrī. Baghdad, 1948.
Durūs fil-Iqtiṣād. Tehran, 1403/1983.
Eccel, A. Chris. *Egypt, Islam and Social Change: al-Azhar in Conflict and Accommodation*. Berlin, 1984.
Ely, John Hart. *Democracy and Distrust*. Cambridge, 1980.
Enayat, Hamid. *Modern Islamic Political Thought*. Austin, 1982.
Encyclopaedia of Islam. Leiden, 1st edn, 1913–38; 2nd edn, 1960 ff.
Engels, Friedrich. *The Origin of the Family, Private Property and the State*. London, 1940.
Esposito, John L., ed. *Voices of Resurgent Islam*. New York, 1983.
Etienne, Bruno. *L'Islamisme Radical*. Paris, 1987.
Faḍlallāh, Muḥammad Ḥusayn. *Āfāq Islāmiyya wa-Mawāḍī' Ukhrā*. Beirut, 1400/1980.
'Alā Ṭarīq Karbalā'. Beirut, 1404/1984.
Al-Islām wa-Manṭiq al-Quwwa. Beirut, 1979.
Min Waḥī al-Qur'ān. 17 vols. Beirut, 1988.
Al-Faḍlī, 'Abdel-Hādī. *Naḥū Adab Islāmī*. Najaf, 1391/1971.
Al-Fahri, Aḥmad. *Baḥth Ḥawl Awliyā' al-Amr wal-Wilāya*. Beirut, 1405/1985.
Le Fait Ethnique en Iran et en Afghanistan. Paris, 1988.
Al-Faqīh, Muḥammad Taqī. *Jāmi'at an-Najaf fi 'Aṣrihā al-Ḥāḍir*. Tyre, Lebanon, n.d.
Al-Fāsī, 'Allāl. *Fil-Madhāhib al-Iqtiṣādiyya*. Rabat, 1971.
Al-Fāsī, Zarūq. *Sharḥ Ṣaḥīḥ al-Bukhārī*. Vol.4, Beirut, 1973.
Al-Fayyāḍ, A. *Ath-Thawra al-'Irāqiyya al-Kubrā*. Baghdad, 1963.
Febvre, Lucien. *Le Problème de l'Incroyance au Seizième Siècle*. Paris, 1947.
The Federalist Papers. New York, 1961.
Fisher, Michael. *Iran: From Religious Dispute to Revolution*. Cambridge, Mass., 1980.
Gilsenan, Michael. *Recognizing Islam*. London, 1982.
Göbel, Karl Heinrich. *Moderne Schiitische Politik und Staadsidee*. Leske, 1984.
Goitein, S.D. *A Mediterranean Society*, vol. 1, *Economic Foundations*. Berkeley, 1967.
Goldziher, Ignaz. *Muhammedanische Studien*. 2 vols., Hildesheim, 1961. Originally published in 1888.
Vorlesungen über den Islam. Heidelberg, 1910.

Die Zahiriten. Leipzig, 1884.
Ḥaidar, H. *Mādha Ja'a Ḥawla Kitāb Falsafatunā?* Qum, 1403/1983.
Hairi, Abdul Hadi. *Shi'ism and Constitutionalism in Iran*. Leiden, 1977.
Al-Ḥakīm, Muḥammad Bāqir. *Al-Mustashriqūn wa Shubahātuhum ḥawl al-Qur'ān*. Beirut, 1405/1985.
Qatl al-'Ulamā' fil-'Irāq Yujassid az-Zāhira al-Far'ūniyya. Tehran, 1404/1984.
Al-Ḥakīm, Muḥammad Taqī. *Al-Uṣūl al-'Āmma lil-Fiqh al-Muqāran*. Beirut, 1963.
Al-Ḥakīm, Muḥsin aṭ-Ṭabāṭabā'i. *Minhāj aṣ-Ṣāliḥīn: Qism al-'Ibādāt*. Beirut, 1396/1976.
Minhāj aṣ-Ṣāliḥīn: Qism al-Mu'āmalāt. Beirut, 1400/1980.
Halliday, Fred. *Iran: Dictatorship and Development*. London, 1979.
Hamon, Léo. *Les Juges de la Loi*. Paris, 1987.
Al-Ḥasanī, 'Abd ar-Razzāq. *Al-'Irāq Qadīman wa-Ḥadīthan*. Saida, 1956.
Ta'rīkh al-'Irāq as-Siyāsī al-Ḥadīth. 3 vols. Saida, 1948.
Ta'rīkh al-Wizārāt al-'Irāqiyya. 10 vols. Saida, 1933–.
Ath-Thawra al-'Irāqiyya al-Kubrā. 3rd edn, Saida, 1972.
Al-Hāshimī, Maḥmūd. *Aṣ-Ṣawm Tarbiya wa Hidāya*. Najaf, 1390/1970.
Ta'aruḍ al-Adilla ash-Shar'iyya. Beirut, 2nd edn, 1980.
Hill, Enid. *Sanhuri and Islamic Law*. Cairo, 1987.
Hiro, Dilip. *Iran under the Ayatollahs*. London, 1985.
Holt, P.M. ed. *Political and Social Change in Modern Egypt*. London, 1968.
Homoud, Sami. *Islamic Banking*. London, 1985.
Hooglund, Eric. *Land and Revolution in Iran*, 1960–1980. Austin, 1982.
Hourani, Albert. *Arabic Thought in the Liberal Age*, 1789–1939. Cambridge, 1983.
Hoveyda, F. *The Fall of the Shah*. London, 1980.
Hunter, Shireen ed. *The Politics of Islamic Revivalism*. Bloomington, 1988.
Hyman, Anthony. *Muslim Fundamentalism*. London, 1985.
Ibn Ḥazm. *al-Muḥallā*. Vol.8, n.p., n.d.
Ibn Khaldūn. *al-Muqaddima*. Cairo, n.d.
Irfani, Suroosh. *Revolutionary Islam in Iran: Popular Liberation or Religious Dictatorship?* London, 1983.
Islamic Banking Conference. *Proceedings*. New York, 1985.
Jafri, Sayed Husein. *Origins and Early Development of Shi'a Islam*. London, 1979.
Al-Jammāl, Muḥammad 'Abd al-Mun'im. *Mawsū'at al-Iqtiṣād al-Islāmī*. Beirut, 1400/1980.
Jansen, J.J.G. *The Neglected Duty; the Creed of Sadat's Assassins and Islamic Resurgence in the Middle East*. New York, 1986.
Al-Jazzār, Ja'far. *Al-Bunūk fil-'Ālam*. Beirut, 1404/1984.
Johansen, Baber. *The Islamic Law on Land Tax and Rent*. London, 1988.
Kamāl ad-Dīn, Muḥammad. *Ath-Thawra al-'Irāqiyya al-Kubrā li-Sanat* 1920. Najaf, 1971.
Kamali, M.H. *Principles of Islamic Jurisprudence*. Malaysia, 1989.
Al-Kāsānī. *Badā'e' aṣ-Ṣanā'e' fī Tartīb ash-Sharā'e'*. 8 vols. Cairo, 1910.
Kāshif al-Ghiṭā', Muḥammad Ḥusayn. *Aṣl ash-Shī'a wa Uṣūluhā*. n.p., n.d.
Muḥāwarāt al-Imām al-Muṣliḥ Kāshif al-Ghiṭā' ash-Shaykh Muḥammad al-Ḥusayn Ma' as-Safīrayn al-Brīṭānī wal-Amrīkī. 4th edn, Najaf, 1954.
Taḥrīr al-Majalla. 5 vols. in 4. Najaf, 1940–3.
Al-Muthul al-'Ulyā fil-Islām lā fī Bḥamdūn. Tehran, 1983. Originally written in 1954.
The Shia: Origin and Faith. Pakistan, 1982.

Kasravī, Aḥmad. *Tārīkh-e Mashrūṭe-ye Irān.* 5th edn, Tehran, 1961.
Al-Kātib, Aḥmad. *Tajrubat ath-Thawra al-Islāmiyya fil-'Irāq Mundhu* 1920 *Ḥatta* 1980. Tehran, 1402/1981.
Kāẓimī, 'Alī. *Karbalā' al-Muqaddasa Kamā Ra'ayt.* Ja'far al-Ḥā'irī tr. Beirut, 1390/1970.
Keddie, Nikki R. ed. *Religion and Politics in Iran: Shi'ism from Quietism to Revolution.* New Haven, 1983.
Religion and Rebellion in Iran: the Tobacco Protest of 1891–1892. London, 1966.
Kedourie, Elie. *The Chatham House Version.* London, 1970.
Kepel, Gilles. *Le Prophète et le Pharaon.* Paris, 1984.
Kerr, Malcolm. *Islamic Reform: the Political and Legal Theories of Muhammad Abduh and Rashid Rida.* Berkeley, 1966.
Khadduri, Majid. *War and Peace in the Law of Islam.* Baltimore, 1955.
Khalidi, Tarif ed. *Land Tenure and Social Transformation in the Middle East.* Beirut, 1984.
Al-Khalil, Samir. *The Republic of Fear.* London, 1989.
Khalīlī, J. ed. *Mausū'at al-'Atabāt al-Muqaddasa, Qism an-Najaf.* 3 vols., Beirut, 1964.
Khan, Muhammad Akram. *Islamic Economics.* Leicester, 1983.
Khan, Waqar Masood. *Towards an Interest-Free Islamic Economic System.* Leicester, 1985.
Kharūfa, 'Alā' ad-Dīn. *ar-Ribā wal-Fā'ida.* Baghdad, 1962.
Al-Khaṭṭāb, R. *Al-'Irāq Bayna* 1921 *wa* 1927. Najaf, 1976.
Al-Khū'ī, Abul-Qāsim. *Al-Masā'il al-Muntakhaba.* Beirut, 22nd edn, 1405/1985.
Minhāj aṣ-Ṣāliḥīn. 2 vols., 10th edn, Beirut, 1985.
Al-Khumainī, Rūḥallāh. *Du'ā'-e Siḥr.* Tehran, 1359/1980.
Al-Ḥukūma al-Islāmiyya. Beirut, 1979.
Islam and Revolution. Trans. and annotated by Hamid Algar. Berkeley, 1981.
Jihād an-Nafs aw al-Jihād al-Akbar. 1980.
Miṣbāḥ al-Hidāya ilā al-Khilāfa wal-Wilāya. Beirut, 1403/1983.
Taḥrīr al-Wasīla. 2 vols., 2nd edn, Beirut, 1405/1985.
The Selected Messages of Imam Khomeini Concerning Iraq and the War Iraq Imposed upon Iran. Tehran, 1981.
Velāyat-e Faqīh. Tehran, 1357/1979.
Wilāyat al-Faqīh. Beirut, 1979.
Kotobi, Mortéza, ed. *Iran: une Première République.* Paris, 1983.
Kramer, Martin. *Islam Assembled: the Advent of the Muslim Congresses.* New York, 1986.
ed. *Shi'ism, Resistance and Revolution.* Boulder Co., 1987.
Kühn, Thomas. *The Structure of Scientific Revolutions.* Chicago, 1962, new edn, 1970.
Al-Kulaynī. *Al-Uṣūl minal-Jāmi' al-Kāfī.* n.p., n.d.
Labovitz, J. *Presidential Impeachment.* New Haven, 1978.
Lambton, Ann. *The Persian Land Reform* 1962–1966. Oxford, 1969.
State and Government in Medieval Islam. Oxford, 1985. 1st edn, 1981.
Lammens, Henri. *Etudes sur le Siècle des Omeyyades.* Beirut, 1930.
Laoust, Henri. *Les Schismes dans l'Islam.* Paris, 1965.
Lapidus, Ira. *Contemporary Islamic Movements in Historical Perspective.* Berkeley, 1983.
Linant de Bellefonds, Y. *Traité de Droit Musulman Comparé.* Vol. 1, Paris, 1965.

Lockhart, W., Kamisar, Y., and Choper, J. eds. *Constitutional Law, Cases, Comments, Questions*. 3rd edn, Chicago, 1970, 1st edn, 1964.

Luchaire, François. *Le Conseil Constitutionnel*. Paris, 1980.

McCloskey, Robert G. *The American Supreme Court*. Chicago, 1960.

Macdonald, Duncan B. *Development of Muslim Theology, Jurisprudence and Constitutional Theory*. Lahore, 1972. 1st edn, 1903.

MacLachlan, Keith. *The Neglected Garden*. London, 1988.

Madanī, Jalāl ad-Dīn. *Hūqūq-e Asāsī dar Jumhūri-ye Islāmi-ye Irān*. Vol.4. *Quwwe-ye Muqannene-ye Shūra-ye Negahbān*. Tehran, 1366/1988.

Maḥbūba, Ja'far. *Māḍī an-Najaf wa Ḥaḍiruhā*. 3 vols. Najaf, 1955–8.

Maḥmaṣānī, Subḥī. *Al-Awḍā' at-Tashrī'iyya fil-Bilād al-'Arabiyya*. Beirut, 1957.

Falsafat at-Tashrī' fil-Islām. Beirut, 1946.

Les Idées Economiques d'Ibn Khaldoun. Essai Historique, Analytique et Critique. Lyon, 1932.

Makkī, Muḥammad Kāẓem. *Al-Ḥaraka al-Fikriyya wal-Adabiyya fī Jabal 'Āmil*. Beirut, 1982. 1st edn, 1963.

Mallat, Chibli, ed. *Islamic Law and Finance*. London, 1988.

Shi'i Thought from the South of Lebanon. Oxford, 1988.

Mann, Hans-Dietrich. *Lucien Febvre: la Pensée Vivante d'un Historien*. Paris, 1971.

Al-Marjānī, Ḥaydar Ṣāleḥ. *Al-Khumainī wal Khumainiyyūn*. Iraq, 1982.

Marr, Phebe. *The Modern History of Iraq*. Boulder, 1985.

Martens, André. *L'Economie des Pays Arabes*. Paris, 1983.

Martin, Richard ed. *Approaches to Islam in Religious Studies*. Tucson, 1985.

Martin, Vanessa. *Islam and Modernism: the Iranian Revolution of* 1906. London, 1989.

Marx, Karl. *Le Capital*. Vol. 1, Paris. 1969.

Contribution to the Critique of Political Economy. London, 1973.

Marx, Karl and Engels, Friedrich. *Selected Works*. 2 vols. Moscow, 1951.

Al-Maṣrī, 'Abd al-Samīh. *Naẓariyyat al-Islām al-Iqtiṣādiyya*. Egypt, 1391/1971.

Al-Māwardī. *al-Aḥkām aṣ-Ṣulṭāniyya*. 2nd edn, Cairo, 1966.

Michalak, Laurence and Salacuse, Jeswald eds. *Social Legislation in the Contemporary Middle East*. Berkeley, 1986.

Al-Mīlānī, Muḥammad Hādī. *Muḥāḍarāt fi-Fiqh al-Imāmiyya, Kitāb al-Khums*. F. Mīlānī ed., n.p., 1400/1800.

Milliot, Louis ed. *Travaux de la Semaine Internationale de Droit Musulman*. Paris, 1953.

Mitchell, Richard. *The Society of the Muslim Brothers*. Oxford, 1969.

Miyānjī, 'Alī Aḥmadī. *Uṣūl-e Mālikiyyat Dar Islām*. Vol. 1. *Mālikiyyat-e Khuṣūṣī*. Tehran, 1361.

Uṣūl-e Mālikiyyat Dar Islām. Vol. 2. *Mālikiyyat-e Khuṣūṣī Zamīn*. Tehran, 1361.

Momen, Mojan. *An Introduction to Shi'i Islam*. New Haven, 1985.

Montesquieu. *Oeuvres Complètes*. Paris, 1964.

Mortimer, Edward. *Faith and Power*. London, 1982.

Mottahedeh, Roy. *The Mantle of the Prophet: Learning and Power in Modern Iran*. London, 1986.

Mughniyya, Muḥammad Jawād. *Allāh wal-'aql*. Beirut, 3rd edn, 1959.

Fiqh al-Imām Ja'far aṣ-Ṣādiq. Beirut, n.d.

Imāmat 'Alī bayn al-'Aql wa l-Qur'ān. Beirut, 1970.

Al-Islām wa-l-'Aql. Beirut, rpt 1984 .

Isrā'īliyyāt al-Qur'ān. Beirut, 1981.

Al-Khumainī wad-Dawla al-Islāmiyya. Beirut, 1979.

Min Hunā wa Hunāk. Beirut, n.d. Original Najaf, 1957.
Ash-Shī'a wal-Ḥākimūn. 5th edn, Beirut, 1981.
Tajārib. Beirut, 1980.
Al-Waḍ' al-Ḥāḍir li-Jabal 'Āmil. Beirut, 1947.
Al-Mūsawī, Ra'd. *Intifāḍat Ṣafar al-Islāmiyya*. n.p. 1402/1982.
Muslehuddin, Mohammad. *Insurance and Islamic Law*. New Delhi, 1982. 1st edn, 1969.
Muṭahharī, A. *Mustanad Tahrīr al-Wasīla*. Qum, 1403/1983.
Al-Muẓaffar, Muḥammad Riḍa. *Uṣūl al-Fiqh*. 2 vols., rpt al-Qutayf.
An-Nafīsī, 'Abdallāh. *Dawr ash-Shī'a fi Taṭawwur Al-'Irāq as-Siyāsī al-Ḥadīth*. Beirut, 1973.
Nā'inī, Muḥammad Ḥusayn. *Tanbīh al-Umma wa Tanzīh al-Millat. Ḥukūmat az Naẓar-e Islām*. Tehran, 1374/1955.
An-Najjār, Aḥmad. *Bunūk Bilā Fā'ida lit-Tanmiya al-Iqtiṣādiyya wal-Ijtimā'iyya fid-Duwal al-Islāmiyya*. Cairo, 1972.
Nashat, Guity ed. *Women and Revolution in Iran*. Boulder Co., 1983.
Ne'me, 'Abdallāh. *Falāsifat ash-Shī'a*. Beirut, 1971.
Newman, Andrew. *The Development and Political Significance of the Rationalist (Usuli) and Traditionalist (Akhbari) School in Imami Shi'i History from the third/ninth to the tenth/sixteenth Century A.D.* Ph.D. thesis, 2 vols., Los Angeles, 1986.
Nienhaus, Volker. *Literature on Islamic Economics in English and in German*. Cologne, 1982.
Nizār, Ja'far Husain. *'Adhrā' al-'Aqīda wal-Mabda': ash-Shahīda Bint al-Hudā*. n.p., 1405/1985.
Norton, Augustus. *Amal and the Shi'a: Struggle for the Soul of Lebanon*. Texas, 1987.
Olson, Robert. *The Siege of Mosul and Ottoman–Persian Relations 1718–1843*. Bloomington, Indiana, 1975.
Philip, Loic and Favoreu, Louis. *Les Grandes Décisions du Conseil Constitutionnel*. 4th edn, Paris, 1986.
Pipes, Daniel. *In the Path of God: Islam and Political Power*. New York, 1983.
Piscatori, James ed. *Islam and the Political Process*. Cambridge, 1983.
Islam in a World of Nation-States. Cambridge, 1986.
Pohl-Schöberlein, Monika. *Die Schiitische Gemeinschaft des SüdLibanon (Gabal 'Amil) innerhalb des Libanesischen Konfessionellen Systems*. Berlin, 1986.
Powers, David. *Studies in Qur'an and Hadith*. Berkeley, 1986.
Qadri Bāsha, Muḥammad. *al-Aḥkām ash-Shar'iyya fil-Aḥwāl ash-Shakhṣiyya*. Alexandria, 1875.
Murshid al-Ḥayrān ilā Ma'rifat Aḥwāl al-Insān fil-Mu'āmalāt ash-Shar'iyya. Cairo, 1891.
Qānun al-'Adl wal-Inṣāf lil-Qaḍā' 'alā Mushkilat al-Awqāf. Cairo, 1896.
Al-Qā'inī, 'Alī al-Fāḍil. *'Ilm al-Uṣūl Tārikhan wa Taṭawwuran*. Tehran, 1405.
Al-Qānūn al-Madanī: Majmū'at al- A'māl at-Taḥḍīriyya. Vols. 1 and 2, Cairo, 1952.
Al-Qazwīnī, Mahdī. *Umniyat al-Mūqin*. Jawdat Al-Qazwīnī ed., Beirut, 2nd edn, 1407/1987.
Al-Qudūrī. *Al-Mukhtaṣar*. India, 1847.
Quṭb, Sayyid. *Fi Zilāl al-Qur'ān*. Beirut, new edn, 1973.
Al-'Adāla al-Ijtimā'iyya fil-Islām. Cairo, 1949.
Rabbath, Edmond. *La Constitution Libanaise, Origines, Textes et Commentaires*. Beirut, 1982.

Randal, Jonathan. *The Tragedy of Lebanon*. London, 1983.
Rawls, John. *A Theory of Justice*. Cambridge, 1971.
Reid, Donald. *Lawyers and Politics in the Arab World* 1880–1960. Chicago, 1981.
Riḍā, Muḥammad Rashīd. *Al-Khilāfa wal-Imāma al-'Uẓmā*. Cairo, 1923.
Tafsīr al-Manār. 12 vols., Egypt, 3rd edn, 1367/1947.
Ar-Rīḥānī, Amīn. *Mulūk al-'Arab*. 2 vols. Beirut, 1929.
Rodinson, Maxime. *Islam et Capitalisme*. Paris, 1966.
Ruḥānī, Ḥāmid. *Nahzat-e Imām Khumainī*. 2 vols., Tehran, 1364/1985.
Aṣ-Ṣadr, Muḥammad. *Falsafat al-Ḥajj wa Maṣāliḥuhu fil-Islām*. Najaf, 1969.
Aṣ-Ṣadr, Muḥammad Bāqer. *Ahl al-Bayt*. Beirut, 1388/1968.
Baḥth Ḥawla al-Mahdī. Beirut, 3rd edn, 1401/1981. 1st edn, 1397/1977.
Baḥth Ḥawla al-Wilāya. Beirut, 3rd edn, 1401/1981. 1st edn, 1397/1977.
Al-Bank al-la-Ribawī fil-Islām. Beirut, 8th edn, 1403/1983.
Buḥūth fi Sharḥ al-'Urwā al-Wuthqā. 3 vols., Najaf, 1971.
Le Chiisme: Prolongement Naturel de la Ligne du Prophète. Abbas al-Bostani tr. Paris, 1983.
Dawr al-A'imma fil-Ḥayāt al-Islāmiyya. Tehran, 1400/1980.
Durūs fi-'Ilm al-Uṣūl. 3 vols. in 4 parts. Beirut, 1978–80.
Fadak fit-Tārīkh. Beirut, 1403/1983. 1st edn, Najaf, 1955.
Falsafatunā. Beirut, 10th edn, 1400/1980.
Al-Fatāwa al-Wāḍiḥa. Vol. 1, Beirut, 3rd edn, 1977.
Ghāyat al-Fikr fi Uṣūl al-Fiqh: Mabāḥith al-Ishtighāl. Beirut, 1988.
Ikhtarnā Lak. Beirut, 2nd edn, 1400/1980. 1st edn, 1395/1975.
Iqtiṣādimā. vol. 1, Muḥammad Kāẓim Mūsavi tr., Tehran, 1971.
Iqtiṣādimā. vol. 2, 'Abdul-'Alī Ispahbūdī tr., Tehran, 1978.
Iqtiṣādunā. Beirut, 1398/1977.
Iqtiṣādunā. English translation, Tehran, 4 vols., 1982–4.
Jawānib min al-Mas'ala al-Ijtimā'iyya. S. Jurayshī ed., Tunis, n.d. [1988?].
Khilāfat al-Insān wa Shahādat al-Anbiyā'. Beirut, 2nd edn, 1399/1979.
Khuṭūt Tafṣīliyya 'an Iqtiṣād al-Mujtama' al-Islāmī. Beirut, 2nd edn, 1399/1979.
Lamḥa Fiqhiyya Tamhīdiyya 'an Mashrū' Dustūr al-Jumhūriyya al-Islāmiyya fi Īrān. Beirut, 1979.
Al-Ma'ālim al-Jadīda fil-Uṣūl. Beirut, 1385/1964.
Mabāḥith al-Uṣūl. Kāẓim al-Ḥusaynī al-Hā'irī ed. Vol. 1, Part 1. Qum, 1407/1987.
Al-Madrasa al-Islāmiyya. Beirut, 3rd edn, 1400/1980. 1st edn, 1393/1973.
Al-Madrasa al-Qur'āniyya. Beirut, 2nd edn, 1981.
Al-Manṭiq al-Waḍ'ī wal-Yaqīn ar-Riyaḍī fil-Falsafa. Tehran, 1400/1980.
Al-Majmū'a al-Kāmila li-Mu'allafāt as-Sayyed Muḥammad Bāqer aṣ-Ṣadr. Beirut, 15 vols., 1980-
Mūjaz Aḥkām al-Ḥajj. n.p., 1395/1975.
Mūjaz fi-Uṣūl ad-Dīn. Beirut, 1401/1981.
Naẓra 'Āmma fil-'Ibādāt. Beirut, 3rd edn, 1401/1981. 1st edn, 1397/1977.
An-Nubuwwa al-Khātima. Beirut, 3rd edn, 1405/1985.
Our Philosophy. Shams Inati tr. London, 1987.
Risālatunā. Tehran, 1402/1982.
Ṣūra 'an Iqtiṣād al-Mujtama' al-Islāmī. Beirut, 2nd edn, 1399/1979.
Unsere Wirtschaft, Eine Gekürzte Kommentierte Ubersetzung des Buches Iqtiṣādunā. A. Rieck tr., Berlin, 1984.
Al-Usus al-'Āmma lil-Bank fil-Mujtama' al-Islāmī. Beirut, 2nd edn, 1399/1979.
Al-Usus al-Manṭiqiyya lil-Istiqrā'. Beirut, 4th edn, 1397/1977. 1st edn, 1391/1972.

Said, Edward. *Orientalism*. London, 1978.
Salāmeh, Ghassān. *As-Siyāsa al-Khārijiyya as-Sa'ūdiyya mundhu 'ām* 1945. Beirut, 1980.
Saleh, Nabil. *Unlawful Gain and Legitimate Profit in Islamic Law*. Cambridge, 1986.
Ṣāleḥ, Ṣubḥī. *'Ulūm al-Ḥadīth wa Muṣṭalaḥuhu*. 2nd edn, Damascus, 1963.
As-Sanhūrī, 'Abd ar-Razzāq. *Le Califat*. Paris, 1926.
Maṣādir al-Ḥaqq fil-Fiqh al-Islāmī. 6 vols., Cairo, 1954–9.
As-Sarakhsī. *al-Mabsūṭ*. 30 vols., Cairo, 1906–12.
Schacht, Joseph. *Introduction to Islamic Law*. Oxford, 1964.
Schirazi, Asghar. *The Problem of the Land Reform in the Islamic Republic of Iran*. Berlin, 1987.
ed. *Texte zur Agrargesetzgebung in der Islamischen Republik Iran*. Berlin, 1988.
Schulze, Rheinhardt. *Islamischer Internationalismus in 20. Jahrhundert; Untersuchungen zur Geschichte der Islamischen Weltliga (Mekka)*. Leiden, 1990.
Shakespeare, William. *Hamlet*. G. Hibbard ed., Oxford, 1987.
Shaltūt, Maḥmūd. *Fatāwā*. Cairo, 1964.
Shamseddīn, Muḥammad Ja'far. *Iqtiṣādunā, Talkhīṣ wa Tawḍīḥ*. 4 vols. Beirut, 1406/1986.
Shamseddīn, Muḥammad Mahdī. *Dirāsa fil-'Aqīda al-Islāmiyya*. Beirut, 1977.
Al-'Ilmāniyya. Beirut, 2nd edn, 1403/1983. 1st edn, 1400/1980.
Mawāqif wa Ta'ammulāt fi Qaḍāyā al-Fikr was-Siyāsa. Beirut, 1405/1984.
Naẓam ad-Dīmuqrātiyya al-'Adadiyya al-Qā'ima 'alā Mabda' ash-Shūrā. Beirut, 1985.
Thawrat al-Ḥusayn fil-Wujdān ash-Sha'bī. Beirut, 1980.
Thawrat al-Ḥusayn, Ẓurūfuhā al-Ijtimā'iyya wa Āthāruhā al-Insāniyya. Beirut, 3rd edn, 1974.
Sharī'atī, 'Alī. *Ḥusayn Varīth-e Ādam*. Tehran, n.d.
Tashayyu'-e 'Alavī va Tashayyu'-e Ṣafavī. Tehran, 2nd edn, 1350/1971.
Ash-Shaybānī. *Sharḥ Kitāb as-Siyar al-Kabīr*, with comments by Sarakhsī, Ṣ. Munajjid ed., 3 vols., Cairo, 1971.
Shaykh al-Muqāwama al-Islāmiyya ash-Shaykh ash-Shahīd Rāgheb Ḥarb. Beirut, 1407/1987.
Le Shi'isme Imamite. Paris, 1970.
Ash-Shīrāzī, Ḥasan. *Al-Iqtiṣād*. Beirut, 2nd edn, 1400/1980. 1st edn, n.p. 1960.
Ash-Shīrāzī, Muḥammad al-Ḥusaynī. *Taqrīb al-Qur'ān ilal-Adhhān*. 30 vols. Beirut, 1980.
Ash-Shīrāzī, Ṣādeq. *Aṭ-Ṭarīq Ilā Bank Islāmī*. Beirut, 1392/1972.
Ash-Shirbāṣī, Aḥmad. *Al-Mu'jam al-Iqtiṣādi al-Islāmī*. Beirut, 1401 /1981.
Sick, Gary. *All Fall Down*. London, 1985.
Siddiqui, K., ed. *Issues in the Islamic Movement* 1980–1981. London, 1981.
Sivan, Emmanuel. *Radical Islam*. New Haven, Conn., 1985
Sluglett, Peter. *Britain in Iraq* 1914–1932. London, 1976.
Sluglett, Peter and Farouk-Sluglett, Marion. *Iraq since* 1958: *from Revolution to Dictatorship*. London, 1987.
Sou'al, ed. *L'Islamisme Aujourd'hui*. Paris, 1985.
Stark, Freya. *Baghdad Sketches*. London, 1947, 1st edn, 1937.
Aṭ-Ṭabarī. *Tafsīr*. Vol.10, Cairo, n.d.
Aṭ-Ṭabārsī. *Majma' al-Bayān fi Tafsīr al-Qur'ān*. Vols. 6–7, Beirut, n.d.
At-Tabataba'i, Hossein Modarressi. *An Introduction to Shi'i Law*. London, 1984.

Aṭ-Ṭabāṭabā'ī, Muḥammad Ḥusayn. *Al-Mīzān fi Tafsīr al-Qur'ān*. 20 vols. Beirut, 1970–.

Naẓariyyat as-Siyāsa wal-Ḥukm fil-Islām. Beirut, 1402/1982.

Risālat al-Wilāya. Beirut, 1407/1987.

Shi'ite Islam. Hossein Nasr tr., Albany, New York, 1977. 1st edn, 1975.

Aṭ-Ṭabāṭabā'ī al-Yazdī, Muḥammad Kāẓim. *al-'Urwā al-Wuthqā*. n.p., n.d.

Taheri, Amir. *Khomeiny*. Paris, 1985.

Taleghani [Ṭāliqānī], Maḥmūd. *Society and Economics in Islam*. R. Campbell tr. Berkeley, 1982.

Islām va Mālekiyyat. 10th edn, Tehran, 1965.

Jihād va Shahādat. Tehran, 1963.

Aṭ-Ṭihrānī, Āgha Buzurg. *Adh-Dharī'a ilā Taṣānīf ash-Shī'a*. Vol. 16, 3rd edn, Beirut, n.d.

At-Tirmidhī: al-Jāme' aṣ-Ṣaḥīḥ. Muḥammad 'Abd al-Bāqī edn, Cairo, 1937.

Tribe, Laurence. *American Constitutional Law*. Mineola, USA, 1978.

Constitutional Choices. Cambridge, Mass., 1985.

Aṭ-Ṭūṣī, Abū Ja'far. *At-Tibyān*. Vol. 3, Najaf, n.d.

Tyan, Emile. *Histoire de l'Organisation Judiciaire en Pays d'Islam*. Vol. 1, Paris, 1938.

Udovitch, Abraham ed. *The Islamic Middle East 700–1900. Studies in Economic and Social History*. Princeton, 1981.

Partnership and Profit in Medieval Islam. Princeton, 1970.

Al-'Umar, 'Abd al-Jabbār. *Al-Khumainī bayn ad-Dīn wad-Dawla*. Bagdad, n.d.

Wansbrough, John. *Qur'anic Studies*. Oxford, 1977.

The Sectarian Milieu. Oxford, 1978.

Al-Wardī, 'Alī. *Tārīkh al-'Irāq al-Ḥadīth*. Vol. 1 *Min Bidāyat al-'Ahd al-'Uthmāni Ḥatta Muntaṣaf al-Qarn at-Tāsi' 'Ashar*. Baghdad, 1967.

Tārīkh al-'Irāq al-Ḥadīth. Vol. 5 *Ḥawla Thawrat al-'Ishrīn*. Baghdad, 1976.

Tārīkh al-'Irāq al-Ḥadīth. Vol. 6 *Min 'Ām* 1920 *ilā 'Ām* 1924. Baghdad, 1978.

Waṭanī, M. ed. *Majmū'e-ye Kāmel-e Qavānin-e Madanī-Asāsī*. Tehran, 1364/1985.

Wohlers-Scharf, Traute. *Les Banques Arabes et Islamiques*. Paris, 1983.

Az-Zuḥailī, Wahbe. *Naẓariyyat aḍ-Ḍamān fil-Fiqh al-Islāmī*. Damascus, 1970.

Articles

'Abdallāh, Muḥammad. 'Dawlat wilāyat al-faqīh', *Dirāsat wa Buḥūth*, 2:8, 1403/1983, 97–127.

Akhavi, Shahrough. 'Shari'ati's social thought', in N. Keddie ed., *Religion and Politics in Iran*, New Haven, 1983, pp. 125–43.

Algar, Hamid. 'The oppositional role of the ulama in twentieth-century Iran', in N. Keddie ed., *Scholars, Saints and Sufis*, Berkeley, 1972, pp. 231–55.

'Social justice in the ideology and legislation of the Islamic revolution of Iran', in L. Michalak and J. Salacuse eds., *Social Legislation in the Contemporary Middle East*, Berkeley, 1986, pp. 17–60.

Althusser, Louis. 'Avertissement aux lecteurs du Livre I du Capital', in K. Marx, *Le Capital*, Paris, 1969.

Amoretti, Biancamaria. 'Pour une analyse politique de l'économie islamique', *La Pensée*, 229, 1982, 62–70.

Anderson, Norman. 'A law of personal status for Iraq', *International and Comparative Law Quarterly*, 1960, 542–63.

'Changes in the law of personal status in Iraq', *International and Comparative Law Quarterly*, 1963, 1026–31.
'Recent developments in shari'a law i-x', *The Muslim World*, xl-xliii, 1950–2.
'Reforms in family law in Morocco', *Journal of African Law*, 1958, 146–59.
'The Syrian law of personal status', *Bulletin of the School of Oriental and African Studies*, 1955, 34–49.
'The shari'a and civil law', *Islamic Quarterly*, 1:1, 1954, 29–46.
Ashtor, Emmanuel. 'Le taux d'intérêt dans l'orient médiéval', in *The Medieval Near East: Social and Economic History*, London, 1978, pp. 197–213.
Al-Badawī, Ibrāhīm Zakī, 'Naẓariyyat ar-ribā al-muḥarram', *Majallat al-Qānūn wal-Iqtiṣād*, 1939, 387–447, 533–66.
Baḥr al-'Ulūm, Muḥammad. 'Ad-dirāsa wa tārīkhuhā fin-Najaf', in J. Khalīlī ed., *Mausū'at al-'Atabāt al-Muqaddasa, Qism an-Najaf*, vol. 2, Beirut, 1964.
Bakhash, Shaul. 'Islam and social justice in Iran', in M. Kramer, ed., *Shi'ism, Resistance and Revolution*, Boulder Co., 1987, pp. 95–116.
'The politics of land, law and social justice in Iran', *Middle East Journal*, 43:2, 1989, 186–201.
'Baqir al-Sadr's last message on the unity of the Ummah', in K. Siddiqui ed., *Issues in the Islamic Movement*, London, 1981, p. 57.
Bar'am, Amazia. 'The shi'ite opposition in Iraq under the Ba'th, 1968–1984', in *Colloquium on Religious Radicalism and Politics in the Middle East*, Hebrew University, Jerusalem, 13–15 May 1985.
Batatu, Hanna. 'Iraq's underground Shi'a movements: characteristics, causes and prospects, *Middle East Journal*, 35:4, 1981, 577–94.
Bayat, Mangol. 'Mahmud Taleqani and the Iranian revolution', in M. Kramer ed., *Shi'ism, Resistance and Revolution*, Boulder Co., 1987, pp. 67–94.
Bengio, Ofra. 'Shi'is and politics in Ba'thi Iraq', *Middle Eastern Studies*, 1985, 2–11.
Braudel, Fernand. 'Histoire et sciences sociales: la longue durée', *Annales E.S.C.*, 4, 1958, 725–53, reprinted in *Ecrits sur l'Histoire*, Paris, 1969, 41–83.
Brunschvig, Robert. 'Les usul al-fiqh imamites à leur stade ancien', in *Le Shi'isme Imamite*, Paris, 1970.
Cagatay, Nesh'et. 'Riba and interest concept and banking in the Ottoman empire', *Studia Islamica*, 32, 1970, 53–68.
Cahen, Claude. 'L'histoire économique et sociale de l'Orient musulman médiéval', *Studia Islamica*, 3, 1955, 93–115.
'Réflexions sur l'usage du mot "féodalité"', *Journal of the Economic and Social History of the Orient*, 3, 1960, 2–20.
Calder, Norman. 'Accommodation and revolution in Imami Shi'i jurisprudence: Khumayni and the classical tradition', *Middle East Studies*, 18, 1982.
'Khums in Imami Shi'i jurisprudence, from the tenth to the sixteenth century AD', *Bulletin of the School of Oriental and African Studies*, 45, 1982, 39–47.
'Zakat in Imami Shi'i jurisprudence, from the tenth to the sixteenth century', *Bulletin of the School of Oriental and African Studies*, 64, 1981.
Cappelletti, Mauro. 'Who watches the watchmen', *American Journal of Comparative Law*, 31, 1983, 1 ff.
Carter v. *Carter Coal Co.*, 298 US 238 (1936).
Chalmeta, Pedro. 'Au sujet des théories économiques d'Ibn Khaldun', *Rivista degli Studi Orientali*, 1983, 93–120.
Chehata, Chafik. 'La théorie de l'abus des droits chez les jurisconsultes musulmans', *Revue Marocaine de Droit*, 1953, 105–13.

Cole, Juan. 'Shi'i clerics in Iraq and Iran 1722–1780: the Akhbari–Usuli controversy reconsidered', *Iranian Studies*, 18:1, 1985, 3–34.

Connors, Jane. 'Towards a system of Islamic finance in Malaysia', in C. Mallat ed., *Islamic Law and Finance*, London, 1988.

Ad-Dajāwī, Yūsuf. 'Mu'āmalāt at-tujjār wamā fīhā min ar-ribā', *Nūr al-Islām*, Vol. 3:6, 1354/1935, 324–8.

'Al-Qirāḍ', *Nūr al-Islām*, vol. 3:6, 1354/1935, 183–7.

Daoualibi, M. 'Usure et droit musulman', in L. Milliot ed., *Travaux de la Semaine Internationale de Droit Musulman*, Paris, 1953, pp. 139–42.

'Decision on shari'a and riba', *Arab Law Quarterly*, 1:1, 1985, 100–8.

Donohue, John. 'Notre économie', *Cahiers de l'Orient*, 8–9, 1987–8, 179 ff.

'La nouvelle Constitution syrienne et ses détracteurs', *Travaux et Jours*, 47, 1973, 93–111.

'Dossier: Aux sources de l'islamisme chiite- Muhammad Baqer al-Sadr', *Cahiers de l'Orient*, issue 8–9, 1987–8, 115–202.

Edge, Ian. 'Shari'a and commerce in contemporary Egypt', in C. Mallat ed., *Islamic Law and Finance*, London, 1988.

Enayat, Hamid. 'Iran: Khumayni's concept of the "Guardianship of the Jurisconsult", in J. Piscatori ed., *Islam and the Political Process*, Cambridge, 1982, pp. 160–80.

Engels, Friedrich. 'Letter to J. Bloch, 21–22 September 1890', in Karl Marx and F. Engels, *Selected Works*, Moscow, 1951, vol. 2.

'Faṣl fī ḥikmat taḥrīm ar-ribā', *al-Manār*, 1906, pp. 332–50.

Haeri, Shahla. 'The institution of mut'a marriage in Iran: a formal and historical perspective', in G. Nashat ed., *Women and Revolution in Iran*, Boulder Co., 1983, pp. 231–51.

'Power of ambiguity: cultural improvisation on the theme of temporary marriage', *Iranian Studies*, 19:2, 1986, 123–54.

Hā'irī, Kaẓem. 'Tarjamat ḥayāt as-sayyid ash-shahīd', in Muḥammad Bāqer aṣ-Ṣadr, *Mabaḥeth al-Uṣūl*, Hā'irī ed., Qum, 1407/1987, pp. 11–168.

Hallaq, Wael. 'The development of logical structure in Sunni legal theory', *Der Islam*, 64, 1987, 42–67.

'On the origins of the controversy about the existence of mujtahids and the gate of ijtihad', *Studia Islamica*, 63, 1986, 129–42.

'Was the Gate of Ijtihad ever closed?', *International Journal of Middle Eastern Studies*, 1984, 1–33.

Halliday, Fred. 'Iranian foreign policy since 1979: internationalism and nationalism in the Islamic revolution', in Cole and Keddie eds., *Shi'ism and Social Protest*, New Haven, 1987, pp. 88–107.

Hill, Enid. 'Islamic law as a source for the development of a comparative jurisprudence: theory and practice in the life and work of Sanhuri', in A. Azmeh ed., *Islamic Law: Social and Historical Contexts*, London, 1988.

Homoud, Sami. 'Islamic Banking and Social Development', in Islamic Banking Conference, *Proceedings*, New York, 1985.

Honigmann, E. 'Al-Nadjaf', *Encyclopedia of Islam*, 1st ed, Leiden 1936, vol. 3, pp. 815–16.

Howard, Ian tr., 'The Islamic Economy I–VII', *al-Serat*, 1981–5.

Ibrahim, Saad Eddin. 'Anatomy of Egypt's militant groups: methodological note and preliminary findings', *International Journal of Middle Eastern Studies*, 12, 1980, 423–53.

'Al-imām ash-shahīd as-sayyid Muḥammad Bāqer aṣ-Ṣadr', *Ṭarīq al-Haqq*, 2:12, Feb. 1982, 5–20.

Jamali, Fadel. 'The theological colleges of Najaf', *The Muslim World*, 50, 1960, 15–22.

Al-Jibālī, I. 'Ar-Ribā', *Nūr al-Islām*, vol. 2, 1931–2, pp. 358–75; 425–31; 488–96; Vol.3, 1932–3, pp. 424–9.

Katouzian, Homa. 'Shi'ism and Islamic Economics', in N. Keddie ed., *Religion and Politics in Iran*, New Haven, 1983.

Kedourie, Elie. 'The Kingdom of Iraq: a retrospect', in *The Chatham House Version*, London, 1970.

Khan, Mohammad. 'Mohamedan Laws against usury and how they are evaded', *Journal of Comparative Law*, 1929, 233–44.

Khomeini [Khumainī], Ruhallah. 'Imam Khomeini's message on hearing of the martyrdom of Ayatollah Sayyid Baqir Sadr at the hands of the American puppet Saddam Husain', in *The Selected Messages of Imam Khomeini Concerning Iraq and the War Iraq Imposed upon Iran*, Tehran, 1981, p. 47.

'Matn-e kāmel-e vaṣiyyatnāme-ye ilāhī-siyāsī Imām Khumainī', *Keyhān Havā'i*, 14 June 1989, p. 2.

Kohlberg, 'From Imamiyya to Ithna 'ashariyya', *Bulletin of the School of Oriental and African Studies*, 39, 1976, 521–34.

Koorooshy, J. 'Agrarverfassung der Islamischen Republik Iran', *Orient*, 28, 1987, 229–43.

Kramer, Martin. 'Tragedy in Mecca', *Orbis*, 32:2, 1988, 231–47.

Küppers, N. 'Das Irakische Zivilgesetzbuch', *Zeitschrift für Vergleichende Rechtswissenschaft*, 62, 1960, 181–98; 63, 1961, 1–44.

Kuran, Timur. 'The economic system in contemporary Islamic thought: interpretation and assessment', *International Journal of Middle Eastern Studies*, 18, 1980, 135–64.

'On the notion of economic justice in contemporary Islamic thought', *International Journal of Middle Eastern Studies*, 21, 1989, 171–91.

Lambton, Ann. 'Quis custodiet custodes? some reflections on the Persian theory of government', *Studia Islamica*, 5, 1955, 125–48; 6, 1956, 125–46.

'A reconsideration of the position of the marja' al-taqlid and the religious institution', *Studia Islamica*, 20, 1964, 115–35.

Linant de Bellefonds, Y. ''Abd al-Razzaq al-Sanhuri: Maṣādir al-Haq fil-Fiqh al-Islāmī', *Revue Internationale de Droit Comparé*, 10, 1958, 476–9 and 11, 1959, pp. 633–9.

'Le code du statut personnel irakien du 30 décembre 1959', *Studia Islamica*, 13, 1960, 79–135.

'Le droit musulman et le nouveau code civil égyptien', *Revue Algérienne, Tunisienne et Marocaine de Législation et de Jurisprudence*, 1956, 211–22.

Loutfi el-Sayed, Afaf. 'The role of the 'ulama in Egypt during the early nineteenth century', in P. M. Holt ed., *Political and Social Change in Modern Egypt*, London, 1968.

Mahmassani [Maḥmaṣānī], Subhi. 'Les principes de droit international à la lumière de la doctrine islamique', *Académie de Droit International, Recueil des Cours*, 117, 1966, 205–328

Makdisi, George. 'The significance of the Sunni schools of law in Islamic religious history', *International Journal of Middle Eastern Studies*, 11, 1979, 1–8.

Mallāṭ, Chiblī. 'A l'origine de la guerre Iran-Irak: l'axe Najaf-Téhéran', *Les Cahiers de l'Orient*, Autumn 1986, 119–36.

'Contemporary Qur'anic exegesis between London and Najaf; a view from the law', unpublished communication, SOAS, 21 October 1987.

'Le féminisme islamique de Bint al-Houdâ', *Maghreb-Machrek*, 116, 1987, 45–58.

'Al-maḥkama al-'ulyā al-amīrkiyya fin-niqāsh al-qānūnī al-mu'āṣir', *Proche-Orient Etudes Juridiques*, 1987, 9–26.

'Political Islam and the 'ulama in Iraq', MS, Berkeley, 1986. Published in part in S. Hunter ed., *The Politics of Islamic Revivalism: Diversity and Unity*, Bloomington, Indiana, pp. 71–87.

'Religious militancy in contemporary Iraq: Muhammad Baqer as-Sadr and the Sunni-Shi'a paradigm', *Third World Quarterly*, 10:2, April 1988, 699–729.

'Sunnism and Shi'ism in Iraqi Islamic family law – Revisiting the codes', in J. Connors and C. Mallat eds., *Islamic Family Law*, London, 1990.

Mandaville, Jon. 'Usurious piety: the cash waqf controversy in the Ottoman Empire', *International Journal of Middle Eastern Studies*, 10, 1979, 289–308.

Marbury v. *Madison*, 1 Cranch 137 (1803).

Martin, Pierre. 'Une grande figure de l'islamisme en Irak', *Cahiers de l'Orient*, 8–9, 1987–8, pp. 117–35.

Mayer, Ann. 'Islamic banking and credit policies in the Sadat era: the social origins of Islamic banking in Egypt', *Arab Law Quarterly*, 1:1, 1985, 32–50.

Mirakhor, Abbas. 'The progress of Islamic banking: the case of Iran and Pakistan', in C. Mallat ed., *Islamic Law and Finance*, London, 1988.

Morony, Michael. 'Landholding and social change: lower al-'Iraq in the early Islamic period', in T. Khalidy ed., *Land Tenure and Social Transformation in the Middle East*, Beirut, 1984.

'Landholding in seventh-century Iraq: late Sasanian and early Islamic patterns', in A. Udovitch ed., *The Islamic Middle East 700–1900. Studies in Economic and Social History*, Princeton, 1981.

Mughniyya, Muḥammad Jawād. 'An-Najaf fi alf 'ām', in *Min Hunā wa Hunāk*, Beirut, n.d., pp. 48–50.

Muḥammad, Yaḥyā. 'Naẓarāt falsafiyya fi fikr ash-shahīd aṣ-Ṣadr', *Dirāsāt wa Buḥūth*, 2:6, 1983, 173 ff.

Mundy, Marsha. 'The family, inheritance, and Islam: a reexamination of the sociology of fara'id law', in A. Azmeh ed., *Islamic Law: Social and Historical Contexts*, London, 1988, pp. 1–123.

Al-Muẓaffar, Muḥammad Riḍā. 'Jāmi'at an-Najaf al-ashraf wa jāmi'at al-Qarawiyyīn', *Majallat al-Majma' al-'Ilmī*, 1964, 293–301.

National Labor Relations v. *Jones Steel Corp.*, 301 US 57 (1937).

Nienhaus, Volker. 'The performances of Islamic banks: trends and cases', in C. Mallat ed., *Islamic Law and Finance*, London, 1988.

Powers, David. 'The historical evolution of Islamic inheritance law', in J. Connors and C. Mallat eds., *Islamic Family Law*, London, 1990.

Railroad Retirement Board v. *Alton Railroad Co.*, 295 US 330 (1935).

Reissner, J. 'Der Imam und die Verfassung; zur politischen und staatsrechtlichen Bedeutung der Direktive Imam Khomeinis vom 7. Januar 1988', *Orient*, 29:2, 1988, 213–36.

'Ribḥ Ṣundūq at-tawfīr', *al-Manār*, 1917, pp. 526–8.

Richard, Yann. 'Du nationalisme à l'islamisme: dimensions de l'identité ethnique en Iran', in *Le Fait Ethnique en Iran et en Afghanistan*, Paris, 1988, pp. 267–75.

Ar-Rifā'ī, 'Abd al-Jabbār. 'Fihrist al-Iqtiṣād al-Islāmī I-VII', *Tawḥīd*, 20–7, 1986–7.
Rippin, Andrew. 'The exegetical genre Asbāb al-Nuzūl: a bibliographical and terminological survey', *Bulletin of the School of Oriental and African Studies*, 48, 1985, 1–15.
'Ibn 'Abbās's al-Lughāt fil-Qur'ān', *Bulletin of the School of Oriental and African Studies*, 44, 1981.
'Literary analysis of Qur'ān, Tafsīr, and Sīra: the methodologies of John Wansbrough', in R. Martin ed., *Approaches to Islam in Religious Studies*, Tucson, 1985, pp. 151–63.
Rose, Gregory. 'Velayat-e Faqih and the recovery of Islamic identity in the thought of Ayatollah Khomeini', In N. Keddie ed., *Religion and Politics in Iran*, New Haven, 1983, pp. 166–88.
Salīm, 'Izz ad-Dīn. 'Ash-shahīd aṣ-Ṣadr, rā'ed ḥarakat at-taghyīr fil-umma', *Tawḥīd*, 27, 1407/1987, 25–39.
Al-Saud, Mohamad. 'Luncheon Address', in Islamic banking conference, *Proceedings*, New York, 1985.
Scarcia, G. 'Intorno alle controversie tra ahbari e usuli presso gli imamiti di Persia', *Rivista degli Studi Orientali*, 33, 1958, 211–50.
Schlechter Poultry Corp. v. *US*, 295 U.S. 495 (1935).
Spengler, J. 'Economic thought in Islam: Ibn Khaldun', *Comparative Studies in Society and History*, 1963–4, 268–306.
'Ṣundūq at-tawfīr fi idārat al-barīd', *al-Manār*, 1904, 28–9.
Ṭabāṭabā'ī, Muḥammad Ḥusayn. 'Ijtihād va taqīd dar islām va shī'a', in *Bahthī dar Barāy-e Marja'iyyat va Rūḥāniyyat*, Tehran, 1963.
'Vilāyat va za'amat', in *Bahthī dar Barāy-e Marja'iyyat va Rūḥāniyyat*, Tehran, 1963.
Tribe, Laurence. 'Towards a syntax of the unsaid: construing the sounds of congressional and constitutional silence', *Indiana Law Journal*, 57, 1982, 515 ff.
Turan, O. 'A legal document concerning money-lending for interest in Seljukian Turkey', *Professor Muhammad Shafi Presentation Volume*, Lahore, 1955, pp. 255–65.
Yavari d'Hellencourt, N. 'Le radicalisme shi'ite de 'Ali Shari'ati', in O. Carré and P. Dumont eds., *Radicalismes Islamiques*, vol. 1, Paris, 1986.
Az-Zain, 'Alī. 'Aḍwā' 'alal-madāres ad-dīniyya fin-Najaf', *al-'Irfān*, 58:3–4, 1970, 307–17.
Zubaida, Sami. 'The ideological conditions for Khomeini's doctrine of government', *Economy and Society*, 11:2, 1982.

Index

'Abduh, Muhammad, 64–6, 124, 159, 163, 165
Abu Bakr, 128
Abu Hanifa, 138, 167
Abu Tammam, 2
al-Adwa', 16
'Ali Ibn Abi Talib, 43, 44, 65, 68
'Amili, Sadr ad-Din al-, 8
'Amili, Jawad, 133, 138
'aql, 29 n.16, 30, 33, 34
Ardabili, 'Abd al-Ghani al-, 8
Ardebili, 105
Ansari, Murtada al-, 40, 41, 42
Asfahani, 138
Asifi, Muhammad Mahdi al-, 189
Azhar, 111
'Aziz, Tariq, 18

Bahr al-'Ulum, Muhammad, 26–34, 189
Bakhtiar, Shapur, 69
Bakr, Ahmad Hasan al-Bakr, 17
Bani-Sadr, Abul-Hasan, 146
banking (Islamic)
  bank structure, 164–73
  and capitalism, 166, 183
  cheques, 174–5, 178–9
  commercial papers, 182
  compensation (*muqassa*), 174, 177
  deposits, depositors, 168–9, 173–4, 175–6, 181, 168–71
  foreign currency, 180
  in Islamic environment, 183
  as intermediary, 168–70
  investors–agents, 168, 171–2
  ju'ala, 140, 165, 166
  letters of credit, 182
  loans, 168–9, 173–4
  mudaraba, 116, 140, 159, 163–5, 169–73, 184
  profits, profit-sharing, 170, 172
  receipt (*qabd*, *tasallum*), 177
  riba, 111, 114, 116, 141, 143, 158, 162
  riba an-nasi'a, 158, 161
  riba al-fadl, 158, 161, 180
  transfer (*hawala*), 179
  and Western banking, 168
Banna, Hasan al-, 65

Barzani, Mulla Mustafa, 18
Bazergan, Mahdi, 81
Behbehani, 26, 28, 30
Bint al-Huda, 15, 16, 18, 189
Britain, ambassador of, 9

causality, 11–12
civil society, 35 n. 42, 46 n. 90
communism, 9, 12, 16, 36, 37
Corbin, Henry, 5

dar al-harb/dar as-silm, 4, 24

economics (Islamic), see also *Iqtisaduna*, Islamic law, banking (Islamic)
  anfal, 130, 149
  distribution, 119, 127, 135–6
  ihya', 128, 135, 156–7
  justice, injustice, 119, 122, 137–9, 141
  khalduniana, 111
  kharaj, 128, 129, 131, 145
  labour, 120, 131, 135, 139, 148, 164
  land, 127, 131, 149, 156–7
  literature on, 4–5, 111
  madhhab, 121, 125
  mantaqat al-faragh, 67, 124, 140–1, 144
  method, 115, 117, 121–4, 135–6, 138–40, 186–7
  minerals, 133–4
  moral dimension, 115, 116–17
  need, 120–1
  'not a science', 117–8
  and Shi'i-Sunni controversy, 124, 128, 143–6
  tasq, 129, 145
  'ushr, 145
  wali al-amr (ruler)'s role, 119, 128, 129, 140–1
  water, 134–5
Egyptian Civil Code, 111, 158–62
Egyptian Supreme Constitutional Court, 146
Ely, John Hart, 85, 104
Engels, 71

Fadak, episode of, 8–9
Fadlallah, Muhammad Husayn, 16, 17

Falsafatuna, 10–11
Faqih, Muhammad Taqi, 40, 41, 43, 56, 58, 77, 107
Fatima, 44
Firdawsi, 2
French Conseil d'Etat, 60
French Conseil Constitutional, 80

Ha'iri, Kazem, 8, 10
Hafiz, 2
Hakim, Mahdi, 18, 189
Hakim, Muhammad Baqer, 17, 18, 189
Hakim, Muhammad Taqi, 41
Hakim, Muhsin, 13, 15, 18, 84
hajj, 4
Hamilton, A., 85, 86
Harak, Abul-Majd, 143
haraka jawhariyya, 11–12
Harb, Ragheb, 189
Hasan Ibn ash-Shahid ath-Thani, 40, 138
Hashimi, Mahmud, 10, 17, 189
Hilli, al-'Allama al-, 40, 133, 138
Hilli, al-Muhaqqiq al-, 137
Hobbes, 71
Husaini, 'Aref, 189
Hussein, Saddam, 17, 18

'ibadat, 4, 13
Ibn al-Athir, 2
Ibn al-Barraj, 132
Ibn Hamza, 132
Ibn Hazm, 146
Ibn Hisham, 40
Ibn Khaldun, 2, 85, 111, 185
Ibn Malik, 40
Ibn Manzur, 2
Ibn an-Nazim, 40
Ibn Qudama, 138, 146
ihtiyat, 36–37
ijma', 33 n. 32
ijtihad, 29–34, 55, 56, 124, 126
  bab al-ijtihad, 34 n. 39
Iqtisaduna, 68, 103, 113–57, see also economics (Islamic)
  criticism of, 141–6
  impact, 142–3
  and capitalism, 113–14, 137, 139, 147
  on *riba*, 162
  and socialism, 113–14, 117, 120, 137, 139–40, 142, 147
  property (ownership), 114, 121, 140
  structure, 113
Iran, see also Iraq
  agrarian reform, 83, 101, 107
  as locus of Islamic revival, 4–6
  1979 constitution, 59–62, 69–107
  Civil Code, 162
  constitutional crisis, 80
  Experts, Assembly of (*majles-e khubregan*), 76, 77, 107
  Guardians, Council of (*shura-ye negahban*), 79, 82, 148, 149 n. 53
  land reform, 146, 149–57
  Leader, Leadership (*rahbar*), 80, 84, 87
  majma'-e tashkhis-e maslahat (Council for the Discernment of the Republic's interest), 105, 153
  mashruta, 6, 59, 60, 61
  Parliament (*majles*), 72–3, 88, 92–6, 148
  Presidency, 73, 80, 88
  separation of powers, 72, 73, 153 n. 62
  Supreme Judicial Council, 82
  Tobacco revolt, 60
Iraq, see also Iran
  Ba'th party in, 17, 51, 54
  Najaf v. Baghdad, 18, 38, 188
  personal status code, 16
  war with Iran, 18, 23
Islam, see also Islamic law
  as civilization, 1
  disciplines in, 2
  as ideology, 7–9
  and Panarabism, 24
  Panislamism, 24
Islamic law (*shari'a, fiqh*), see also economics (Islamic), banking (Islamic), Iran
  classification, 13
  codification, 3
  constitutional law, 4–5, 25–6
  constrained, 91–6
  criminal law in, 4, 116
  definition, 2–3,
  foundation for economic theory, 122, 124
  and international law, 4, 24
  labour, 83, 102, 107
  necessity, 153–5
  primary v. secundary injunctions in, 91, 118
  Qur'an, as basis of, 62–5
  succession in, 3
  slavery in, 3
  usul al-fiqh, 9–10

Jawahiri, Jawad al-, 59

Kamal, Yusuf, 143
Karrubi, Mehdi, 106
Kashif al-Ghita', 'Ali, 18
Kashif al-Ghita', Muhammad Husayn, 9, 188
Khalisi, Mahdi, 15
Khamene'i, 'Ali, 89, 105, 107
Khoiniha, 105, 106
Khu'i, Abul-Qasem, 16, 44, 46, 53, 56, 84
Khumaini, Ahmad, 103, 105, 106
Khumaini, Ruhullah, 6–7, 18, 19, 50–2, 107, 149
khums, 14
Khurasani, Muhammad Kazem, 41, 42

Kufa university, 17
Kulayni, al-, 134
Kurds, 18

Locke, 71

Mahdavi-Kani, 106
Mahmasani, Subhi, 111
Majalla (Ottoman civil code), 49
Maliki school, 146
Marshall, John, 83, 97
Maqrizi, 2
Marbury v. *Madison*, 96–8
Mawardi, 133
mudhakara, 42
Mughniyya, Muhammad Jawad, 38
Mujtama'una, 16
Muntazeri, Hussein, 54, 92, 149
Musavi, Husain, 102, 105, 106
Mutanabbi, 2
Muzaffar, 40, 41, 48

Na'ini, 42, 57
Najafi, 138
Naser, Jamal 'Abd an-, 24
Nasef, 'Ali an-Najdi, 143
Nation-state, 23
Nuri, 'Abdallah, 106

Politzer, 142

Qasem, 'Abdel-Karim, 15, 16
Quduri, 145
Qummi, 41, 134
Qutb, Sayyid, 64–6, 145

Rafsanjani, 'Ali Hashemi, 100–1, 105, 106
Radi, 40
ra'i, 36–7
Razi, 40
Rida, Muhammad Rashid, 64–6, 159, 163
Rieck, Andreas, 142
Risalatuna, 16
Rousseau, 6, 71

Sadr, Haydar, 8
Sadr, Isma'il, 8, 57
Sadr, Muhammad, 59
Sadr, Muhammad Baqer, *passim*
  arrest, 18
  on banking, 158–84
  biography, 8–19
  on constitution, 59–79
  on economics, 111–46, 156–7
  execution, 18–19
  and Khumaini, 50–4
Sane'i Hasan, 106
Sane'i, Yusuf, 106
Sanhuri, 159, 161
Sarakhsi, 138, 146

slaves, law of, 3
Shafi'i, 133, 134, 146
shahada (diploma), 39, 42–6
Shahid ath-Thani, ash-, 40, 41
Shari'ati, 'Ali, 5
Shaybani, 25, 18
Shi'ism
  bahth al-kharej, 41
  as civil society, 44–5
  colleges, 35, 38, 39, 47–9
  legal structure, 30, 32–58
  in Southern Iraq, 18
  and Iranian Presidency, 81
  marja', *marja'iyya*, 38, 43, 54–8
  muqallid/mujtahid in, 35–7, 44–7, 81–2, 90
  recognition of scholarship in, 35, 46, 52–6
  revenues of *'ulama* in, 38 n. 58, 44, 46
  Shi'i 'international', 15, 19, 45–6, 55, 188–9
  Shi'i-Sunni relations, 64 n. 24, 9, 29 n. 14, 124, 128
  social structure, 31, 35, 46, 52
  Usuli-Akhbari controversy, 26, 28–30, 32, 46
Shirazi, Hasan, 189
Shirazi, Muhammad, 189
Shirazi, Muhammad Husayn, 65, 66
social contract, 6
sovereignty, 69–73
Stalin, 142
sufism, 5
Sunduq at-tawfir affair, 158–60
Sunnism, see Shi'ism
Suyuti, 40

Tabari, 2
Tabataba'i, Muhamad Husayn, 5, 65–6, 84
Tabataba'i, Muhamad Kazem, 13, 40
Taftazani, 40
Taliqani, Mahmud, 61, 69, 145, 149
Talmasani, 'Umar, 63
Tavasoli, Muhammad Reza, 105, 106
Tusi, Abu Ja'far at-, 38, 138, 144
Tusi, Muhammd Ibn Hasan at-, 128

United States, ambassador of, 9
United States Supreme Court, 60, 80, 82–3, 96, 101 n. 35

Voltaire, 6

Wahhabis, 4
wilayat al-faqih, 6, 27, 59–62, 89–90

zakat, 14
Zionism, 36
Zubaydi, 2

Cambridge Middle East Library

29 CHIBLI MALLAT
The renewal of Islamic law
Muhammad Baqer as-Sadr, Najaf and the Shi'i International

28 MADIHA RASHID AL MADFAI
Jordan, the United States and the Middle East peace process 1974–1991

27 KENNETH M. CUNO
The Pasha's peasants
Land, society and economy in lower Egypt, 1740–1858

26 LOUISE L'ESTRANGE FAWCETT
Iran and the Cold War
The Azerbaijan crisis of 1946

25 GLEN BALFOUR-PAUL
The end of empire in the Middle East
Britain's relinquishment of power in her last three Arab dependencies

24 JILL CRYSTAL
Oil and politics in the Gulf
Rulers and merchants in Kuwait and Qatar

23 DONALD MALCOLM REID
Cairo University and the making of modern Egypt

22 EHUD R. TOLEDANO
State and society in mid-nineteenth-century Egypt

21 FRED HALLIDAY
Revolution and foreign policy
The case of South Yemen 1967–1987

20 GERSHON SHAFIR
Land, labor and the origins of the Israeli–Palestinian conflict 1882–1914

19 MAHFOUD BENNOUNE
The making of contemporary Algeria, 1830–1987
Colonial upheavals and post-independence development

18 DANIEL J. SCHROETER
Merchants of Essaouira
Urban society and imperialism in southwestern Morocco, 1844–1886

17 TIMOTHY MITCHELL
Colonising Egypt

16 NADIA HIJAB
Womanpower
The Arab debate on women at work

15 BENNY MORRIS
The birth of the Palestinian refugee problem, 1947–1949

14 MIRIAM COOKE
War's other voices
Women writers on the Lebanese civil war

13 MARY C. WILSON
King Abdullah, Britain and the making of Jordan

12 SEVKET PAMUK
The Ottoman empire and European capitalism 1820–1913
Trade, investment and production

11 JOHN C. WILKINSON
The Imamate tradition of Oman

10 SAMIR A. MUTAWI
Jordan in the 1967 war

9 NORMAN N. LEWIS
Nomads and settlers in Syria and Jordan, 1800–1980

8 OLIVIER ROY
Islam and resistance in Afghanistan

7 JUDITH E. TUCKER
Women in nineteenth-century Egypt

6 RAYMOND A. HINNEBUSCH JR
Egyptian politics under Sadat
The post-populist development of an authoritarian-modernizing state

5 HELENA COBBAN
The Palestinian Liberation Organisation
People, power and politics

4 AFAF LUTFI AL-SAYYID MARSOT
Egypt in the reign of Muhammad Ali

3 PHILIP S. KHOURY
Urban notables and Arab nationalism
The politics of Damascus 1860–1920

2 NANCY ELIZABETH GALLAGHER
Medicine and power in Tunisia, 1780–1900

1 YORAM PERI
Between battles and ballots
Israeli military in politics

6655565R0

Made in the USA
Lexington, KY
08 September 2010